這本書該如何使用

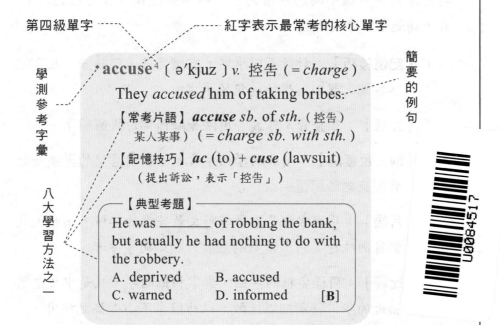

第四級單字 ········ ──── 紅字表示最常考的核心單字

學測參考字彙

八大學習方法之一

簡要的例句

*accuse⁴ 〔ə'kjuz〕v. 控告（= charge）

They *accused* him of taking bribes.

【常考片語】*accuse* sb. of sth.（控告某人某事）（= *charge* sb. *with* sth.）

【記憶技巧】*ac* (to) + *cuse* (lawsuit)（提出訴訟，表示「控告」）

【典型考題】
He was ＿＿＿＿ of robbing the bank, but actually he had nothing to do with the robbery.
A. deprived　　B. accused
C. warned　　　D. informed　　[B]

　　教育部國教署通過課綱中，明訂高中生畢業前要會 4500 個單字，以往是 7000 字。現在同學熟背最常用的 4500 個字，也就是 7000 字的 1～4 級，升大學考試詞彙題就可得滿分。而整份試題的範圍，約在 7000 字左右。背了 4500 個字，一般文章約可看懂 80%，背了 7000 字，大約 90%，背到五萬字，只有 95%，所以，最划得來的，是先背 4500 字，再不斷地做以 7000 字爲範圍的試題。目前使用中的英文單字，有 17 萬 1,476 個，一字又多義，無人能背好。同學應集中力量，以熟背最常用的 4500 個單字爲第一目標。

Vocabulary size	% of content in OEC	Example
10	25%	the, of, and, to, that, have
100	50%	from, because, go, me, our, well, way
1000	75%	girl, win, decide, huge, difficult, series
4500	**80%**	**humidity, species, protein, multiple, ingredient**
7000	90%	tackle, peak, crude, purely, dude, modest
50,000	95%	saboteur, autocracy, calyx, conformist
>100,000	99%	laggardly, endobenthic

※ 本資料來自牛津英語語料庫（OEC）。

「高中生必背 4500 字」除了重要字彙皆附有例句外，最大的特色是提供八種不同的學習方式，同學能選擇適合自己的學習方式，讀起來快樂沒負擔。

① 【記憶技巧】：針對不同單字，有諧音法、口訣法，及字根字首法，幫助同學快速記憶單字。

② 【注意】：在發音、釋義、用法等細節部份提醒同學。

③ 【同、反義詞】：增加同學的字彙量，相同意思的單字一起背，有助於記憶。

④ 【片語】：片語常常是同學學英文最苦惱的部份，為此，我們特別統計，列出常考的重要片語給同學參考。

⑤ 【比較】：同樣字根的字組、拼字相似的字，或是中文意思相近的字，特別加以比較，以防同學不小心搞混誤用。

⑥ 【衍伸詞】：須注意的詞類變化，以及從單字本身衍伸出來生活常見的名詞都歸納於此，讓同學能舉一反三。

⑦ 【典型考題】：同學不用攜帶試題本，背完單字即可自我測驗，立即驗收學習成果。特別加入歷年升大學經典試題，讓同學掌握考題大方向，成為考場大贏家。

⑧ 【重要知識】：坊間一般的字典、教材內容大多過時，許多單字的唸法已不符現代人的習慣，這項補充教你如何 *talk like Americans*。另外，收錄美國人一些生活用語，講出來道地有成就感，越學越開心。

　　本書在編審及校對的每一階段，花費了很長的時間，我們力求完善，但恐有疏漏之處，誠盼各界先進不吝批評指正。

編者　謹識

A a

abandon[4] 〔ə'bændən〕v. 拋棄
(= *give up*)
They *abandoned* the car when they ran out of gas.
【記憶技巧】諧音法：a｜ban｜don
（嗯便當要「拋棄」）

【典型考題】
The girl had to _____ her journey because of her father's illness.
A. abandon　　B. remove
C. mention　　D. inspect　　[A]

abdomen[4] 〔'æbdəmən〕n. 腹部
(= *belly*)
He feels a dull pain in the lower *abdomen*.

ability[2] 〔ə'bɪlətɪ〕n. 能力

able[1] 〔'ebḷ〕adj. 能夠的
Nick is not *able* to come to the party.
【片語】*be able to* (能夠)

aboard[3] 〔ə'bord〕adv. 在車（船、飛機）上
"All *aboard*!" shouted the conductor, and every passenger rushed for the train.
【記憶技巧】*a* (on) + *board* (甲板)
（上了甲板，即「在船上」）

abroad[2] 〔ə'brɔd〕adv. 到國外
Have you ever traveled *abroad*?
【記憶技巧】*ab* (away) + *road* (way)
（離開平常走的路，就是「到國外」）

absence[2] 〔'æbsns〕n. 缺席；不在
(= *time off*)；缺乏 (= *lack*)；沒有
Ms. Lin marks the *absence* of students every day.

absent[2] 〔'æbsn̩t〕adj. 缺席的
(= *away*)
Bill is *absent* from school today.
【記憶技巧】*ab* (away) + *s* (be) + *ent* (*adj.*) (不在這裡，就是「缺席的」)
【反義詞】present (出席的)

absolute[4] 〔'æbsə‚lut〕adj. 絕對的；完全的 (= *complete*)
People say that Einstein was an *absolute* genius.

【典型考題】
A child has _____ trust in his mother.
A. opposite　　B. fatal
C. absolute　　D. tense　　[C]

absorb[4] 〔əb'sɔrb〕v. 吸收 (= *suck in*)
The sponge quickly *absorbed* the liquid.
【記憶技巧】*ab* (away) + *sorb* (suck in) (把東西吸進去，就是「吸收」)

【典型考題】
The earth was so dry that it quickly _____ the rain.
A. soaked　　B. evaporated
C. absorbed　　D. contained　　[C]

abstract[4] 〔'æbstrækt〕adj. 抽象的
What you said was too *abstract* for Jenny. She is only three.
【反義詞】concrete (具體的)

academic[4] 〔‚ækə'dɛmɪk〕adj. 學術的 (= *scholastic*)
His *academic* performance is poor; he usually gets bad grades.

A

* **accent**[4] 〔'æksɛnt〕 n. 口音
(= *pronunciation*)
The speaker's strong *accent* makes
it difficult to understand him.
【記憶技巧】 *ac* (to) + *cent* (sing)

* **accept**[2] 〔ək'sɛpt〕 v. 接受 (= *receive*)
He dislikes Peter; he would not
accept his offer.
【記憶技巧】 *ac* (to) + *cept* (take)
（把東西拿過來，就是「接受」）

【典型考題】
Mike was ecstatic when his book was
————— for publication.
A. accepted   B. expected
C. rejected   D. postponed   [A]

* **acceptable**[3] 〔ək'sɛptəbḷ〕 adj.
可接受的 (= *satisfactory*)

* **acceptance**[4] 〔ək'sɛptəns〕 n. 接受
(= *accepting*)

* **access**[4] 〔'æksɛs〕 n. 接近或使用權
(= *admission*)   v. 存取（資料）
The suspect claimed that he had not
been allowed *access* to a lawyer
after he was arrested.
【常考片語】 *have access to* (有接近或
使用…的權利)

‡ **accident**[3] 〔'æksədənt〕 n. 意外；
車禍 (= *crash*)
【記憶技巧】 *ac* (to) + *cid* (fall) + *ent*
(n.)（事情突然落到身上來，就是「意外」）

【典型考題】
I saw a traffic ————— on my way to
school. Many people got hurt.
A. accident   B. jam
C. light   D. rule   [A]

* **accidental**[4] 〔ˌæksə'dɛntḷ〕 adj.
意外的；偶然的 (= *unintentional*)
His remark was *accidental*; he didn't
mean to reveal the secret.

accompany[4] 〔ə'kʌmpənɪ〕 v. 陪伴；
伴隨 (= *go with*)
The rain was *accompanied* by a
strong wind.
【記憶技巧】 *ac* (to) + *company* (同伴)
（去當別人的同伴，就是「陪伴」）

【典型考題】
The president is always ————— by
several bodyguards wherever he goes.
A. accomplished   B. accompanied
C. accustomed   D. accounted   [B]

* **accomplish**[4] 〔ə'kɑmplɪʃ〕 v. 完成
(= *achieve*)
Although everyone expected Stan to
accomplish great things, he ended
up doing little with his life.

* **accomplishment**[4] 〔ə'kɑmplɪʃmənt〕
n. 成就 (= *achievement*)

* **according to**[1] 根據
According to the forecast, it will be
colder tomorrow.

* **account**[3] 〔ə'kaunt〕 n. 帳戶
【記憶技巧】 *ac* (to) + *count* (count)
（「帳戶」就是用來計算金錢的收付）

* **accountant**[4] 〔ə'kauntənt〕 n.
會計師 (= *bookkeeper*)

* **accuracy**[4] 〔'ækjərəsɪ〕 n. 準確
(= *precision*)

A

*accurate[3] 〔'ækjərɪt 〕 *adj.* 準確的
（＝ *precise* ）

It is important to make sure that your calculations are *accurate* before you write the final answer.

【記憶技巧】 *ac* (to) + *cur* (take care) + *ate* (*adj.*) (做事小心，才會「準確的」)

【典型考題】

Facts and figures, even when _____, can often be misleading.
A. accurate　　　B. mistaken
C. detailed　　　D. careful　　　[A]

*accuse[4] 〔ə'kjuz 〕 *v.* 控告 （＝ *charge* ）

They *accused* him of taking bribes.

【常考片語】 *accuse sb. of sth.* (控告某人某事)（＝ *charge sb. with sth.* ）

【記憶技巧】 *ac* (to) + *cuse* (lawsuit) (提出訴訟，表示「控告」)

【典型考題】

He was _____ of robbing the bank, but actually he had nothing to do with the robbery.
A. deprived　　　B. accused
C. warned　　　D. informed　　　[B]

*ache[3] 〔 ek 〕 *v.n.* 疼痛

Eva complained that her back *ached*.

【衍伸詞】 toothache (牙痛)
　　　　 headache (頭痛)
　　　　 stomachache (胃痛)
　　　　 backache (背痛)

*achieve[3] 〔 ə'tʃiv 〕 *v.* 達到
（＝ *accomplish* ）

In order to *achieve* your goal, you must work hard.

*achievement[3] 〔 ə'tʃivmənt 〕 *n.* 成就
（＝ *accomplishment* ）

*acid[4] 〔'æsɪd 〕 *adj.* 酸性的 （＝ *sour* ）；尖酸刻薄的

Acid rain is a serious environmental problem that affects large parts of the US.

【比較】 acid 是指物體本身帶有的酸性，sour (酸的) 則指因腐敗而產生的酸性。

*acquaint[4] 〔 ə'kwent 〕 *v.* 使認識；使熟悉

Before classes start, you had better get *acquainted* with one another.

【片語】 *get acquainted with sb.* (認識某人)

【記憶技巧】 *ac* (to) + *quaint* (know) (知道某一個人，就是「認識」)

【典型考題】

The professor did his best to _____ the students with new ideas.
A. witness　　　B. review
C. acquaint　　　D. display　　　[C]

*acquaintance[4] 〔 ə'kwentəns 〕 *n.* 認識的人

【衍伸詞】 *a nodding acquaintance* (點頭之交)

*acquire[4] 〔 ə'kwaɪr 〕 *v.* 獲得；學會

I *acquired* three new stamps for my collection while I was abroad.

【記憶技巧】 *ac* (to) + *quire* (seek) (去尋找，就會「獲得」)

【典型考題】

If you can use a word correctly and effectively, that means you have _____ it.
A. developed　　　B. expressed
C. mimicked　　　D. acquired　　　[D]

*acre[4] 〔'ekə 〕 *n.* 英畝

The rich man owns 500 *acres* of land.

A

‡**act**[1] 〔 ækt 〕 *n.* 行為（ = *deed* ）
　　v. 行動；表現得；演戲

‡**action**[1] 〔'ækʃən 〕 *n.* 行動（ = *step* ）；
　行為（ = *act* ）
　Actions speak louder than words.

‡**active**[2] 〔'æktɪv 〕 *adj.* 活躍的
　（ = *lively* ）；主動的
　Although he is over 80, he's still
　very *active*.
　【記憶技巧】*act* (act) + *ive* (adj.)

‡**activity**[3] 〔 æk'tɪvətɪ 〕 *n.* 活動
　Watching television is a popular
　activity in many homes, especially
　in large cities.

‡**actor**[1] 〔'æktɚ 〕 *n.* 演員（ = *performer* ）
　He is a famous film *actor*.

‡**actress**[1] 〔'æktrɪs 〕 *n.* 女演員
　（ = *female performer* ）
　Sarah wants to be an *actress*.

*　**actual**[3] 〔'æktʃʊəl 〕 *adj.* 實際的（ = *real* ）
　Could you tell me the *actual* number?
　【衍伸詞】actually（實際上）

　ad[3] 〔 æd 〕 *n.* 廣告（ = *advertisement* ）

*　**adapt**[4] 〔 ə'dæpt 〕 *v.* 適應（ = *adjust* ）；
　改編（ = *change* ）
　The immigrant *adapted* to life in his
　new country.
　【記憶技巧】*ad* (to) + *apt* (fit)
　　　（去符合一個環境，也就是「適應」）
　【比較】adopt（採用）；adept（熟練的）
　┌─【典型考題】──────────
　│During the process of evolution, man
　│has shown remarkable ability to
　│────── to the environment.
　│A. adorn　　　B. adopt
　│C. adore　　　D. adapt　　　[D]
　└──────────────

*　**add**[1] 〔 æd 〕 *v.* 增加（ = *increase* ）
　The fire is going out; will you *add*
　some wood?

*　**addition**[2] 〔 ə'dɪʃən 〕 *n.* 增加
　（ = *increasing* ）
　These houses have been improved
　by the *addition* of bathrooms.
　【衍伸詞】*in addition*（此外）

*　**additional**[3] 〔 ə'dɪʃənḷ 〕 *adj.* 附加的；
　額外的（ = *extra* ）
　The price includes an *additional* tax.

‡**address**[1] 〔 ə'drɛs ,'ædrɛs 〕 *n.* 地址
　（ = *location* ）；演講（ = *speech* ）
　v. 向…講話
　Sue's *address* is written on the
　envelope.
　【重要知識】這個字作「地址」解時，有兩種
　發音，美國人 58% 唸作〔 ə'drɛs 〕，42% 唸
　作〔'ædrɛs 〕。

*　**adequate**[4] 〔'ædəkwɪt 〕 *adj.* 足夠的
　（ = *enough* = *sufficient* ）
　There is no need to write a long paper;
　two or three pages will be *adequate*.

*　**adjective**[4] 〔'ædʒɪktɪv 〕 *n.* 形容詞

*　**adjust**[4] 〔 ə'dʒʌst 〕 *v.* 調整（ = *adapt* ）
　Please *adjust* the color on the TV; the
　picture looks too red.
　【記憶技巧】*ad* (to) + *just* (right)（矯正
　　錯誤，就是要「調整」）

*　**adjustment**[4] 〔 ə'dʒʌstmənt 〕 *n.*
　調整（ = *alteration* ）

* **admirable**[4] 〔'ædmərəbḷ〕 *adj.* 值得
讚賞的；令人欽佩的(= *praiseworthy*)
Although he failed, his effort was
admirable.
【記憶技巧】 *ad* (at) + *mir* (wonder) +
able (*adj.*) (表現令人驚奇，表示「值得
讚賞的」)
【典型考題】
Their determination to fight to the
last man was really _____.
A. admirable B. disposable
C. replaceable D. portable [A]

* **admiration**[4] 〔ˌædmə'reʃən〕 *n.* 欽佩
(= *respect*)；讚賞

* **admire**[3] 〔əd'maɪr〕 *v.* 欽佩
(= *respect*)；讚賞

* **admission**[4] 〔əd'mɪʃən〕 *n.* 入場
(許可)；入學 (許可)(= *access*)
Clark was denied *admission* to the
movie because he is only 15 years old.
【記憶技巧】 *ad* (to) + *miss* (send) +
ion (*n.*) (被送進去某場所，就是「入場」)
【片語】 *deny admission to sb.* (不准
某人進入)

* **admit**[3] 〔əd'mɪt〕 *v.* 承認(= *confess*)；
准許進入 (= *allow*)
I have to *admit* that I have made some
mistakes in dealing with the matter.

* **adopt**[3] 〔ə'dɑpt〕 *v.* 採用(= *take on*)；
領養 (= *take in*)
They *adopted* the child as one of their
own.
【記憶技巧】背 ad<u>opt</u> (領養；採用)，想到
s<u>on</u>；背 ad<u>apt</u>，想到 <u>adjust</u> (適應)。

【典型考題】
The government is determined to
_____ measures to prevent inflation
from rising any further.
A. adopt B. adapt
C. addict D. adorn [A]

‡ **adult**[1] 〔ə'dʌlt〕 *n.* 成人
An *adult* has more responsibility
than a child.

* **advance**[2] 〔əd'væns〕 *v.* 前進
(= *progress*) *n.* 進步
The troops have now *advanced* to
within five miles of the city.
【記憶技巧】 *adv* (from) + *ance*
(before) (從「以前」來到「現在」，
就是「前進」)
【反義詞】 retreat (後退；撤退)

advanced[3] 〔əd'vænst〕 *adj.* 高深的；
先進的 (= *up-to-date*)
He went abroad for *advanced* studies.
【衍伸詞】 *advanced studies* (深造)
an advanced country (先進國家)

* **advantage**[3] 〔əd'væntɪdʒ〕 *n.* 優點
(= *benefit*)
He has the *advantage* of good health.
【反義詞】 disadvantage (缺點)

* **adventure**[3] 〔əd'vɛntʃɚ〕 *n.* 冒險
My grandfather enjoys talking about
his boyhood *adventures*.
【記憶技巧】 *ad* (to) + *vent* (come) +
ure (*n.*) (去面臨危險，就是「冒險」)
【典型考題】
The old man always spins tales about
his _____ in remote areas in his youth.
A. delivery B. designs
C. adventures D. command [C]

A

* **adverb**[4] 〔'ædvɝb 〕 *n.* 副詞
  【記憶技巧】 *ad* + *verb* (動詞) = adverb

* **advertise**[3] 〔'ædvɚ͵taɪz 〕 *v.* 登廣告
  (= *publicize*)

* **advertisement**[3] 〔͵ædvɚ'taɪzmənt 〕
  n. 廣告 (= *ad*)；平面廣告
  Advertisements help to sell goods.

  ┌─【典型考題】─────
  │ The _____ was so convincing that
  │ I decided to try the product.
  │ A. personal   B. confidence
  │ C. advertisement   D. ingredient   **[C]**
  └────────────────

* **advice**[3] 〔 əd'vaɪs 〕 *n.* 勸告；建議
  (= *suggestion*)
  I need your *advice* on the matter.
  【注意】 advice 為不可數名詞，可用單位名詞
       piece 表示「數」的概念。

* **advise**[3] 〔 əd'vaɪz 〕 *v.* 勸告；建議
  (= *suggest*)
  He *advised* his daughter not to marry
  in a hurry.
  【記憶技巧】 *ad* (to) + *vise* (see)
       (看見別人的行為，因而給予「勸告」)

  adviser[3] 〔 əd'vaɪzɚ 〕 *n.* 顧問
  (= *counselor*)；導師 (= *advisor*)

* **affair**[2] 〔 ə'fɛr 〕 *n.* 事情 (= *matter*)
  All of us should be concerned with
  public *affairs* to make our society a
  better place.

  ┌─【典型考題】─────
  │ He always knows how to handle his
  │ own _____.
  │ A. motions   B. phrases
  │ C. genders   D. affairs   **[D]**
  └────────────────

* **affect**[3] 〔 ə'fɛkt 〕 *v.* 影響 (= *influence*)
  The power failure *affected* thousands
  of people, forcing them to live in the
  dark.
  【比較】 effect 〔 ɪ'fɛkt 〕 *n.* 影響

* **afford**[3] 〔 ə'fɔrd 〕 *v.* 負擔得起
  This is not expensive, so I can *afford*
  to buy it.

* **afraid**[1] 〔 ə'fred 〕 *adj.* 害怕的
  Don't be *afraid* of my puppy.

* **afterward(s)**[3] 〔'æftɚwɚd(z) 〕 *adv.*
  後來；之後
  Let's have dinner first and go to a
  movie *afterwards*.
  【比較】 downward(s) (向下地)
          northward(s) (向北地)
          outward(s) (向外地)

* **against**[1] 〔 ə'gɛnst 〕 *prep.* 反對
  Are you for or *against* it?

* **age**[1] 〔 edʒ 〕 *n.* 年紀 (= *years*)；時代
  v. 變老 (= *grow old*)

* **agency**[4] 〔'edʒənsɪ 〕 *n.* 代辦處
  (= *company*)
  Employment *agencies* help workers
  to get jobs, and find workers for
  people who need them.
  【衍伸詞】 *travel agency* (旅行社)
         employment agency (職業介
         紹所)

* **agent**[4] 〔'edʒənt 〕 *n.* 代理人；經紀人
  (= *representative*)；密探
  Mr. White is my *agent*; he can make
  decisions for me.
  【衍伸詞】 *travel agent* (旅遊業者)

* **aggressive**[4] 〔 ə'grɛsɪv 〕 *adj.* 有攻擊性的 (= *offensive*)；積極進取的
The audience gasped when the lion made an *aggressive* move toward its trainer.
【記憶技巧】 *ag* (to) + *gress* (walk) + *ive* (adj.) (走進別人的領域，是「有攻擊性的」行為)

─【典型考題】─────
Please keep a safe distance. When startled, the tamed animal can become very _____.
A. aggressive B. possible
C. attentive   D. permissive [A]

‡ **agree**[1] 〔 ə'gri 〕 *v.* 同意 (= *concur*)
Gao Xingjian, who won the Nobel Prize for literature in 2000, has *agreed* to teach in eastern Taiwan this summer.
【記憶技巧】 *a* (to) + *gree* (please) (「同意」對方的想法，會讓對方高興)

agreeable[4] 〔 ə'griəbḷ 〕 *adj.* 令人愉快的 (= *pleasant*)

* **agreement**[1] 〔 ə'grimənt 〕 *n.* 協議 (= *treaty*)

* **agriculture**[3] 〔 'æɡrɪ͵kʌltʃɚ 〕 *n.* 農業 (= *farming*)
【記憶技巧】 *agri* (field) + *culture* (文化)(田野文化，即「農業」)

‡ **ahead**[1] 〔 ə'hɛd 〕 *adv.* 在前方
John ran *ahead* of the other boys.
【片語】 *ahead of* (在…之前)

* **aid**[2] 〔 ed 〕 *n. v.* 幫助 (= *help*)
He deserves our *aid*.

* **AIDS**[4] 〔 edz 〕 *n.* 愛滋病；後天免疫不全症候群

AIDS stands for Acquired Immune Deficiency Syndrome.

‡ **aim**[2] 〔 em 〕 *n.* 目標 (= *goal*)
My *aim* is to become an English teacher.

‡ **air**[1] 〔 ɛr 〕 *n.* 空氣 (= *atmosphere*)
I need some fresh *air*.

‡ **air conditioner**[3] 〔 'ɛrkən'dɪʃənɚ 〕 *n.* 冷氣機
We need a new *air conditioner*.

* **aircraft**[2] 〔 'ɛr͵kræft 〕 *n.* 飛機
【集合名詞】(= *plane*)
The *aircraft* was damaged by lightning and had to make an emergency landing.

* **airlines**[2] 〔 'ɛr͵laɪnz 〕 *n.* 航空公司
I often travel by China *Airlines*.
【注意】通常以複數形當單數用，作「航空公司」解 (= *airways*)。

* **airmail**[1] 〔 'ɛr͵mel 〕 *n.* 航空郵件
【片語】 *by airmail* (以航空郵寄)

‡ **airplane**[1] 〔 'ɛr͵plen 〕 *n.* 飛機
(= *plane* = *aircraft*)
He took a trip by *airplane*.

‡ **airport**[1] 〔 'ɛr͵port 〕 *n.* 機場
(= *airfield*)
An *airport* is a busy place.
【記憶技巧】 *air* + *port* (港口)(空港，即「機場」)

‡ **alarm**[2] 〔 ə'lɑrm 〕 *v.* 使驚慌 *n.* 警鈴
We were *alarmed* by the loud thunder.
【記憶技巧】 *al* (to) + *arm* (weapons) (拿著武器，會使別人「驚慌」)
【衍伸詞】 *alarm clock* (鬧鐘)

A

* **album**[2] 〔'ælbəm〕 *n.* 專輯(= *record*)；剪貼本；(照片、郵票、手稿等的) 專册；黏貼本

* **alcohol**[4] 〔'ælkə,hɔl〕 *n.* 酒 (= *liquor*)；酒精
It is illegal to sell *alcohol* to minors.

* **alert**[4] 〔ə'lɝt〕 *adj.* 機警的 (= *attentive*)   *v.* 使警覺   *n.* 警報
The *alert* guard prevented a robbery.

【典型考題】
The government issued a travel
———— for Taiwanese in response to
the outbreak of civil war in Syria.
A. alert   B. monument
C. exit   D. circulation   [A]

* **alike**[2] 〔ə'laɪk〕 *adj.* 相像的 (= *similar*)
The two sisters look very much *alike*.

* **alive**[2] 〔ə'laɪv〕 *adj.* 活的 (= *living*)；有活力的
People have a better chance of remaining *alive* in a car accident if they use seat belts.
【反義詞】 dead (死的)

* **alley**[3] 〔'ælɪ〕 *n.* 巷子 (= *lane*)
There is an *alley* behind her house.

* **allow**[1] 〔ə'laʊ〕 *v.* 允許 (= *permit*)
We were not *allowed* to wear short skirts in our school days.

* **allowance**[4] 〔ə'laʊəns〕 *n.* 零用錢 (= *pocket money*)
My parents give me an *allowance* for daily expenses.

almond[2] 〔'æmənd〕 *n.* 杏仁

* **almost**[1] 〔'ɔl,most〕 *adv.* 幾乎
Dinner is *almost* ready.

* **alone**[1] 〔ə'lon〕 *adj.* 單獨的 *adv.* 單獨地
Parents should never leave children *alone* at night.

* **along**[1] 〔ə'lɔŋ〕 *prep.* 沿著
She walked *along* the street with her mother.

* **aloud**[2] 〔ə'laʊd〕 *adv.* 出聲地 (= *out loud*)
Please read *aloud*. (請唸出聲音來。)
Please speak *loudly*. (請大聲說。)
【記憶技巧】 *a* (intensive) + *loud*
【注意】 aloud 的主要意思是「出聲地」，作「大聲地」解，是古語用法，現在不用，要用 loudly 來取代。

* **alphabet**[2] 〔'ælfə,bɛt〕 *n.* 字母系統
The Phoenician *alphabet* was the most useful method of writing ever invented.

* **although**[2] 〔ɔl'ðo〕 *conj.* 雖然
Although it was raining, Joan still wanted to go out.

* **altogether**[2] 〔,ɔltə'gɛðɚ〕 *adv.* 總共 (= *all*)；完全地 (= *completely*)
There are seven of us *altogether*.

* **aluminum**[4] 〔ə'lumɪnəm〕 *n.* 鋁

* **always**[1] 〔'ɔlwez〕 *adv.* 總是

* **a.m.**[4] 〔'e'ɛm〕 *abbr.* 上午 (= *am* = *A.M.* = *AM*)
I will meet you at 8:15 *a.m.*

* **amateur**[4] 〔ˈæməˌtʃur 〕 *adj.* 業餘的
(= *nonprofessional*) *n.* 業餘愛好者
Mr. Shaw is an *amateur* photographer.
【記憶技巧】*amat* (love) + *eur* (人)
(只是愛好者，沒有將嗜好當成職業，所以
是「業餘的」)
【反義詞】professional (職業的)

* **amaze**[3] 〔 əˈmez 〕 *v.* 使驚訝
(= *astonish*)
Donna *amazed* the judges with her
excellent performance.
【記憶技巧】*a* (intensive) + *maze*
(confuse) (當一個人驚訝時，會感到
非常困惑)

* **amazement**[3] 〔 əˈmezmənt 〕 *n.* 驚訝
(= *astonishment*)

* **ambassador**[3] 〔 æmˈbæsədɚ 〕 *n.*
大使 (= *representative*)
Mr. Lee is our *ambassador* to South
Africa.
【衍伸詞】embassy (大使館)

* **ambition**[3] 〔 æmˈbɪʃən 〕 *n.* 抱負；
野心 (= *goal* = *wish*)
His *ambition* is to be a millionaire.
【記憶技巧】*amb* (about) + *it* (go) +
ion (n.) (為了「抱負」，就要到處奔波)

* **ambitious**[4] 〔 æmˈbɪʃəs 〕 *adj.*
有抱負的；有野心的 (= *aspiring*)

* **amid**[4] 〔 əˈmɪd 〕 *prep.* 在…之中
(= *amidst*)
Ivan sat *amid* the fans, watching the
performance with delight.
【記憶技巧】*a* (on) + *mid* (middle)

** **among**[1] 〔 əˈmʌŋ 〕 *prep.* 在…之間
She was sitting *among* the boys.

* **amount**[2] 〔 əˈmaunt 〕 *n.* 數量
He paid a large *amount* of money.

* **amuse**[4] 〔 əˈmjuz 〕 *v.* 娛樂 (= *please*)
A clown was hired to *amuse* the
children.
【記憶技巧】*a* + *muse* (Muse (繆斯女神)，
掌管音樂、美術等，有「娛樂」性質的學問)

* **amusement**[4] 〔 əˈmjuzmənt 〕 *n.* 娛樂

* **analysis**[4] 〔 əˈnæləsɪs 〕 *n.* 分析
(= *study*)
A careful *analysis* of the substance
was made in the laboratory.
【記憶技巧】*ana* (back) + *lys* (loosen)
+ *is* (n.) (「分析」就是將錯綜複雜的事情
解開回到原來的樣子)

* **analyze**[4] 〔ˈænḷˌaɪz 〕 *v.* 分析
(= *research*)
┌【典型考題】─────────
│ Faced with a problem, you have to
│ ────── it first, and then try to find
│ a solution.
│ A. resemble   B. analyze
│ C. concentrate   D. substitute   [B]
└──────────────────

* **ancestor**[4] 〔ˈænsɛstɚ 〕 *n.* 祖先
(= *forefather*)
Our *ancestors* were French, but
none of us speak the language.
【記憶技巧】*an* (before) + *ces* (go) +
tor (n.) (走在前面的人，也就是「祖先」)

** **ancient**[2] 〔ˈenʃənt 〕 *adj.* 古代的
Museums have *ancient* and modern
art.

A

‡**angel**[3] 〔ˈendʒəl〕 n. 天使

In pictures *angels* are usually dressed in white and have wings.

【比較】angle（角度）

‡**anger**[1] 〔ˈæŋgɚ〕 n. 生氣；憤怒（= *rage* = *fury*） v. 使生氣；激怒

The two boys were full of *anger*.

***angle**[3] 〔ˈæŋgl̩〕 n. 角度（= *slope*）；觀點

Looking at the painting from this *angle*, we can see a hidden image.

【衍伸詞】tri**angle**（三角形）

‡**animal**[1] 〔ˈænəml̩〕 n. 動物（= *creature*）

The earliest form of man's wealth was *animals* and tools.

‡**ankle**[2] 〔ˈæŋkl̩〕 n. 腳踝

Sam hurt his *ankle*.

***anniversary**[4] 〔͵ænəˈvɝsərɪ〕 n. 週年紀念（= *remembrance*）

The couple celebrated their wedding *anniversary* with a trip abroad.

【記憶技巧】*anni* (year) + *vers* (turn) + *ary* (n.)（每年都來一次，也就是「週年紀念」）

***announce**[3] 〔əˈnauns〕 v. 宣佈（= *declare*）

The former singer has *announced* his candidacy.

【記憶技巧】*an* (to) + *nounce* (report)（向大眾報告，就是「宣佈」）

【比較】de**nounce**（譴責）
pro**nounce**（發音）
re**nounce**（放棄）

***announcement**[3] 〔əˈnaunsmənt〕 n. 宣佈（= *declaration*）；公告

***annoy**[4] 〔əˈnɔɪ〕 v. 使心煩（= *bother* = *irritate*）

Annoyed by the children's loud voices, Mrs. Davis told them to speak softly.

***annual**[4] 〔ˈænjuəl〕 adj. 一年一度的（= *once a year*）；一年的

That contract must be renewed every year; it is an *annual* one.

‡**another**[1] 〔əˈnʌðɚ〕 adj. 另一個

The shirt is too small; I need *another* one.

‡**answer**[1] 〔ˈænsɚ〕 v. 回答

The question is so difficult that we can't *answer* it.

‡**ant**[1] 〔ænt〕 n. 螞蟻

An *ant* is a small insect.

***anxiety**[4] 〔æŋˈzaɪətɪ〕 n. 焦慮（= *worry*）；令人擔心的事

The dentist tried to relieve his patient's *anxiety* by telling him his teeth were in good shape.

┌─【典型考題】─────────
I felt a bit of ＿＿＿＿ the day school began.
A. anxious   B. anxiously
C. anxiety   D. anxieties   [C]
└────────────────────

***anxious**[4] 〔ˈæŋkʃəs〕 adj. 焦慮的（= *worried*）；渴望的（= *eager*）

【片語】*be anxious to V*.（渴望…）

‡**anybody**[2] 〔'ɛnɪˌbɑdɪ 〕*pron.* 任何人

***anyhow**[2] 〔'ɛnɪˌhau 〕*adv.* 無論如何
Anyhow, let's try again.

‡**anyone**[2] 〔'ɛnɪˌwʌn 〕*pron.* 任何人
If *anyone* calls, tell him I'll be back at five.

‡**anything**[1] 〔'ɛnɪˌθɪŋ 〕*pron.* 任何事

***anytime**[2] 〔'ɛnɪˌtaɪm 〕*adv.* 任何時候
You are welcome to visit us *anytime*.

***anyway**[2] 〔'ɛnɪˌwe 〕*adv.* 無論如何
Anyway, it's not fair.

‡**anywhere**[2] 〔'ɛnɪˌhwɛr 〕*adv.* 任何地方
Lisa has never been *anywhere* outside her country.

***apart**[3] 〔 ə'pɑrt 〕*adv.* 相隔；分開地
My sister and I live twenty miles *apart*.
【記憶技巧】 *a* (to) + *part* (分開)

‡**apartment**[2] 〔 ə'pɑrtmənt 〕*n.* 公寓
(= *flat*)
Ben and his sister lived in an *apartment*.

***ape**[1] 〔 ep 〕*n.* 猿   *v.* 模仿 (= *imitate*)

‡**apologize**[4] 〔 ə'pɑləˌdʒaɪz 〕*v.* 道歉
(= *say sorry*)
There's nothing to *apologize* for.
【記憶技巧】 *apo* (off) + *log* (speak) + *ize* (v.) (為免去罪過而説話，就是「道歉」)

【典型考題】
The boy _____ to the teacher for his improper behavior.
A. apologized   B. appealed
C. approached   D. attached   **[A]**

***apology**[4] 〔 ə'pɑlədʒɪ 〕*n.* 道歉
(= *regret*)

***apparent**[3] 〔 ə'pærənt 〕*adj.* 明顯的
(= *obvious*)
Old age is the *apparent* cause of death.
【記憶技巧】 *ap* (to) + *par* (appear) + *ent* (adj.) (讓東西顯現出來，就是變得「明顯的」)

***appeal**[3] 〔 ə'pil 〕*v.* 吸引
His performance didn't *appeal* to me.
【常考片語】 *appeal to* 吸引 (= *attract*)

‡**appear**[1] 〔 ə'pɪr 〕*v.* 出現
(= *show up*)；似乎 (= *seem*)
AIDS is caused by a kind of virus, but signs of the disease may not *appear* until several years after a person is infected.

***appearance**[2] 〔 ə'pɪrəns 〕*n.* 外表
(= *look*)；出現
You must not judge things by *appearances*.

***appetite**[2] 〔'æpəˌtaɪt 〕*n.* 食慾
(= *hunger*)；渴望
A good *appetite* is a good sauce.

【典型考題】
Eating snacks between meals may kill your _____.
A. energy   B. character
C. quality   D. appetite   **[D]**

‡**apple**[1] 〔'æpl 〕*n.* 蘋果
An *apple* a day keeps the doctor away.

***appliance**[4] 〔 ə'plaɪəns 〕*n.* 家電用品
(= *device*)
Refrigerators, washing machines, toasters, and irons are household *appliances*.

A

* **applicant**[4] 〔'æpləkənt 〕 *n.* 申請人；
應徵者 (= *candidate*)
Displaying your knowledge about the corporation may make you stand out from other *applicants*.

┌─【典型考題】────────
When you put in for a job, you are a(n) _____ for it.
A. client   B. applicant
C. accountant   D. customer   [B]
└────────────────────

* **application**[4] 〔,æplə'keʃən 〕 *n.* 申請
(= *request*)；申請書；應用
【衍伸詞】 *application form* (申請表)

* **apply**[2] 〔 ə'plaɪ 〕 *v.* 申請 (= *request*)；
應徵；運用 (= *use*)
【片語】 *apply for* (申請；應徵)
          apply to (適用於)

* **appoint**[4] 〔 ə'pɔɪnt 〕 *v.* 指派(= *assign*)
【記憶技巧】 *ap* (to) + *point* (指)
          (被指到的就派出去)

* **appointment**[4] 〔 ə'pɔɪntmənt 〕 *n.*
約會 (= *meeting*)；約診
I'm sorry I can't have lunch with you; I have a prior *appointment*.
【注意】男女之間的約會，則是 date。

* **appreciate**[3] 〔 ə'priʃɪ,et 〕 *v.* 欣賞；
感激 (= *be grateful for*)
I really *appreciate* what you have done for me.

* **appreciation**[4] 〔 ə,priʃɪ'eʃən 〕 *n.*
欣賞；感激 (= *gratitude*)

* **approach**[3] 〔 ə'protʃ 〕 *v.* 接近
(= *come to*)   *n.* 方法 (= *method*)
A beggar *approached* me for alms today.

【記憶技巧】 *ap* (to) + *proach* (near)
(向～靠近，也就是「接近」)
【比較】cockroach-approach-reproach 這
三個字要一起背，口訣是：「蟑螂」「接近」
就「責備」牠。

┌─【典型考題】────────
Many students find it hard to focus on their studies when holidays are _____.
A. approaching   B. dismissing
C. expanding   D. presenting   [A]
└────────────────────

* **appropriate**[4] 〔 ə'proprɪɪt 〕 *adj.*
適當的 (= *suitable* = *proper*)
Screaming doesn't seem to be an *appropriate* response to this situation.
【記憶技巧】 *ap* (to) + *propri* (proper)
     + *ate* (*adj.*)

┌─【典型考題】────────
It is not _____ for Chinese to attend a funeral wearing loud clothing.
A. permanent   B. insistent
C. appropriate   D. hospitable   [C]
└────────────────────

* **approval**[4] 〔 ə'pruvl 〕 *n.* 贊成
(= *consent*)

* **approve**[3] 〔 ə'pruv 〕 *v.* 贊成；批准
(= *agree to*)
The school has *approved* his application.
【記憶技巧】 *ap* (to) + *prove* (證明)
【反義詞】 disapprove (不贊成)

*** **April**[1] 〔'eprəl 〕 *n.* 四月

* **apron**[2] 〔'eprən 〕 *n.* 圍裙
My mother always puts on her *apron* before she starts cooking.

* **aquarium**[3] 〔 ə'kwɛrɪəm 〕 *n.* 水族箱;水族館

The water in the *aquarium* looks cloudy. When did you last clean the tank?

【記憶技巧】*aqua* (water) + *rium* (place)(有水的地方,即「水族箱」)

* **arch**[4] 〔 ɑrtʃ 〕 *n.* 拱門 (= *archway*)

* **area**[1] 〔'ɛrɪə , 'erɪə 〕 *n.* 地區 (= *region*)

* **argue**[2] 〔'ɑrgju 〕 *v.* 爭論 (= *quarrel*);主張

I'm not going to *argue* with you tonight.

* **argument**[2] 〔'ɑrgjəmənt 〕 *n.* 爭論 (= *quarrel*);論點 (= *reason*)

* **arise**[4] 〔 ə'raɪz 〕 *v.* 發生 (= *happen*)

If you often borrow money from friends, problems are bound to *arise*.

【片語】*arise from* (起因於;由於)

* **arithmetic**[3] 〔 ə'rɪθmə,tɪk 〕 *n.* 算術 (= *science of numbers*);計算

I believe this number is incorrect. Please check your *arithmetic*.

【記憶技巧】*arithmet* (number) + *ic* (學術用語的字尾)(關於數字的學術)

* **arm**[1,2] 〔 ɑrm 〕 *n.* 手臂 (= *upper limb*) *v.* 武裝;配備 (= *equip*)

He fell down and hurt his left *arm*.

* **armchair**[2] 〔'ɑrm,tʃɛr 〕 *n.* 扶手椅

The woman is resting in the *armchair*.

* **arms**[4] 〔 ɑrmz 〕 *n. pl.* 武器

The government supplies its soldiers with *arms*.

* **army**[1] 〔'ɑrmɪ 〕 *n.* 軍隊;陸軍 (= *soldiers*);大批

There they formed an *army* of about two thousand men.

* **around**[1] 〔 ə'raʊnd 〕 *prep.* 環繞

He walked *around* the park three times.

* **arouse**[4] 〔 ə'raʊz 〕 *v.* 喚起 (= *inflame*);喚醒 (= *awaken*)

Mary's interest was *aroused* when she saw the other children rollerblading.

* **arrange**[2] 〔 ə'rendʒ 〕 *v.* 安排 (= *plan*);排列 (= *put in order*)

The meeting has been *arranged* for tonight.

【記憶技巧】*ar* (to) + *range* (rank)

【典型考題】

Jessica ＿＿＿＿ the chairs in a circle so that the participants could see one another.
A. displayed   B. located
C. removed   D. arranged   [D]

* **arrangement**[2] 〔 ə'rendʒmənt 〕 *n.* 安排 (= *plan*);排列 (= *display*)

【衍伸詞】*flower arrangement* (插花)

* **arrest**[2] 〔 ə'rɛst 〕 *v.* 逮捕 (= *capture*);吸引 *n.* 逮捕

The man was *arrested* for drunk driving.

【記憶技巧】*ar* (to) + *re* (back) + *st* (stand)(警察在「逮捕」犯人時,都會叫他們站住,再把他們抓回來)

【典型考題】

The drug dealer was ＿＿＿＿ by the police while he was selling cocaine to a high school student.
A. motivated   B. demonstrated
C. arrested   D. endangered   [C]

A

* **arrival**[3] 〔 ə'raɪvḷ 〕 n. 到達
（= coming）; 出現

‡ **arrive**[2] 〔 ə'raɪv 〕 v. 到達（= come）
The train starts at five, arriving at ten.

* **arrow**[2] 〔'æro 〕 n. 箭（= dart）
Time flies like an arrow.
【比較】bow（弓）

‡ **art**[1] 〔 art 〕 n. 藝術（品）（= artwork）;
技巧 pl. 文科【文學、藝術等學科】
Drawing pictures is an art.

* **article**[2,4] 〔'artɪkḷ 〕 n. 文章（= essay）;
物品（= thing）
He contributed articles to the
newspaper frequently.

* **artificial**[4] 〔ˌartə'fɪʃəl 〕 adj. 人造的;
人工的（= man-made）
The artificial flowers look almost real.
【記憶技巧】**arti**（skill）+ **fic**（make）
+ **ial**（adj.）（用技術去製造，即「人造的」）
【反義詞】natural（自然的; 未加工的）
┌─【典型考題】───────────────
The organic food products are made
of natural ingredients, with no
_____ flavors added.
A. accurate   B. regular
C. superficial   D. artificial   [D]
└──────────────────────────

‡ **artist**[2] 〔'artɪst 〕 n. 藝術家
（= creator）; 畫家

* **artistic**[4] 〔 ar'tɪstɪk 〕 adj. 藝術的
（= creative）; 有藝術鑑賞力的
┌─【典型考題】───────────────
Few people were conscious of the
_____ value of Vincent van
Gogh's paintings until he died.
A. artistic   B. athletic
C. insecure   D. ignorant   [A]
└──────────────────────────

‡ **as**[1] 〔 əz , æz 〕 prep. 身為… conj. 雖然
（= although）; 因為（= because）

* **ash**[3] 〔 æʃ 〕 n. 灰
They poured water on the ashes of
the fire.

* **ashamed**[4] 〔 ə'ʃemd 〕 adj. 感到羞恥
的（= feeling shame）; 感到慚愧的
Billy was ashamed of his bad behavior.
【記憶技巧】**a** + **shame**（羞恥）+ **d**

* **aside**[3] 〔 ə'saɪd 〕 adv. 在一邊
Put your book aside and go out and play.

‡ **ask**[1] 〔 æsk 〕 v. 問

‡ **asleep**[2] 〔 ə'slip 〕 adj. 睡著的
As soon as Mary went to bed, she was
able to fall asleep.
【片語】**fall asleep**（睡著）

* **aspect**[4] 〔'æspɛkt 〕 n. 方面（= point）;
外觀
Confidence is the most obvious aspect
of his character.
【記憶技巧】**a**（to）+ **spect**（see）
（看事情，可從各「方面」去看）

* **aspirin**[4] 〔'æspərɪn 〕 n. 阿斯匹靈
You can buy aspirin at a drugstore.

* **assemble**[4] 〔 ə'sɛmbḷ 〕 v. 集合
（= gather）; 裝配（= put together）
Please assemble the students in the
gymnasium.
【記憶技巧】**as**（to）+ **semble**（same）
（到相同地點，就是「集合」）
【比較】resemble（像）
┌─【典型考題】───────────────
He can _____ a motorcycle if he
is given all the parts.
A. transmit   B. assemble
C. reform   D. proceed   [B]
└──────────────────────────

* **assembly**[4] 〔ə'sɛmblɪ〕 *n.* 集會
  (= *meeting*)；裝配
  【衍伸詞】 *assembly line*（裝配線）

* **assign**[4] 〔ə'saɪn〕 *v.* 指派（= *appoint*）
  Margaret has been *assigned* to work
  in Germany.

* **assignment**[4] 〔ə'saɪnmənt〕 *n.* 作業
  (= *homework*)；任務（= *task*）

* **assist**[3] 〔ə'sɪst〕 *v.* 幫助（= *help*）
  I offered to *assist* my father with
  the gardening.
  【記憶技巧】 *as* (to) + *sist* (stand)
  （站在旁邊，給予「幫助」）
  【比較】 insist（堅持）；persist（堅持）；
  consist（組成）；exist（存在）；
  resist（抵抗）

* **assistance**[4] 〔ə'sɪstəns〕 *n.* 幫助

‡ **assistant**[2] 〔ə'sɪstənt〕 *n.* 助手

* **associate**[4] 〔ə'soʃɪ͵et〕 *v.* 聯想；
  使有關連
  People often *associate* the color
  red with love and passion.
  【片語】 *associate* A *with* B（把 A 和 B
  聯想在一起）
  be associated with 和…有關

  【典型考題】
  Chinese people always ＿＿＿＿ the
  color yellow with emperors.
  A. decorate   B. communicate
  C. award   D. associate   **[D]**

* **association**[4] 〔ə͵soʃɪ'eʃən〕 *n.* 協會
  (= *group*)

‡ **assume**[4] 〔ə's(j)um〕 *v.* 假定；認爲
  (= *presume*)；承擔
  If we receive a call during sleeping
  hours, we *assume* it is a very
  important matter.

  【記憶技巧】 *as* (to) + *sume* (take)
  （拿取想法，也就是「認爲」）
  【比較】 consume（消耗）
  presume（假定）
  resume（恢復；再繼續）

  【典型考題】
  The problem with Larry is that he
  doesn't know his limitations; he just
  ＿＿＿＿ he can do everything.
  A. convinces   B. disguises
  C. assumes   D. evaluates   **[C]**

* **assurance**[4] 〔ə'ʃurəns〕 *n.* 保證
  (= *promise*)；把握
  【比較】 insurance（保險）

* **assure**[4] 〔ə'ʃur〕 *v.* 向～保證
  (= *promise to*)
  I *assure* you that it will never
  happen again.

  【典型考題】
  I was worried about my first overseas
  trip, but my father ＿＿＿＿ me that
  he would help plan the trip so that
  nothing would go wrong.
  A. rescued   B. assured
  C. inspired   D. conveyed   **[B]**

* **athlete**[3] 〔'æθlit〕 *n.* 運動員
  (= *sportsperson*)

* **athletic**[4] 〔æθ'lɛtɪk〕 *adj.* 運動員的；
  強壯靈活的（= *strong*）
  Terry is so *athletic* that she can beat
  any other runner in our school.

  【典型考題】
  Maxwell has a(n) ＿＿＿＿ build. He is
  tall and fit. Besides, he seems to be
  able to perform energetic movements
  easily.
  A. monstrous   B. insecure
  C. amazed   D. athletic   **[D]**

A

* **ATM**[4] *n.* 自動提款機
  (= *automated teller machine*
  = *automatic teller machine*)

* **atmosphere**[4] 〔'ætməs,fɪr 〕 *n.*
  大氣層;氣氛
  A person who travels beyond the earth's *atmosphere* in a rocket-driven capsule is an astronaut.
  【記憶技巧】 *atmo* (vapor) + *sphere*
  (ball) (地球四周的氣體,就是「大氣層」)

* **atom**[4] 〔'ætəm 〕 *n.* 原子
  【比較】 molecule (分子)

* **atomic**[4] 〔 ə'tɑmɪk 〕 *adj.* 原子的
  The idea of *atomic* power frightens some people.
  【記憶技巧】 *a* (not) + *tom* (divide) + *ic*
  (*adj.*) (不能再分割的,就是「原子的」)
  【衍伸詞】 *atomic bomb* (原子彈)

* **attach**[4] 〔 ə'tætʃ 〕 *v.* 附上 (= *adhere*);
  綁
  I will *attach* the report to my next e-mail.
  【片語】 *attach* A *to* B (把 A 附到 B 上)
  【記憶技巧】 *at* (to) + *tach* (stake)
  (把東西栓上去,即「附上」)

* **attachment**[4] 〔 ə'tætʃmənt 〕 *n.*
  附屬品 (= *accessory*);附件;喜愛

‡ **attack**[2] 〔 ə'tæk 〕 *n. v.* 攻擊 (= *assault*)
  The tiger *attacked* and killed a deer for food.

* **attempt**[3] 〔 ə'tɛmpt 〕 *n. v.* 企圖;嘗試
  (= *try*)
  The climbers made several *attempts* to reach the top of the mountain.
  【比較】 tempt (誘惑) -attempt-contempt
  (輕視) 這三個字要一起背。

【典型考題】
George at first had difficulty swimming across the pool, but he finally succeeded on his fourth _____ .
A. attempt   B. process
C. instance   D. display   [A]

* **attend**[2] 〔 ə'tɛnd 〕 *v.* 參加 (= *go to*);
  上 (學);服侍
  I was unable to *attend* my niece's wedding because I was sick.
  【記憶技巧】 *at* (to) + *tend* (stretch)
  (往有人的地方伸展,就是「參加」)

‡ **attention**[2] 〔 ə'tɛnʃən 〕 *n.* 注意力
  (= *notice*)
  Pay *attention* to what you're doing. Don't let your thoughts wander.
  【片語】 *pay attention to* (注意)

【典型考題】
Dr. Chu's speech on the new energy source attracted great _____ from the audience at the conference.
A. attention   B. fortune
C. solution   D. influence   [A]

* **attitude**[3] 〔'ætə,tjud 〕 *n.* 態度
  (= *manner*)
  Danny always has a positive *attitude*.

* **attract**[3] 〔 ə'trækt 〕 *v.* 吸引
  (= *appeal to*)
  This new product has *attracted* a lot of attention.
  【記憶技巧】 *at* (to) + *tract* (draw)
  (把眾人的目光拉過來,就是「吸引」)

【典型考題】
Her beautiful dress _____ everyone's attention.
A. attracts   B. accepts
C. attaches   D. attends   [A]

A

* **attraction**[4] 〔 ə'trækʃən 〕 *n.* 吸引力
（ = *appeal* ）；有吸引力的東西

* **attractive**[3] 〔 ə'træktɪv 〕 *adj.* 吸引人的（ = *charming* ）

* **audience**[3] 〔 'ɔdɪəns 〕 *n.* 觀眾
（ = *spectators* ）
The *audience* was pleased with the excellent performance.
【記憶技巧】 *audi* (hear) + *ence* (*n.*)
（聆聽觀看的人，就是「觀眾」）

* **audio**[4] 〔 'ɔdɪ‚o 〕 *adj.* 聽覺的

‡ **August**[1] 〔 'ɔgəst 〕 *n.* 八月

‡ **aunt**[1] 〔 ænt 〕 *n.* 阿姨
My *aunt* is coming to see us.

* **author**[3] 〔 'ɔθɚ 〕 *n.* 作者（ = *writer* ）
v. 寫作；創作
【記憶技巧】 *auth* (make to grow) + *or* （人）（使事物產生的人，即「作者」）

* **authority**[4] 〔 ə'θɔrətɪ 〕 *n.* 權威；權力
The traffic police have the *authority* to issue tickets for traffic violations.
【衍伸詞】 *the authorities concerned* （有關當局）

* **auto**[3] 〔 'ɔto 〕 *n.* 汽車（ = *automobile* ）

* **autobiography**[4] 〔‚ɔtəbaɪ'ɑgrəfɪ 〕 *n.* 自傳（ = *life story* ）
We call the story of a person's life written by himself his *autobiography*.
【記憶技巧】 *auto* (self) + *bio* (life) + *graph* (write) + *y* (*n.*) （寫關於自己一生的書，也就是「自傳」）
【比較】 biography （傳記）

* **automatic**[3] 〔‚ɔtə'mætɪk 〕 *adj.* 自動的（ = *self-acting* ）
You can withdraw the money from the *automatic* teller machine at any time.
【記憶技巧】 *auto* (self) + *mat* (think) + *ic* (*adj.*) （可以自己動腦去想的，就是「自動的」）

* **automobile**[3] 〔 'ɔtəmə‚bil 〕 *n.* 汽車（ = *car* ）
【記憶技巧】 *auto* (self) + *mobile* （可移動的）

‡ **autumn**[1] 〔 'ɔtəm 〕 *n.* 秋天（ = *fall* ）
Autumn is the season between summer and winter.

‡ **available**[3] 〔 ə'veləbl̩ 〕 *adj.* 可獲得的
The hotel is full. There are no rooms *available*.

【典型考題】
If you want to borrow magazines, tapes, or CDs, you can visit the library. They are all _____ there.
A. sufficient　　B. vacant
C. able　　　　D. available　　[D]

* **avenue**[3] 〔 'ævə‚nju 〕 *n.* 大道；…街；途徑
The restaurant is located on First *Avenue*.
【記憶技巧】 *a* (to) + *venue* (come)
【比較】 revenue （收入；國家的歲收）

* **average**[3] 〔 'ævərɪdʒ 〕 *n.* 平均（數）
adj. 一般的

【典型考題】
The _____ of 18, 13, and 14 is 15.
A. division　　B. balance
C. average　　D. total　　[C]

A

‡**avoid**[2] 〔ə'vɔɪd〕 v. 避免

Women should *avoid* driving alone at night.

【典型考題】

It is not safe to swim in the sea, so Susan's mother asked her to _____ it.
A. invite   B. draw
C. avoid   D. join   [C]

* **await**[4] 〔ə'wet〕 v. 等待 (= *wait for*)

You may *await* your visitors in the Arrival Hall.

* **awake**[3] 〔ə'wek〕 v. 醒來 (= *wake up*)
adj. 醒著的

Larry *awoke* from his nap when the phone rang.

* **awaken**[3] 〔ə'wekən〕 v. 喚醒
(= *wake up*)

* **award**[3] 〔ə'wɔrd〕 v. 頒發 (= *give*)
n. 獎 (= *prize*)

Dr. Yang Chen was *awarded* the 1957 Nobel Prize for physics.

【比較】award 和 reward 要一起背，口訣是：「頒發」「獎賞」。

* **aware**[3] 〔ə'wɛr〕 adj. 知道的
(= *conscious*)

A good salesperson is *aware* of his strengths and weaknesses, and constantly tries to improve his sales skills.

【片語】 *be aware of* (知道；察覺到)

‡**away**[1] 〔ə'we〕 adv. 離開

They're *away* on holiday.

* **awful**[3] 〔'ɔfḷ〕 adj. 可怕的
(= *terrible* = *horrible*)

A scene of mass poverty is an *awful* sight.

* **awkward**[4] 〔'ɔkwəd〕 adj. 笨拙的
(= *clumsy*)；不自在的

Tom is terribly shy and he feels *awkward* in the presence of women.

【記憶技巧】 *awk* (wrong) + *ward* (表示方向)（做事情時，結果總是往錯誤的方向發展，表示「笨拙的」）

ax[3] 〔æks〕 n. 斧頭 (= *axe*)

B b

‡**baby**[1] 〔'bebɪ〕 n. 嬰兒 (= *infant*)

The hungry *baby* was crying.

* **baby-sit**[2] 〔'bebɪ,sɪt〕 v. 當臨時褓姆

I asked Melissa to *baby-sit* the children while we go out to dinner.

‡**baby-sitter**[2] 〔'bebɪ,sɪtə〕 n. 臨時褓姆

Lucy's part-time job is being a *baby-sitter*.

‡**back**[1] 〔bæk〕 n. 背面 (= *rear*)

The price is on the *back* of the book.

【反義詞】 front (前面)

* **background**[3] 〔'bæk,graʊnd〕 n. 背景；經驗 (= *experience*)

She made it to the top despite her *background*.

* **backpack**[4] 〔'bæk,pæk〕 n. 背包

‡backward(s)[2] 〔ˈbækwəd(z)〕 *adv.*
向後
She looked *backward* over her shoulder.
【反義詞】 forward(s)（向前）

*bacon[3] 〔ˈbekən〕 *n.* 培根

*bacteria[3] 〔bækˈtɪrɪə〕 *n.pl.* 細菌
（= *microorganisms*）
【注意】單數為 bacterium。
Many diseases are spread by *bacteria*.

‡bad[1] 〔bæd〕 *adj.* 不好的（= *harmful*）
The weather was really *bad*.

*badly[3] 〔ˈbædlɪ〕 *adv.* 差勁地；嚴重地
He was *badly* injured.

‡badminton[2] 〔ˈbædmɪntən〕 *n.*
羽毛球；羽毛球運動
Badminton is a very interesting sport.

‡bag[1] 〔bæg〕 *n.* 袋子
Tom carried a *bag* to school.

*baggage[3] 〔ˈbægɪdʒ〕 *n.* 行李
（= *luggage*）
The customs officer examined my
baggage.
【比較】baggage 和 luggage 都是集合
名詞，不加 s，而 bag 也可作「行李」解，
是可數名詞。

*bait[3] 〔bet〕 *n.* 餌（= *attraction*）；
誘惑
The fisherman claims that worms
are the best *bait*.

‡bake[2] 〔bek〕 *v.* 烘烤
I like to *bake* cakes from time to time.

‡bakery[2] 〔ˈbekərɪ〕 *n.* 麵包店
（= *bakeshop*）

There is a very good *bakery* near my
house.

【典型考題】
I like bread very much and I usually
buy my breakfast at the _____
near my home.
A. bakery　　　B. bank
C. fire station　　D. post office　　**[A]**

*balance[3] 〔ˈbæləns〕 *n.* 平衡
（= *evenness*）
The acrobat lost his *balance* and fell
off the tightrope.

【典型考題】
We should keep a _____ between
doing what we want and doing what
we should.
A. balance　　　B. benefit
C. content　　　D. influence　　**[A]**

‡balcony[2] 〔ˈbælkənɪ〕 *n.* 陽台
（= *terrace*）；包廂
You can see the ocean from our
balcony.
【記憶技巧】*balcon*（房子較突出的一角）
+ *y* (place)

*bald[4] 〔bɔld〕 *adj.* 禿頭的（= *hairless*）
The driver was a tall, *bald* man.
【比較】bold（大膽的）

‡ball[1] 〔bɔl〕 *n.* 球；舞會
We need a *ball* to play basketball.

*ballet[4] 〔bæˈle〕 *n.* 芭蕾舞

*balloon[1] 〔bəˈlun〕 *n.* 氣球
They blew up *balloons* for the party.

*bamboo[2] 〔bæmˈbu〕 *n.* 竹子
【衍伸詞】*a bamboo shoot*（竹筍）

B

‡banana[1] 〔bəˈnænə〕*n.* 香蕉
Monkeys like to eat *bananas*.

‡band[1] 〔bænd〕*n.* 樂隊；一群
The *band* is playing.

bandage[3] 〔ˈbændɪdʒ〕*n.* 繃帶
（= *dressing*）　*v.* 用繃帶包紮
You'd better put a *bandage* on that
cut finger.
【記憶技巧】*band* (bind) + *age* (*n.*)
（用來捆綁的東西，就是「繃帶」）
【比較】要連 band-aid（OK 繃）一起背

bang[3] 〔bæŋ〕*v.* 重擊
He *banged* the table with his fist.

‡bank[1] 〔bæŋk〕*n.* 銀行；河岸

banker[2] 〔ˈbæŋkɚ〕*n.* 銀行家
（= *financier*）

bankrupt[4] 〔ˈbæŋkrʌpt〕*adj.* 破產的
（= *broke*）
The man claimed he could not pay
his bills because he was *bankrupt*.
【記憶技巧】*bank* + *rupt* (break)
（銀行倒閉的，代表「破產的」）
【片語】*go bankrupt*（破產）
┌─【典型考題】────────────┐
The recession has made many small
companies go ＿＿＿＿.
A. bankrupt   B. balanced
C. conceptual   D. essential   [A]
└────────────────────┘

bar[1] 〔bar〕*n.* 酒吧（= *pub*）；
（巧克力、肥皂等）條；棒　*v.* 禁止

‡barbecue[2] 〔ˈbarbɪˌkju〕*n.* 烤肉
（= *Bar-B-Q*）
We'll have a *barbecue* this Friday.

barber[1] 〔ˈbarbɚ〕*n.* 理髮師
【記憶技巧】*barb* (beard) + *er*（人）
（負責修剪鬍子的人，是「理髮師」）
【比較】hairdresser（美髮師）

bare[3] 〔bɛr〕*adj.* 赤裸的（= *naked*）
The storm covered the *bare* ground
with three inches of snow.
┌─【典型考題】────────────┐
On a sunny afternoon last month, we
all took off our shoes and walked on
the grass with ＿＿＿＿ feet.
A. bare   B. raw
C. tough   D. slippery   [A]
└────────────────────┘

barely[3] 〔ˈbɛrlɪ〕*adv.* 幾乎不
（= *hardly*）
The old men *barely* talked to each
other.

bargain[4] 〔ˈbargɪn〕*v.* 討價還價
（= *negotiate*）　*n.* 便宜貨；協議
It's necessary to *bargain* if you want
to get a good price.
┌─【典型考題】────────────┐
In traditional markets, you can get
better deals if you know how to ＿＿＿＿
with the vendors.
A. recover   B. scream
C. bargain   D. beg   [C]
└────────────────────┘

‡bark[2] 〔bark〕*v.*（狗、狐狸等）吠叫
（= *howl*）　*n.* 樹皮（= *covering*）
What are the dogs *barking* at?

barn[3] 〔barn〕*n.* 穀倉

barrel[3] 〔ˈbærəl〕*n.* 一桶
Oil is sold by the *barrel*.

* **barrier**[4] 〔ˈbærɪə〕 *n.* 障礙
(= *obstacle*)
Humanitarians tried to remove all the
barriers.
【記憶技巧】*bar* (bar) + *rier* (用來防
禦的柵欄,就是「障礙」)

‡ **base**[1] 〔bes〕 *n.* 基地 (= *post*);基礎
(= *foundation*);(棒球) 壘
He used Stephen King's novel as the
base of his movie.

* **baseball**[1] 〔ˈbesˌbɔl〕 *n.* 棒球

‡ **basement**[2] 〔ˈbesmənt〕 *n.* 地下室
(= *underground room*)
A house with a *basement* is for sale.

┌─【典型考題】────────
│ After the rain, the residents found the
│ _____, where they parked their cars,
│ full of water.
│ A. balcony   B. attic
│ C. closet   D. basement   [D]
└──────────────────

‡ **basic**[1] 〔ˈbesɪk〕 *adj.* 基本的
(= *fundamental*)
The *basic* topic of these fairy tales
never changes.

* **basin**[4] 〔ˈbesn̩〕 *n.* 臉盆;盆地(= *valley*)

* **basis**[2] 〔ˈbesɪs〕 *n.* 基礎 (= *base*);
根據 (= *agreement*)
The farmers form the *basis* of a nation.

┌─【典型考題】────────
│ His ideas have no _____ in reality.
│ They are not practical at all.
│ A. basis   B. reform
│ C. career   D. argument   [A]
└──────────────────

‡ **basket**[1] 〔ˈbæskɪt〕 *n.* 籃子;一籃的量
This *basket* is made of bamboo.

‡ **basketball**[1] 〔ˈbæskɪtˌbɔl〕 *n.* 籃球
We play *basketball* every day.

‡ **bat**[1] 〔bæt〕 *n.* 球棒;蝙蝠
Ben used a *bat* to hit the ball in the
game.

‡ **bath**[1] 〔bæθ〕 *n.* 洗澡
Sue took a *bath* because she was dirty.
【比較】shower (淋浴)

* **bathe**[1] 〔beð〕 *v.* 洗澡

‡ **bathroom**[1] 〔ˈbæθˌrum〕 *n.* 浴室;
廁所 (= *lavatory*)
She went into the *bathroom* and took
a shower.

【重要知識】因為 toilet 含有馬桶的意思,
美國人稱廁所為 bathroom(原意為浴室),
是種文雅的說法。

* **battery**[4] 〔ˈbætərɪ〕 *n.* 電池;連續猛
擊;【律】毆打

* **battle**[2] 〔ˈbætl̩〕 *n.* 戰役 (= *fight*)
v. 奮戰;競爭
After a fierce fight, the *battle* came
to an end.

* **bay**[3] 〔be〕 *n.* 海灣 (= *gulf* 〔gʌlf〕)
Several sailboats are moored in the
bay.

‡ **beach**[1] 〔bitʃ〕 *n.* 海灘 (= *seaside*)
John likes to go to the *beach*.

* **bead**[2] 〔bid〕 *n.* 有孔的小珠
Barbara wore a black *bead* necklace
at the party.

* **beak**[4] 〔bik〕 *n.* 鳥嘴
The parrot picked up a sunflower
seed with its *beak*.

B

B

* **beam**[3,4] 〔 bim 〕 *n.* 光線（= *ray* ）；
横樑（= *rafter* ）　 *v.* 眉開眼笑
The guard shone a *beam* of light
on the car.

‡ **bean**[2] 〔 bin 〕 *n.* 豆子（= *seed* ）
A *bean* is a vegetable.

‡ **bear**[2,1] 〔 bɛr 〕 *v.* 忍受（= *endure* =
stand = *tolerate* = *put up with* ）　 *n.* 熊
【注意】三態變化：bear–bore–borne
I can't *bear* the noise anymore.
A *bear* is a wild animal.

┌─【典型考題】─────────┐
She couldn't _____ to leave and
cried all the way to the airport.
A. scatter   B. pay
C. exist   D. bear   **[D]**
└────────────────────┘

‡ **beard**[2] 〔 bɪrd 〕 *n.* 鬍子（= *whiskers* ）
My uncle has a long black *beard*.

* **beast**[3] 〔 bist 〕 *n.* 野獸
We are not sure what kind of *beast*
killed the goat.

‡ **beat**[1] 〔 bit 〕 *v.* 打；打敗　 *n.* 心跳；
節拍
He *beat* the drum with a stick.
【注意】三態變化：beat–beat–beat

‡ **beautiful**[1] 〔 ˈbjutəfəl 〕 *adj.* 美麗的
（= *pretty* ）

‡ **beauty**[1] 〔 ˈbjutɪ 〕 *n.* 美；美女

‡ **because**[1] 〔 bɪˈkɔz 〕 *conj.* 因為
Linda was late *because* it was raining.

‡ **become**[1] 〔 bɪˈkʌm 〕 *v.* 變成
They *became* good friends at once.

‡ **bed**[1] 〔 bɛd 〕 *n.* 床
I fell off my *bed* last night.

‡ **bedroom**[2] 〔 ˈbɛdˌrum 〕 *n.* 臥房
I have my own *bedroom*.

‡ **bee**[1] 〔 bi 〕 *n.* 蜜蜂
A *bee* is an insect which makes
honey.
【衍伸詞】beehive（蜂窩）
【片語】 *as busy as a bee*（非常忙碌）

‡ **beef**[2] 〔 bif 〕 *n.* 牛肉
You can buy *beef* from a butcher.

beep[2] 〔 bip 〕 *n.* 嗶嗶聲
v. 發出嗶嗶聲

* **beer**[2] 〔 bɪr 〕 *n.* 啤酒（= *brew* ）
Buy me a *beer*, Jack.

* **beetle**[2] 〔 ˈbitḷ 〕 *n.* 甲蟲

* **beg**[2] 〔 bɛg 〕 *v.* 乞求（= *ask for* ）
Timmy *begged* his mother to let
him watch the movie.

* **beggar**[3] 〔 ˈbɛgɚ 〕 *n.* 乞丐

‡ **begin**[1] 〔 bɪˈgɪn 〕 *v.* 開始（= *start* ）

* **beginner**[2] 〔 bɪˈgɪnɚ 〕 *n.* 初學者
（= *starter* ）；創辦人
He drives better than most *beginners*.

* **behave**[3] 〔 bɪˈhev 〕 *v.* 行為舉止（= *act* ）
Jim always *behaves* well.

* **behavior**[4] 〔 bɪˈhevjɚ 〕 *n.* 行為
（= *conduct*〔ˈkɑndʌkt 〕）
Everyone was impressed by his
polite *behavior*.

┌─【典型考題】─────────┐
Jane and I were ashamed of Tom's
rude _____ on the formal occasion.
A. attachment   B. behavior
C. time   D. harm   **[B]**
└────────────────────┘

‡**behind**[1] 〔 bɪ'haɪnd 〕 *prep.* 在…之後
【記憶技巧】*be* (by) + *hind* (在後的)

***being**[3] 〔'biɪŋ 〕 *n.* 存在
Scientists believe that they will one day be able to bring a human clone into *being*.
【片語】*come into being* (產生)
【衍伸詞】*human beings* (人類)

***belief**[2] 〔 bɪ'lif 〕 *n.* 相信 (= *trust*)；信仰 (= *faith*)
She was beautiful beyond *belief*.
【片語】*beyond belief* (令人難以置信地)

***believable**[2] 〔 bɪ'livəbl̩ 〕 *adj.* 可信的
(= *credible* 〔'krɛdəbl̩ 〕)

‡**believe**[1] 〔 bɪ'liv 〕 *v.* 相信 (= *trust*)
I *believe* in God.
【片語】*believe in* (相信…的存在；信任)

‡**bell**[1] 〔 bɛl 〕 *n.* 鐘；鈴
I can hear the church *bell* ringing.

***belly**[3] 〔'bɛlɪ 〕 *n.* 肚子 (= *stomach*)

‡**belong**[1] 〔 bə'lɔŋ 〕 *v.* 屬於
(= *be owned by*)
This book *belongs* to me.

‡**below**[1] 〔 bə'lo 〕 *prep.* 在…之下
Students who have marks *below* 60 will have to take the exam again.

‡**belt**[2] 〔 bɛlt 〕 *n.* 皮帶 (= *strap*)；地帶
Rose gave a *belt* to her father on his birthday.

‡**bench**[2] 〔 bɛntʃ 〕 *n.* 長椅 (= *long seat*)
The man has been sitting on the *bench* all day long.

***bend**[2] 〔 bɛnd 〕 *v.* 彎曲 (= *turn*)
Since the accident, Glen has been unable to *bend* his knee without pain.

***beneath**[3] 〔 bɪ'niθ 〕 *prep.* 在…之下
There are still many mysteries *beneath* the sea.
【記憶技巧】*be* (by) + *neath* (down)

***benefit**[3] 〔'bɛnəfɪt 〕 *n.* 利益；好處
(= *advantage*)　*v.* 對…有益；受益
Two weeks of paid vacation is one of the *benefits* of this job.

***berry**[3] 〔'bɛrɪ 〕 *n.* 漿果
The hikers found some *berries* in the woods and decided to pick them.
【比較】strawberry (草莓)

‡**beside**[1] 〔 bɪ'saɪd 〕 *prep.* 在…旁邊
Pat and Paul sat *beside* each other in class.

‡**besides**[2] 〔 bɪ'saɪdz 〕 *adv.* 此外
(= *moreover*)
It's too late to go out now. *Besides*, it's beginning to rain.

***best**[1] 〔 bɛst 〕 *adj.* 最好的

***bet**[2] 〔 bɛt 〕 *v.* 打賭 (= *gamble*)
My father likes to *bet* on the horse races.

***better**[1] 〔'bɛtɚ 〕 *adj.* 更好的

‡**between**[1] 〔 bə'twin 〕 *prep.* 在 (兩者) 之間
【記憶技巧】*be* (by) + *tween* (two)

【典型考題】
March is the third month of the year. It comes ＿＿＿＿＿ February and April.
A. about　　　B. before
C. during　　　D. between　　[D]

※**beyond**[2] 〔bɪ'jɑnd〕*prep.* 超過

Many people don't go on working *beyond* the age of 65.

＊**Bible**[3] 〔'baɪbl̩〕*n.* 聖經（= *Word of God*）；（小寫）權威書籍；經典

※**bicycle**[1] 〔'baɪsɪkl̩〕*n.* 腳踏車（= *bike*）

Do you know who stole the *bicycle*?

【記憶技巧】 *bi* (two) + *cycle* (circle)

※**big**[1] 〔bɪg〕*adj.* 大的；重要的

※**bike**[1] 〔baɪk〕*n.* 腳踏車（= *bicycle*）

※**bill**[2] 〔bɪl〕*n.* 帳單（= *charges*）；紙鈔（= *banknote*）；法案

The man is looking at the *bill*.

＊**billion**[3] 〔'bɪljən〕*n.* 十億

"How many people are there in the world?" "It has a population of more than 7.4 *billion*."

【比較】 trillion（兆）

＊**bind**[2] 〔baɪnd〕*v.* 綁（= *tie*）；包紮

【注意】 三態變化：bind-bound-bound

The package was *bound* with a string.

＊**bingo**[3] 〔'bɪŋgo〕*n.* 賓果遊戲

My grandmother was very excited when she won the *bingo* game.

＊**biography**[4] 〔baɪ'ɑgrəfɪ〕*n.* 傳記（= *life story*）

If you want to know more about Picasso, you should read his *biography*.

【記憶技巧】 *bio* (life) + *graph* (write) + *y* (*n.*)（記錄人的一生，就是「傳記」）

※**biology**[4] 〔baɪ'ɑlədʒɪ〕*n.* 生物學

※**bird**[1] 〔bɜd〕*n.* 鳥

＊**birth**[1] 〔bɜθ〕*n.* 出生；誕生

December 25 is Christmas Day. It celebrates the *birth* of Jesus approximately 2000 years ago.

＊**biscuit**[3] 〔'bɪskɪt〕*n.* 餅乾（= *cookie*）

Don't eat too many *biscuits* before dinner!

＊**bit**[1] 〔bɪt〕*n.* 一點點（= *a small amount*）

Just give me a *bit* of that soup. I'm not very hungry.

※**bite**[1] 〔baɪt〕*v.* 咬

【注意】 三態變化：bite–bit–bitten

My puppy always *bites* my shoes.

＊**bitter**[2] 〔'bɪtə〕*adj.* 苦的

The medicine tastes *bitter*.

※**black**[1] 〔blæk〕*adj.* 黑的（= *dark*）

Sue's hair is *black*.

【衍伸詞】 black sheep（害群之馬）

※**blackboard**[2] 〔'blæk,bord〕*n.* 黑板（= *chalkboard* 〔'tʃɔk,bord〕）

The teacher writes a sentence on the *blackboard*.

blade[4] 〔bled〕*n.* 刀鋒

The *blade* of this knife is so dull that it can't cut anything.

‡**blame**[3]〔blem〕v. 責備（＝*impute*）
n. 責難；責任

He *blamed* you for being late.

【片語】*be to blame*（應受責備；應該怪…）
blame sb. *for* sth.（為…責備某人）

【典型考題】
Ted dropped the ball and now everyone
_____ him for losing the game.
A. accuses　　　B. complains
C. demands　　　D. blames　　　[D]

‡**blank**[2]〔blæŋk〕adj. 空白的
（＝*empty*）　　n. 空格

He handed in a *blank* piece of paper.

【片語】*go blank*（腦中變得一片空白）

【典型考題】
My mind went _____ when I saw
the questions on the test paper.
A. blank　　　B. backwards
C. brief　　　D. calm　　　[A]

‡‡**blanket**[3]〔'blæŋkɪt〕n. 毯子（＝*cover*）

The baby is covered with the *blanket*.

***bleed**[3]〔blid〕v. 流血

After Gina fell on the sidewalk, her
knee was *bleeding*.

【記憶技巧】「流血」（bleed）很痛，所以字
中的「ee」像半瞇的眼；而看到「血」（blood）
會嚇一跳，眼睛張得很大，故字中是「oo」。

***blend**[4]〔blɛnd〕v. 混合（＝*mix*）；
調和

First *blend* the butter and sugar and
then add the flour.

***bless**[3]〔blɛs〕v. 祝福

***blessing**[4]〔'blɛsɪŋ〕n. 恩賜；幸福

This rain is a *blessing*; we no longer
have to worry about a drought.

‡‡**blind**[2]〔blaɪnd〕adj. 瞎的

Blind children have to go to special
schools.

***blink**[4]〔blɪŋk〕v. 眨眼（＝*wink*）

The moviegoers *blinked* their eyes
in the bright light as they left the
theater.

‡‡**block**[1]〔blɑk〕n. 街區

The store is three *blocks* away.

‡**blood**[1]〔blʌd〕n. 血

A lot of people are afraid of the
sight of *blood*.

***bloody**[2]〔'blʌdɪ〕adj. 血腥的
（＝*cruel*）

It was a *bloody* fight in which many
were wounded.

【記憶技巧】*blood*（血）+ *y*（adj.）
【比較】cloudy（多雲的）；windy（風大的）

***bloom**[4]〔blum〕v. 開花（＝*blossom*）；
繁盛；容光煥發　　n. 開花；盛開

This shrub usually *blooms* in May.

【比較】bloom 指「果樹開花」，一般植物「開
花」，用 flower。

【典型考題】
This is a Christmas cactus, so you
can expect it to _____ in December.
A. bloom　　　B. stare
C. wither　　　D. donate　　　[A]

***blossom**[4]〔'blɑsəm〕n. 花

The room was decorated with
beautiful pink *blossoms*.

【衍伸詞】*cherry blossom*（櫻花）

‡**blouse**[3]〔blaʊz〕n. 女用上衣

Wendy wears a white *blouse* to
school.

‡**blow**[1] 〔 blo 〕 *v.* 吹

She *blows* her hair dry.

‡**blue**[1] 〔 blu 〕 *adj.* 藍色的

Helen is wearing a *blue* dress.

【片語】*out of the blue*（突然地）

***blush**[4] 〔 blʌʃ 〕 *n.* 臉紅；腮紅

v. 臉紅 (= *turn red*)

The girls applied *blush* and lipstick to their faces.

┌─【典型考題】─────────
│ Jenny _____ when she was praised
│ by her teacher for writing an
│ excellent English composition.
│ A. blushed   B. bloomed
│ C. blamed   D. blessed   **[A]**
└──────────────────

***board**[2] 〔 bord 〕 *v.* 上（車、船、飛機）

The passengers *boarded* the plane at London Airport.

【比較】aboard（在車、船，或飛機上）

***boast**[4] 〔 bost 〕 *v.* 自誇 (= *brag*)；
以擁有…自豪   *n.* 自誇；誇耀

It is not polite to *boast* of your successes.

┌─【典型考題】─────────
│ Jack is very proud of his fancy new
│ motorcycle. He has been _____ to
│ all his friends about how cool it looks
│ and how fast it runs.
│ A. boasting   B. proposing
│ C. gossiping   D. confessing   **[A]**
└──────────────────

‡**boat**[1] 〔 bot 〕 *n.* 船

‡**body**[1] 〔'bɑdɪ 〕 *n.* 身體

Eat right and you will have a healthy *body*.

‡**boil**[2] 〔 bɔɪl 〕 *v.* 沸騰

The water is *boiling*.

***bold**[3] 〔 bold 〕 *adj.* 大膽的 (= *daring*)；
厚臉皮的

Cheryl made a *bold* move and won the chess game.

【比較】bald（禿頭的）

‡**bomb**[2] 〔 bɑm 〕 *n.* 炸彈 (= *explosive*)
v. 轟炸

A *bomb* exploded and destroyed many houses.

【比較】bomb 像 comb（梳子）、tomb
（墳墓）一樣，字尾的 b 都不發音。

***bond**[4] 〔 bɑnd 〕 *n.* 束縛；關係
(= *relation*)；公債；債券
v. 建立感情

The prisoner tried in vain to loosen his *bonds*.

‡**bone**[1] 〔 bon 〕 *n.* 骨頭

An old woman doesn't have strong *bones*.

***bony**[2] 〔'bonɪ 〕 *adj.* 骨瘦如柴的
(= *skinny*)

The fish has a nice taste but it is too *bony* for me.

‡**book**[1] 〔 bʊk 〕 *n.* 書   *v.* 預訂

I *booked* a room for him at a hotel.

┌─【典型考題】─────────
│ Having saved enough money, Joy
│ _____ two trips for this summer
│ vacation, one to France and the other
│ to Australia.
│ A. booked   B. observed
│ C. enclosed   D. deposited   **[A]**
└──────────────────

***bookcase**[2] 〔'bʊk‚kes 〕 *n.* 書架

Can you put the *bookcase* over there?

B

***boot**³〔but〕*n.* 靴子（= *overshoe*）
v. 啟動
Boot your computer.

***border**³〔'bɔrdɚ〕*n.* 邊界
I live on the *border* between North Hills and South Hills, so it is convenient for me to go to either city.

***bore**³〔bor〕*v.* 使無聊（= *tire*）
n. 令人厭煩的人
Science class *bores* me so much that I can barely stay awake.

‡**born**¹〔bɔrn〕*adj.* 出生的；天生的
Connie is a *born* singer.

‡**borrow**²〔'baro〕*v.* 借（入）
May I *borrow* your bicycle for a day?

‡**boss**¹〔bɔs〕*n.* 老闆
The new *boss* is very strict.

‡**both**¹〔boθ〕*pron.* 兩者
Sharon and Mark *both* came to class late.

***bother**²〔'baðɚ〕*v.* 打擾（= *disturb*）
Don't *bother* Tina with that now—she is busy.

‡**bottle**²〔'batḷ〕*n.* 瓶子（= *glass container*） *v.* 把…裝入瓶中
Harry is pouring a drink from a *bottle*.

‡**bottom**¹〔'batəm〕*n.* 底部
The ship sank to the *bottom* of the sea.
【衍伸詞】bottom line（底線；要點）

***bounce**⁴〔baʊns〕*v.* 反彈
The ball *bounced* off the wall.

‡‡**bow**²〔baʊ〕*v.* 鞠躬（= *bend*）
n. 船首 〔bo〕*n.* 弓；蝴蝶結
The student *bowed* to his teacher.

‡**bowl**¹〔bol〕*n.* 碗
He has finished five *bowls* of rice.

***bowling**²〔'bolɪŋ〕*n.* 保齡球
Bowling is Jeff's favorite sport.

‡**box**¹〔baks〕*n.* 箱子；耳光
She got a *box* on the cheek for telling a lie.
【衍伸詞】box office（售票處；票房）

‡**boy**¹〔bɔɪ〕*n.* 男孩；小伙子

***bracelet**⁴〔'breslɪt〕*n.* 手鐲（= *wristlet*）

***brain**²〔bren〕*n.* 頭腦（= *mind*）
pl. 智力
She has a good *brain* and beauty.

***brake**³〔brek〕*n.* 煞車
The *brakes* on this car must be repaired before it is safe to drive.

‡**branch**²〔bræntʃ〕*n.* 樹枝（= *shoot*）；分店（= *office*）；分支

***brand**²〔brænd〕*n.* 品牌（= *trademark*）
Julie is willing to pay more for a good *brand* of shampoo.

***brass**³〔bræs〕*n.* 黃銅

***brassiére**⁴〔brə'zɪr , ‚bræsɪ'ɛr〕*n.* 胸罩（= *bra*）
【重要知識】這個字來自法文，縮寫成 bra。美國人都用 bra，較少用 brassiére。

B

‡ **brave**[1] 〔 brev 〕 *adj.* 勇敢的
　Firemen are *brave* people.
　【反義詞】 timid (膽小的)

* **bravery**[3] 〔'brevərɪ 〕 *n.* 勇敢

‡ **bread**[1] 〔 brɛd 〕 *n.* 麵包

‡ **break**[1] 〔 brek 〕 *v.* 打破 (= *smash*)
　n. 休息

‡ **breakfast**[1] 〔'brɛkfəst 〕 *n.* 早餐
　We always have *breakfast* at 7:00 a.m.

* **breast**[3] 〔 brɛst 〕 *n.* 胸部 (= *chest*)
　They had chicken *breasts* for lunch.

* **breath**[3] 〔 brɛθ 〕 *n.* 呼吸
　Take a deep *breath* and count to ten,
　and then you will feel calmer.

┌─【典型考題】──────────────┐
│ Before John got on the stage to give a │
│ speech, he took a deep _____ to │
│ calm himself down. │
│ A. order　　　　 B. rest │
│ C. effort　　　　 D. breath　　 **[D]** │
└──────────────────────────┘

* **breathe**[3] 〔 brið 〕 *v.* 呼吸

* **breed**[4] 〔 brid 〕 *v.* 繁殖；養育
　The zookeepers tried in vain to
　breed the pandas.

* **breeze**[3] 〔 briz 〕 *n.* 微風

‡ **brick**[2] 〔 brɪk 〕 *n.* 磚頭

* **bride**[3] 〔 braɪd 〕 *n.* 新娘
　【衍伸詞】 bridesmaid (伴娘)

* **bridegroom**[4] 〔'braɪd,grum 〕 *n.* 新郎
　(= *groom*)
　The *bridegroom* stood waiting at
　the altar.
　【比較】 ***best man*** (伴郎)

‡ **bridge**[1] 〔 brɪdʒ 〕 *n.* 橋 (= *overpass*)
　v. 彌補；消除

* **brief**[2] 〔 brif 〕 *adj.* 簡短的 (= *short*)
　He gave a *brief* talk to the students.

┌─【典型考題】──────────────┐
│ All the new students are given one │
│ minute to _____ introduce │
│ themselves to the whole class. │
│ A. briefly　　　　 B. famously │
│ C. gradually　　　 D. obviously　 **[A]** │
└──────────────────────────┘

‡ **bright**[1] 〔 braɪt 〕 *adj.* 明亮的
　(= *shining*)；聰明的
　The box was painted *bright* green.
　【反義詞】 dark (暗的)

* **brilliant**[3] 〔'brɪljənt 〕 *adj.* 燦爛的；
　聰明的 (= *intelligent*)
　Sunglasses will protect your eyes
　from the *brilliant* light of the sun.

‡ **bring**[1] 〔 brɪŋ 〕 *v.* 帶來 (= *take*)
　I *brought* the book you wanted.

* **broad**[2] 〔 brɔd 〕 *adj.* 寬的 (= *wide*)
　This street is *broad*.
　【反義詞】 narrow (窄的)

* **broadcast**[2] 〔'brɔd,kæst 〕 *v.* 廣播；
　播送 (= *air*)
　The TV station *broadcasts* the show
　every day.
　【記憶技巧】 ***broad*** + ***cast*** (throw)
　　(廣泛地投射出去，就是「播送」)

broil[4] 〔 brɔɪl 〕 *v.* 烤 (= *grill*)
　My mother decided to *broil* a
　chicken for dinner.

* **broke**[4] 〔 brok 〕 *adj.* 沒錢的；破產的
（ = *bankrupt* ）
Ted spent all his money on that stereo. Now he's *broke* until payday.

* **brook**[3] 〔 bruk 〕 *n.* 小溪 (= *creek*)
The horse stopped to drink from the *brook*.
【注意】在 k 前的 oo 都讀 /ʊ/。

* **broom**[3] 〔 brum 〕 *n.* 掃帚
Do you believe that witches can fly on *brooms*?

‡ **brother**[1] 〔 'brʌðɚ 〕 *n.* 兄弟
These two boys are *brothers*.

* **brow**[3] 〔 braʊ 〕 *n.* 眉毛 (= *eyebrow*)；額頭 (= *forehead*)

‡ **brown**[1] 〔 braʊn 〕 *adj.* 棕色的
John likes to wear *brown* shoes.

‡ **brunch**[2] 〔 brʌntʃ 〕 *n.* 早午餐
We are used to eating *brunch* on weekends.
〔breakfast + lunch = brunch〕

‡ **brush**[2] 〔 brʌʃ 〕 *n.* 刷子 (= *sweeper*)
William used a small *brush* to paint his house.

* **brutal**[4] 〔 'brutl̩ 〕 *adj.* 殘忍的
(= *cruel*)；令人不快的；不講情面的
The people cheered when the *brutal* dictator was overthrown.
【記憶技巧】*brut* (禽獸) + *al* (adj.)
（像禽獸一樣的，就是「殘忍的」）

* **bubble**[3] 〔 'bʌbl̩ 〕 *n.* 泡泡
Soap *bubbles* filled the sink.

‡ **bucket**[3] 〔 'bʌkɪt 〕 *n.* 水桶 (= *pail*)；一桶的量
Pat carries water with his small *bucket*.

* **budget**[3] 〔 'bʌdʒɪt 〕 *n.* 預算 (= *funds*)
Paul was forced to cut his *budget* after he lost his part-time job.

* **buffalo**[3] 〔 'bʌfl̩ˏo 〕 *n.* 水牛
【比較】bison (美洲野牛)

‡ **buffet**[3] 〔 bʌ'fe 〕 *n.* 自助餐
They had a *buffet* at the wedding.

‡ **bug**[1] 〔 bʌg 〕 *n.* 小蟲；(機器) 故障
v. 竊聽

‡ **build**[1] 〔 bɪld 〕 *v.* 建造
They can *build* a house in one week.

* **building**[1] 〔 'bɪldɪŋ 〕 *n.* 建築物

* **bulb**[3] 〔 bʌlb 〕 *n.* 燈泡；球根 (= *tuber*)
This *bulb* should produce a beautiful tulip in the spring.

bulge[4] 〔 bʌldʒ 〕 *v.* 鼓起；裝滿
(= *swell*)   *n.* 鼓起
His luggage *bulged* with clothes.

* **bull**[3] 〔 bul 〕 *n.* 公牛

* **bullet**[3] 〔 'bulɪt 〕 *n.* 子彈
The bank robber fired three *bullets*.
【記憶技巧】*bul* (ball) + *let* (small)
（球狀的小東西，就是「子彈」）

* **bulletin**[4] 〔 'bulətɪn 〕 *n.* 佈告(= *report*)
There is an advertisement on the *bulletin* board.
【衍伸詞】*bulletin board* (佈告欄)
bulletin board system (電子公佈欄【即 BBS】)
【比較】bull-bullet-bulletin 要一起背。

* **bump**[3] 〔 bʌmp 〕 v. 撞上

The waiter *bumped* into the table, knocking over a glass of wine.

【片語】 ***bump into*** (撞上；碰巧遇見)

** **bun**[2] 〔 bʌn 〕 n. 小圓麵包

* **bunch**[3] 〔 bʌntʃ 〕 n. 一群；一夥 (人)

一束 (花) (= *bouquet* 〔 bu'ke 〕);

一串 (香蕉、葡萄、鑰匙) (= *cluster*)

This *bunch* of bananas looks ripe.

【重要知識】 "Thanks a ***bunch***." 可能是非常感謝的意思，也可能是語帶諷刺的說法。

** **bundle**[2] 〔 'bʌndl̩ 〕 n. 一大堆

(= *heap*);(尤指為了攜帶方便而紮成的) 捆；包   v. 把⋯捆起來

I have a *bundle* of clothes to wash.

【片語】 ***a bundle of*** (一大堆)

* **burden**[3] 〔 'bɝdn̩ 〕 n. 負擔

(= *trouble*)

The porter struggled under the *burden* of three heavy suitcases.

** **burger**[2] 〔 'bɝgɚ 〕 n. 漢堡

(= *hamburger*)

Burgers are my favorite food.

* **burglar**[3] 〔 'bɝglɚ 〕 n. 竊賊 (= *thief*)

This alarm system will protect your house from *burglars*.

【記憶技巧】 ***burgl(e)*** (竊盜) + ***ar*** (人)

【注意】 字尾有 ar 大多不是好人，如 begg<u>ar</u> (乞丐)、li<u>ar</u> (說謊者)。

* **burn**[2] 〔 bɝn 〕 v. 燃燒 (= *set on fire*)

n. 燙傷；灼傷

In winter, people *burn* wood to keep warm.

* **burst**[2] 〔 bɝst 〕 v. 爆破 (= *explode*)

【注意】 三態變化：burst–burst–burst

My sister's balloon *burst*.

* **bury**[3] 〔 'bɛrɪ 〕 v. 埋；埋藏

I wish the dog wouldn't *bury* bones in the yard.

** **bus**[1] 〔 bʌs 〕 n. 公車

* **bush**[3] 〔 buʃ 〕 n. 灌木叢

** **business**[2] 〔 'bɪznɪs 〕 n. 生意

(= *dealings*)

We didn't do much *business* with the firm.

** **busy**[1] 〔 'bɪzɪ 〕 adj. 忙碌的

(= *occupied with*)

** **butter**[1] 〔 'bʌtɚ 〕 n. 奶油

Mom put some *butter* in the corn soup.

** **butterfly**[1] 〔 'bʌtɚˌflaɪ 〕 n. 蝴蝶

A *butterfly* is an insect with wings full of bright colors.

【比較】 dragonfly (蜻蜓)

* **button**[2] 〔 'bʌtn̩ 〕 n. 按鈕 (= *switch*);

鈕扣 (= *fastener*)

I pushed the *button* to turn on the light.

** **buy**[1] 〔 baɪ 〕 v. 買;【口語】接受;相信

If you say it's true, I'll *buy* it.

* **buzz**[3] 〔 bʌz 〕 v. 發出嗡嗡聲 (= *hum*)

n. 嗡嗡聲;嘈雜聲

There was a wasp *buzzing* around me in the garden.

【片語】 give *sb.* a buzz (打電話給某人)

C c

***cabbage**² 〔'kæbɪdʒ 〕 *n.* 包心菜；
高麗菜；大白菜
Joe hates to eat *cabbage*.

【重要知識】美國人不分大白菜或高麗菜等，
都稱 cabbage。有些字典翻成「甘藍菜」，是
大陸人的用語。

* **cabin**³ 〔'kæbɪn 〕 *n.* 小木屋 (= *hut*)；
船艙；機艙
The hunter lived in a *cabin* in the
woods.

* **cabinet**⁴ 〔'kæbənɪt 〕 *n.* 櫥櫃
(= *locker*)；(大寫) 內閣
He bought a record *cabinet* last
month.

***cable**² 〔'kebḷ 〕 *n.* 電纜 (= *line*)；鋼索
This new bridge is supported by
hundreds of *cables*.
　　【衍伸詞】 ***cable TV*** (第四台)
　　　　　　 cable car (纜車)

┌─【典型考題】────────┐
The best way to appreciate the
beauty of the waterfall is to take the
_____ car.
A. cabbage　　　B. cable
C. cancer　　　　D. castle　　　[B]
└─────────────────┘

* **cafe**² 〔kə'fe 〕 *n.* 咖啡店 (= *café*)

***cafeteria**² 〔ˌkæfə'tɪrɪə 〕 *n.* 自助餐廳
(= *a self-service restaurant*)
There is a *cafeteria* in our school.

***cage**¹ 〔kedʒ 〕 *n.* 籠子 (= *enclosure*)
There are two lions in the *cage*.

***cake**¹ 〔kek 〕 *n.* 蛋糕
Chocolate *cake* is my favorite dessert.

* **calculate**⁴ 〔'kælkjəˌlet 〕 *v.* 計算
(= *count*)
We have to *calculate* the cost of
this plan.
　　【記憶技巧】 ***calc*** (lime) + ***ul*** (small) +
　　　　ate (*v.*) (古時候用小石頭來「計算」)

* **calculation**⁴ 〔ˌkælkjə'leʃən 〕 *n.*
計算 (= *estimate*)

* **calculator**⁴ 〔'kælkjəˌletɚ 〕 *n.*
計算機
May I use your *calculator* to work
out this math problem?

***calendar**² 〔'kæləndɚ 〕 *n.* 日曆
Holidays are often printed in red on
the *calendar*.
　　【衍伸詞】 ***lunar calendar*** (農曆)

***call**¹ 〔kɔl 〕 *v.* 叫 (= *speak loudly*)；
打電話給 (某人)　　*n.* 喊叫；打電話
My mother *called* me into the house.

***calm**² 〔kɑm 〕 *adj.* 冷靜的
They were *calm* in the face of the
disaster.

calorie⁴ 〔'kælərɪ 〕 *n.* 卡路里
(= *calory*)

* **camel**¹ 〔'kæmḷ 〕 *n.* 駱駝
【記憶技巧】 ***came*** + ***l*** = camel

***camera**¹ 〔'kæmərə 〕 *n.* 照相機；
攝影機

***camp**¹ 〔kæmp 〕 *v.* 露營
We will *camp* in the park tonight.

C

C

* **campaign**[4] 〔 kæm'pen 〕 *n.* 活動

The old man was constantly making speeches in political *campaigns* when he was young.

‡ **campus**[3] 〔'kæmpəs 〕 *n.* 校園

The students are running around the *campus*.

【記憶技巧】 *camp* + *us*（我們一起在「校園」中露營）

‡ **can**[1] 〔 kæn 〕 *aux.* 能夠（= *be able to*）
n. 罐子；罐頭

Wendy *can* type 80 words per minute.

‡ **cancel**[2] 〔'kænsl̩ 〕 *v.* 取消（= *call off*）；撤銷；廢除

Mr. Jackson *cancelled* his order for the books.

【典型考題】
When my boss told me I could not take a vacation next month, I _____ my flight.
A. terminated　　B. cancelled
C. resumed　　　 D. reserved　　[B]

‡ **cancer**[2] 〔'kænsɚ 〕 *n.* 癌症（= *tumor*）；弊端；（大寫）巨蟹座

My aunt died of *cancer*.

* **candidate**[4] 〔'kændə,det 〕 *n.* 候選人（= *nominee*）；有望做…的人

The former senator declared that he was a *candidate* for president.

【記憶技巧】 *cand* (white) + *id* (adj.) + *ate*（人）（古代政治人物穿白袍）

【典型考題】
Three people are running for mayor. All three _____ seem confident that they will be elected, but we won't know until the outcome of the election is announced.
A. particles　　B. receivers
C. candidates　 D. containers　　[C]

‡ **candle**[2] 〔'kændl̩ 〕 *n.* 蠟燭

Michelle has twelve *candles* on her birthday cake.

【記憶技巧】 *cand* (bright) + *le* (small thing)（會發光的小東西，就是「蠟燭」）

‡ **candy**[1] 〔'kændɪ 〕 *n.* 糖果

* **cane**[3] 〔 ken 〕 *n.* 手杖（= *stick*）；藤條

Furniture made out of *cane* is very light.

* **canoe**[3] 〔 kə'nu 〕 *n.* 獨木舟

Fifty miles is a long way to paddle a *canoe*.

* **canyon**[3] 〔'kænjən 〕 *n.* 峽谷（= *valley*）

【衍伸詞】 *the Grand Canyon*（大峽谷）

‡ **cap**[1] 〔 kæp 〕 *n.*（無邊的）帽子

Don't forget to wear a *cap* if you go out in the sun.

* **capable**[3] 〔'kepəbl̩ 〕 *adj.* 能夠的

Ben is *capable* of running a twenty-mile marathon.

【片語】 *be capable of*（能夠）

* **capacity**[4] 〔 kə'pæsətɪ 〕 *n.* 容量（= *space*）；能力

The *capacity* of the hall is 500 people.

【片語】 *be filled to capacity*（客滿）

【典型考題】
The memory _____ of the new computer has been increased so that more information can be stored.
A. capacity　　　B. occupation
C. attachment　　D. machinery　　[A]

* **cape**[4] 〔 kep 〕 *n.* 披風；海角

A *cape* is an important part of a vampire costume.

【記憶技巧】 c + ape（猿）= cape

* **capital**[3,4] ﹝'kæpət﹞ *n.* 首都;資本
Mr. Kim moved to the *capital* after he won the election.

* **capitalism**[4] ﹝'kæpət͟l͵ɪzəm﹞ *n.* 資本主義

capitalist[4] ﹝'kæpət͟lɪst﹞ *n.* 資本家

‡ **captain**[2] ﹝'kæptən﹞ *n.* 船長;機長;隊長
He is the *captain* of our team.
【記憶技巧】 *capt* (head) + *ain* (人)
(帶頭的人,就是「船長」)

* **capture**[3] ﹝'kæptʃɚ﹞ *v.* 抓住
(= *catch*)
Police and firefighters worked with the zookeepers in an attempt to *capture* the escaped lion.
【記憶技巧】 *cap* (catch) + *ture* (*v.*)
【反義詞】 release (釋放)

‡ **car**[1] ﹝kɑr﹞ *n.* 汽車
(= *auto* = *automobile*)
Tom drives an old *car*.

‡ **card**[1] ﹝kɑrd﹞ *n.* 卡片 *pl.* 撲克牌遊戲;卡片
Danny sent a Christmas *card* to me.

‡ **care**[1] ﹝kɛr﹞ *v.* 在乎 *n.* 注意;照料
I don't *care* what happens.

* **career**[4] ﹝kə'rɪr﹞ *n.* 職業 (= *job* = *vocation* = *occupation* = *profession*)
She abandoned her *career* as a teacher.

‡ **careful**[1] ﹝'kɛrfəl﹞ *adj.* 小心的
(= *cautious*)
Be *careful* when you drive the car.

* **cargo**[4] ﹝'kɑrgo﹞ *n.* 船貨;(裝載的) 貨物 (= *goods*)
The ship was carrying a *cargo* of steel.

* **carpenter**[3] ﹝'kɑrpəntɚ﹞ *n.* 木匠
(= *woodworker*)

‡ **carpet**[2] ﹝'kɑrpɪt﹞ *n.* 地毯
A cat was sleeping on a *carpet*.
【比較】 rug (小塊的地毯)

* **carriage**[3] ﹝'kærɪdʒ﹞ *n.* 四輪馬車;火車車廂;運輸;運費
Four horses pulled the *carriage*.
【記憶技巧】 *carri* (car) + *age* (*n.*)

carrier[4] ﹝'kærɪɚ﹞ *n.* 運送人;郵差;帶菌者;運輸公司;運輸工具

‡ **carrot**[2] ﹝'kærət﹞ *n.* 胡蘿蔔
We grow *carrots* in our garden.

‡ **carry**[1] ﹝'kærɪ﹞ *v.* 攜帶;拿著 (= *take*)
Linda *carried* a big box.

* **cart**[2] ﹝kɑrt﹞ *n.* 手推車
The farmers carried their vegetables to market in a *cart*.

‡ **cartoon**[2] ﹝kɑr'tun﹞ *n.* 卡通
(= *animation*)
My children enjoy *cartoons*.

* **carve**[4] ﹝kɑrv﹞ *v.* 雕刻 (= *cut*)
He *carved* his name on the tree.

‡ **case**[1] ﹝kes﹞ *n.* 情況 (= *condition*);例子 (= *example*);盒子
(= *container*)
That's a very unusual *case*.

‡ **cash**[2] ﹝kæʃ﹞ *n.* 現金 (= *money*)
Roy pays *cash* for his clothes.

C

‡cassette[2]〔kæ'sɛt〕n. 卡式錄音帶

I bought a lot of *cassettes* yesterday.

*cast[3]〔kæst〕v. 投擲（= *throw*）；扔 n. 演員陣容；石膏

We *cast* bread into the water to attract fish.

‡castle[2]〔'kæsḷ〕n. 城堡

Long ago, kings lived in *castles*.

*casual[3]〔'kæʒʊəl〕adj. 非正式的 （= *informal*）；輕鬆的；休閒的

The party is *casual*, so don't dress up.

‡cat[1]〔kæt〕n. 貓

*catalogue[4]〔'kætḷͺɔg〕n. 目錄 （= *catalog*）　v. 將…編目分類

If something is not available in our store, you can order it from the *catalogue*.

【記憶技巧】*cata* (fully) + *logue* (say) （有詳細敘述內容的東西，就是「目錄」）

‡catch[1]〔kætʃ〕v. 抓住（= *seize*）； 吸引（注意）（= *attract*）　n. 陷阱

Jenny keeps a cat to *catch* mice.

【典型考題】────────
A large poster in beautiful colors
───── the attention of many
people.
A. called   B. caught
C. charted   D. caused   **[B]**

*caterpillar[3]〔'kætəͺpɪlə〕n. 毛毛蟲

The *caterpillar* will eventually turn into a beautiful butterfly.

*cattle[3]〔'kætḷ〕n. 牛（= *cows*）

These *cattle* have been marked for slaughter.

【注意】cattle 爲集合名詞，當複數用，不加 s。

‡cause[1]〔kɔz〕n. 原因　v. 造成 （= *lead to*）

What was the *cause* of the accident?

【反義詞】result（結果）

*cave[2]〔kev〕n. 洞穴（= *hollow*）

This *cave* is so large that it has not been fully explored yet.

*CD[4] n. 雷射唱片（= *compact disk*）

*cease[4]〔sis〕v. 停止（= *stop*）

The colonel ordered the men to *cease* firing.

*ceiling[2]〔'silɪŋ〕n. 天花板

A lamp is hanging from the *ceiling*.

【片語】*hit the ceiling*（勃然大怒）

【典型考題】────────
Last night the glass lamp, hanging
from the ─────, dropped and hit
him on the head.
A. calendar   B. dew
C. director   D. ceiling   **[D]**

‡celebrate[3]〔'sɛləͺbret〕v. 慶祝 （= *commemorate*）

We *celebrated* Judy's birthday yesterday.

【記憶技巧】*celebr* (populous) + *ate* (v.)（「慶祝」活動中，有很多人參與）

*celebration[4]〔ͺsɛlə'breʃən〕n. 慶祝 活動（= *commemoration*）

* **cell**[2] 〔 sɛl 〕 *n.* 細胞；小牢房；小蜂窩；電池；手機 (= *cell phone*)

All animals are made of *cells*.

* **cement**[4] 〔 sə'mɛnt 〕 *n.* 水泥 (= *mortar* 〔'mɔrtɚ 〕) *v.* 鞏固

The *cement* wall was cracked by the earthquake.

‡ **cent**[1] 〔 sɛnt 〕 *n.* 分 (= *penny*)

There are 100 *cents* to a dollar.

‡ **center**[1] 〔'sɛntɚ 〕 *n.* 中心 (= *middle* = *centre*【英式用法】)

New York is a *center* of trade.

‡ **centimeter**[3] 〔'sɛntə,mitɚ 〕 *n.* 公分 (= *cm* = *centimetre*【英式用法】)

Children under 110 *centimeters* need not pay any fare.

【記憶技巧】*centi* (hundred) + *meter* (公尺的百分之一，就是「公分」)

‡ **central**[2] 〔'sɛntrəl 〕 *adj.* 中央的 (= *middle*)

The railroad station is in the *central* part of the city.

【記憶技巧】*centr* (center) + *al* (*adj.*)

* **century**[2] 〔'sɛntʃərɪ 〕 *n.* 世紀

We live in the twenty-first *century*.

【記憶技巧】*cent* (hundred) + *ury* (*n.*) (一百年就是一「世紀」)

ceramic[3] 〔 sə'ræmɪk 〕 *adj.* 陶器的 *n.* 陶瓷

The *ceramic* plate broke when I dropped it.

‡ **cereal**[2] 〔'sɪrɪəl 〕 *n.* 穀類食品；麥片

I've just bought a box of *cereal*.

* **certain**[1] 〔'sɝtṇ 〕 *adj.* 確定的 (= *sure*)

I am not *certain* whether he will come today.

【典型考題】
The teacher didn't teach the next formula until he made _____ everyone understood this one.
A. awake   B. believe
C. certain   D. rush   [C]

* **chain**[3] 〔 tʃen 〕 *n.* 連鎖店；鏈子 (= *tether* 〔'tɛðɚ 〕)

Terry put the dog on a *chain* in the backyard.

【衍伸詞】*chain store* (連鎖店)

‡ **chair**[1] 〔 tʃɛr 〕 *n.* 椅子

‡ **chalk**[2] 〔 tʃɔk 〕 *n.* 粉筆

My teacher is writing with a piece of *chalk*.

【注意】chalk 中的 l 不發音，而粉筆的量詞為 piece，例如 two pieces of chalk (兩支粉筆)。

* **challenge**[3] 〔'tʃælɪndʒ 〕 *n.* 挑戰 (= *test*)

【典型考題】
In this ever-changing world, we must be prepared to face all kinds of _____.
A. agency   B. challenges
C. wilderness   D. grades   [B]

* **chamber**[4] 〔'tʃembɚ 〕 *n.* 房間 (= *room*)；會議廳；議會

* **champion**[3] 〔'tʃæmpɪən 〕 *n.* 冠軍 (= *winner*)

championship[4] 〔'tʃæmpɪən,ʃɪp 〕 *n.*
冠軍資格

chance[1] 〔 tʃæns 〕 *n.* 機會
（ = *opportunity* ）
At the party every child has a
chance to win a prize.

change[2] 〔 tʃendʒ 〕 *v.* 改變（ = *alter* ）
n. 零錢
I will not *change* my mind.

changeable[3] 〔'tʃendʒəbl̩ 〕 *adj.*
可改變的（ = *variable* ）；善變的

channel[3] 〔'tʃænl̩ 〕 *n.* 頻道；海峽
（ = *strait* ）
What's on *Channel* 55 tonight?
【衍伸詞】 **the English Channel**（ 英吉
利海峽 ）

chapter[3] 〔'tʃæptɚ 〕 *n.* 章（ = *section* ）
The book consists of ten *chapters*.

character[2] 〔'kærɪktɚ 〕 *n.* 性格
（ = *personality* ）
She has a changeable *character*.

characteristic[4] 〔,kærɪktə'rɪstɪk 〕
n. 特性（ = *feature* ）

charge[2] 〔 tʃɑrdʒ 〕 *v.* 收費（ = *bill* ）；
控告（ = *accuse* ） *n.* 費用；控告
He *charged* me five dollars for a
cup of coffee.
【常考片語】 *charge sb. with*（ 控告某人~ ）

┌─【典型考題】──────────
This hotel is quite reasonable. It
———— only NT$ 800 for a single
room per night.
A. charges   B. changes
C. chooses   D. charts   **[A]**
└──────────────────

charity[4] 〔'tʃærətɪ 〕 *n.* 慈善機構
（ = *charitable organization* ）
The Red Cross is an international
charity.

charm[3] 〔 tʃɑrm 〕 *n.* 魅力
【衍伸詞】 charming（ 迷人的 ）

chart[1] 〔 tʃɑrt 〕 *n.* 圖表（ = *diagram* ）
The result is shown on *chart* 2.

chase[1] 〔 tʃes 〕 *v.* 追趕；追求
（ = *pursue* ）
A dog was *chasing* a motorcycle.

chat[3] 〔 tʃæt 〕 *v.* 聊天（ = *talk* ）

cheap[2] 〔 tʃip 〕 *adj.* 便宜的
【反義詞】 expensive（ 昂貴的 ）

cheat[2] 〔 tʃit 〕 *v.* 欺騙（ = *deceive* ）；
作弊
Kim was *cheated* by the stranger.

check[1] 〔 tʃɛk 〕 *v.* 檢查（ = *examine* ）
n. 支票（ = *cheque* ）
Please *check* the door before going
to bed.
I wrote my son a *check* for $10,000.

cheek[3] 〔 tʃik 〕 *n.* 臉頰

cheer[3] 〔 tʃɪr 〕 *v.* 使振作（ = *hearten* ）；
使高興；使感到安慰；歡呼
Going to a KTV after the exam will
cheer me up.
【片語】 *cheer sb. up*（ 使某人振作精神 ）

cheerful[3] 〔'tʃɪrfəl 〕 *adj.* 愉快的
（ = *pleasant* ）

cheese[3] 〔 tʃiz 〕 *n.* 起司
I'm fond of French *cheese*.

C

* **chemical**[2] 〔'kɛmɪkḷ 〕 *n.* 化學物質
 (= *compound*)　*adj.* 化學的
 Joe decided to be a *chemical* engineer.
 【衍伸詞】 *agricultural chemicals* (農藥)

‡ **chemistry**[4] 〔'kɛmɪstrɪ 〕 *n.* 化學
 【比較】 physics (物理學)

* **cherish**[4] 〔'tʃɛrɪʃ 〕 *v.* 珍惜
 (= *treasure*)；心中懷有

* **cherry**[3] 〔'tʃɛrɪ 〕 *n.* 櫻桃

‡ **chess**[2] 〔 tʃɛs 〕 *n.* 西洋棋
 My younger brother loves playing
 chess.

* **chest**[3] 〔 tʃɛst 〕 *n.* 胸部 (= *breast*)

* **chew**[3] 〔 tʃu 〕 *v.* 嚼 (= *munch*)
 【衍伸詞】 *chewing gum* (口香糖)

* **chick**[1] 〔 tʃɪk 〕 *n.* 小雞
 【比較】 kitten (小貓)；puppy (小狗)

‡ **chicken**[1] 〔'tʃɪkən 〕 *n.* 雞；雞肉
 I like to eat fried *chicken*.

* **chief**[1] 〔 tʃif 〕 *adj.* 主要的 (= *main*)
 n. 首長 (= *head*)；酋長

‡ **child**[1] 〔 tʃaɪld 〕 *n.* 小孩
 【注意】 複數形是 children

‡ **childhood**[3] 〔'tʃaɪld,hud 〕 *n.* 童年
 Her early *childhood* had been very
 happy.
 【記憶技巧】 *child* (兒童) + *hood* (表
 示「時期」)

‡ **childish**[2] 〔'tʃaɪldɪʃ 〕 *adj.* 幼稚的
 (= *immature*)
 It's *childish* of you to say that.

【記憶技巧】 *child* (兒童) + *ish* (帶有
 ～性質)

* **childlike**[2] 〔'tʃaɪld,laɪk 〕 *adj.* 純眞的
 She looked at me with her *childlike*
 eyes.
 【記憶技巧】 *child* (兒童) + *like* (像～
 樣的)

 chill[3] 〔 tʃɪl 〕 *n.* 寒冷 (= *coldness*)；
 害怕的感覺
 His words sent a *chill* down her spine.

* **chilly**[3] 〔'tʃɪlɪ 〕 *adj.* 寒冷的 (= *cold*)

* **chimney**[3] 〔'tʃɪmnɪ 〕 *n.* 煙囪

‡ **chin**[2] 〔 tʃɪn 〕 *n.* 下巴
 John fell down and scraped his *chin*.

* **chip**[3] 〔 tʃɪp 〕 *n.* 薄片；晶片；籌碼；
 碎片　*v.* 碰出缺口
 【衍伸詞】 *potato chips* (洋芋片)

* **chirp**[3] 〔 tʃɝp 〕 *v.* 發出啁啾聲；
 嘰嘰喳喳地說　*n.* 啁啾聲；鳥叫聲

‡ **chocolate**[2] 〔'tʃɔkəlɪt 〕 *n.* 巧克力
 adj. 巧克力的
 My sister made a *chocolate* cake
 yesterday.

‡ **choice**[2] 〔 tʃɔɪs 〕 *n.* 選擇 (= *selection*)
 Be careful in your *choice* of friends.

* **choke**[3] 〔 tʃok 〕 *v.* 使窒息；噎住
 (= *suffocate*)
 Don't let the baby put a marble in
 his mouth; he might *choke* on it.

‡ **choose**[2] 〔 tʃuz 〕 *v.* 選擇 (= *select*)
 Sally has to *choose* the dress she
 likes best.

* **chop**[3] 〔tʃɑp〕 v. 砍；剁碎（= cut）
n. 小肉片；（帶骨的）小塊肉
The cook *chopped* the meat into smaller pieces.

‡ **chopsticks**[2] 〔'tʃɑp,stɪks〕 n.pl. 筷子
Most Asians eat with *chopsticks*.

* **chore**[4] 〔tʃor〕 n. 雜事（= task）
Taking out the garbage is one of the *chores* that I must do at home.
【衍伸詞】 *household chores*（家事）

* **chorus**[4] 〔'korəs〕 n. 合唱團

‡ **Christmas**[1] 〔'krɪsməs〕 n. 聖誕節
（= Xmas）

‡ **church**[1] 〔tʃɝtʃ〕 n. 教堂
（= chapel〔'tʃæpḷ〕）
People go to *church* to pray.

cigar[4] 〔sɪ'gɑr〕 n. 雪茄

* **cigarette**[3] 〔'sɪgə,rɛt〕 n. 香煙
【比較】 tobacco（煙草）

* **cinema**[4] 〔'sɪnəmə〕 n. 電影
（= movie）

‡ **circle**[2] 〔'sɝkḷ〕 n. 圓圈（= ring）
Peter drew a *circle* in my book.

* **circular**[4] 〔'sɝkjələ〕 adj. 圓的
（= round）

* **circulate**[4] 〔'sɝkjə,let〕 v. 循環
（= flow）
【記憶技巧】 *circul*（circle）+ *ate*（v.）
（表示「循環」的形狀就像是一個圓圈）

* **circulation**[4] 〔,sɝkjə'leʃən〕 n. 循環
（= flow）；發行量

【典型考題】
If you exercise regularly, your blood
_____ will be improved, and you
will feel more energetic.
A. fatigue   B. tranquility
C. fragrance   D. circulation   [D]

* **circumstance**[4] 〔'sɝkəm,stæns〕
n. 情況（= condition = situation）
【常考片語】 *under no circumstances*
（在任何情況下都不；絕不）
【記憶技巧】 *circum*（around）+ *stan*
（stand）+ *ce*（n.）（關於某事或某人周圍
的「情況」）

* **circus**[3] 〔'sɝkəs〕 n. 馬戲團；
（古羅馬的）圓形競技場

* **citizen**[2] 〔'sɪtəzn̩〕 n. 公民（= civilian）
Many Chinese in the United States
have become American *citizens*.
【記憶技巧】 *citiz*（城市）+ *en*（人）
【衍伸詞】 *senior citizen*（老人）

‡ **city**[1] 〔'sɪtɪ〕 n. 城市（= town）

civil[3] 〔'sɪvḷ〕 adj. 公民的（= civic）；
平民的；（非軍用而是）民用的

civilian[4] 〔sə'vɪljən〕 n. 平民；
老百姓；非軍警人員   adj. 平民的

* **civilization**[4] 〔,sɪvḷaɪ'zeʃən〕 n. 文明
（= culture）

* **claim**[2] 〔klem〕 v. 宣稱（= assert）；
要求（= demand）；認領
He *claimed* his answer was correct.
【比較】 exclaim（大叫；呼喊）

‡ **clap**[2] 〔klæp〕 v. 鼓掌（= applaud）
Alice *clapped* when the music ended.

* **clarify**[4] 〔'klærə,faɪ 〕 *v.* 清楚地說明
（ = *explain* ）
Not understanding what Jim meant by systematic problems, I asked him to *clarify*.

* **clash**[4] 〔klæʃ 〕*v.* 起衝突 (= *conflict*)；不相稱；爭吵
Joe and Tony *clashed* at the meeting.
This shirt *clashes* with my trousers.

** **class**[1] 〔klæs 〕*n.* 班級；(班級的) 上課 (時間)；等級
There are thirty students in our *class*.

* **classic**[2] 〔'klæsɪk 〕*adj.* 第一流的 (= *first-class*)；經典的；古典的
Pride and Prejudice is a *classic* work.

* **classical**[3] 〔'klæsɪkl̩ 〕*adj.* 古典的 (= *classic*)
My mother loves *classical* music.

* **classification**[4] 〔,klæsəfə'keʃən 〕*n.* 分類 (= *categorization*)

* **classify**[4] 〔'klæsə,faɪ 〕*v.* 分類 (= *categorize*)
【記憶技巧】 *class* (等級) + *ify* (*v.*)
【衍伸詞】 *classified ads* (分類廣告)

* **claw**[2] 〔klɔ 〕*n.* 爪
【記憶技巧】 c + law (法律) = claw

【典型考題】
Koalas are cute. But you have to watch out for their ＿＿＿ when you hold them.
A. claws   B. dumplings
C. duties   D. cereals   [A]

* **clay**[2] 〔kle 〕*n.* 黏土
【記憶技巧】 c + lay (下蛋；放置) = clay

** **clean**[1] 〔klin 〕*adj.* 乾淨的 (= *hygienic*)   *v.* 打掃；清理
The air is not *clean* in big cities.
【反義詞】 dirty (髒的)

cleaner[2] 〔'klinɚ 〕*n.* 清潔工；乾洗店

** **clear**[1] 〔klɪr 〕*adj.* 清楚的；清澈的
The sea is so *clear* that I can see the fish.

** **clerk**[2] 〔klɝk 〕*n.* 店員；職員
My mother works as a *clerk* in the shop.

【典型考題】
I like to go shopping in that store because the ＿＿＿ there are very polite and nice.
A. clerks   B. doctors
C. fans   D. passengers   [A]

** **clever**[2] 〔'klɛvɚ 〕*adj.* 聰明的 (= *smart* = *intelligent*)
He seems to have a lot of *clever* ideas.

* **click**[3] 〔klɪk 〕*n.* 喀嗒聲 (= *clack*)
【記憶技巧】 c + lick (舔) = click

* **client**[3] 〔'klaɪənt 〕*n.* 客戶

* **cliff**[4] 〔klɪf 〕*n.* 懸崖 (= *crag*)
It's very dangerous to get too close to the edge of the *cliff*.

** **climate**[2] 〔'klaɪmɪt 〕*n.* 氣候
She doesn't like to live in a hot *climate*.
【比較】 weather (天氣)

C

* **climax**[4] (ˈklaɪmæks) *n.* 高潮
(= *culmination*)
Everyone in the theater held his
breath at the *climax* of the movie.
【記憶技巧】 *cli* (bend) + *max* (largest)
（情緒曲線彎曲幅度最大的位置，就代表
情緒的「高潮」）

【典型考題】
The _____ of the story was when
the dog saved the little girl from
the bad man.
A. version　　　　B. climax
C. attempt　　　　D. system　　　[B]

‡ **climb**[1] (klaɪm) *v.* 爬；攀登 (= *mount*)
We will *climb* Mt. Jade this summer.

* **clinic**[3] (ˈklɪnɪk) *n.* 診所
【記憶技巧】 *clin* (bed) + *ic*
（提供病床的地方，就是「診所」）

* **clip**[3] (klɪp) *v.* 修剪 (= *trim*)；夾住
n. 迴紋針 (= *paper clip*)；夾子
I have to *clip* my nails before they
get any longer.
【衍伸詞】 clippers（指甲刀）
【注意】夾小東西用 clip，夾大東西，或使東
西固定，用 clamp。pliers（鉗子），則
須用複數形。

‡ **clock**[1] (klɑk) *n.* 時鐘
I'm going to buy a new *clock* this
weekend.

‡ **close**[1] (kloz) *v.* 關上 (= *shut*)
(klos) *adj.* 接近的 (= *near*)
Close the door, please.

‡ **closet**[2] (ˈklɑzɪt) *n.* 衣櫥
Hang your coat in the *closet*.

* **cloth**[2] (klɔθ) *n.* 布 (= *fabric*)

* **clothe**[2] (kloð) *v.* 穿衣 (= *dress*)

‡ **clothes**[2] (kloz) *n. pl.* 衣服 (= *dress*)
We need cloth to make *clothes*.

* **clothing**[2] (ˈkloðɪŋ) *n.* 衣服【集合名詞】

‡ **cloud**[1] (klaʊd) *n.* 雲
The top of Mt. Ali was covered
with *clouds*.

‡ **cloudy**[2] (ˈklaʊdɪ) *adj.* 多雲的
Today is a *cloudy* day.

* **clown**[2] (klaʊn) *n.* 小丑
【比較】 crown（皇冠）

‡ **club**[2] (klʌb) *n.* 俱樂部；社團
Jessica belongs to the drama *club*.

* **clue**[3] (klu) *n.* 線索
The police found a *clue* to her
whereabouts.

* **clumsy**[4] (ˈklʌmzɪ) *adj.* 笨拙的
(= *awkward* (ˈɔkwəd))
It was so *clumsy* of me to knock that
vase over.

【典型考題】
Johnny is a _____ boy. He often spills
the milk at breakfast and makes a mess.
A. rodent　　　　　B. pessimistic
C. majestic　　　　D. clumsy　　　[D]

* **coach**[2] (kotʃ) *n.* 教練
Ted is my swimming *coach*.

* **coal**[2] (kol) *n.* 煤
【比較】 charcoal（木炭）

* **coarse**[4] (kors) *adj.* 粗糙的 (= *rough*)
I don't like to wear this shirt
because the material feels *coarse*.
【反義詞】 smooth（平滑的）

‡ **coast**[1] 〔kost〕 *n.* 海岸 (= *shore*)
They live on the *coast*.

‡ **coat**[1] 〔kot〕 *n.* 外套；大衣 (= *jacket*)
v. 覆蓋；塗在…上面

* **cock**[2] 〔kɑk〕 *n.* 公雞 (= *rooster*)

* **cockroach**[2] 〔'kɑk͵rotʃ〕 *n.* 蟑螂
(= *roach*)
Lucy is afraid of *cockroaches*.

* **cocktail**[3] 〔'kɑk͵tel〕 *n.* 雞尾酒
【重要知識】cocktail 源自古時的「雞尾酒」上面會用公雞的羽毛裝飾。

* **coconut**[3] 〔'kokənət〕 *n.* 椰子

‡ **coffee**[1] 〔'kɔfɪ〕 *n.* 咖啡

* **coin**[2] 〔kɔɪn〕 *n.* 硬幣 (= *metal money*)

‡ **Coke**[1] 〔kok〕 *n.* 可口可樂
(= *Coca-Cola*)
I would like to have a *Coke*.

‡ **cola**[1] 〔'kolə〕 *n.* 可樂 (= *coke*)

‡ **cold**[1] 〔kold〕 *adj.* 寒冷的 (= *chilly*)
n. 冷空氣；感冒
We had a *cold* winter.

* **collapse**[4] 〔kə'læps〕 *v.* 倒塌；倒下
(= *fall down*)；崩潰；瓦解
As soon as the marathon runner crossed the finish line, he *collapsed* on the ground.
【記憶技巧】*col* (together) + *lapse* (glide down) (整體滑落，表示「倒塌」)

【典型考題】
The kingdom began to ＿＿＿ after the death of its ruler, and was soon taken over by a neighboring country.
A. collapse　　　B. dismiss
C. rebel　　　　D. withdraw　　　[A]

* **collar**[3] 〔'kɑlɚ〕 *n.* 衣領 (= *neckband*)
The house owner seized the thief by the *collar*.
【比較】sleeve (袖子)

‡ **collect**[2] 〔kə'lɛkt〕 *v.* 收集 (= *gather*)
Why do you *collect* dolls?

* **collection**[3] 〔kə'lɛkʃən〕 *n.* 收集；收藏品

【典型考題】
This museum is famous for its ＿＿＿ of modern paintings.
A. construction　B. reduction
C. affection　　　D. collection　　[D]

* **college**[3] 〔'kɑlɪdʒ〕 *n.* 大學
(= *university*)；學院
What do you plan to do after *college*?

* **colony**[3] 〔'kɑlənɪ〕 *n.* 殖民地
(= *settlement*)

‡ **color**[1] 〔'kʌlɚ〕 *n.* 顏色 (= *colour*)
adj. 彩色的

* **colorful**[2] 〔'kʌlɚfəl〕 *adj.* 多彩多姿的
(= *colourful*【英式用法】)
In order to live a *colorful* life, you have to make some changes to your life.

* **column**[3] 〔'kɑləm〕 *n.* 專欄
(= *article*)；圓柱 (= *pillar*)
She writes a *column* for an English newspaper.

‡ **comb**[2] 〔kom〕 *n.* 梳子
We use a *comb* to make our hair tidy.
【注意】comb 字尾的 b 不發音。

* **combination**[4] 〔͵kɑmbə'neʃən〕
  n. 結合 (= *association*)
  【典型考題】
  Almost everybody is a ＿＿＿ of
  many different "selves"; we show
  different faces to different people.
  A. combination   B. communication
  C. complication   D. competition   [A]

* **combine**[3] 〔kəm'baɪn〕 *v.* 結合
  (= *associate*)
  【記憶技巧】 *com* (together) + *bine*
  (two)(把兩件事放在一起，也就是「結合」)

‡ **come**[1] 〔kʌm〕 *v.* 來 (= *arrive*)

* **comedy**[4] 〔'kɑmədɪ〕 *n.* 喜劇
  【反義詞】 tragedy (悲劇)

* **comfort**[3] 〔'kʌmfət〕 *n.* 舒適 (= *ease*)
  v. 安慰 (= *console*)
  【記憶技巧】 *com* (wholly) + *fort*
  (strong) (全身強壯，就不會感到不舒服)

‡ **comfortable**[2] 〔'kʌmfətəbḷ〕 *adj.*
  舒適的；舒服的 (= *at ease*)
  This chair doesn't look *comfortable*.
  【典型考題】
  In summer it is ＿＿＿ to stay in
  my parents' room because it is
  air-conditioned.
  A. comfortable   B. gentle
  C. impossible   D. serious   [A]

‡ **comic**[4] 〔'kɑmɪk〕 *n.* 漫畫
  (= *comic book*)
  【衍伸詞】 *comic strip* (連環漫畫)

* **comma**[3] 〔'kɑmə〕 *n.* 逗點
  (= *a punctuation mark*)
  【比較】 period (句點)

‡ **command**[3] 〔kə'mænd〕 *v.* 命令
  (= *order*)；俯瞰 (= *overlook*)
  n. 精通 (= *proficiency*)
  The captain *commanded* his men to
  start at once.
  【片語】 have a good command of
  (精通)

* **commander**[4] 〔kə'mændə〕 *n.* 指揮官
  (= *commandant*)

‡ **comment**[4] 〔'kɑmɛnt〕 *n.* 評論
  (= *remark*)
  He made no *comment* on the topic.
  【記憶技巧】 *com* (thoroughly) + *ment*
  (mind) (徹底表達出心中的想法，即是
  一種「評論」)
  【衍伸詞】 *No comment.* (不予置評。)
  【典型考題】
  Since I do not fully understand your
  proposal, I am not in a position to
  make any ＿＿＿ on it.
  A. difference   B. solution
  C. demand   D. comment   [D]

* **commerce**[4] 〔'kɑmɝs〕 *n.* 商業
  【記憶技巧】 *com* (together) + *merce*
  (trade) (共同交易，就是「商業」)

* **commercial**[3] 〔kə'mɝʃəl〕 *adj.* 商業的
  n. (電視、廣播的) 商業廣告
  【比較】 報紙、雜誌的「平面廣告」，則是
  advertisement。
  【典型考題】
  Most businessmen are more interested
  in the ＿＿＿ success of their
  products than their educational value.
  A. cultural   B. commercial
  C. classical   D. criminal   [B]

C

C

* **commit**[4] 〔kə'mɪt〕v. 委託；致力於；犯（罪）(= *perpetrate* 〔'pɝpə,tret〕)
The burglar promised that he would not *commit* any more crimes.
【常考片語】*commit suicide* (自殺)

* **committee**[3] 〔kə'mɪtɪ〕n. 委員會
(= *commission*)
【記憶技巧】*commit* (委託) + *t* + *ee* (被 ~的人)(受委託的人，就是「委員會」)

* **common**[1] 〔'kɑmən〕adj. 常見的
(= *usual*)；共同的
Smith is a very *common* last name in England.
【反義詞】rare (罕見的)
【常考片語】*in common* (共同的)

* **communicate**[3] 〔kə'mjunə,ket〕v.
溝通；聯繫 (= *contact*)

* **communication**[4]
〔kə,mjunə'keʃən〕n. 溝通；通訊
(= *contact*)

【典型考題】
With e-mail and telephones, ＿＿＿＿ has become easier, and the world is getting smaller.
A. experience　　B. communication
C. difference　　D. software　　**[B]**

* **community**[4] 〔kə'mjunətɪ〕n. 社區
(= *neighborhood*)；社會

* **companion**[4] 〔kəm'pænjən〕n.
同伴；朋友 (= *partner*)
【記憶技巧】*com* (together) + *pan* (bread) + *ion* (*n.*) (貧困的時候，願意把麵包拿出來分享的人，就是「同伴」)
【注意】company 作「同伴」解時，為不可數名詞；而 companion 則是可數名詞。

【典型考題】
A man is known by his ＿＿＿＿, so we should be careful in choosing friends.
A. companies　　B. competitors
C. proponents　　D. companions　　**[D]**

* **company**[2] 〔'kʌmpənɪ〕n. 公司
(= *firm* = *corporation* = *enterprise*)；
同伴；朋友
Tony has worked for this *company* for 18 years.

* **compare**[2] 〔kəm'pɛr〕v. 比較
(= *contrast*)；比喻
He *compared* my painting with his.
Some people *compared* books to friends.

* **comparison**[3] 〔kəm'pærəsṇ〕n.
比較 (= *contrast*)
【片語】*in comparison with* (和…相比)

* **compete**[3] 〔kəm'pit〕v. 競爭
(= *contend*)
【記憶技巧】*com* (together) + *pete* (strive) (一起爭鬥，即「競爭」)

* **competition**[4] 〔,kɑmpə'tɪʃən〕n.
競爭 (= *contest*)
【衍伸詞】*keen competition* (激烈的 競爭)

【典型考題】
At the Olympic Games, our representatives are in ＿＿＿＿ with the best athletes from all over the world.
A. competent　　B. competition
C. compliment　　D. compare　　**[B]**

* **competitive**[4]〔kəm'pɛtətɪv〕*adj.*
競爭的；競爭激烈的
【典型考題】
Living in a highly _____ society,
you definitely have to arm yourself
with as much knowledge as possible.
A. tolerant　　B. permanent
C. favorable　　D. competitive　[D]

* **competitor**[4]〔kəm'pɛtətɚ〕*n.*
競爭者（= *contender*）

* **complain**[2]〔kəm'plen〕*v.* 抱怨
（= *grumble*）
John is always *complaining.*
【記憶技巧】*com* (together) + *plain*
(beat the breast)（想「抱怨」時，因
為內心充滿怒火，會想要捶胸頓足）
【片語】*complain about*（抱怨）
（= *complain of*）

* **complaint**[3]〔kəm'plent〕*n.* 抱怨
（= *grumble*）；疾病
【典型考題】
The transportation in this city is
terrible and people have many _____
about it.
A. transcripts　　B. complaints
C. accounts　　　D. results　[B]

* **complete**[2]〔kəm'plit〕*adj.* 完整的；
完成的　　*v.* 完成
His work is *complete.*
【記憶技巧】*com* (with) + *plete* (fill)
（將有空缺的東西填滿後，就會變「完整」）

* **complex**[3]〔kəm'plɛks , 'kamplɛks〕
adj. 複雜的（= *complicated*）

* **complicate**[4]〔'kamplə,ket〕*v.*
使複雜

Thank you for your suggestion, but
I think it would just *complicate* the
situation.
【記憶技巧】*com* (together) + *plic*
(fold) + *ate* (*v.*)（將事情重疊在一起，
就會變得複雜難懂）

* **compose**[4]〔kəm'poz〕*v.* 組成
（= *constitute*）；作（曲）
【記憶技巧】*com* (together) + *pose*
(put)（放置在一起，就是「組成」）
【比較】impose（強加）；expose（暴露）
propose（提議）；oppose（反對）

* **composer**[4]〔kəm'pozɚ〕*n.* 作曲家

* **composition**[4]〔,kampə'zɪʃən〕*n.*
作文（= *writing*）；（音樂、美術等）
作品；構造

** **computer**[2]〔kəm'pjutɚ〕*n.* 電腦
Computers are necessary for everyone.

* **concentrate**[4]〔'kansn̩,tret〕*v.* 專心；
集中（= *focus*）
I asked the children to be quiet so
that I could *concentrate* on my book.
【常考片語】*concentrate on*（專心於）
【記憶技巧】*con* (together) + *centr*
(center) + *ate* (*v.*)（把全部思緒一起
放到中心，也就是「專心」）
【典型考題】
Frank always thinks about too many
things, so he cannot _____ in class.
A. concentrate　　B. imagine
C. preview　　　　D. remember　[A]

* **concentration**[4]〔,kansn̩'treʃən〕*n.*
專心（= *attention*）；集中
【衍伸詞】*concentration camp*（集中營）

C

* **concept**[4] 〔'kɑnsɛpt 〕*n.* 觀念
(= *conception*)

【典型考題】
It is difficult for children to
understand abstract _____;
therefore, teachers use concrete
examples to explain.
A. aspects   B. appetites
C. concepts   D. paces   [C]

* **concern**[3] 〔 kən'sɝn 〕*n.* 關心
(= *care*)；關心的事
He shows no *concern* for his children.
【片語】*main concern* (最關心的事)

* **concerning**[4] 〔 kən'sɝnɪŋ 〕*prep.* 關於
(= *regarding* = *respecting* = *about*)
John's boss wants to talk to him
concerning his salary.

* **concert**[3] 〔'kɑnsɝt 〕*n.* 音樂會；
演唱會
Are you going to attend this *concert?*

* **conclude**[3] 〔 kən'klud 〕*v.* 下結論
(= *decide*)；結束 (= *bring to*
an end)
The speaker *concluded* his remarks by
thanking the audience for listening.
【記憶技巧】*con* (together) + *clude*
(shut) (做關上的動作，表示「結束」)

【典型考題】
When Rita came out of the classroom,
she was smiling, so I _____ that
she had done well on the test.
A. concluded   B. pretended
C. described   D. intended   [A]

* **conclusion**[3] 〔 kən'kluʒən 〕*n.* 結論
【片語】*in conclusion* (總之)

* **concrete**[4] 〔 kɑn'krit , 'kɑnkrit 〕*adj.*
具體的 (= *substantial*)   *n.* 混凝土
There being no *concrete* proof that
the man was guilty, the judge let him
go.
【反義詞】 abstract (抽象的)

* **conductor**[4] 〔 kən'dʌktɚ 〕*n.* 指揮
(= *music director*)；導體

* **cone**[3] 〔 kon 〕*n.* 圓錐體；(冰淇淋)
甜筒

* **conference**[4] 〔'kɑnfərəns 〕*n.* 會議
(= *meeting*)

【典型考題】
Many experts from all over the world
will be invited to attend this year's
_____ on drug control.
A. reference   B. intention
C. conference   D. interaction   [C]

* **confess**[4] 〔 kən'fɛs 〕*v.* 承認；招認
(= *admit*)
I must *confess* myself completely
puzzled by the question.
【記憶技巧】*con* (fully) + *fess* (speak)
(把實情全說出來，也就是「招認」)

* **confidence**[4] 〔'kɑnfədəns 〕*n.* 信心
(= *assurance*)

【典型考題】
All the people in our company have
_____ that the economy will get better.
A. ignorance   B. confidence
C. insecurity   D. attraction   [B]

C

‡**confident**[3] 〔'kɑnfədənt 〕 *adj.*
有信心的（ = *assured* ）

He was *confident* that he would win.

【記憶技巧】 *con* (fully) + *fid* (trust) +
ent (*adj.*) （完全信任的，表示「有信心的」）

***confine**[4] 〔 kən'faɪn 〕 *v.* 限制
（ = *restrict* ）；關閉

We *confine* the dog to the house at
night, but let him go out in the yard
during the day.

【衍伸詞】 *be confined to bed* （臥病
在床）

***confirm**[2] 〔 kən'fɝm 〕 *v.* 確認；證實
（ = *prove* ）

This *confirms* my suspicions.

***conflict**[2] 〔'kɑnflɪkt 〕 *n.* 衝突；爭端；
矛盾 〔 kən'flɪkt 〕 *v.* 牴觸；衝突
（ = *clash* ）

They have a *conflict* in what they
believe.

【記憶技巧】 *con* (together) + *flict*
(strike) （彼此毆打，也就是有「衝突」）

┌─【典型考題】─────────
│ ＿＿＿＿ between good friends
│ should be resolved, not ignored.
│ A. Compliments B. Communication
│ C. Conflicts　　　 D. Connections　[C]
└────────────────────

Confucius[2] 〔 kən'fjuʃəs 〕 *n.* 孔子
（ = *Kong Fuzi* ）

Confucius is the greatest teacher in
Chinese history.

‡**confuse**[3] 〔 kən'fjuz 〕 *v.* 使困惑
（ = *puzzle* = *baffle* = *bewilder* ）

The new rules *confused* the drivers.

【記憶技巧】 *con* (together) + *fuse*
(pour) （太多事情同時注入，會覺得困惑）

***confusion**[4] 〔 kən'fjuʒən 〕 *n.* 困惑
（ = *puzzlement* ）；混亂局面

***congratulate**[4] 〔 kən'grætʃə,let 〕 *v.*
祝賀（ = *compliment* ）

【記憶技巧】 *con* (together) + *gratul*
(please) + *ate* (*v.*) （大家一起讓對方感
到高興，此時會表達「祝賀」）

‡**congratulations**[2]
〔 kən,grætʃə'leʃənz 〕 *n. pl.* 恭喜
（ = *compliments* ）

Please accept my *congratulations*
on your recovery.

***congress**[4] 〔'kɑŋgrəs 〕 *n.* 議會
（ = *council* ）；會議（ = *meeting* ）

The laws in this country are made
by a *congress* of 200 legislators.

【記憶技巧】 *con* (together) + *gress*
(walk) （參加「會議」時，大家會一同
走去開會的地方）

***conjunction**[4] 〔 kən'dʒʌŋkʃən 〕 *n.*
連接詞

【記憶技巧】 *con* (together) + *junct*
(join) + *ion* (*n.*) （將前後文連結在一起，
也就是「連接詞」）

***connect**[3] 〔 kə'nɛkt 〕 *v.* 連接（ = *link* ）

This railway *connects* London and
Edinburgh.

【記憶技巧】 *con* (together) + *nect*
(bind) （連結在一起，即「連接」）

【反義詞】 disconnect （切斷；分開）

C

* **connection**[3] 〔kə'nɛkʃən〕 n. 關聯
(= *link*)
【片語】*in connection with* (關於)

【典型考題】
He has made a good plan in
_____ with marketing strategies.
A. ambition   B. connection
C. possession   D. instruction   [B]

* **conquer**[4] 〔'kɑŋkɚ〕 v. 征服
【記憶技巧】*con* (wholly) + *quer*
(seek) (完全求得，就是「征服」)

* **conscience**[4] 〔'kɑnʃəns〕 n. 良心
【注意發音】(= *moral sense*)
The thief eventually returned the
man's wallet because his *conscience*
was bothering him.
【記憶技巧】背這個字，只要背 con +
science (科學)。

* **conscious**[3] 〔'kɑnʃəs〕 *adj.* 知道的；
察覺到的 (= *aware*)
【片語】*be conscious of* (知道；
察覺到)

* **consequence**[4] 〔'kɑnsə,kwɛns〕 n.
後果 (= *result*)
One *consequence* of losing the game
was that we were eliminated from
the competition.
【記憶技巧】*con* (with) + *sequ*
(follow) + *ence* (n.)
【比較】背這個字要和 sequence (連續)
一起背。

* **consequent**[4] 〔'kɑnsə,kwɛnt〕 *adj.*
接著發生的 (= *subsequent*)

In the *consequent* confusion after
the earthquake, many fires broke out.

* **conservative**[4] 〔kən'sɝvətɪv〕 *adj.*
保守的 (= *traditional* = *conventional*)
【記憶技巧】*con* (together) + *serv*
(keep) + *ative* (adj.) (把事情放在心
裡不說出來，顯示這個人是很「保守的」)

** **consider**[2] 〔kən'sɪdɚ〕 v. 認為
(= *think*)；考慮 (= *think about*)
Please *consider* my offer.
【常考片語】*consider* A (*to be*) B (認為
A 是 B)

* **considerable**[3] 〔kən'sɪdərəbl̩〕 *adj.*
相當大的 (= *large*)
【衍伸詞】considerably (相當大地)

【典型考題】
The ideas about family have changed
_____ in the past twenty years. For
example, my grandfather was one of
ten children in his family, but I am the
only child.
A. mutually   B. narrowly
C. considerably   D. scarcely   [C]

* **consideration**[3] 〔kən,sɪdə'reʃən〕 n.
考慮 (= *deliberation*)
【片語】*take…into consideration*
(考慮到…)

* **consist**[4] 〔kən'sɪst〕 *v.* 由…組成 < *of* >
(= *comprise*)；在於 < *in* >
The house *consists* of two bedrooms
and one bathroom.
【常考片語】*consist of* (由…組成)
(= *be made up of* = *be composed of*)

C

* **consistent**[4] ﹝kənˈsɪstənt﹞ *adj.* 一致的
(= *compatible*)；前後連貫的
(= *coherent*)
【片語】 *be consistent with* (和…一致)

【典型考題】

I'm afraid we can't take your word,
for the evidence we've collected so far
is not _____ with what you said.
A. familiar   B. durable
C. consistent   D. sympathetic   [C]

* **consonant**[4] ﹝ˈkɑnsənənt﹞ *n.* 子音
【記憶技巧】 *con* (together) + *son*
(sound) + *ant* (*n.*) (連在一起發音，
不分音節的，就是「子音」)
【比較】 vowel (母音)

* **constant**[3] ﹝ˈkɑnstənt﹞ *adj.* 不斷的
(= *continuous*)；持續的；忠誠的

【典型考題】

Women's fashions are _____ changing.
One season they favor pantsuits, but
the next season they may prefer
miniskirts.
A. lately   B. shortly
C. relatively   D. constantly   [D]

* **constitute**[4] ﹝ˈkɑnstəˌtjut﹞ *v.* 構成
(= *comprise* = *compose* = *make up*)
24 hours *constitute* a day.
【記憶技巧】 *con* (together) + *stitute*
(stand) (站在一起，就是「構成」)

* **constitution**[4] ﹝ˌkɑnstəˈtjuʃən﹞ *n.* 憲
法 (= *fundamental law*)；構成；構造

* **construct**[4] ﹝kənˈstrʌkt﹞ *v.* 建造
(= *build*)；建築；建設
【記憶技巧】 *con* (together) + *struct*
(build)
【比較】 in<u>struct</u> (教導)；ob<u>struct</u> (阻礙)

* **construction**[4] ﹝kənˈstrʌkʃən﹞ *n.*
建設 (= *building*)

* **constructive**[4] ﹝kənˈstrʌktɪv﹞ *adj.*
建設性的 (= *positive*)
【反義詞】 destructive (破壞性的)

【典型考題】

For hours, we have heard nothing but
negative criticism. Why can't you
say something more _____?
A. ambitious   B. synthetic
C. determined   D. constructive   [D]

* **consult**[4] ﹝kənˈsʌlt﹞ *v.* 請教
(= *confer*)；查閱
【片語】 *consult a dictionary* (查字典)

【典型考題】

Mei-ling has a very close relationship
with her parents. She always _____
them before she makes important
decisions.
A. impresses   B. advises
C. consults   D. motivates   [C]

* **consultant**[4] ﹝kənˈsʌltənt﹞ *n.* 顧問
(= *adviser*)
【記憶技巧】 *con* (together) + *sult* (sit)
+ *ant* (人) (坐在一起提供意見的人，就
是「顧問」)

【典型考題】

After years of hard work, Mandy
finally became the first female
_____ on the staff of City Hospital.
A. visitor   B. humanist
C. consultant   D. follower   [C]

* **consume**[4] ﹝kənˈsum, -ˈsjum﹞ *v.* 消耗
(= *use up*)；吃 (喝) (= *take in*)
【記憶技巧】 *con* (wholly) + *sume*
(take) (完全取用耗盡，也就是「消耗」)

C

* **consumer** [4] (kən'sumɚ , -'sjumɚ) *n.*
  消費者 (= *buyer*)
  【比較】customer (顧客)

* **contact** [2] ('kɑntækt) *v. n.* 聯絡;接觸
  (= *touch*)
  【記憶技巧】*con* (together) + *tact*
  (touch)
  【片語】*keep in contact with* (與…
  保持聯絡)

  ┌─【典型考題】────────
  │ Since I graduated from college, I
  │ have lost _____ with my best
  │ friend, Julie.
  │ A. distance   B. division
  │ C. contact   D. conflict   [C]
  └───────────────────

* **contain** [2] (kən'ten) *v.* 包含
  (= *hold* = *include*)
  Beer *contains* alcohol.
  【記憶技巧】*con* (with) + *tain* (hold)

  ┌─【典型考題】────────
  │ Each of these bottles _____
  │ 1,000 cc of mineral water, and sells
  │ for NT$50.
  │ A. attains   B. remains
  │ C. sustains   D. contains   [D]
  └───────────────────

* **container** [4] (kən'tenɚ) *n.* 容器
  (= *holder*)

* **content** [4] ('kɑntɛnt) *n.* 內容;
  (*pl.*)目錄
  (kən'tɛnt) *adj.* 滿足的 (= *satisfied*)
  【片語】*the table of contents* 目錄

  ┌─【典型考題】────────
  │ When I open a book, I look first at the
  │ table of _____ to get a general idea
  │ of the book and to see which chapters
  │ I might be interested in reading.
  │ A. contract   B. contents
  │ C. contest   D. contact   [B]
  └───────────────────

* **contentment** [4] (kən'tɛntmənt) *n.*
  滿足 (= *satisfaction*)
  Happiness lies in *contentment*.

* **contest** [4] ('kɑntɛst) *n.* 比賽
  (= *competition*)
  【衍伸詞】*a speech contest* (演講比賽)
           a beauty contest (選美比賽)

* **context** [4] ('kɑntɛkst) *n.* 上下文
  (= *framework*);背景;環境
  (= *circumstances*)
  【記憶技巧】*con* (together) + *text*
  (weave) (編排在一起的文字)

  ┌─【典型考題】────────
  │ A good reader can often figure out
  │ what new words mean by using
  │ _____.
  │ A. contact   B. context
  │ C. conflict   D. contest   [B]
  └───────────────────

* **continent** [3] ('kɑntənənt) *n.* 洲;大陸

* **continual** [4] (kən'tɪnjʊəl) *adj.* 連續的
  (= *constant*)

* **continue** [1] (kən'tɪnju) *v.* 繼續
  (= *go on*)
  He *continued* to write the novel.
  【記憶技巧】*con* (with) + *tinue* (hold)
  (保持某個動作,表示「繼續」)

* **continuous** [4] (kən'tɪnjʊəs) *adj.*
  連續的 (= *constant*)

  【比較】continual 是「有間斷的」的連續,
  continuous 是「沒間斷的」連續。

  ┌─【典型考題】────────
  │ The river flows _____ for seven
  │ months of the year, but it flows
  │ intermittently in the dry season.
  │ A. rapidly   B. urgently
  │ C. continuously D. temporarily   [C]
  └───────────────────

‡ contract[3] 〔ˈkɑntrækt 〕 *n.* 合約
（ = *agreement* ）
〔 kənˈtrækt 〕 *v.* 收縮；感染
We have a *contract* with that company.
【記憶技巧】 *con* (together) + *tract* (draw) （「合約」是雙方簽訂的文件）

* contrast[4] 〔ˈkɑntræst 〕 *n.* 對比
（ = *opposition* ）；對照；比較
I like the *contrast* between the two colors.
【記憶技巧】 *contra* (against) + *st* (stand) （站在相反的立場，形成「對比」）

* contribute[4] 〔 kənˈtrɪbjut 〕 *v.* 貢獻；捐獻 （ = *give* ）
【片語】 *contribute to* （對…有貢獻；有助於）
【比較】 attribute （歸因於）
distribute （分配；分發）

* contribution[4] 〔ˌkɑntrəˈbjuʃən 〕 *n.*
貢獻；捐贈 （ = *donation* ）

‡ control[2] 〔 kənˈtrol 〕 *v. n.* 控制
（ = *rule* ）
This plane was *controlled* by the computer system.
【常考片語】 *keep…under control* （控制住…）

controller[2] 〔 kənˈtrolɚ 〕 *n.* 管理者

* convenience[4] 〔 kənˈvinjəns 〕 *n.*
方便
【片語】 *at one's convenience* （在某人方便的時候）

【典型考題】
It is urgent, so please call me back at your earliest _____.
A. custom   B. development
C. convenience D. trust [C]

‡‡ convenient[2] 〔 kənˈvinjənt 〕 *adj.*
方便的 （ = *handy* ）
Is Friday *convenient* for you?
【衍伸詞】 convenience （方便）

* convention[4] 〔 kənˈvɛnʃən 〕 *n.* 代表
大會 （ = *meeting* = *conference*
= *congress* ）；習俗 （ = *custom* ）
The next sales *convention* will be held in Palm Springs in January.

* conventional[4] 〔 kənˈvɛnʃənl̩ 〕 *adj.*
傳統的 （ = *traditional* ）；一般的

【典型考題】
I think more people will like this _____ design than the innovative one.
A. conventional B. considerable
C. revolutionary D. removable [A]

‡ conversation[2] 〔ˌkɑnvɚˈseʃən 〕 *n.*
對話 （ = *talk* ）
Mark and Mike are having a *conversation* over the telephone.

【典型考題】
The woman likes to show off and criticize people. She really should learn more about the art of _____.
A. interest   B. conversation
C. stranger   D. country [B]

* converse[4] 〔 kənˈvɝs 〕 *v.* 談話
（ = *talk* ）
〔ˈkɑnvɝs 〕 *adj.* 逆的；相反的

C

* **convey**[4] 〔 kən've 〕 v. 傳達
  (= *communicate*)；運輸；傳遞；
  搬運；運送
  No words can *convey* my feelings.
  【記憶技巧】*con* (together) + *vey* (way)

* **convince**[4] 〔 kən'vɪns 〕 v. 使相信
  (= *persuade*)
  【記憶技巧】*con* (thoroughly) + *vince*
  (conquer) (完全征服對方，使對方相信)
  【常考片語】*convince sb. of sth.* (使某
  人相信某事)

‡ **cook**[1] 〔 kʊk 〕 v. 做菜   n. 廚師

* **cooker**[2] 〔'kʊkɚ 〕 n. 烹調器具

‡ **cookie**[1] 〔'kʊkɪ 〕 n. (甜的) 餅乾

‡ **cool**[1] 〔 kul 〕 adj. 涼爽的；很酷的
  Please keep the medicine in a *cool*
  and dry place.

* **cooperate**[4] 〔 ko'apə,ret 〕 v. 合作
  (= *work together*)
  【記憶技巧】*co* (together) + *oper*
  (work) + *ate* (v.)

* **cooperation**[4] 〔 ko,apə're∫ən 〕 n.
  合作 (= *teamwork*)

* **cooperative**[4] 〔 ko'apə,retɪv 〕 adj.
  合作的 (= *joint*)

* **cope**[4] 〔 kop 〕 v. 應付；處理 (= *deal*)
  【常考片語】*cope with* (應付；處理)

* **copper**[4] 〔'kapɚ 〕 n. 銅

‡ **copy**[2] 〔'kapɪ 〕 v. 影印；抄寫；模仿；
  複製 (= *reproduce*)
  n. 影本 (= *print*)；複製品
  (= *reproduction*)
  Copy down the questions in your
  notebook.

* **cord**[4] 〔 kɔrd 〕 n. 細繩 (= *rope*)

* **cork**[4] 〔 kɔrk 〕 n. 軟木塞

‡ **corn**[1] 〔 kɔrn 〕 n. 玉米
  (= *maize* 〔 mez 〕)
  【衍伸詞】*cornflakes* (玉米薄片)

‡ **corner**[2] 〔'kɔrnɚ 〕 n. 角落；轉角
  The post office is right on the
  corner.

‡ **correct**[1] 〔 kə'rɛkt 〕 adj. 正確的
  (= *right*)
  All the answers are *correct*.
  【記憶技巧】*cor* (wholly) + *rect* (right)

* **correspond**[4] 〔,kɔrə'spand 〕 v. 通信
  (= *write*)；符合 (= *match*)
  Matt and Denise *corresponded*
  regularly after leaving school.
  【記憶技巧】*cor* (together) + *respond*
  (answer) (相互回信，即「通信」)
  【片語】*correspond with* (和…通信)
  　　　correspond to (符合)

‡ **cost**[1] 〔 kɔst 〕 n. 費用 (= *price*)
  v. 花費；值… (= *be priced at*)
  How much will it *cost* to repair
  this car?

* **costly**[2] 〔'kɔstlɪ 〕 adj. 昂貴的
  (= *expensive*)

***costume**[4] 〔'kɑstjum 〕 n. 服裝
(= *outfit* = *clothes*)
【衍伸詞】*costume ball* (化妝舞會)

***cottage**[4] 〔'kɑtɪdʒ 〕 n. 農舍 (= *cabin*)

****cotton**[2] 〔'kɑtn̩ 〕 n. 棉
This cloth is made from *cotton*.

****couch**[3] 〔kaʊtʃ 〕 n. 長沙發 (= *sofa*)
There is a cat on the *couch*.
【注意】「雙人沙發」稱作 loveseat,「單人沙發」稱作 armchair (扶手椅),全部通稱 sofa (沙發)。

****cough**[2] 〔kɔf 〕 n. v. 咳嗽
The child has a bad *cough*.
【衍伸詞】*cough syrup* (止咳糖漿)

***council**[4] 〔'kaʊnsl̩ 〕 n. 議會
(= *committee*)
【記憶技巧】*coun* (together) + *cil*
(call) (共同召集,是要參加「議會」)
【注意】council (議會) 和 counsel (建議) 讀音相同,但議會要召集 (call a meeting) 才會有人來,所以是 coun**cil**。
【衍伸詞】*the city council* (市議會)

****count**[1] 〔kaʊnt 〕 v. 數 (= *add up*);
重要 (= *matter*)
My little sister can *count* from one to ten.
It is quality, not quantity that *counts*.

***countable**[3] 〔'kaʊntəbl̩ 〕 adj. 可數的
(= *numerable*)
【衍伸詞】*a countable noun* (可數名詞)

***counter**[4] 〔'kaʊntɚ 〕 n. 櫃台

****country**[1] 〔'kʌntrɪ 〕 n. 國家
(= *nation*);鄉下
I would like to live in the *country*.

***countryside**[2] 〔'kʌntrɪ,saɪd 〕 n. 鄉間
(= *rural areas*)
The Japanese *countryside* looks its best in October.

***county**[2] 〔'kaʊntɪ 〕 n. 郡;縣
(= *district*)
Tony wants to move to the *county* of Essex.
【記憶技巧】country 是國家,少一個 r,就是比較小的 county (郡;縣)。

****couple**[2] 〔'kʌpl̩ 〕 n. 一對男女
(= *pair*);夫婦 (= *husband and wife*)
We saw many young *couples* walking in the park.

****courage**[2] 〔'kɝɪdʒ 〕 n. 勇氣 (= *bravery*)
He is a man of *courage*.

***courageous**[4] 〔kə'redʒəs 〕 adj.
勇敢的 (= *brave*)

****course**[1] 〔kors 〕 n. 課程 (= *classes*)
She took a *course* in French literature.

****court**[2] 〔kort 〕 n. 法院;(網球) 球場
(= *field*);天井;宮廷;庭院
(= *courtyard*)
Our school has a tennis *court*.

***courteous**[4] 〔'kɝtɪəs 〕 adj. 有禮貌的
(= *polite*)

【典型考題】
Jim is a ＿＿＿＿ person: he is polite, kind, and always shows respect for others.
A. courteous   B. handsome
C. hateful   D. sensitive   **[A]**

* **courtesy**[4]〔ˈkɝtəsɪ〕*n.* 禮貌
(= *politeness*)

【典型考題】

Out of _____ and consideration, I always write a thank-you note when someone sends me a gift.
A. convenience   B. concentration
C. courtesy   D. courtship   [C]

‡ **cousin**[2]〔ˈkʌzn̩〕*n.* 表（堂）兄弟姊妹
I have six *cousins* on my mother's side.

‡ **cover**[1]〔ˈkʌvɚ〕*v.* 覆蓋（ = *mask* ）；
涵蓋   *n.* 蓋子
The car is *covered* with snow.

‡ **cow**[1]〔kaʊ〕*n.* 母牛
You can see *cows* on the farm.
【比較】bull（公牛）

* **coward**[3]〔ˈkaʊɚd〕*n.* 懦夫(= *chicken*)
【記憶技巧】*cow*（母牛）+ *ard*（人）

‡ **cowboy**[1]〔ˈkaʊˌbɔɪ〕*n.* 牛仔
(= *cattleman*)
I'll be a *cowboy* at the party.

‡ **crab**[2]〔kræb〕*n.* 螃蟹
Crab is my favorite seafood.

* **crack**[4]〔kræk〕*v.* 使破裂（ = *break* ）；
說（笑話）(= *tell*)
【片語】*crack a joke*（說笑話）
        crack down on（嚴格取締）

* **cradle**[3]〔ˈkredl̩〕*n.* 搖籃

* **craft**[4]〔kræft〕*n.* 技藝；技術（ = *skill* ）
The sculptor worked with fine *craft*.

* **cram**[4]〔kræm〕*v.* 填塞（ = *jam* ）；
K 書   *n.* 填鴨式的用功

I don't think all of this stuff will fit in my suitcase, but I will try to *cram* it in.
【衍伸詞】*cram school*（補習班）

* **crane**[2]〔kren〕*n.* 起重機；鶴

* **crash**[3]〔kræʃ〕*v. n.* 墜毀；撞毀
(= *smash*)   *n.* 汽車相撞聲
Bobby *crashed* his car, but he was unhurt.
【衍伸詞】*air crash*（空難）

* **crawl**[3]〔krɔl〕*v.* 爬行（ = *creep* ）

【典型考題】

It being a tiring day, as soon as I got home, I locked the door and _____ into bed.
A. skinned   B. stirred
C. crawled   D. crouched   [C]

* **crayon**[2]〔ˈkreən〕*n.* 蠟筆

‡ **crazy**[2]〔ˈkrezɪ〕*adj.* 瘋狂的（ = *mad* ）
She went *crazy* with fear.

* **cream**[2]〔krim〕*n.* 奶油
Do you take *cream* in your coffee?

* **create**[2]〔krɪˈet〕*v.* 創造（ = *make* ）
He *created* wonderful characters in his novels.
【記憶技巧】*cre* (make) + *ate* (v.)

* **creation**[4]〔krɪˈeʃən〕*n.* 創造
(= *production*)
【比較】recreation（娛樂）

* **creative**[3]〔krɪˈetɪv〕*adj.* 有創造力的
(= *inventive*)

*creativity[4] 〔͵krieˈtɪvətɪ〕 *n.* 創造力
　　(= *imagination* = *originality*)

【典型考題】
The writing teacher has found that
reading fantasies such as J. K.
Rowling's Harry Potter may inspire her
students to think and write with _____.
A. creativity　　　B. generosity
C. superstition　　D. foundation　　**[A]**

creator[3] 〔krɪˈetɚ〕 *n.* 創造者
　　(= *maker*)

*creature[3] 〔ˈkritʃɚ〕 *n.* 生物
　　(= *living thing*)；動物 (= *animal*)

*credit[3] 〔ˈkrɛdɪt〕 *n.* 信用 (= *trust*)
　　【衍伸詞】 *credit card* (信用卡)

*creep[3] 〔krip〕 *v.* 悄悄地前進
　　(= *sneak*)；爬行　　*n.* 爬行；(*pl.*) 毛
　　骨悚然的感覺
　　The cat *crept* up on the bird silently.

*crew[3] 〔kru〕 *n.* (船、飛機的) 全體
　　工作人員
　　The sailboat has a *crew* of seven.

*cricket[3] 〔ˈkrɪkɪt〕 *n.* 蟋蟀

**crime[2] 〔kraɪm〕 *n.* 罪 (= *offense*)
　　He committed a serious *crime*.

*criminal[3] 〔ˈkrɪmənḷ〕 *n.* 罪犯
　　(= *lawbreaker*)

*cripple[4] 〔ˈkrɪpḷ〕 *n.* 跛子；瘸子
　　(= *a disabled person*)　　*v.* 使殘廢
　　(= *disable*)

*crisis[2] 〔ˈkraɪsɪs〕 *n.* 危機
　　(= *emergency*)
　　This country faced a political *crisis*.
　　【注意】複數形為 crises。

【典型考題】
In times of _____, one finds out who
one's real friends are.
A. condition　　　B. situation
C. mischief　　　D. crisis　　**[D]**

*crispy[3] 〔ˈkrɪspɪ〕 *adj.* 酥脆的

*critic[4] 〔ˈkrɪtɪk〕 *n.* 評論家
　　(= *reviewer*)；批評者

*critical[4] 〔ˈkrɪtɪkḷ〕 *adj.* 批評的
　　(= *fault-finding*)；危急的 (= *risky*)
　　【衍伸詞】 *a critical moment* (關鍵
　　　　　　　時刻)

*criticism[4] 〔ˈkrɪtəͺsɪzəm〕 *n.* 批評
　　(= *disapproval*)

*criticize[4] 〔ˈkrɪtəͺsaɪz〕 *v.* 批評
　　(= *find fault with*)

【典型考題】
People who don't like to _____
others are popular.
A. notice　　　B. tell
C. send　　　　D. criticize　　**[D]**

*crop[2] 〔krɑp〕 *n.* 農作物

**cross[2] 〔krɔs〕 *v.* 越過 (= *go across*)
　　n. 十字架
　　We *crossed* a lake in a boat.
　　【衍伸詞】 *the Red Cross* (紅十字會)

*crow[1,2] 〔kro〕 *n.* 烏鴉　*v.* (公雞) 啼
　　叫 (= *cry*)

‡**crowd**[2] 〔kraʊd〕 *n.* 群眾（= *group*）；人群（= *people*）

There are *crowds* of people at the market.

【衍伸詞】crowded（擁擠的）

***crown**[3] 〔kraʊn〕 *n.* 皇冠

‡**cruel**[2] 〔ˈkruəl〕 *adj.* 殘忍的（= *brutal*）

Don't be *cruel* to animals.

cruelty[4] 〔ˈkruəltɪ〕 *n.* 殘忍（= *inhumane treatment*）

***crunchy**[3] 〔ˈkrʌntʃɪ〕 *adj.* 鬆脆的（= *crispy*）

Look at all the fresh, *crunchy* vegetables at the salad bar!

***crush**[4] 〔krʌʃ〕 *v.* 壓扁（= *smash*）；壓碎；摧毀 *n.* 迷戀

I accidentally sat on the bag and *crushed* the tomatoes that were inside.

【片語】*have a crush on*（迷戀）

***crutch**[3] 〔krʌtʃ〕 *n.* 枴杖

【片語】*walk on crutches*（撐著枴杖走路）

‡**cry**[1] 〔kraɪ〕 *v.* 哭

The little babies always *cry*.

***cub**[1] 〔kʌb〕 *n.* 幼獸

cube[4] 〔kjub〕 *n.* 立方體

【比較】tube（管子）

***cucumber**[4] 〔ˈkjukʌmbɚ〕 *n.* 黃瓜

***cue**[4] 〔kju〕 *v.* 暗示（= *hint*）

The director *cued* the actors to begin their scene.

***cultural**[3] 〔ˈkʌltʃərəl〕 *adj.* 文化的

‡**culture**[2] 〔ˈkʌltʃɚ〕 *n.* 文化

Every nation has its own *culture*.

【典型考題】

It is difficult for a Westerner to understand and appreciate Chinese _____.

A. situation B. comet
C. telescope D. culture [D]

***cunning**[4] 〔ˈkʌnɪŋ〕 *adj.* 狡猾的（= *sly*〔slaɪ〕）

It was very *cunning* of you to trick Jane into doing your work.

‡**cup**[1] 〔kʌp〕 *n.* 杯子

I broke my *cup* yesterday.

***cupboard**[3] 〔ˈkʌbɚd〕 *n.* 碗櫥

【注意發音】

‡**cure**[2] 〔kjur〕 *v. n.* 治療（= *heal*）

This medicine will *cure* your cold.

***curiosity**[4] 〔ˌkjurɪˈɑsətɪ〕 *n.* 好奇心（= *interest*）

Curiosity killed the cat.

【典型考題】

Deep inside the human heart is the _____ about what other people do in private. That's why the media pursue and people peep.

A. attraction B. curiosity
C. dependence D. experiment [B]

‡**curious**[2] (ˈkjʊrɪəs) *adj.* 好奇的
(= *interested*)
She is too *curious* about other
people's business.

*__curl__[4] (kɝl) *n.* 捲曲 (= *twist*)

*__curse__[4] (kɝs) *v.* 詛咒 (= *swear*)
n. 詛咒 (= *swearword*)
Henry is so unlucky that it seems
as though he is *cursed.*

‡**curtain**[2] (ˈkɝtn̩) *n.* 窗簾

*__curve__[4] (kɝv) *n.* 曲線
The child drew *curves* on the paper.

*__cushion__[4] (ˈkʊʃən) *n.* 墊子 (= *pad*)

‡**custom**[2] (ˈkʌstəm) *n.* 習俗
(= *practice*)

It's a *custom* for Japanese to bow
when they meet their acquaintances.

【典型考題】
There are different ＿＿＿＿ in
different countries. That is why the
proverb goes, "Do in Rome as the
Romans do."
A. wonders　　　B. tourists
C. strangers　　　D. customs　　　[D]

‡**customer**[2] (ˈkʌstəmɚ) *n.* 顧客
(= *guest*)
The store has a lot of *customers.*

‡**cut**[1] (kʌt) *v.* 切；割
She *cut* her finger with a knife.

‡**cute**[1] (kjut) *adj.* 可愛的 (= *lovely*)
She is such a *cute* girl.

*__cycle__[3] (ˈsaɪkl̩) *n.* 循環
【記憶技巧】 *cycle* (circle)

D d

‡**dad**[1] (dæd) *n.* 爸爸
(= *daddy* = *papa* = *pa* = *pop*)
Dad told me a strange story.

‡**daddy**[1] (ˈdædɪ) *n.* 爸爸

*__daily__[2] (ˈdelɪ) *adj.* 每天的
I am paid on a *daily* basis.
【片語】 *on a daily basis* (每天)

*__dairy__[3] (ˈdɛrɪ) *adj.* 乳製品的
n. 酪農場
【比較】 diary (日記)
【衍伸詞】 *dairy product* (乳製品)

*__dam__[3] (dæm) *n.* 水壩

‡**damage**[2] (ˈdæmɪdʒ) *v.* 損害 (= *harm*)
When a road is *damaged,* someone
must do the necessary repairs.

*__damn__[4] (dæm) *v.* 詛咒 (= *curse*)
Once he became a drug addict, he
was *damned* to a life of misery.

*__damp__[4] (dæmp) *adj.* 潮濕的 (= *wet*)
Sheila wiped the counter with a
damp cloth.

‡**dance**[1] (dæns) *v.* 跳舞
We can *dance* at the party tomorrow.

*__dancer__[1] (ˈdænsɚ) *n.* 舞者

D

‡**danger**[1] (ˈdendʒɚ) *n.* 危險 (= *risk*)
A jungle is full of *danger*.
【反義詞】security (安全)

‡**dangerous**[2] (ˈdendʒərəs) *adj.* 危險
的 (= *risky*)

【典型考題】

It is ＿＿＿＿ to go out on a typhoon
day. The sky is dark and the wind
is strong.
A. careful   B. fashionable
C. dangerous   D. convenient   [C]

*·**dare**[3] (dɛr) *v.* 敢 (= *have the courage*)
I have never *dared* to speak to him.

‡**dark**[1] (dɑrk) *adj.* 黑暗的
The house is very *dark* at night.

*·**darling**[3] (ˈdɑrlɪŋ) *n.* 親愛的人

*·**dash**[3] (dæʃ) *v.* 猛衝 (= *rush*)
n. 破折號 (—)
He *dashed* to get the last train.

*·**data**[2] (ˈdetə) *n. pl.* 資料
Thank you for giving me the *data*.
【注意】單數為 datum (ˈdetəm)。

‡**date**[1] (det) *n.* 日期；約會
What is your *date* of birth?

‡**daughter**[1] (ˈdɔtɚ) *n.* 女兒
Lucy is the only *daughter* of the
family.

‡**dawn**[2] (dɔn) *n.* 黎明
We set out at *dawn*.

‡**day**[1] (de) *n.* 天
What *day* is today?

‡**dead**[1] (dɛd) *adj.* 死的
His father has been *dead* for nearly
ten years.
【反義詞】alive (活的)

*·**deadline**[4] (ˈdɛd,laɪn) *n.* 最後期限
(= *time limit*)
Setting *deadlines* is the best way to
do things efficiently.

‡**deaf**[2] (dɛf) *adj.* 聾的
He is unable to hear you because
he is *deaf*.
【記憶技巧】仔細看 deaf 這個字，中間是
ea(r) (耳朵)，所以是「聾的」。
【比較】blind (瞎的)
           dumb (啞的)

deafen[3] (ˈdɛfən) *v.* 使聾
(= *make deaf*)

‡**deal**[1] (dil) *v.* 處理
I'm busy, and there are still a lot of
things that I have to *deal* with.
【常考片語】***deal with*** (應付；處理)

dealer[3] (ˈdilɚ) *n.* 商人

‡**dear**[1] (dɪr) *adj.* 親愛的
Alice is my *dear* friend.

*·**death**[1] (dɛθ) *n.* 死亡
Her *death* was a shock to him.

*·**debate**[2] (dɪˈbet) *v.* 辯論
We are *debating* which was best.
【記憶技巧】*de* (down) + *bate* (beat)
(「辯論」就是要打倒對方)

D

** **debt**[2]〔 dɛt 〕*n.* 債務

If they paid me their *debts*, I should be quite well off.

【注意】字中的 b 不發音。

** **decade**[3]〔'dɛked 〕*n.* 十年

Over the last *decade*, writer-director David Mamet has made many great films.

【記憶技巧】*deca* (ten) + *de* (*n.*)

‡**December**[1]〔 dɪ'sɛmbɚ 〕*n.* 十二月

‡**decide**[1]〔 dɪ'saɪd 〕*v.* 決定

(= *make up one's mind*)

Just as I got down to work, my friends *decided* to visit me.

【記憶技巧】*de* (off) + *cide* (cut)

（從一堆想法中把自己想要的部分割開並拿走，表示「決定」）

‡**decision**[2]〔 dɪ'sɪʒən 〕*n.* 決定

(= *conclusion*)

【片語】*make a decision* (做決定)

** **deck**[3]〔 dɛk 〕*n.* 甲板；一副 (紙牌)

【衍伸詞】*a deck of cards* (一副紙牌)

** **declare**[4]〔 dɪ'klɛr 〕*v.* 宣佈

(= *announce*)

Carl was *declared* the winner of the boxing match.

【記憶技巧】*de* (fully) + *clare* (clear)

（向大家表示得十分清楚，也就是「宣佈」）

【典型考題】

The Olympic chairperson _____ the Games open.
A. declared   B. departed
C. discovered   D. deserved   [A]

‡**decorate**[2]〔'dɛkə,ret 〕*v.* 裝飾

(= *adorn*)

The hotel room was *decorated* with flowers.

【記憶技巧】*decor* (ornament) + *ate* (*v.*)

【典型考題】

Mr. Lin usually _____ his restaurant with lights and flowers before the New Year.
A. celebrates   B. decorates
C. examines   D. notices   [B]

** **decoration**[4]〔,dɛkə'reʃən 〕*n.* 裝飾

(= *adornment*)

‡**decrease**[4]〔 dɪ'kris 〕*v. n.* 減少 (= *cut*)

We should *decrease* the amount of our trash.

【反義詞】 increase (增加)

** **deed**[3]〔 did 〕*n.* 行為 (= *action*)；功績

The bystander who stopped the thief was praised for his brave *deed*.

‡**deep**[1]〔 dip 〕*adj.* 深的

The ocean is very *deep*.

【反義詞】 shallow (淺的)

deepen[3]〔'dipən 〕*v.* 加深

‡**deer**[1]〔 dɪr 〕*n.* 鹿【單複數同形】

A *deer* is an animal with horns.

** **defeat**[4]〔 dɪ'fit 〕*v.* 打敗 (= *beat*)

He *defeated* his opponents in this election.

【記憶技巧】*de* (away) + *feat* (功績)

（把別人的功績拿走，就是「打敗」）

** **defend**[4]〔 dɪ'fɛnd 〕*v.* 保衛 (= *protect*)

The forest ranger carries a rifle to *defend* himself against bears.

【記憶技巧】*de* (away) + *fend* (strike)

（把敵人打跑，就是「保衛」自己）

* defense[4]〔 dɪ'fɛns 〕 *n.* 防禦
（ = *protection* ）
【反義詞】 offense（攻擊）
【衍伸詞】 *national defense*（國防）

【典型考題】
Every country needs strong national
_____ against enemy invasions.
A. defense　　　B. balance
C. analysis　　　D. response　　[A]

* defensible[4]〔 dɪ'fɛnsəbḷ 〕 *adj.* 可防
禦的

* defensive[4]〔 dɪ'fɛnsɪv 〕 *adj.* 防禦的
（ = *protective* ）

* define[3]〔 dɪ'faɪn 〕 *v.* 下定義
How would you *define* your role in
the group?
【記憶技巧】 *de* (completely) + *fine*
(limit)（把限制完全說出，就是「下定義」）

* definite[4]〔 'dɛfənɪt 〕 *adj.* 明確的
（ = *certain* ）
I want a *definite* answer right now.

【典型考題】
We cannot give you a _____
answer now; there are still many
uncertainties on this issue.
A. definite　　　B. familiar
C. courteous　　D. hollow　　[A]

* definition[3]〔 ˌdɛfə'nɪʃən 〕 *n.* 定義
（ = *explanation* ）

* degree[2]〔 dɪ'gri 〕 *n.* 程度；度
To what *degree* are you interested
in fishing?
【片語】 *to ~ degree*（到~程度）
　　　（ = *to ~ extent* ）

* delay[2]〔 dɪ'le 〕 *v.* 延遲（ = *put off* ）；
耽誤（ = *hold up* ）
What *delayed* you so long
yesterday?
【記憶技巧】 *de* (away) + *lay* (leave)
（離開到較遠的地方，就會「延遲」）

* delicate[4]〔 'dɛləkət, -kɪt 〕 *adj.* 細緻的
（ = *refined* ）
What a *delicate* piece of
embroidery!

* delicious[2]〔 dɪ'lɪʃəs 〕 *adj.* 美味的
（ = *tasty* ）
What a *delicious* dinner we enjoyed
tonight!
【記憶技巧】 *de* (intensive) + *lic*
（ entice 引誘 ）+ *ious* (adj.)
（食物有著強烈的誘惑，表示「美味的」）

* delight[4]〔 dɪ'laɪt 〕 *n.* 高興（ = *joy* ）
Tina smiled in *delight* when she saw
her boyfriend approach.

【典型考題】
The children were so _____ to see
the clown appear on stage that they
laughed, screamed, and clapped their
hands happily.
A. admirable　　B. fearful
C. delighted　　D. intense　　[C]

* delightful[4]〔 dɪ'laɪtfəl 〕 *adj.* 令人高興
的（ = *pleasant* ）

* deliver[2]〔 dɪ'lɪvɚ 〕 *v.* 遞送（ = *bring* ）
The postman *delivers* letters to our
home every day.
【記憶技巧】背這個字要順便背 liver（肝
臟）。

D

D

* **delivery**[3]〔 dɪ'lɪvərɪ 〕*n.* 遞送

【典型考題】

The special ＿＿＿＿ postal service is very efficient. A package sent can be received in a couple of hours.
A. delivery　　　B. directory
C. discovery　　D. dormitory　　[A]

* **demand**[4]〔 dɪ'mænd 〕*v.* 要求
（ ＝ *ask for* ）

The irate customers *demanded* to speak to the store manager.

【記憶技巧】 *de* (completely) ＋ *mand* (order)（完全以下令的方式，就是「要求」）

【比較】 command (命令)

* **democracy**[3]〔 də'makrəsɪ 〕*n.* 民主政治

After the dictator was overthrown, *democracy* was established.

【記憶技巧】 *demo* (people) ＋ *cracy* (rule)（由人民來管理，就是「民主」）

* **democratic**[3]〔,dɛmə'krætɪk 〕*adj.* 民主的

* **demonstrate**[4]〔'dɛmən,stret 〕
v. 示威（ ＝ *march in protest* ）；示範
The swimming teacher first *demonstrated* the stroke and then asked all of us to try it.

【記憶技巧】 *de* (fully) ＋ *monstr* (show) ＋ *ate* (*v.*)（完整地表演給大家看，就是「示範」）

* **demonstration**[4]〔,dɛmən'streʃən 〕
n. 示威（ ＝ *protest* ）；示範
（ ＝ *show* ）

* **dense**[4]〔 dɛns 〕*adj.* 濃密的；密集的
There was little light in the *dense* forest.

【反義詞】 sparse (稀疏的)

** **dentist**[2]〔'dɛntɪst 〕*n.* 牙醫
Dentists take care of people's teeth and treat diseases of the mouth.

* **deny**[2]〔 dɪ'naɪ 〕*v.* 否認（ ＝ *negate*)；拒絕

* **depart**[4]〔 dɪ'part 〕*v.* 離開（ ＝ *leave* ）
Buses *depart* for the airport every twenty minutes.

【記憶技巧】 *de* (from) ＋ *part* (分開)
（ 從某處分開，就是「離開」）

** **department**[2]〔 dɪ'partmənt 〕*n.* 部門
（ ＝ *section* ）；系（ ＝ *division* ）
Eddie teaches in the literature *department*.

【衍伸詞】 *department store* (百貨公司)

* **departure**[4]〔 dɪ'partʃ⋗ 〕*n.* 離開
（ ＝ *leaving* ）；出發

【典型考題】

The airport was closed because of the snowstorm, and our ＿＿＿＿ for Paris had to be delayed until the following day.
A. movement　　B. registration
C. tendency　　D. departure　　[D]

** **depend**[2]〔 dɪ'pɛnd 〕*v.* 依賴；依靠
（ ＝ *rely* ）
You cannot *depend* on your parents forever.

【常考】 *depend on* (依賴；視…而定)

【記憶技巧】 *de* (down) ＋ *pend* (hang)
（ 懸掛東西需要「依賴」支撐物 ）

D

* **dependable**[4] 〔 dɪˈpɛndəbl̩ 〕 *adj.*
可靠的 (= *reliable*)

* **dependent**[4] 〔 dɪˈpɛndənt 〕 *adj.*
依賴的 (= *reliant*)

* **deposit**[3] 〔 dɪˈpɑzɪt 〕 *n.* 存款
We had better make a bank *deposit*
before we write any more checks.
【記憶技巧】 *de* (down) + *posit* (put)
（將錢放置在銀行，這筆錢就是「存款」）

* **depress**[4] 〔 dɪˈprɛs 〕 *v.* 使沮喪
(= *upset* = *discourage*)
When you *depress* someone, you
make him or her sad.
【記憶技巧】 *de* (down) + *press* (press)
（壓到谷底，就是「使沮喪」）

* **depression**[4] 〔 dɪˈprɛʃən 〕 *n.* 沮喪
(= *sadness*)；不景氣 (= *recession*)

* **depth**[2] 〔 dɛpθ 〕 *n.* 深度 (= *deepness*)；
深厚；(*pl.*) 深處

** **describe**[2] 〔 dɪˈskraɪb 〕 *v.* 描述
(= *portray*)
He was *described* as being very
clever.
【記憶技巧】 *de* (fully) + *scribe*
(write) (寫得很詳細，也就是「描述」)

* **description**[3] 〔 dɪˈskrɪpʃən 〕 *n.* 描述
(= *portrayal*)

** **desert**[2] 〔ˈdɛzɚt 〕 *n.* 沙漠
〔 dɪˈzɝt 〕 *v.* 拋棄 (= *abandon*)
There are many camels in the *desert*.

Ray *deserted* his wife and children.
【記憶技巧】 *de* (off) + *sert* (join)
（脫離連結，就是「拋棄」）

【典型考題】
You can't ＿＿＿＿ your dog in the
park just because it is old and sick.
A. exercise   B. encourage
C. divide   D. desert   [D]

* **deserve**[4] 〔 dɪˈzɝv 〕 *v.* 應得
You've been working all morning—
you *deserve* a rest.

【典型考題】
The landslide after the typhoon
signals that environmental protection
＿＿＿＿ our attention.
A. accuses   B. stretches
C. obtains   D. deserves   [D]

** **design**[2] 〔 dɪˈzaɪn 〕 *v. n.* 設計 (= *plan*)
Adam *designs* clothes for me.
【記憶技巧】 *de* (out) + *sign* (mark)
（把符號畫出來，就是「設計」）

* **designer**[3] 〔 dɪˈzaɪnɚ 〕 *n.* 設計師
(= *stylist*)

desirable[3] 〔 dɪˈzaɪrəbl̩ 〕 *adj.* 合意的
【典型考題】
Everyone in our company enjoys
working with Jason. He's got all the
qualities that make a ＿＿＿＿ partner.
A. desirable   B. comfortable
C. frequent   D. hostile   [A]

** **desire**[2] 〔 dɪˈzaɪr 〕 *n.* 渴望；慾望
Paul has a *desire* to help people.

** **desk**[1] 〔 dɛsk 〕 *n.* 書桌
My grandfather made this *desk* for me.

***desperate**[4] (ˈdɛspərɪt) *adj.* 絕望的 (= *hopeless*); (因絕望) 不顧一切的

【典型考題】
Most of the refugees are ______ because life is very hard for them.
A. sarcastic B. insured
C. decomposed D. desperate [D]

***despite**[4] (dɪˈspaɪt) *prep.* 儘管 (= *in spite of*)
Despite her bad cold, Ellen insisted on going to work.

****dessert**[2] (dɪˈzɝt) *n.* 甜點
"What do we have for *dessert*?" "Ice cream."
【記憶技巧】***des*** (apart) + ***sert*** (serve)
(與主食分開端上的食物，就是「甜點」)

***destroy**[3] (dɪˈstrɔɪ) *v.* 破壞 (= *ruin*)
The house was *destroyed* by fire.
【記憶技巧】***de*** (down) + ***stroy*** (build)
(使建築物倒下，也就是「破壞」)

***destruction**[4] (dɪˈstrʌkʃən) *n.* 破壞 (= *ruin*)
The earthquake caused widespread *destruction*.

***detail**[3] (ˈditel , dɪˈtel) *n.* 細節
In writing an order letter, you should be careful to give every *detail* necessary for it to be filled accurately.
【記憶技巧】***de*** (entirely) + ***tail*** (cut)
(將一件事徹底分割，就是「細節」)
【比較】entail (必然伴有；需要)
retail (零售)

****detect**[2] (dɪˈtɛkt) *v.* 偵查 (= *investigate*)；偵測；查出 (= *discover*)；查明；察覺 (= *notice*)
He soon *detected* the problem.
【注意】這個字在許多字典上多作「發現」解，事實上它是 detective 的動詞，應翻成「偵查」。

***detective**[4] (dɪˈtɛktɪv) *n.* 偵探

***determination**[4] (dɪˌtɝməˈneʃən) *n.* 決心 (= *resolution*)

【典型考題】
A person of great ______ usually can achieve his goal.
A. affirmation B. determination
C. information D. imitation [B]

***determine**[3] (dɪˈtɝmɪn) *v.* 決定 (= *decide*)；決心 (= *make up one's mind*)
The judge will *determine* which side is at fault.
【片語】***be determined to V.*** (決心…)

****develop**[2] (dɪˈvɛləp) *v.* 發展 (= *grow*)；研發
His company has *developed* a new kind of battery.
【記憶技巧】***de*** (undo) + ***velop*** (wrap)
(解開束縛，才能「研發」出新東西)

【典型考題】
Modern technology has finally succeeded in ______ a bomb that destroys people but does no harm to buildings.
A. rearing B. raising
C. discovering D. developing [D]

***development**[2] (dɪˈvɛləpmənt) *n.* 發展 (= *growth*)

***device**[4] (dɪˈvaɪs) *n.* 裝置
This is an ingenious *device*.

* **devil**[3] 〔ˈdɛvḷ 〕 *n.* 魔鬼 (= *demon*)
  Many horror movies are stories about the *devil*.

* **devise**[4] 〔 dɪˈvaɪz 〕 *v.* 設計 (= *design*) ; 發明 (= *invent*)

* **devote**[4] 〔 dɪˈvot 〕 *v.* 使致力於 (= *dedicate*)
  The students are *devoted* to their studies.
  【常考片語】 ***be devoted to*** (致力於)
  【記憶技巧】 ***de*** (from) + ***vote*** (vow) (發誓要做某件事，就是「致力於」)

  dew[2] 〔 dju 〕 *n.* 露水

* **dial**[2] 〔ˈdaɪəl 〕 *v.* 撥 (號)
  The first step in making a phone call is *dialing* the number.

* **dialogue**[3] 〔ˈdaɪəˌlɔg 〕 *n.* 對話 (= *conversation*)
  The story contains an interesting *dialogue* between the main characters.
  【記憶技巧】 ***dia*** (between) + ***logue*** (speak) (兩人之間的言語，就是「對話」)

* **diamond**[2] 〔ˈdaɪəmənd 〕 *n.* 鑽石
  Diamonds are a girl's best friend.

  diaper[4] 〔ˈdaɪəpɚ 〕 *n.* 尿布 (= *nappy*)
  【衍伸詞】 ***disposable diapers*** (免洗尿布)

* **diary**[2] 〔ˈdaɪərɪ 〕 *n.* 日記 (= *journal*)
  I always write in my *diary* at night.
  【比較】 dairy 〔ˈdɛrɪ 〕 *adj.* 乳製品的

* **dictionary**[2] 〔ˈdɪkʃənˌɛrɪ 〕 *n.* 字典
  Cindy looks up every word in the *dictionary*.

【典型考題】
John is an active language learner. He always takes a ———— with him.
A. story   B. determination
C. dictionary   D. sentence   [C]

* **die**[1] 〔 daɪ 〕 *v.* 死 (= *pass away*)
  My grandmother *died* in 1998.

* **diet**[3] 〔ˈdaɪət 〕 *n.* 飲食
  He eats a well-balanced *diet*.
  【片語】 ***go on a diet*** (節食)

* **differ**[4] 〔ˈdɪfɚ 〕 *v.* 不同 (= *be dissimilar*)
  【記憶技巧】 ***dif*** (apart) + ***fer*** (carry)

* **difference**[2] 〔ˈdɪfərəns 〕 *n.* 不同 (= *dissimilarity*)
  What is the *difference* between a lemon and a lime?

【典型考題】
There is a big ———— between understanding a language and speaking it.
A. business   B. prescription
C. difference   D. dessert   [C]

* **different**[1] 〔ˈdɪfərənt 〕 *adj.* 不同的 (= *dissimilar*)

* **difficult**[1] 〔ˈdɪfəˌkʌlt 〕 *adj.* 困難的 (= *hard*)
  English is not too *difficult* to learn.

* **difficulty**[2] 〔ˈdɪfəˌkʌltɪ 〕 *n.* 困難 (= *trouble*)
  【常考】 ***have difficulty (in) + V-ing*** (很難…)

D

‡**dig**[1] 〔 dɪg 〕 *v.* 挖 (= *hollow out*)

The gardener has to *dig* a hole to plant a tree.

【典型考題】

Our dog always hides food under the ground. She ——— it out when she needs it.
A. digs   B. hands
C. knocks   D. packs   [A]

* **digest**[4] 〔 daɪˈdʒɛst 〕 *v.* 消化 (= *absorb*)
〔ˈdaɪdʒɛst 〕 *n.* 文摘；綱要

【記憶技巧】 *di* (apart) + *gest* (carry)
(吃下去的東西要分開，才能「消化」)

* **digestion**[4] 〔 daɪˈdʒɛstʃən 〕 *n.* 消化
(= *absorption*)

Too much heavy food may interfere with your *digestion*.

* **digital**[4] 〔ˈdɪdʒətl̩ 〕 *adj.* 數位的

A *digital* thermometer will give you an accurate measure of the temperature.

* **dignity**[4] 〔ˈdɪgnətɪ 〕 *n.* 尊嚴 (= *pride*)

She maintained her *dignity* throughout the trial.

【記憶技巧】 *dign* (worthy) + *ity* (n.)
(「尊嚴」是有價值的東西)

【典型考題】

A man's ——— depends not upon his wealth or rank but upon his character.
A. dignity   B. personal
C. intellect   D. eloquence   [A]

* **diligence**[4] 〔ˈdɪlədʒəns , ˈdɪlɪ- 〕
n. 勤勉 (= *industry*)；用功

* **diligent**[3] 〔ˈdɪlədʒnt , ˈdɪlɪ- 〕 *adj.*
勤勉的 (= *hard-working*)；用功的

He is *diligent* in his studies.

* **dim**[3] 〔 dɪm 〕 *adj.* 昏暗的 (= *dark*)

The light was too *dim* for the boy to read the book.

【反義詞】 bright (明亮的)

* **dime**[3] 〔 daɪm 〕 *n.* 一角硬幣

* **dine**[3] 〔 daɪn 〕 *v.* 用餐 (= *eat*)

Our group will *dine* at eight and then go to an after-dinner show.

‡**dinner**[1] 〔ˈdɪnɚ 〕 *n.* 晚餐

I would like to eat noodles for *dinner*.

* **dinosaur**[2] 〔ˈdaɪnəˌsɔr 〕 *n.* 恐龍

He is interested in *dinosaurs*.

【記憶技巧】 *dino* (terrible) + *saur* (lizard) (「恐龍」的形狀就像大型蜥蜴)

* **dip**[3] 〔 dɪp 〕 *v.* 沾；浸 (= *immerse*)

The candy maker *dipped* the strawberries in chocolate.

* **diploma**[4] 〔 dɪˈplomə 〕 *n.* 畢業證書

The principal will hand you your *diplomas* as you cross the stage.

【記憶技巧】 *di* (double) + *ploma* (folded)

【典型考題】

Most young people in Taiwan are not satisfied with a high school ——— and continue to pursue further education in college.
A. maturity   B. diploma
C. foundation   D. guarantee   [B]

‡diplomat[4] 〔ˈdɪpləˌmæt 〕 *n.* 外交官

I want to be a *diplomat* in the future.

【記憶技巧】*diploma*（畢業證書）+ *t*
（要當外交官，必須拿到「畢業證書」）

‡direct[1] 〔 dəˈrɛkt 〕 *adj.* 直接的
（= *straight* ）

He is in *direct* contact with the mayor.

【反義詞】 indirect（間接的）

┌─【典型考題】─────────
Eyes are sensitive to light. Looking at
the sun _____ could damage our
eyes.
A. hardly   B. specially
C. totally   D. directly   [D]
└──────────────────

‡direction[2] 〔 dəˈrɛkʃən 〕 *n.* 方向
（= *way* ）

【片語】*in all directions*（向四面八方）

┌─【典型考題】─────────
He has a very good sense of _____.
When he arrives in a new city, he
doesn't have to depend too much on
a map.
A. education   B. element
C. direction   D. department   [C]
└──────────────────

director[2] 〔 dəˈrɛktɚ 〕 *n.* 導演；主任

dirt[3] 〔 dɝt 〕 *n.* 污垢（= *filth* ）

‡dirty[1] 〔ˈdɝtɪ 〕 *adj.* 髒的（= *filthy* ）

disadvantage[4] 〔ˌdɪsədˈvæntɪdʒ 〕
n. 缺點（= *weakness* ）；不利的條件

Not having finished high school
turned out to be a great *disadvantage*
when he tried to find a job.

【記憶技巧】*dis* (negative) +
advantage（負面的利益，就是「不利
的條件」）

【片語】*to one's disadvantage*（對某
人不利）

disagree[2] 〔ˌdɪsəˈgri 〕 *v.* 不同意

We *disagree* on what the best place
to spend our vacation would be.

disagreement[2] 〔ˌdɪsəˈgrimənt 〕
n. 意見不合（= *argument* ）

‡disappear[2] 〔ˌdɪsəˈpɪr 〕 *v.* 消失
（= *vanish* ）

The cat *disappeared* in the dark.

【反義詞】 appear（出現）

disappoint[3] 〔ˌdɪsəˈpɔɪnt 〕 *v.* 使失望
（= *let down* ）

The children expect presents at
Christmas and we can't *disappoint*
them.

【記憶技巧】*dis* (undo) + *appoint*（沒
有達成指派的任務，就是「使失望」）

disappointment[3]
〔ˌdɪsəˈpɔɪntmənt 〕 *n.* 失望
（= *dejection* ）

disaster[4] 〔 dɪzˈæstɚ 〕 *n.* 災難
（= *catastrophe* ）

The bad harvest is a *disaster* for
this poor country.

【記憶技巧】*dis* (away) + *aster* (star)
（這個字源自占星學，當星星不在正確的
位置上時，會造成「災難」）

【衍伸詞】*natural disaster*（天災）

discipline[4] 〔ˈdɪsəplɪn 〕 *n.* 紀律
（= *control* ）；訓練（= *training* ）

His pupils showed good *discipline*.

disco[3] 〔ˈdɪsko 〕 *n.* 迪斯可舞廳
（= *discotheque* 〔ˈdɪskəˌtɛk 〕）

D

* **disconnect**[4] 〔͵dɪskə'nɛkt〕 v. 切斷
(= *shut off*)

Our cable service was *disconnected* when we did not pay the bill.

【記憶技巧】 *dis* (not) + *con* (together) + *nect* (bind)

【典型考題】

John had failed to pay his phone bill for months, so his telephone was _____ last week.
A. interviewed   B. discriminated
C. excluded   D. disconnected   [D]

* **discount**[3] 〔'dɪskaʊnt〕 n. 折扣
(= *cut price*)

To celebrate its 20th anniversary, this department store is selling everything at a *discount*.

【記憶技巧】 *dis* (away) + *count* (計算)
(要減掉計算出來的數字，就是「折扣」)

* **discourage**[4] 〔dɪs'kɝɪdʒ〕 v. 使氣餒
(= *dishearten*)

Don't let the failure *discourage* you.

【記憶技巧】 *dis* (deprive of) + *courage* (剝奪勇氣，會「使人氣餒」)

【典型考題】

John's poor math score must have _____ him a lot because he is not attending the class any more.
A. expelled   B. discouraged
C. impressed   D. finished   [B]

* **discouragement**[4] 〔dɪs'kɝɪdʒmənt〕
n. 氣餒 (= *disheartenment*)

‡ **discover**[1] 〔dɪ'skʌvɚ〕 v. 發現
(= *find out*)

In the last hundred years, we have *discovered* how to use natural gas for cooking and heating.

【記憶技巧】 *dis* (deprive of) + *cover* (遮蓋)(使失去掩蓋，也就是「發現」)

* **discovery**[3] 〔dɪ'skʌvərɪ〕 n. 發現
(= *finding*)

‡ **discuss**[2] 〔dɪ'skʌs〕 v. 討論
(= *talk about*)

Let's sit down to *discuss* this matter, OK?

【記憶技巧】 *dis* (apart) + *cuss* (beat)
(把事情攤開來說，就是「討論」)

‡ **discussion**[2] 〔dɪ'skʌʃən〕 n. 討論
(= *talk*)

* **disease**[3] 〔dɪ'ziz〕 n. 疾病 (= *illlness* = *complaint* = *disorder* = *ailment*)

The mosquito is a common carrier of *disease*.

【記憶技巧】 *dis* (apart) + *ease* (輕鬆)
(感染「疾病」，就無法輕鬆)

* **disguise**[4] 〔dɪs'gaɪz〕 v. n. 偽裝
(= *camouflage* 〔'kæmə͵flɑʒ〕)

He fled the city by *disguising* himself as a woman.

【記憶技巧】 *dis* (apart) + *guise* (appearance)(在別人面前以不同的樣子出現，就是「偽裝」)

【衍伸詞】 *a blessing in disguise* (因禍得福)

【典型考題】

The thief went into the apartment building and stole some jewelry. He then _____ himself as a security guard and walked out the front gate.
A. balanced   B. calculated
C. disguised   D. registered   [C]

*__disgust__[4] 〔 dɪsˈɡʌst 〕 v. 使厭惡
(= *sicken*)
The smell of rotten meat *disgusted* us.
【記憶技巧】 *dis* (apart) + *gust* (taste)
(讓人不想品嚐，表示「厭惡」)
【衍伸詞】 disgusting (令人噁心的)

‡‡__dish__[1] 〔 dɪʃ 〕 n. 盤子 (= *plate*)；菜餚
Used *dishes* are put in the sink.

*__dishonest__[2] 〔 dɪsˈɑnɪst 〕 adj. 不誠實的
He is a *dishonest* man.

*__disk__[3] 〔 dɪsk 〕 n. 光碟 (= *disc*)

*__dislike__[3] 〔 dɪsˈlaɪk 〕 v. 不喜歡
Nick *dislikes* vegetables but loves
junk food.
【比較】 unlike (不像)

*__dismiss__[4] 〔 dɪsˈmɪs 〕 v. 解散 (= *free*)；
下 (課)；不予考慮：解雇
The teacher *dismissed* his class
when the bell rang.
Class *dismissed*.
【記憶技巧】 *dis* (away) + *miss* (send)
(把學生送走，就是讓他們「下課」)

*__disorder__[4] 〔 dɪsˈɔrdɚ 〕 n. 混亂；疾病
After the party, the house was in
great *disorder*.
【記憶技巧】 *dis* (away) + *order* (秩序)
(沒有秩序，就是「混亂」)
【衍伸詞】 *a stomach disorder* (胃病)

*__display__[2] 〔 dɪˈsple 〕 v.n. 展示
(= *show*)
If you carry a large sum of cash,
don't *display* it openly.

【記憶技巧】 *dis* (apart) + *play* (fold)
(將重疊的東西展開來，讓別人看到，就
是「展示」)
【片語】 *on display* (展示的)

【典型考題】
At the Book Fair, exhibitors from 21
countries will _____ textbooks,
novels, and comic books.
A. predict   B. require
C. display   D. target   [C]

*__dispute__[4] 〔 dɪˈspjut 〕 v. 爭論
(= *argue about*)；否認   n. 爭論；
糾紛
Economists *disputed* whether
consumer spending was as strong as
the figure suggested.
【記憶技巧】 *dis* (apart) + *pute* (think)
(大家擁有不同的想法，就會開始「爭論」)

**__distance__[2] 〔ˈdɪstəns 〕 n. 距離
(= *space*)
When you make a long-*distance* call,
you have to dial the area code first.
【重要知識】 *at a distance* 是指「在稍遠處
的地方」，而 *in the distance* 則是指「在遠
方」。

**__distant__[2] 〔ˈdɪstənt 〕 adj. 遙遠的
(= *remote*)
The sun is *distant* from the earth.
【記憶技巧】 *di* (apart) + *st* (stand) +
ant (adj.) (分開站著，即「遙遠的」)

*__distinct__[4] 〔 dɪˈstɪŋkt 〕 adj. 獨特的；
不同的 (= *different*)
I like this brand of ice cream
because it has a very *distinct* flavor.

D

*distinguish[4] 〔 dɪ'stɪŋgwɪʃ 〕 *v.* 分辨
　(= *differentiate*); 區分; 看出
　The twins were so much alike that
　it was impossible to *distinguish*
　one from the other.
　【記憶技巧】*dis* (apart) + *tingu* (prick)
　+ *ish* (v.) (以戳穿的方式來「分辨」)
　┌─【典型考題】───────
　│ To avoid being misled by news
　│ reports, we should learn to _____
　│ between facts and opinions.
　│ A. distinguish　　B. complicate
　│ C. reinforce　　　D. speculate　　[A]
　└────────────────

*distinguished[4] 〔 dɪ'stɪŋgwɪʃt 〕
　adj. 卓越的 (= *excellent*); 傑出的;
　著名的

*distribute[4] 〔 dɪ'strɪbjut 〕 *v.* 分配
　(= *hand out*); 分發; 配送; 分佈
　We will *distribute* the new product
　to as many drugstores as possible.
　【記憶技巧】*dis* (apart) + *tribute* (give)
　　(將東西分送出去,表示「分配」)
　┌─【典型考題】───────
　│ The candidate found every way to
　│ _____ her election materials to
　│ the voters.
　│ A. operate　　　B. recognize
　│ C. distribute　　D. cultivate　　[C]
　└────────────────

*distribution[4] 〔 ,dɪstrə'bjuʃən 〕 *n.*
　分配 (= *spreading*); 分發; 配送;
　傳播

*district[4] 〔 'dɪstrɪkt 〕 *n.* 地區
　(= *area*); 行政區
　The schools in this *district* are among
　the best in the country.

*disturb[4] 〔 dɪ'stɝb 〕 *v.* 打擾
　(= *bother*)
　Sorry to *disturb* you, but I need to
　ask you an important question.
　┌─【典型考題】───────
　│ Mr. Smith won't tolerate talking
　│ during class; he says it _____ others.
　│ A. disturbs　　　B. deserves
　│ C. destroys　　　D. dismisses　　[A]
　└────────────────

*ditch[3] 〔 dɪtʃ 〕 *n.* 水溝; 壕溝
　As the tornado approached, the
　farmer threw himself into a *ditch*
　beside the road.

*dive[3] 〔 daɪv 〕 *v.* 潛水
　Our swimming teacher says that we
　will learn how to *dive* next week.

*divide[2] 〔 də'vaɪd 〕 *v.* 劃分
　(= *separate*); 分割
　Mom *divided* the pizza into four
　pieces for us to share.
　【片語】*divide…into* ~ (把…分成~)
　【記憶技巧】*di* (apart) + *vide*
　(separate) (把東西分開,就是「分割」)

*divine[4] 〔 də'vaɪn 〕 *adj.* 神聖的
　(= *sacred*)
　The spring is said to have a *divine*
　power to heal the sick.

*division[2] 〔 də'vɪʒən 〕 *n.* 劃分
　(= *separation*); 分配
　┌─【典型考題】───────
　│ Kate shared the cake with her sisters,
　│ but her _____ was not equal.
　│ A. gratitude　　　B. removal
　│ C. division　　　D. contribution　　[C]
　└────────────────

*__divorce__[4] 〔 dəˋvɔrs 〕 *n. v.* 離婚

The Petersons are said to be getting a *divorce*.

‡__dizzy__[2] 〔ˋdɪzɪ 〕 *adj.* 頭暈的

When he got up, he felt *dizzy*.

‡__do__[1] 〔 du 〕 *v.* 做

I *do* my homework every day.

*__dock__[3] 〔 dɑk 〕 *n.* 碼頭 (= *port*)

The passengers waved good-bye to the islanders as their ship moved away from the *dock*.

‡__doctor__[1] 〔ˋdɑktɚ 〕 *n.* 醫生 (= *Dr.* = *doc* = *physician*)；博士

She went to see the *doctor* at two o'clock.

‡__dodge__[3] 〔 dɑdʒ 〕 *v. n.* 躲避 (= *avoid*)

Unable to *dodge* the punch, the boxer was hit in the face.

【衍伸詞】*dodge ball* (躲避球)

‡__dog__[1] 〔 dɔg 〕 *n.* 狗

We keep two *dogs* at home.

‡__doll__[1] 〔 dɑl 〕 *n.* 洋娃娃

Most girls like to play with *dolls*.

【典型考題】

Victoria's little daughter has beautiful big eyes. Everyone says she is just like a pretty ＿＿＿＿.
A. ball   B. doll
C. pair   D. poster   [B]

‡__dollar__[1] 〔ˋdɑlɚ 〕 *n.* 元

One *dollar* is the same as 100 cents.

*__dolphin__[2] 〔ˋdɑlfɪn 〕 *n.* 海豚

*__domestic__[3] 〔 dəˋmɛstɪk 〕 *adj.* 國內的 (= *home*)；家庭的

We are going to take a *domestic* flight to Tainan.

【反義詞】 foreign (外國的)

【典型考題】

If you fly from Taipei to Tokyo, you'll be taking an international flight, rather than a ＿＿＿＿ one.
A. liberal   B. domestic
C. connected   D. universal   [B]

*__dominant__[4] 〔ˋdɑmənənt 〕 *adj.* 支配的 (= *controlling*)；佔優勢的；統治的；最有勢力的 (= *powerful*)

Our bank is the *dominant* company in the field of investment management.

【記憶技巧】*domin* (rule) + *ant* (adj.) (有統治力量的，表示「最有勢力的」)

【典型考題】

Buddhism is the ＿＿＿＿ religion in Thailand, with 90% of the total population identifying as Buddhist.
A. racial   B. competitve
C. modest   D. dominant   [D]

*__dominate__[4] 〔ˋdɑməˌnet 〕 *v.* 支配；控制 (= *control*)

A man of strong will often *dominates* others.

【典型考題】

Matt is ＿＿＿＿ by his older brother and always does what he says.
A. respected   B. dominated
C. depressed   D. approved   [B]

‡__donkey__[2] 〔ˋdɑŋkɪ 〕 *n.* 驢子 (= *ass*)

Don't be dumb like a *donkey*.

D

‡**door**[1] 〔 dɔr 〕 *n.* 門
Please lock the *door* when you come in.

***dormitory**[4,5] 〔'dɔrmə,torɪ 〕 *n.* 宿舍 (= *dorm*)
Students have a choice of living in the *dormitory* or finding an apartment off campus.
【記憶技巧】 *dormit* (sleep) + *ory* (place) (睡覺的地方，也就是「宿舍」)

***dose**[3] 〔 dos 〕 *n.* (藥的) 一劑；服用量
Don't take more than the prescribed *dose* of this medicine.

‡**dot**[2] 〔 dɑt 〕 *n.* 點
Her skirt is green with red *dots*.
【片語】 *polka dot* (衣料的) 圓點花樣

‡**double**[2] 〔'dʌbḷ 〕 *adj.* 兩倍的 *v.* 變成兩倍
His income is *double* what it was last year.
【記憶技巧】 *dou* (two) + *ble* (fold) (twofold 就是「兩倍的」)

‡**doubt**[2] 〔 daʊt 〕 *v. n.* 懷疑；不相信 (= *distrust*)
I *doubt* that he will succeed.
【注意】 字中的 b 不發音。
【常考】 *no doubt* (無疑地)

***doubtful**[3] 〔'daʊtfəl 〕 *adj.* 懷疑的；不確定的 (= *uncertain*)
【典型考題】
Because Mr. Chang has been busy these days, it's _____ that he will come to the party.
A. suspenseful　B. conceivable
C. doubtful　　D. inevitable　[C]

‡**doughnut**[2] 〔'do,nʌt 〕 *n.* 甜甜圈

***dove**[1] 〔 dʌv 〕 *n.* 鴿子 (= *pigeon*)

‡**down**[1] 〔 daʊn 〕 *adv.* 向下

***download**[4] 〔'daʊn,lod 〕 *v.* 下載
You can *download* this program from our website.
【記憶技巧】 *down* (向下) + *load* (carry)
【反義詞】 upload (上傳)

‡**downstairs**[1] 〔'daʊn'stɛrz 〕 *adv.* 到樓下
He fell *downstairs* and broke his leg.

‡**downtown**[2] 〔'daʊn'taʊn 〕 *adv.* 到市中心
We went *downtown* to buy some new clothes.

***doze**[4] 〔 doz 〕 *v.* 打瞌睡 *n.* 瞌睡
Grandmother *dozed* in her chair by the fire.
【比較】 只要記得睡著的符號是 z，就不會搞混 doze (打瞌睡) 和 dose (一劑)。

‡**dozen**[1] 〔'dʌzn̩ 〕 *n.* 一打
Karen has a *dozen* roses.
【記憶技巧】 *do* (two) + *zen* (ten)

‡**Dr.**[2] 〔'dɑktɚ 〕 *n.* 醫生；博士 (= *Doctor*)

***draft**[4] 〔 dræft 〕 *n.* 草稿 (= *outline*)；匯票；徵兵 *v.* 草擬；徵召…入伍

***drag**[2] 〔 dræg 〕 *v.* 拖 (= *pull*)
Not able to lift the suitcase, he *dragged* it down the hall.

‡**dragon**[2] 〔'drægən 〕 *n.* 龍
In fairy tales, *dragons* are dangerous animals.
【比較】 phoenix (鳳凰)

***dragonfly**[2] 〔'drægən,flaɪ 〕 *n.* 蜻蜓

*drain³〔dren〕*n.* 排水溝 (= *ditch*)
v. 排出…的水
We *drain* the swimming pool in the winter and refill it at the beginning of the summer.

‡drama²〔'drɑmə, 'dræmə〕*n.* 戲劇 (= *play*)
He wrote many great *dramas*.

*dramatic³〔drə'mætɪk〕*adj.* 戲劇性的；誇張的 (= *exaggerated*)
【衍伸詞】*dramatically* (戲劇性地；相當大地)

‡draw¹〔drɔ〕*v.* 拉 (= *pull*)；吸引 (= *attract*)；畫 (= *make a picture*)
Amy is *drawing* a tree with a pencil.
【片語】*draw one's attention to* (吸引某人注意)

‡drawer²〔drɔr〕*n.* 抽屜；製圖者
I put the book in the left-hand *drawer*.

*drawing²〔'drɔɪŋ〕*n.* 圖畫 (= *picture*)

*dread⁴〔drɛd〕*v.* 害怕 (= *fear*)
Most of us *dread* a visit to the dentist.

‡dream¹〔drim〕*n.* 夢 *v.* 做夢

‡dress²〔drɛs〕*n.* 衣服 (= *clothing*)；洋裝
Linda ironed her *dress* before wearing it.

*drift⁴〔drɪft〕*v.* 漂流 (= *float*)
The fisherman took down his sail, content to *drift* with the current.

*drill⁴〔drɪl〕*n.* 鑽孔機 (= *borer*)；練習 (= *practice*)；演習 *v.* 鑽孔

‡drink¹〔drɪŋk〕*v.* 喝；喝酒 *n.* 飲料 (= *beverage*)
I *drink* water when I am thirsty.

*drip³〔drɪp〕*v.* 滴下
Water *dripped* constantly from the faucet, so we had it replaced.

‡drive¹〔draɪv〕*v.* 開車；驅使 (=*force*)
She *drives* very cautiously.

‡driver¹〔'draɪvɚ〕*n.* 駕駛人

‡drop²〔drɑp〕*v.* 落下 (= *fall*)
n. 一滴
The book *dropped* from the desk to the floor.

*drown³〔draʊn〕*v.* 淹死；使淹死
There were only ten survivors; the rest of the ferry passengers *drowned*.

*drowsy³〔'draʊzɪ〕*adj.* 想睡的 (= *sleepy*)；使人昏昏欲睡的
The cold medicine made Edith feel *drowsy*.

*drug²〔drʌg〕*n.* 藥
Scientists are always developing new *drugs* for a variety of diseases.

drugstore²〔'drʌg,stor〕*n.* 藥房
In the U.S.A., *drugstores* often also sell cosmetics, candy, magazines, etc.

┌─【典型考題】─────────┐
She went into the _____ for some cough medicine.
A. drugstore   B. material
C. service   D. package   [A]
└──────────────────┘

‡drum²〔drʌm〕*n.* 鼓

D

****drunk**[3] 〔 drʌŋk 〕 *adj.* 喝醉的
After four glasses of wine, he was clearly *drunk*.
【衍伸詞】 *drunk driving*（酒醉駕車）

‡**dry**[1] 〔 draɪ 〕 *adj.* 乾的
When Joan arrived, her umbrella was wet but her clothes were *dry*.
【反義詞】 wet（濕的）

‡**dryer**[2] 〔 ˈdraɪɚ 〕 *n.* 烘乾機（= *drier*）
【衍伸詞】 *hair dryer*（吹風機）

‡**duck**[1] 〔 dʌk 〕 *n.* 鴨子
Alice is feeding the *ducks* in the pond.

****duckling**[1] 〔 ˈdʌklɪŋ 〕 *n.* 小鴨
【衍伸詞】 *ugly duckling*（醜小鴨）

****due**[3] 〔 dju 〕 *adj.* 到期的（= *payable*）；預定的；應得的；適當的
The gas bill is *due*, so you had better pay it right away.
【衍伸詞】 *due reward*（應得的報酬）
【片語】 *due to*（由於）

****dull**[2] 〔 dʌl 〕 *adj.* 笨的（= *stupid*）；遲鈍的（= *insensitve*）
Jake thinks he is too *dull* to succeed in math, but I think he just needs to study harder.

‡**dumb**[2] 〔 dʌm 〕 *v.* 啞的（= *mute*）；笨的（= *stupid*）
He can't answer your question because he is *dumb*.

****dump**[3] 〔 dʌmp 〕 *v.* 傾倒（= *throw away*）；拋棄（= *desert*） *n.* 垃圾場
The truck *dumped* the sand next to the building site.
【片語】 *down in the dumps*（悶悶不樂）

‡**dumpling**[2] 〔 ˈdʌmplɪŋ 〕 *n.* 水餃

****durable**[4] 〔 ˈdjurəbl̩ 〕 *adj.* 耐用的（= *tough*）；持久的
When times are good and incomes high, *durable* goods will have the greatest increase in sales.
【記憶技巧】 *dur* (last) + *able* (*adj.*)
（可以持續用下去，表示「耐用的」）

┌─【典型考題】──────────
This pot is made of strong steel and is very _____. I've used it for years.
A. scary   B. weak
C. hot   D. durable   [D]
└──────────────────────

‡‡**during**[1] 〔 ˈdjurɪŋ 〕 *prep.* 在…期間
Albert always sleeps *during* class.

****dust**[3] 〔 dʌst 〕 *n.* 灰塵 *v.* 除去…的灰塵

dusty[4] 〔 ˈdʌstɪ 〕 *adj.* 滿是灰塵的

‡**duty**[2] 〔 ˈdjutɪ 〕 *n.* 責任；關稅
The *duty* of a student is to study.
【衍伸詞】 duty-free（免稅的）

****DVD**[4] *n.* 數位影音光碟（= *digital video disk*）

****dye**[4] 〔 daɪ 〕 *v.* 染（= *color*）
n.（用於衣服、頭髮等）染劑；染料
She has *dyed* her hair brown.

****dynamic**[4] 〔 daɪˈnæmɪk 〕 *adj.* 充滿活力的（= *energetic*）；不斷變化的；動力的
We need an experienced and *dynamic* man for this job.
【記憶技巧】 *dynam* (power) + *ic* (*adj.*)

****dynasty**[4] 〔 ˈdaɪnəstɪ 〕 *n.* 朝代；王朝
Under the Ming *dynasty* China had a prosperous economy.

E e

‡**each**[1] 〔itʃ〕 *adj.* 每個
Each student in the class got a present.

***eager**[3] 〔'igɚ〕 *adj.* 渴望的
The birthday boy was so *eager* to open his present that he even forgot to say thank you.

‡**eagle**[1] 〔'igḷ〕 *n.* 老鷹

‡**ear**[1] 〔ɪr〕 *n.* 耳朵

‡**early**[1] 〔'ɝlɪ〕 *adj.* 早的   *adv.* 早

***earn**[2] 〔ɝn〕 *v.* 賺（= *be paid*）
How much do you *earn* a week?

***earnest**[4] 〔'ɝnɪst〕 *adj.* 認眞的
（= *serious*）
Most mothers are very *earnest* about their children's education.
【片語】*in earnest*（認眞地）

┌─【典型考題】────────
He made a(n) ———— attempt to lose weight.
A. arrogant   B. manual
C. earnest   D. poisonous   [C]
└──────────────────

‡**earnings**[3] 〔'ɝnɪŋz〕 *n. pl.* 收入
（= *income*）

***earphone**[4] 〔'ɪr͵fon〕 *n.* 耳機
（= *headphone*）

‡**earth**[1] 〔ɝθ〕 *n.* 地球
We live on *earth*.

***earthquake**[2] 〔'ɝθ͵kwek〕 *n.* 地震
In those island nations, *earthquakes* happen once in a while.

***ease**[1] 〔iz〕 *n.* 容易；輕鬆
v. 減輕；舒緩
He solved the math problem with *ease*.
【片語】*with ease*（輕易地）

‡**east**[1] 〔ist〕 *n.* 東方

***eastern**[2] 〔'istɚn〕 *adj.* 東方的

‡**easy**[1] 〔'izɪ〕 *adj.* 容易的

‡**eat**[1] 〔it〕 *v.* 吃

***echo**[3] 〔'ɛko〕 *n.* 回音（= *resonance*）；重複；共鳴   *v.* 發出回聲；附和
The *echo* of our shouts gradually diminished.

***economic**[4] 〔͵ikə'nɑmɪk〕 *adj.* 經濟的
（= *financial*）
An *economic* system must settle the questions of what goods shall be produced and who shall get them.

***economical**[4] 〔͵ikə'nɑmɪkḷ〕
adj. 節省的（= *inexpensive*）；節儉的（= *thrifty* = *frugal*）
Economical shoppers wait for special sales.

┌─【典型考題】────────
My sister doesn't like to waste money and is very ———— when she goes shopping.
A. financial   B. extravagant
C. economical   D. careless   [C]
└──────────────────

***economics**[4] 〔͵ikə'nɑmɪks〕 *n.* 經濟學

***economist**[4] 〔ɪ'kɑnəmɪst〕 *n.* 經濟學家

* **economy**[4] 〔 ɪˈkɑnəmɪ 〕 *n.* 經濟
（ = *financial system* ）

‡ **edge**[1] 〔 ɛdʒ 〕 *n.* 邊緣（ = *brink* ）；優勢
（ = *advantage* ）
The *edge* of the plate was broken.

* **edit**[3] 〔ˈɛdɪt 〕 *v.* 編輯
Laura *edits* English books.
【記憶技巧】 *e* (out) + *dit* (give)

* **edition**[3] 〔 ɪˈdɪʃən 〕 *n.* （發行物的）版
（ = *version* ）
【衍伸詞】 *limited edition* （限定版）

* **editor**[3] 〔ˈɛdɪtɚ 〕 *n.* 編輯（ = *compiler* ）
The *editor* made a few changes to
the reporter's story.

* **educate**[3] 〔ˈɛdʒəˌket 〕 *v.* 教育
（ = *teach* ）
Their son was *educated* in
Switzerland and only recently
returned home.
【記憶技巧】 *e* (out) + *ducate* (lead)
（引導出才能，也就是「教育」）

‡ **education**[2] 〔ˌɛdʒəˈkeʃən 〕 *n.* 教育
（ = *teaching* ）

* **educational**[3] 〔ˌɛdʒəˈkeʃənḷ 〕
adj. 教育的（ = *teaching* ）；
有教育意義的（ = *instructive* ）

* **effect**[2] 〔 ɪˈfɛkt 〕 *n.* 影響
（ = *influence* = *impact* ）
The accident had a direct *effect* on us.
【片語】 *have an effect on* （對⋯有影響）

【記憶技巧】 *ef* (out) + *fect* (make)
（產生出來的結果，表示「影響」）

* **effective**[2] 〔 ɪˈfɛktɪv 〕 *adj.* 有效的
【反義詞】 ineffective （無效的）
┌─【典型考題】────────
The teacher's way of keeping those
students quiet is really _____.
A. willing   B. affecting
C. eager   D. effective   [D]
└──────────────────

* **efficiency**[4] 〔 əˈfɪʃənsɪ 〕 *n.* 效率
The increase in the output of Factory
B is due to the *efficiency* of its
production methods.

* **efficient**[3] 〔 əˈfɪʃənt 〕 *adj.* 有效率的
【比較】 pro<u>ficient</u> （精通的）
su<u>fficient</u> （足夠的）
┌─【典型考題】────────
Cars in the future will be characterized
by their _____ use of gasoline.
A. affective   B. efficient
C. immediate   D. traditional   **[B]**
└──────────────────

‡ **effort**[2] 〔ˈɛfɚt 〕 *n.* 努力
We can do nothing without *effort*.
【記憶技巧】 *ef* (out) + *fort* (strong)
（使出力量，就是「努力」）
┌─【典型考題】────────
Actually it takes everyone's _____
to reduce noise in the neighborhood.
A. effort   B. improvement
C. information   D. connection   **[A]**
└──────────────────

‡ **egg**[1] 〔 ɛg 〕 *n.* 蛋

‡ **either**[1] 〔ˈiðɚ 〕 *adv.* ⋯或～；也（不）
I don't have *either* a cat or a dog.
If you do not go, I shall not, *either*.
【片語】 *either* A *or* B （A或B）

E

* **elastic**[4] 〔 ɪˈlæstɪk 〕 *adj.* 有彈性的
（ = *flexible* ）；可變通的
Victor was prepared because he wore pants with an *elastic* waist to the all-you-can-eat buffet.

* **elbow**[3] 〔ˈɛlˌbo 〕 *n.* 手肘
【記憶技巧】 *el* (forearm) + *bow* (弓)
（ 前臂可以弓起來的部分，就是「手肘」）

‡ **elder**[2] 〔ˈɛldɚ 〕 *adj.* 年長的　　*n.* 年長者
She is my *elder* sister.
【衍伸詞】 *one's elders* (長輩)

* **elderly**[3] 〔ˈɛldɚlɪ 〕 *adj.* 年老的
【衍伸詞】 *the elderly* (老人)

‡ **elect**[2] 〔 ɪˈlɛkt 〕 *v.* 選舉
We *elected* him as our mayor.
【記憶技巧】 *e* (out) + *lect* (choose)
（ 選出想要的，就是「選舉」）

* **election**[3] 〔 ɪˈlɛkʃən 〕 *n.* 選舉

‡ **electric**[3] 〔 ɪˈlɛktrɪk 〕 *adj.* 電的
The *electric* light went out.

* **electrical**[3] 〔 ɪˈlɛktrɪkl̩ 〕 *adj.* 與電有關的

* **electrician**[4] 〔 ɪˌlɛkˈtrɪʃən 〕 *n.* 電工

* **electricity**[3] 〔 ɪˌlɛkˈtrɪsətɪ 〕 *n.* 電
（ = *power* ）
The air-conditioner is run by *electricity*.

* **electronic**[3] 〔 ɪˌlɛkˈtranɪk 〕 *adj.* 電子的

* **electronics**[4] 〔 ɪˌlɛkˈtranɪks 〕
n. 電子學
The silicon chip has revolutionized *electronics*.

* **elegant**[4] 〔ˈɛləgənt 〕 *adj.* 優雅的
（ = *graceful* ）
Her *elegant* manners impressed everyone at the party.

* **element**[2] 〔ˈɛləmənt 〕 *n.* 要素
（ = *factor* ）
Constant practice is an important *element* of developing good speaking skills.

* **elementary**[4] 〔ˌɛləˈmɛntərɪ 〕 *adj.*
基本的 (= *basic*)
【衍伸詞】 *elementary school* (小學)

‡ **elephant**[1] 〔ˈɛləfənt 〕 *n.* 大象
Elephants are found in Asia and Africa.

* **elevator**[2] 〔ˈɛləˌvetɚ 〕 *n.* 電梯
（ = *lift* ）；升降機
【比較】 escalator (電扶梯)

‡ **eleven**[1] 〔 ɪˈlɛvən 〕 *n.* 十一

* **eliminate**[4] 〔 ɪˈlɪməˌnet 〕 *v.* 除去
（ = *remove* ）；淘汰；排除
In order to lose weight, Ricky decided to *eliminate* all sweets from his diet.
【記憶技巧】 *e* (out) + *limin* (門檻) + *ate* (*v.*) (排除在門檻以外，表示「除去」)

┌─【典型考題】──────
I tried out for the school play but I was ＿＿ in the second round of auditions.
A. chosen　　　B. eliminated
C. improved　　D. involved　　[**B**]

‡ **else**[1] 〔 ɛls 〕 *adj.* 其他的　　*adv.* 其他

* **elsewhere** [4] (ˈɛlsˌhwɛr) *adv.* 在別處
  I'm afraid we don't have that book in stock; you'll have to look *elsewhere*.

‡ **e-mail** [4] (ˈiˌmel) *n.* 電子郵件
  (= *electronic mail*)

‡ **embarrass** [4] (ɪmˈbærəs) *v.* 使尷尬
  (= *abash*)
  Your question did *embarrass* me.
  I don't want to answer it.
  【記憶技巧】這個字很容易拼錯，最好分段背：emb-arr-ass。

* **embarrassment** [4] (ɪmˈbærəsmənt)
  n. 尷尬 (= *shame*)

* **embassy** [4] (ˈɛmbəsɪ) *n.* 大使館
  There is tight security at most foreign *embassies*.
  【衍伸詞】ambassador (大使)

* **emerge** [4] (ɪˈmɝdʒ) *v.* 出現 (= *appear*)
  The chicks *emerged* slowly from the eggs.
  【記憶技巧】e (out of) + *merge* (sink)
  (從沉沒狀態跑出來，表示「出現」)
  【比較】im**merge** (使沉浸)
  　　　　sub**merge** (沉入水中)

* **emergency** [3] (ɪˈmɝdʒənsɪ) *n.* 緊急情況 (= *crisis*)
  It is important to remain calm in an *emergency*.

‡ **emotion** [2] (ɪˈmoʃən) *n.* 情緒
  (= *feeling*)；感情
  Love, joy, and hate are all *emotions*.
  【記憶技巧】e (out) + *mot* (move) + *ion* (n.) (內心釋放出的感覺就是「情緒」)

【典型考題】
He has never learned to control his ————. He tends to lose his temper whenever his teammates disagree with him.
A. bundle　　　　B. environment
C. emotions　　　D. damage　　[C]

* **emotional** [4] (ɪˈmoʃənḷ) *adj.* 感情的；感動人的；激動的

* **emperor** [3] (ˈɛmpərɚ) *n.* 皇帝

* **emphasis** [4] (ˈɛmfəsɪs) *n.* 強調
  (= *stress*)
  【片語】*put emphasis on* (強調)

‡ **emphasize** [3] (ˈɛmfəˌsaɪz) *v.* 強調
  (= *stress*)
  Which word should I *emphasize*?

* **empire** [4] (ˈɛmpaɪr) *n.* 帝國
  (= *kingdom*)
  【記憶技巧】*em* (in) + *pire* (order)

‡ **employ** [3] (ɪmˈplɔɪ) *v.* 雇用 (= *hire*)
  The company *employs* 500 workers.

* **employee** [3] (ˌɛmplɔɪˈi) *n.* 員工
  (= *worker*)

* **employer** [3] (ɪmˈplɔɪɚ) *n.* 雇主
  (= *boss*)
  【注意】字尾 ee 表「被動」；er 表「主動」。

* **employment** [3] (ɪmˈplɔɪmənt)
  n. 雇用；工作 (= *work*)

‡ **empty** [3] (ˈɛmptɪ) *adj.* 空的
  The box was *empty*.
  【反義詞】full (滿的)

* **enable** [3] (ɪnˈebḷ) *v.* 使能夠 (= *allow*)
  Cell phones *enable* us to stay in touch with others easily.

* **enclose**[4]〔ɪnˋkloz〕v.（隨函）附寄
（= *send with*）
We *enclosed* some recent photos of
the baby in the letter.
【記憶技巧】*en* (in) + *close*（在把信封黏
起來之前，將東西放進去，就是「附寄」）

* **encounter**[4]〔ɪnˋkaʊntɚ〕v. 遭遇
（= *come across*）
The travelers *encountered* many tough
problems but finally solved them.
【記憶技巧】*en* (in) + *counter* (against)
（進入衝突狀態，表示「遭遇」）

* **encourage**[2]〔ɪnˋkɝɪdʒ〕v. 鼓勵
（= *inspire*）
Many people worry that the
computerized Taiwan Lottery will
encourage gambling.

* **encouragement**[2]〔ɪnˋkɝɪdʒmənt〕
n. 鼓勵（= *inspiration*）

‡ **end**[1]〔ɛnd〕n. v. 結束

* **endanger**[4]〔ɪnˋdendʒɚ〕v. 危害
（= *put in danger*）
Don't *endanger* others by driving
drunk.

* **ending**[2]〔ˋɛndɪŋ〕n. 結局

* **endure**[4]〔ɪnˋdjʊr〕v. 忍受（= *bear*）
I have *endured* your unfair treatment
for too long. I want out.
【記憶技巧】*en* (in) + *dure* (last)
（處於持續狀態，表示「忍受」）

‡ **enemy**[2]〔ˋɛnəmɪ〕n. 敵人
He has many *enemies* in the
political world.
【記憶技巧】*en* (not) + *emy* (friend)
（不是朋友，也就是「敵人」）

* **energetic**[3]〔͵ɛnɚˋdʒɛtɪk〕adj. 充滿活
力的（= *active*）
He is young and *energetic*.

* **energy**[2]〔ˋɛnɚdʒɪ〕n. 活力（= *power*）
【記憶技巧】*en* (at) + *erg* (work) +
y (n.)（工作時，最需要的就是「活力」）

【典型考題】
Let's have some ice cream, so we may
have more ＿＿＿ to do the shopping.
A. cookies B. money
C. energy D. time [C]

* **enforce**[4]〔ɪnˋfors〕v. 實施；執行
There is a traffic officer stationed at
the intersection to *enforce* the rule
against jaywalking.
【記憶技巧】*en* (in) + *force* (strong)
（用力做事，就是「執行」）

* **enforcement**[4]〔ɪnˋforsmənt〕n. 實施
（= *implementation*）；執行

* **engage**[3]〔ɪnˋgedʒ〕v. 從事；訂婚
They *engaged* in a long discussion.
【片語】*engage in*（從事；參與）

* **engagement**[3]〔ɪnˋgedʒmənt〕
n. 訂婚

‡ **engine**[3]〔ˋɛndʒən〕n. 引擎（= *motor*）
This car has a new *engine*.

‡ **engineer**[3]〔͵ɛndʒəˋnɪr〕n. 工程師
The car was designed by *engineers*.

* **engineering**[4]〔͵ɛndʒəˋnɪrɪŋ〕n.
工程學

‡ **English**[1]〔ˋɪŋglɪʃ〕n. 英語
Ellen studies *English* every Sunday.

E

E

‡**enjoy**[2] 〔 ɪn'dʒɔɪ 〕 *v.* 享受；喜歡
(= *take pleasure in*)
How did you *enjoy* your trip?

* **enjoyable**[3] 〔 ɪn'dʒɔɪəbḷ 〕 *adj.* 令人
愉快的 (= *pleasant*)

* **enjoyment**[2] 〔 ɪn'dʒɔɪmənt 〕 *n.*
樂趣

* **enlarge**[4] 〔 ɪn'lɑrdʒ 〕 *v.* 擴大；放大
She *enlarged* her restaurant.

┌─【典型考題】────────────┐
These two photographs are too small.
Let's have them _____.
A. increased　　B. formalized
C. enlarged　　 D. enclosed　　[C]
└─────────────────────┘

* **enlargement**[4] 〔 ɪn'lɑrdʒmənt 〕
n. 擴大 (= *expansion*)；放大

* **enormous**[4] 〔 ɪ'nɔrməs 〕 *adj.* 巨大的
(= *huge*)
The construction was estimated to
cost an *enormous* amount of
money.
【記憶技巧】*e* (out of) + *norm* (標準)
+ *ous* (*adj.*) (超出標準，即「巨大的」)

‡**enough**[1] 〔 ɪ'nʌf , ə'nʌf 〕 *adj.* 足夠的
adv. 足夠地
Have you got *enough* money to pay
for this meal?

‡**enter**[1] 〔 'ɛntɚ 〕 *v.* 進入 (= *go into*)

* **entertain**[4] 〔 ,ɛntɚ'ten 〕 *v.* 娛樂
(= *amuse*)
The host *entertained* all the guests
with his funny tricks.

┌─【典型考題】────────────┐
The book is not only informative but
also _____, making me laugh and
feel relaxed while reading it.
A. understanding　B. infecting
C. entertaining　　D. annoying　　[C]
└─────────────────────┘

* **entertainment**[4] 〔 ,ɛntɚ'tenmənt 〕
n. 娛樂 (= *amusement*)

┌─【典型考題】────────────┐
Movies, sports, and reading are forms
of _____.　They help us relax.
A. tournament　　B. entertainment
C. asset　　　　　D. contest　　[B]
└─────────────────────┘

* **enthusiasm**[4] 〔 ɪn'θjuzɪ,æzəm 〕
n. 熱忱
John loves to study, and he does all
his schoolwork with *enthusiasm*.
【記憶技巧】這個字要分音節背 en-thu-
si-asm，才不會拼錯。
【衍伸詞】enthusiastic (熱心的)

* **entire**[2] 〔 ɪn'taɪr 〕 *adj.* 整個的 (= *whole*)

┌─【典型考題】────────────┐
She spent the _____ day shopping
with her friends.
A. entire　　　　　B. classic
C. central　　　　 D. broad　　[A]
└─────────────────────┘

‡**entrance**[2] 〔 'ɛntrəns 〕 *n.* 入口
(= *way in*)；入學資格 (= *admission*)
We used the back *entrance* to the
building.
【反義詞】exit (出口)

* **entry**[3] 〔 'ɛntrɪ 〕 *n.* 進入 (= *entering*)

‡**envelope**[2] 〔 'ɛnvə,lop 〕 *n.* 信封
Nancy forgot to write the address on
the *envelope*.
【記憶技巧】「信封」是把信件從頭到尾包
起來，所以是 e 開頭 e 結尾。

* **envious**[4] 〔'ɛnvɪəs 〕 *adj.* 羨慕的；嫉妒的

Marla is *envious* of her sister's accomplishments.

【片語】 *be envious of*（羨慕；嫉妒）

* **environment**[2] 〔 ɪn'vaɪrənmənt 〕 *n.* 環境（= *surroundings*）

The *environment* here is good.

【記憶技巧】 *en* (in) + *viron* (circuit) + *ment* (n.)（環繞在周圍，也就是「環境」）

* **environmental**[3] 〔 ɪn͵vaɪrən'mɛntḷ 〕 *adj.* 環境的

【衍伸詞】 *environmental protection*（環保）

* **envy**[3] 〔'ɛnvɪ 〕 *n.* 羨慕；嫉妒（= *jealousy*）

* **equal**[1] 〔'ikwəl 〕 *adj.* 平等的（= *fair*）；相等的（= *the same*） *v.* 等於

Men and women have *equal* rights.

【片語】 *be equal to*（和～相等）

* **equality**[4] 〔 ɪ'kwɑlətɪ 〕 *n.* 相等（= *sameness*）；平等（= *fairness*）

* **equip**[4] 〔 ɪ'kwɪp 〕 *v.* 裝備；使配備（= *supply*）

A vehicle *equipped* for transporting sick or injured people is an ambulance.

* **equipment**[4] 〔 ɪ'kwɪpmənt 〕 *n.* 設備（= *supplies*）

* **era**[4] 〔'ɪrə，'irə 〕 *n.* 時代（= *age*）

【注意發音】

Britain was a great power during the Colonial *era*.

* **erase**[3] 〔 ɪ'res 〕 *v.* 擦掉

The teacher *erased* the old example from the board and wrote a new one.

【記憶技巧】 *e* (out of) + *rase* (scrape 擦去)

* **eraser**[2] 〔 ɪ'resɚ 〕 *n.* 橡皮擦

* **errand**[4] 〔'ɛrənd 〕 *n.* 差事（= *task*）

I have several *errands* to do today, which include mailing this package.

* **error**[2] 〔'ɛrɚ 〕 *n.* 錯誤（= *mistake*）

There are too many *errors* in his report.

【衍伸詞】 *err* 〔 ɝ 〕 *v.* 犯錯

【典型考題】

Be careful. One _____ in the data you record will destroy all our efforts.
A. corner   B. error
C. clown   D. display   **[B]**

* **escalator**[4] 〔'ɛskə͵letɚ 〕 *n.* 電扶梯

It's not a good idea to take your baby's stroller on the *escalator*. Why not use the elevator instead?

* **escape**[3] 〔 ə'skep 〕 *v.* 逃走（= *get away*） *n.* 逃脫

He *escaped* from jail by climbing over a wall.

【記憶技巧】 *es* (out of) + *cape*（無袖的短外套）（迅速脫掉外套，表示「逃走」）

* **especially**[2] 〔 ə'spɛʃəlɪ 〕 *adv.* 特別地

It's *especially* cold today.

【典型考題】

The teacher loved to teach young students, _____ those who were smart.
A. officially   B. especially
C. popularly   D. similarly   **[B]**

E

* **essay**[4] 〔ˈɛse 〕 *n.* 論說文；文章
(= *composition*)

Our teacher asked us to write an *essay* on an important invention of the twentieth century.

essential[4] 〔 əˈsɛnʃəl 〕 *adj.* 必要的
(= *necessary*)；非常重要的
(= *vital*)

Food and water are *essential* to life.

┌─【典型考題】─────
│ Water is ＿＿＿＿ to every living thing.
│ A. cautious　　　 B. miraculous
│ C. observant　　　 D. essential　　　 [D]
└────────────────

* **establish**[4] 〔 əˈstæblɪʃ 〕 *v.* 建立
(= *found*)

This company was *established* in 1974.

【記憶技巧】 *e* + *stabli* (stable) + *sh*
(*v.*) (使穩固，就是「建立」)

* **establishment**[4] 〔 əˈstæblɪʃmənt 〕
n. 建立 (= *founding*)；機構
(= *organization*)

* **estimate**[4] 〔ˈɛstəˌmet 〕 *v.* 估計；估算
(= *calculate*)　〔ˈɛstəmɪt 〕 *n.* 估計

I asked the repairman to *estimate* how long it would take him to finish the job.

* **evaluate**[4] 〔 ɪˈvæljuˌet 〕 *v.* 評估
(= *assess*)

Speech contestants will be *evaluated* on the basis of fluency and speech content.

【記憶技巧】 *e* (out) + *valu*(*e*) (價值)
+ *ate* (*v.*) (算出價值，即「評估」)

* **evaluation**[4] 〔 ɪˌvæljuˈeʃən 〕
n. 評價；評估 (= *assessment*)

‡ **eve**[4] 〔 iv 〕 *n.* (節日的) 前夕

Christmas *Eve* is a happy time for children.

‡ **even**[1] 〔ˈivən 〕 *adv.* 甚至
adj. 平坦的；偶數的
【相反詞】 odd (奇數的)

‡ **evening**[1] 〔ˈivnɪŋ 〕 *n.* 傍晚

‡ **event**[2] 〔 ɪˈvɛnt 〕 *n.* 事件
(= *occurrence*)；大型活動

His visit was quite an *event*.

* **eventual**[4] 〔 ɪˈvɛntʃuəl 〕 *adj.* 最後的
(= *final*)

Although Mr. Adams is only fifty-five now, we should be prepared for his *eventual* retirement.

【衍伸詞】 eventually (最後；終於)

‡ **ever**[1] 〔ˈɛvɚ 〕 *adv.* 曾經

Have you *ever* seen a lion?

‡ **every**[1] 〔ˈɛvrɪ,ˈɛvərɪ 〕 *adj.* 每一個

* **evidence**[4] 〔ˈɛvədəns 〕 *n.* 證據
(= *proof*)

The judge said that there was not enough *evidence* to prove that the man was guilty.

┌─【典型考題】─────
│ There isn't enough ＿＿＿＿ to prove
│ that the woman stole the vase.
│ A. evidence　　　 B. convenience
│ C. influence　　　 D. obedience　　 [A]
└────────────────

* **evident**[4] 〔ˈɛvədənt 〕 *adj.* 明顯的
(= *obvious*)

【記憶技巧】 *e* (out) + *vid* (see) + *ent*
(*adj.*) (可以看到外面的，表示「明顯的」)

E

‡ **evil**[3] 〔'ivḷ〕 *adj.* 邪惡的 (= *wicked*)

The old witch was *evil*.

* **exact**[2] 〔ɪg'zækt〕 *adj.* 精確的
(= *accurate*)

Your description is not very *exact*.

【典型考題】
Can you tell me the ＿＿＿ number of the people who will attend the meeting?
A. dull　　　　B. exact
C. dizzy　　　 D. cruel　　　[B]

* **exaggerate**[4] 〔ɪg'zædʒə͵ret〕 *v.* 誇大
(= *overstate*)

Charles *exaggerated* his role in the game so much that you would think he won it single-handedly.

【記憶技巧】 *ex* (out) + *ag* (to) + *gerate* (carry) (向外擴張，也就是「誇大」)

【典型考題】
Don't take what he says too seriously; he is always ＿＿＿.
A. exaggerating　B. recommending
C. diminishing　 D. associating　[A]

‡ **exam**[1] 〔ɪg'zæm〕 *n.* 考試
(= *examination*)

Students have to take a lot of *exams*.

【片語】 *take an exam* (參加考試)

【典型考題】
Sally worries that she can't pass the final ＿＿＿.
A. exam　　　　B. color
C. dessert　　　D. housework　[A]

* **examination**[1] 〔ɪg͵zæmə'neʃən〕 *n.*
考試 (= *exam*)；檢查
(= *inspection*)

* **examine**[1] 〔ɪg'zæmɪn〕 *v.* 檢查
(= *inspect*)；仔細研究；測驗
(= *test*)

He *examined* the room.

【典型考題】
Jason's car broke down twice yesterday. I think he had better have it ＿＿＿.
A. examined　　B. expressed
C. accepted　　 D. emptied　　[A]

* **examinee**[4] 〔ɪg͵zæmə'ni〕 *n.* 應試者
【記憶技巧】 *ee* 表「被~的人」。

* **examiner**[4] 〔ɪg'zæmɪnɚ〕 *n.* 主考官
(= *tester*)

‡ **example**[1] 〔ɪg'zæmpḷ〕 *n.* 例子
Here is another *example*.
【片語】 *for example* (例如)

* **excellence**[3] 〔'ɛksḷəns〕 *n.* 優秀
(= *superiority*)

【典型考題】
Many people strive all their lives for ＿＿＿ in whatever they do.
A. excellence　　B. keyboard
C. collection　　 D. suffering　　[A]

‡ **excellent**[2] 〔'ɛksḷənt〕 *adj.* 優秀的
(= *outstanding*)

‡ **except**[1] 〔ɪk'sɛpt〕 *prep.* 除了
(= *other than*)

I like all animals *except* snakes.

【記憶技巧】 *ex* (out) + *cept* (take)
(把東西拿掉，即「除了」)

【比較】 besides *prep.* 除了…之外 (還有)

E

* **exception**⁴ 〔 ɪkˈsɛpʃən 〕 *n.* 例外
  (= *exclusion*)

  It is regrettable that there can be no *exception* to this rule.

  【典型考題】
  Everyone in the office must attend the meeting tomorrow. There are no _____ allowed.
  A. exceptions　　B. additions
  C. divisions　　　D. measures　[**A**]

* **exchange**³ 〔 ɪksˈtʃendʒ 〕 *v.* 交換

  Can we *exchange* seats?

  【記憶技巧】 *ex* (fully) + *change*
  (完全變換，就是「交換」)

‡ **excite**² 〔 ɪkˈsaɪt 〕 *v.* 使興奮 (= *thrill*)

  【衍伸詞】 excited (興奮的)
  　　　　　 exciting (令人興奮的；刺激的)

* **excitement**² 〔 ɪkˈsaɪtmənt 〕 *n.* 興奮
  (= *thrill*)

‡ **excuse**² 〔 ɪkˈskjuz 〕 *v.* 原諒
  〔 ɪkˈskjus 〕 *n.* 藉口

  Excuse me for what I said to you yesterday.

‡ **exercise**² 〔ˈɛksɚˌsaɪz 〕 *v.* 運動
  (= *work out*) 　*n.* 運動；練習

  They *exercise* every day so they are healthy.

* **exhaust**⁴ 〔 ɪgˈzɔst 〕 *v.* 使筋疲力盡
  (= *tire out*)；用光 (= *use up*)
  n. 廢氣

  The *exhaust* from various vehicles pollutes the air.

  【記憶技巧】 *ex* (off) + *haust* (draw)
  (從排氣管抽出來的東西，就是「廢氣」)

* **exhibit**⁴ 〔 ɪgˈzɪbɪt 〕 *v.* 展示；展現
  (= *display*)

  They *exhibited* great power of endurance during the climb.

  【記憶技巧】 *ex* (out) + *hibit* (hold)
  (把東西拿出來，就是「展示」)

* **exhibition**³ 〔ˌɛksəˈbɪʃən 〕 *n.* 展覽會
  (= *display*)

‡ **exist**² 〔 ɪgˈzɪst 〕 *v.* 存在 (= *be*)

  The city library has *existed* since 1947.

  【記憶技巧】 *ex* (forth) + *ist* (stand)
  (繼續站在世界上，表示「存在」)

* **existence**³ 〔 ɪgˈzɪstəns 〕 *n.* 存在
  (= *being*)

  【片語】 *come into existence* (產生)

‡ **exit**³ 〔ˈɛgzɪt, ˈɛksɪt 〕 *n.* 出口
  (= *way out*)

  When there is a fire, you can run out through the emergency *exit*.

  【典型考題】
  When you stay at a hotel, to be on the safe side, you must look for its _____ first.
  A. exits　　　　B. restrooms
  C. bathrooms　　D. entries　[**A**]

* **expand**⁴ 〔 ɪkˈspænd 〕 *v.* 擴大
  (= *increase*)

  He is trying to *expand* his business.

  【記憶技巧】 *ex* (out) + *pand* (spread)
  (向外擴展，也就是「擴大」)

  【典型考題】
  We are trying to _____ our market by appealing to teenagers.
  A. please　　　B. expand
  C. trade　　　　D. inflate　[**B**]

* **expansion**[4] 〔 ɪk'spænʃən 〕 n. 擴大
（ = *increase* ）

【典型考題】

The _____ of this empire led to many wars with its neighboring countries.
A. expansion   B. exception
C. experience   D. explanation   [A]

‡ **expect**[2] 〔 ɪk'spɛkt 〕 v. 期待
（ = *anticipate* ）

We did not *expect* the performance to be as excellent as it was.

【記憶技巧】 *ex* (out) + *pect* (look)
（因為「期待」，就會不停向外張望）

【比較】inspect（檢查）
         respect（尊敬）

【典型考題】

I'd rather not go out because I'm _____ my sister to stop by.
A. assuming   B. expecting
C. hesitating   D. arriving   [B]

* **expectation**[3] 〔ˌɛkspɛk'teʃən 〕
n. 期望；期待（ = *anticipation* ）

【片語】 *live up to one's expectations*
（不辜負某人的期望）

【典型考題】

We are positive that his son must have lived up to his _____.
A. examinations   B. examples
C. expressions   D. expectations   [D]

* **expense**[3] 〔 ɪk'spɛns 〕 n. 費用
（ = *cost* ）

‡ **expensive**[2] 〔 ɪk'spɛnsɪv 〕 adj. 昂貴的
（ = *costly* ）

‡ **experience**[2] 〔 ɪk'spɪrɪəns 〕 n. 經驗

* **experiment**[3] 〔 ɪk'spɛrəmənt 〕
n. 實驗（ = *test* ）

We usually perform chemistry *experiments* in the science lab.

* **experimental**[4] 〔 ɪkˌspɛrə'mɛntl̩ 〕
adj. 實驗的

* **expert**[2] 〔'ɛkspɝt 〕 n. 專家

Mechanical engineers are *experts* in machinery.

* **explain**[2] 〔 ɪk'splen 〕 v. 解釋
（ = *make clear* ）

I don't understand what you're talking about. Would you *explain* yourself a little?

【記憶技巧】 *ex* (fully) + *plain* (flatten)
（使所有人的想法一樣平整，就要「解釋」）

* **explanation**[4] 〔ˌɛksplə'neʃən 〕 n.
解釋

* **explode**[3] 〔 ɪk'splod 〕 v. 爆炸
（ = *blow up* ）

Police were able to defuse the bomb before it *exploded*.

* **explore**[4] 〔 ɪk'splor 〕 v. 在…探險；
探測；探討；研究（ = *research* ）

* **explosion**[4] 〔 ɪk'sploʒən 〕 n. 爆炸
（ = *blowup* ）

【典型考題】

The fire in the fireworks factory in Changhua set off a series of powerful _____ and killed four people.
A. explosions   B. extensions
C. inspections   D. impressions   [A]

E

* **explosive**[4] 〔 ɪk'splosɪv 〕 adj. 爆炸性的　n. 炸藥

【典型考題】
To prevent terrorist attacks, the security guards at the airport check all luggage carefully to see if there are any ＿＿＿＿ items or other dangerous objects.
A. dynamic　　　B. identical
C. permanent　　D. explosive　　[D]

* **export**[3] 〔 ɪks'port, ɛks'port 〕 v. 出口
We now *export* all kinds of industrial products.
【反義詞】 import (進口)

* **expose**[4] 〔 ɪk'spoz 〕 v. 暴露
(= *uncover*)；使接觸
(= *lay open to*)
Don't *expose* yourself to the sun too long. It may do harm to your skin.
【記憶技巧】 *ex* (out) + *pose* (put)
(放在外面，就是「暴露」)

【典型考題】
This plant does well in the shade so don't ＿＿＿＿ it to too much sun.
A. expose　　　B. reveal
C. show　　　　D. place　　　[A]

* **exposure**[4] 〔 ɪk'spoʒɚ 〕 n. 暴露；接觸
(= *contact*)

* **express**[2] 〔 ɪk'sprɛs 〕 v. 表達
(= *communicate*)　adj. 快遞的；快速的 (= *speedy*)
I'd like to *express* my deepest gratitude to you.
【記憶技巧】 *ex* (out) + *press* (壓)
(將想法從腦子裡壓出去，即「表達」)
【衍伸詞】 *an express train* (快車)

【典型考題】
In a democratic country, people can ＿＿＿＿ their opinions freely.
A. express　　　B. prefer
C. insist　　　　D. recover　　[A]

* **expression**[3] 〔 ɪk'sprɛʃən 〕 n. 說法；表達 (= *explanation*)；表情 (= *face*)

expressive[3] 〔 ɪk'sprɛsɪv 〕 adj. 表達的 (= *telling*)；富於表情的 (= *vivid*)

* **extend**[4] 〔 ɪk'stɛnd 〕 v. 延伸 (= *make broader*)；延長 (= *make longer*)
They *extended* their visit by another day.
【記憶技巧】 *ex* (out) + *tend* (stretch)

* **extent**[4] 〔 ɪk'stɛnt 〕 n. 程度 (= *degree*)
We have to find out the *extent* of the problem before we can discuss how to solve it.

* **extra**[2] 〔 'ɛkstrə 〕 adj. 額外的
I don't need any *extra* help.

【典型考題】
They were behind schedule and had to apply for ＿＿＿＿ manpower to complete their project in time.
A. basic　　　　B. extra
C. introductory　D. profound　[B]

* **extraordinary**[4] 〔 ɪk'strɔrdn̩ˌɛrɪ 〕 adj. 不尋常的 (= *unusual*)；非常奇怪的；特別的
The job in Japan was an *extraordinary* opportunity for a recent graduate.
【記憶技巧】 *extra* + *ordinary* (普通的)
(超出普通的範圍，即「特別的」)

F f

*__extreme__[3] 〔 ɪkˋstrim 〕 *adj.* 極端的；
偏激的；罕見的　*n.* 極端
Alan was in such *extreme* despair
when his girlfriend left him.

【衍伸詞】 extremely（極度地；非常地）

‡__eye__[1] 〔 aɪ 〕 *n.* 眼睛

*__eyebrows__[2] 〔ˋaɪˏbraʊz 〕 *n. pl.* 眉毛

*__fable__[3] 〔ˋfeb!〕 *n.* 寓言；故事
(= *story*)
【衍伸詞】 *Aesop's Fables*（伊索寓言）

‡__face__[1] 〔 fes 〕 *n.* 臉　*v.* 面對；使面對
【片語】 *be faced with*（面對）

__facial__[4] 〔ˋfeʃəl 〕 *adj.* 臉部的
The judge's *facial* expression didn't
change at all.

*__facility__[4] 〔 fəˋsɪlətɪ 〕 *n.* 設備；設施
(= *equipment*)；廁所【常用複數】
At most schools, *facilities* for
learning and recreation are available
to students.
【重要知識】如果跟外國人說：I need to use
the *facilities*. 他會認為你英文很好。這裡的
facilities 是指「衛生設備」，也就是「廁所」。

‡__fact__[1] 〔 fækt 〕 *n.* 事實 (= *truth*)
A *fact* is something that is true.

*__factor__[3] 〔ˋfæktɚ 〕 *n.* 因素
(= *determinant* = *element*)
Diligence and perseverance were
important *factors* in his success.
【記憶技巧】 *fact* (make) + *or* (*n.*)
（造成的原因，也就是「因素」）

‡__factory__[1] 〔ˋfæktrɪ 〕 *n.* 工廠
(= *workshop*)

The children are going to visit a car
factory.

*__fade__[3] 〔 fed 〕 *v.* 褪色 (= *lose color*)；
逐漸消失
My orange T-shirt *faded* when I
washed it.

【典型考題】
His dark brown jacket had holes in the
elbows, and had ＿＿＿＿ to light
brown, but he continued to wear it.
A. cycled   B. faded
C. loosened   D. divivded   **[B]**

‡__fail__[2] 〔 fel 〕 *v.* 失敗
(= *be unsuccessful*)
Our plan has *failed*.

*__failure__[2] 〔ˋfeljɚ 〕 *n.* 失敗

*__faint__[3] 〔 fent 〕 *v.* 昏倒
The gym was so hot that several
of the students *fainted* during the
assembly.

‡__fair__[2] 〔 fɛr 〕 *adj.* 公平的 (= *impartial*)
The judge made a *fair* decision.
【反義詞】 unfair（不公平的）

*__fairly__[3] 〔ˋfɛrlɪ 〕 *adv.* 公平地
(= *justly*)；相當地 (= *quite*)

F

*fairy[3] 〔'fɛrɪ〕 *n.* 仙女（= *genie*）
An old story says that *fairies* live
in the forest.
【片語】*fairy tale*（童話故事）

*faith[3] 〔feθ〕 *n.* 信念（= *belief*）；
信任（= *trust*）
I have no *faith* in Lisa's ability to
do the job.

*faithful[4] 〔'feθfəl〕 *adj.* 忠實的
（= *loyal*）
【典型考題】
John's vision was direct, concrete, and
simple, and he recorded ＿＿＿ the
incidents of everyday life.
A. universally　　B. scarcity
C. passively　　　D. faithfully　　[D]

*fake[3] 〔fek〕 *adj.* 假的；仿冒的
（= *false*）
Donna paid a lot of money for a
famous painting but it turned out
to be *fake*.

‡fall[1] 〔fɔl〕 *v.* 落下（= *drop down*）
n. 秋天（= *autumn*）
The rain is *falling* from the sky.
I got married in the *fall* of 2007.
【重要知識】秋天落葉，所以有「落下」和「秋天」
兩個意思，也象徵著一年的結束。注意美國人的
季節序是「冬春夏秋」，因為1月份新年是冬天。

‡false[1] 〔fɔls〕 *adj.* 錯誤的（= *wrong*）；
偽造的；假的
It was *false* news. Don't believe it.
【反義詞】true（正確的）

*fame[4] 〔fem〕 *n.* 名聲（= *celebrity*）
The actor's *fame* increased after he
won an Academy Award.

【典型考題】
The popular baseball player's ＿＿＿
grew after his team won the
championship.
A. fame　　　　B. frame
C. blame　　　 D. shame　　　[A]

*familiar[3] 〔fə'mɪljɚ〕 *adj.* 熟悉的
（= *well-known*）
I am not *familiar* with this song.
Do you know who the singer is?
【記憶技巧】*famili*（family）+ *ar*（adj.）
【典型考題】
Although Martha had been away
from home for a long time, when she
came near her house, everything
suddenly became ＿＿＿.
A. functional　　B. impulsive
C. emotional　　D. familiar　　[D]

‡family[1] 〔'fæməlɪ〕 *n.* 家庭（= *home*）；
家人（= *kin*）

‡famous[2] 〔'feməs〕 *adj.* 有名的
（= *notable* = *well-known*）
【典型考題】
Glen is a very ＿＿＿ TV star; even
children know his name.
A. famous　　　B. hungry
C. serious　　　D. weak　　　[A]

‡fan[3,1] 〔fæn〕 *n.*（影、歌、球）迷；
風扇（= *wind blower*）

‡fancy[3] 〔'fænsɪ〕 *adj.* 花俏的
（= *extravagant*）；昂貴的
My boyfriend invited me to a *fancy*
restaurant on Valentine's Day.

‡fantastic[4] 〔fæn'tæstɪk〕 *adj.* 極好的
（= *amazing*）
She's really a *fantastic* girl.

*__fantasy__[4] 〔'fæntəsɪ 〕 *n.* 幻想
(= *dream*)

‡__far__[1] 〔 fɑr 〕 *adj.* 遠的

*__fare__[3] 〔 fɛr 〕 *n.* 車資
Can you tell me what the *fare* from
London to Manchester is?
【比較】fee (學費;會費;入場費)

*__farewell__[4] 〔,fɛr'wɛl 〕 *n.* 告別
Albert said he had to leave and we
bid him *farewell*.

‡__farm__[1] 〔 fɑrm 〕 *n.* 農田

‡__farmer__[1] 〔'fɑrmɚ 〕 *n.* 農夫
(= *peasant*)

*__farther__[3] 〔'fɑrðɚ 〕 *adj.* 更遠的
The bank is on the corner and the
post office is just a little *farther*.

*__fashion__[3] 〔'fæʃən 〕 *n.* 流行(= *vogue*);
時尚 (業);方式　*v.* 精心製成
Narrow trousers are the latest
fashion.

‡__fashionable__[3] 〔'fæʃənəbl̩ 〕
adj. 流行的

‡__fast__[1] 〔 fæst 〕 *adj.* 快的　*adv.* 快速地

*__fasten__[3] 〔'fæsn̩ 〕 *v.* 繫上
You must *fasten* your seat belt if you
want to sit in the front of the car.
【記憶技巧】*fast* (牢固的) + *en* (*v.*)

‡__fat__[1] 〔 fæt 〕 *adj.* 胖的

*__fatal__[4] 〔'fetl̩ 〕 *adj.* 致命的
(= *deadly* = *lethal*)
The patient's family were relieved to
learn that his illness was not *fatal*.

*__fate__[3] 〔 fet 〕 *n.* 命運 (= *destiny*)
It was Holly's *fate* to meet her Mr.
Right in Las Vegas.

‡__father__[1] 〔'fɑðɚ 〕 *n.* 父親

‡__faucet__[3] 〔'fɔsɪt 〕 *n.* 水龍頭 (= *tap*)
Remember to turn off the *faucet*.

‡__fault__[2] 〔 fɔlt 〕 *n.* 過錯 (= *mistake*)
It was his *fault* that the window broke.

┌─【典型考題】──────────
│ I'm sorry for breaking your window.
│ It's all my _____.
│ A. fault　　　　B. idea
│ C. joke　　　　D. question　　[A]
└────────────────

*__favor__[2] 〔'fevɚ 〕 *n.* 恩惠 (= *benefit*);
幫忙 (= *help*)
Please do me the *favor* of turning
off your cell phone.
【片語】*do* sb. *a favor* (幫某人的忙)

*__favorable__[4] 〔'fevərəbl̩ 〕 *adj.* 有利的
(= *advantageous*)
Considering the *favorable* response
of the audience, I think we should
give first prize in the speech contest
to Ian.

‡‡__favorite__[2] 〔'fevərɪt 〕 *adj.* 最喜愛的
(= *preferred*)
【記憶技巧】*favor* (偏愛) + *ite* (*adj.*)
(特別偏愛的,就是「最喜愛的」)

┌─【典型考題】──────────
│ He likes A-mei.　She's his _____
│ singer.
│ A. volunteer　　B. exciting
│ C. favorite　　　D. garbage　　[C]
└────────────────

F

F

*__fax__[3] 〔fæks〕 v. 傳真 (=_facsimile_)

*__fear__[1] 〔fɪr〕 v. n. 害怕；恐懼 (=_dread_)

__fearful__[2] 〔'fɪrfəl〕 adj. 害怕的 (=_afraid_)；可怕的 (=_dreadful_)
We are _fearful_ that the river will flood if it keeps raining.

*__feast__[4] 〔fist〕 n. 盛宴 (=_banquet_ 〔'bæŋkwɪt〕)
It is traditional to enjoy a _feast_ after a wedding.
【記憶技巧】 _f_ + _east_ (東方)

*__feather__[3] 〔'fɛðə〕 n. 羽毛
Birds of a _feather_ flock together.

*__feature__[3] 〔'fitʃə〕 n. 特色 (=_characteristic_) v. 以…為特色
Wet weather is a _feature_ of life in Scotland.

【典型考題】
My apartment has one ＿＿＿ I like. It has a fireplace in the living room.
A. mystery   B. triumph
C. character   D. feature   **[D]**

‡__February__[1] 〔'fɛbju‚ɛrɪ〕 n. 二月
February is the second month of the year.

【重要知識】這字也可唸成〔'fɛbru‚ɛrɪ〕。根據發音字典，現在美國人 64% 唸 /ju/，36% 唸 /ru/。

‡__fee__[2] 〔fi〕 n. 費用 (=_charge_)；服務費；入場費
The entrance _fee_ to the exhibition is 20 dollars.

‡__feed__[1] 〔fid〕 v. 餵
We _feed_ the birds every day.

‡__feel__[1] 〔fil〕 v. 覺得
I _feel_ happy because I am playing with friends.

‡__feeling__[1] 〔'filɪŋ〕 n. 感覺

*__feelings__[1] 〔'filɪŋz〕 n. pl. 感情

*__fellow__[2] 〔'fɛlo〕 n. 傢伙；同伴
We were _fellows_ at school.
【片語】 _fellow at school_ (同學)

‡__female__[2] 〔'fimel〕 n. 女性 (=_woman_) adj. 女性的 (=_feminine_)
【反義詞】 male (男性；男性的)

‡__fence__[2] 〔fɛns〕 n. 籬笆；圍牆
That small house doesn't have a _fence_.

*__ferry__[4] 〔'fɛrɪ〕 n. 渡輪 (=_transportation boat_)

*__fertile__[4] 〔'fɜtl̩〕 adj. 肥沃的
Several types of fruit tree grow in the _fertile_ valley.
【反義詞】 sterile (貧瘠的)

‡__festival__[2] 〔'fɛstəvl̩〕 n. 節日 (=_holiday_)
Christmas is an important church _festival_.

【典型考題】
Easter is one of the biggest ＿＿＿ for Christians. It is a day to celebrate the rebirth of Jesus.
A. festivals   B. funerals
C. fields   D. fortresses **[A]**

*__fetch__[4] 〔fɛtʃ〕 v. 拿來；去拿
We taught our dog to _fetch_ the newspaper from the front yard.

‡fever[2] 〔'fivə 〕 *n.* 發燒
He has a little *fever*.

‡few[1] 〔 fju 〕 *adj.* 很少的

****fiction**[4] 〔'fɪkʃən 〕 *n.* 小說 (= *novel*)；
虛構的事 (= *made-up story*)
As a proverb goes, "Truth is stranger
than *fiction*."
【記憶技巧】 *fict* (feign) + *ion* (*n.*)
(「小說」的內容是不真實的)
【衍伸詞】 fictional (虛構的；小說的)

*** field**[2] 〔 fild 〕 *n.* 田野 (= *land*)
The children are playing in the *field*.

*** fierce**[4] 〔 fɪrs 〕 *adj.* 兇猛的
(= *ferocious*)；激烈的 (= *intense*)
The house is guarded by a *fierce* dog.

【典型考題】
Since the contestants were all very
good, the competition for the first
prize was ＿＿＿＿.
A. sincere   B. fierce
C. radiant   D. efficient   [B]

‡fifteen[1] 〔 fɪf'tin 〕 *n.* 十五

‡fifty[1] 〔'fɪftɪ 〕 *n.* 五十

‡fight[1] 〔 faɪt 〕 *v.* 打架
Dogs always *fight* with cats.

*** fighter**[2] 〔'faɪtə 〕 *n.* 戰士
【衍伸詞】 *fire fighter* (消防隊員)

*** figure**[2] 〔'fɪgjə 〕 *n.* 數字 (= *number*)；
人物 (= *famous person*)
He wrote the date in *figures*.
He became a familiar *figure* to the
townspeople.
【片語】 *figure out* (了解；算出)

*** file**[3] 〔 faɪl 〕 *n.* 檔案 (= *documents*)；
文件夾；縱隊 *v.* 歸檔；提出

‡fill[1] 〔 fɪl 〕 *v.* 使充滿；填補；修補
【片語】 *be filled with* (充滿)
(= *be full of*)

【典型考題】
Newspapers are ＿＿＿＿ with
advertisements for all kinds of
consumer goods.
A. full   B. filled
C. fitted   D. fixed   [B]

*** film**[2] 〔 fɪlm 〕 *n.* 影片 (= *movie*)；
底片；薄層 *v.* 拍攝

‡final[1] 〔'faɪnḷ 〕 *adj.* 最後的 (= *last*)
This is your *final* chance.
【記憶技巧】 *fin* (end) + *al* (*adj.*)
【衍伸詞】 finally (最後；終於)

*** finance**[4] 〔'faɪnæns 〕 *n.* 財務
(= *economic affairs*)   *v.* 資助
The city's *finances* are bad.
We are trying to raise money to
finance a new gym.
【記憶技巧】 *fin* (end) + *ance* (*n.*)
(使結束債務，即「資助」)

【重要知識】現在87％美國人唸成〔'faɪnæns 〕，
13％的人唸成〔 fə'næns 〕。

*** financial**[4] 〔 faɪ'nænʃəl 〕 *adj.* 財務的
【典型考題】
Some students get ＿＿＿＿ aid from
the government to support their
education.
A. financial   B. vocational
C. professional   D. intellectual   [A]

‡find[1] 〔 faɪnd 〕 *v.* 找到

‡fine[1] 〔 faɪn 〕 *adj.* 晴朗的；美麗的；
好的 (= *good*)   *n.* 罰款 *v.* 對…
處以罰款
The weather is *fine*, isn't it?

F

‡**finger**[1] 〔ˈfɪŋɚ〕 *n.* 手指

‡**finish**[1] 〔ˈfɪnɪʃ〕 *v.* 結束；完成
(= *accomplish* = *complete*)
I'll *finish* this work at nine o'clock.

‡**fire**[1] 〔faɪr〕 *n.* 火 (= *burning*)
Are you afraid of *fire*?

* **firecrackers**[4] 〔ˈfaɪrˌkrækɚz〕 *n. pl.*
鞭炮 (= *fireworks*)
The family lit *firecrackers* to
celebrate the new year.
【記憶技巧】*fire* + *crack* (破裂) + *ers*
(「鞭炮」點火之後，碎片會散落一地)

fireman[2] 〔ˈfaɪrmən〕 *n.* 消防隊員
(= *firefighter*)

* **fireplace**[4] 〔ˈfaɪrˌples〕 *n.* 壁爐
(= *hearth*)

* **firework**[3] 〔ˈfaɪrˌwɝk〕 *n.* 煙火
Fireworks lit up the sky on the
Fourth of July.

* **firm**[2] 〔fɝm〕 *adj.* 堅定的　*n.* 公司
Tom was *firm* in his refusal to help
us, so there is no point in talking to
him again.
【比較】confirm (證實)；affirm (斷言)

‡**first**[1] 〔fɝst〕 *adj.* 第一的

‡**fish**[1] 〔fɪʃ〕 *n.* 魚

‡**fisherman**[2] 〔ˈfɪʃɚmən〕 *n.* 漁夫

* **fist**[3] 〔fɪst〕 *n.* 拳頭
The angry man shook his *fist* at them.

‡**fit**[2] 〔fɪt〕 *v.* 適合
The skirt *fits* you well.

‡**fix**[2] 〔fɪks〕 *v.* 修理 (= *repair*)
The machine needs to be *fixed*.

* **flag**[2] 〔flæg〕 *n.* 旗子 (= *banner*)
There are three colors on our
national *flag*.

* **flame**[3] 〔flem〕 *n.* 火焰 (= *fire*)
The *flame* of the candle was our
only light when the electricity was
cut off.
【注意】火舌亂竄，就如同 fl 字群一樣搖擺
不定。flame 是指閃動的「火焰」部分。

* **flash**[2] 〔flæʃ〕 *n.* 閃光；(光的) 閃爍
(= *shimmer*)
We were startled by a *flash* of light
and then realized that it was
lightning.

* **flashlight**[2] 〔ˈflæʃˌlaɪt〕 *n.* 閃光燈
(= *spotlight*)；手電筒

* **flat**[2] 〔flæt〕 *adj.* 平的
(= *level and smooth*)
The floor is quite *flat*.

* **flatter**[4] 〔ˈflætɚ〕 *v.* 奉承；討好
(= *gratify*)
Greg *flattered* Janice by praising
her cooking even though it was
not really very good.

* **flavor**[3] 〔ˈflevɚ〕 *n.* 口味 (= *taste*)
Strawberry is my favorite *flavor* of
ice cream.

* **flea**[3] 〔fli〕 *n.* 跳蚤 (= *bug*)
【衍伸詞】*flea market* (跳蚤市場)

* **flee**[4] 〔 fli 〕 *v.* 逃走（ = *run away* ）；
逃離（ = *escape* ）

The bank robbers *fled* the scene in
a green car.

【注意】三態變化爲：flee-fled-fled

* **flesh**[3] 〔 flɛʃ 〕 *n.* 肉（ = *body tissue* ）

The doctor said it was just a *flesh*
wound and not to worry too much.

【片語】 *flesh wound*（皮肉傷；輕傷）

【注意】活的動物（身體）的肉是 flesh；
而死的動物（食用）的肉則是 meat。

* **flexible**[4] 〔'flɛksəbḷ 〕 *adj.* 有彈性的
（ = *pliable* ）

We like *flexible* working hours.

【記憶技巧】 *flex* (bend) + *ible* (adj.)
（可彎曲的，就是「有彈性的」）

【典型考題】

Nowadays many companies adopt a
_____ work schedule which allows
their employees to decide when to
arrive at work—from as early as 6
a.m. to as late as 11 a.m.
A. relative   B. severe
C. primitive   D. flexible   [D]

* **flight**[2] 〔 flaɪt 〕 *n.* 班機

He took the five o'clock *flight* to
Tokyo.

* **float**[3] 〔 flot 〕 *v.* 飄浮；漂浮
（ = *drift* ）

When he became tired, the swimmer
turned over and *floated* on his back.

* **flock**[3] 〔 flɑk 〕 *v.* 聚集   *n.* (鳥、羊)群

People *flocked* to see the baseball
star.

【典型考題】

Standing on the seashore, we saw a
_____ of seagulls flying over the
ocean before they glided down and
settled on the water.
A. pack   B. flock
C. herd   D. school   [B]

* **flood**[2] 〔 flʌd 〕 *n.* 水災

‡ **floor**[1] 〔 flɔr 〕 *n.* 地板；樓層

This elevator stops at every *floor*.

* **flour**[2] 〔 flaʊr 〕 *n.* 麵粉【注意發音】
（ = *wheat powder* ）

* **flow**[2] 〔 flo 〕 *v.* 流；暢通；飄拂
n. 流動

The water was *flowing* out.

‡ **flower**[1] 〔'flaʊɚ 〕 *n.* 花（ = *bloom* ）

* **flu**[2] 〔 flu 〕 *n.* 流行性感冒（ = *influenza* ）

He is in bed with the *flu*.

* **fluent**[4] 〔'fluənt 〕 *adj.* 流利的
（ = *smooth and articulate* ）

Margaret hopes to become a *fluent*
Japanese speaker so that she can
work as a translator.

【記憶技巧】 *flu* (flow) + *ent* (adj.)
（說話像水流一樣順暢，表示「流利的」）

* **flunk**[4] 〔 flʌŋk 〕 *v.* 使不及格；當掉
（ = *fail* ）

If the average of your scores is not
at least 60 percent, you will *flunk*
this course.

* **flush**[4] 〔 flʌʃ 〕 *v.* 臉紅

His face was *flushed* because he had
run all the way from the dormitory.

F

‡**flute**[2] 〔flut〕 *n.* 笛子
Jason asked his mother to buy a *flute* for him.

‡**fly**[1] 〔flaɪ〕 *v.* 飛 *n.* 蒼蠅

***foam**[4] 〔fom〕 *n.* 泡沫 (= *bubbles*);
泡棉 *v.* 起泡沫
Bill doesn't often drink draft beer because he doesn't like the *foam*.

***focus**[2] 〔'fokəs〕 *n.* 焦點
v. 對準焦點;集中
She always wants to be the *focus* of attention.
【片語】*focus on* (把焦點對準於;集中於)

***fog**[1] 〔fɔg , fag〕 *n.* 霧 (= *heavy mist*)
Fog is a cloud near the ground.

‡**foggy**[2] 〔'fagɪ〕 *adj.* 多霧的

***fold**[3] 〔fold〕 *v.* 摺疊(= *lay in creases*)
Please don't *fold* this paper; put it in a folder to keep it flat.

***folk**[3] 〔fok〕 *n.* 人們 (= *people*)
adj. 民間的

‡**follow**[1] 〔'falo〕 *v.* 跟隨 (= *pursue*);
遵守 (= *observe*)
Follow me.
We should *follow* the rules.

***follower**[3] 〔'faloɚ〕 *n.* 信徒

***following**[2] 〔'faləwɪŋ〕 *adj.* 下列的

***fond**[3] 〔fand〕 *adj.* 喜歡的
Uncle Henry is *fond* of gardening.
【片語】*be fond of* (喜歡)

‡**food**[1] 〔fud〕 *n.* 食物

‡**fool**[2] 〔ful〕 *n.* 傻瓜

He is such a *fool* that he doesn't know what to do.

‡**foolish**[2] 〔'fulɪʃ〕 *adj.* 愚蠢的
【記憶技巧】*ish* 結尾表「帶有～性質」。

‡**foot**[1] 〔fut〕 *n.* 腳;英呎
Wendy hurt her left *foot*.
【注意】複數型是 feet。

‡**football**[2] 〔'fut,bɔl〕 *n.* 橄欖球;足球
Football is an exciting game.

‡**for**[1] 〔fɔr〕 *prep.* 為了;給 *conj.* 因為
This apple is *for* Anne.

***forbid**[4] 〔fɚ'bɪd〕 *v.* 禁止
(= *prohibit* = *ban*)
My parents *forbid* me to go to Internet cafes at night.

***force**[1] 〔fors〕 *n.* 力量 *v.* 強迫

***forecast**[4] 〔'for,kæst〕 *n.* 預測
(= *prediction*) *v.* 預測 (= *predict*)
The weather bureau has *forecast* freezing temperatures for next week.
【記憶技巧】*fore* (before) + *cast* (throw) (事先放出消息,就是「預測」)

***forehead**[3] 〔'for,hɛd〕 *n.* 額頭
Rich is rubbing his *forehead*; maybe he has a headache.
【重要知識】88% 的美國人唸成〔'for,hɛd〕,老一輩的人唸成〔'forɪd〕。

‡**foreign**[1] 〔'forɪn〕 *adj.* 外國的
(= *alien*);外來的
Our new classmate has a *foreign* accent.

【典型考題】
English is studied by us as a _____ language.
A. polite   B. foreign
C. science   D. strange   **[B]**

‡**foreigner**[2] ﹝'fɔrɪnɚ﹞ *adj.* 外國人
(= *alien person*)

‡**forest**[1] ﹝'fɔrɪst﹞ *n.* 森林 (= *woods*)
Monkeys live in a *forest*.
【衍伸詞】*tropical rain forest* (熱帶雨林)

***forever**[3] ﹝fɚ'ɛvɚ﹞ *adv.* 永遠
(= *eternally*)
No one can live *forever*.

‡**forget**[1] ﹝fɚ'gɛt﹞ *v.* 忘記
Robert *forgot* to bring his book to
school.

‡**forgive**[2] ﹝fɚ'gɪv﹞ *v.* 原諒 (= *pardon*)
Mom *forgave* me for stealing her
money.
【衍伸詞】*forgive and forget* (既往不咎)

┌─【典型考題】──────────
│ I will _____ you, but you will have
│ to say you are sorry.
│ A. return   B. avoid
│ C. forgive   D. regret   [C]
└────────────────────────

‡**fork**[1] ﹝fɔrk﹞ *n.* 叉子
When we eat, we use *forks* and knives.

‡**form**[2] ﹝fɔrm﹞ *v.* 形成 (= *shape*)
n. 形式 (= *accepted procedure*)

‡**formal**[2] ﹝'fɔrml̩﹞ *adj.* 正式的
(= *official*)
I wore *formal* clothes to the party.
【記憶技巧】*form* (form) + *al* (*adj.*)
(拘泥形式的，也就是「正式的」)
【反義詞】informal (非正式的)

***formation**[4] ﹝fɔr'meʃən﹞ *n.* 形成
(= *establishment*)
They are discussing the *formation* of
the earth.

***former**[2] ﹝'fɔrmɚ﹞ *n.* 前者
(= *previous one*)   *adj.* 前任的
The *former* is better than the latter.
【反義詞】latter (後者)。

***formula**[4] ﹝'fɔrmjələ﹞ *n.* 公式；式
The chemical *formula* of water is H_2O.

***fort**[4] ﹝fɔrt﹞ *n.* 堡壘 (= *fortress*)

***forth**[3] ﹝forθ, fɔrθ﹞ *adv.* 向前
(= *forward*)
The wind chimes moved back and
forth.
【片語】*back and forth* (來回地)

***fortunate**[4] ﹝'fɔrtʃɪnɪt﹞ *adj.* 幸運的
(= *lucky*)
Alan was *fortunate* to find a job so
quickly.

***fortune**[3] ﹝'fɔrtʃən﹞ *n.* 運氣 (= *fate*)；
財富 (= *wealth*)

‡**forty**[1] ﹝'fɔrtɪ﹞ *n.* 四十

***forward**[2] ﹝'fɔrwɚd﹞ *adv.* 向前
(= *forth* = *forwards*【英式用法】)
adj. 向前的 (= *advancing*)
Go *forward* and you can see the
bookstore on the corner.

***forwards**[2] ﹝'fɔrwɚdz﹞ *adv.* 向前

fossil[4] ﹝'fɑsl̩﹞ *n.* 化石
【衍伸詞】*fossil fuel* (石化燃料)

***found**[3] ﹝faʊnd﹞ *v.* 建立
Mr. Lee *founded* the company in
1954.

***foundation**[4] ﹝faʊn'deʃən﹞ *n.* 建立
(= *establishment*)；基礎 (= *basis*)

F

founder[4] 〔'faʊndɚ〕 *n.* 創立者
(= *establisher*)

fountain[3] 〔'faʊntn̩〕 *n.* 噴泉
(= *spring*)；泉源 (= *source*)
【記憶技巧】 *foun* (spring 泉) + *tain*
(hold) (裝湧泉的地方，即「噴泉」)

fox[2] 〔faks〕 *n.* 狐狸

fragrance[4] 〔'fregrəns〕 *n.* 芳香

fragrant[4] 〔'fregrənt〕 *adj.* 芳香的
The flower smells *fragrant*.

frame[4] 〔frem〕 *n.* 骨架；框架
(= *casing*)
This photograph looks so much
more attractive in a nice *frame*.

frank[2] 〔fræŋk〕 *adj.* 坦白的
(= *honest*)
He is *frank* with me about
everything.

free[1] 〔fri〕 *adj.* 自由的
(= *unrestrained*)；免費的

freedom[2] 〔'fridəm〕 *n.* 自由
(= *liberty*)
He has *freedom* to do what he likes.

freeway[4] 〔'fri,we〕 *n.* 高速公路
(= *expressway*)
【注意】 freeway 比 highway (公路) 速限
更高，開起來更接近 free 的狀態。

freeze[3] 〔friz〕 *v.* 結冰

freezer[2] 〔'frizɚ〕 *n.* 冰箱
There is a lot of food in our *freezer*.

frequency[4] 〔'frikwənsɪ〕 *n.* 頻繁
(= *constancy*)；頻率；次數
Andrea lives nearby so she visits the
coffee shop with great *frequency*.

frequent[3] 〔'frikwənt〕 *adj.* 經常的；
習慣的；屢次的
〔frɪ'kwɛnt〕 *v.* 常去

fresh[1] 〔frɛʃ〕 *adj.* 新鮮的 (= *new*)；
新進的；涼爽的；生氣蓬勃的；沒鹽
分的
The cake is very *fresh*.
【反義詞】 stale (不新鮮的)
【衍伸詞】 *fresh water* (淡水)

freshman[4] 〔'frɛʃmən〕 *n.* 大一新生

Friday[1] 〔'fraɪdɪ〕 *n.* 星期五

friend[1] 〔frɛnd〕 *n.* 朋友
(= *companion*)
Everyone needs a *friend* to share
his feelings with.

friendly[2] 〔'frɛndlɪ〕 *adj.* 友善的
(= *amiable*)

【典型考題】
People in this small town are quite
_____ to strangers; they always try
to help strangers.
A. careful   B. friendly
C. honest   D. successful   [B]

friendship[3] 〔'frɛndʃɪp〕 *n.* 友誼
【記憶技巧】 *friend* + *ship* (抽象名詞
字尾)

fright[2] 〔fraɪt〕 *n.* 驚嚇 (= *horror*)

* **frighten**[2] 〔'fraɪtn̩〕 v. 使驚嚇
(= *horrify*)
I'm sorry I *frightened* you.

‡ **frog**[1] 〔frɑg〕 n. 青蛙
Frogs are jumping in the rain.

‡ **front**[1] 〔frʌnt〕 n. 前面
Don't park your car in *front* of the building.
【片語】 *in front of* (在…前面)

* **frost**[4] 〔frɔst〕 n. 霜；嚴寒 (期)
v. 結霜；在…上灑糖霜
【比較】 defrost (除霜；解凍)

* **frown**[4] 〔fraʊn〕 v. 皺眉頭 (= *wrinkle the brow*)   n. 皺眉；不悅之色
Why are you *frowning*? Is something bothering you?

‡ **fruit**[1] 〔frut〕 n. 水果；果實；成果

* **frustrate**[3] 〔'frʌstret〕 v. 使受挫折
(= *discourage*)
If the lesson is too difficult, it will *frustrate* the students.
【記憶技巧】 *frustr* (in vain) + *ate* (v.)
(所做的一切都白費，便會感到受挫)

【典型考題】
Though Kevin failed in last year's singing contest, he did not feel _____. This year he practiced day and night and finally won first place in the competition.
A. relieved   B. suspected
C. discounted   D. frustated   [D]

* **frustration**[4] 〔frʌs'treʃən〕 n. 挫折
(= *disappointment*)；失望；阻撓

* **fry**[3] 〔fraɪ〕 v. 油炸；油炒；油煎
n. 油炸物
She *fried* a fish.

* **fuel**[4] 〔'fjuəl〕 n. 燃料
A car usually uses gasoline as *fuel*.

* **fulfill**[4] 〔fʊl'fɪl〕 v. 履行 (義務、約定)
實現 (= *accomplish*)
If he's lazy he'll never *fulfill* his ambition to be a doctor.
【記憶技巧】 *ful(l)* + *fill* (填滿)

* **fulfillment**[4] 〔fʊl'fɪlmənt〕 n. 實現
(= *accomplishment*)

【典型考題】
Her dream of being a dancer finally came to _____ when she got the opportunity to perform on the stage.
A. fulfillment   B. department
C. conclusion   D. punishment   [A]

‡ **full**[1] 〔fʊl〕 adj. 充滿的
This river is *full* of fish.
【片語】 *be full of* (充滿)(= *be filled with*)

‡ **fun**[1] 〔fʌn〕 n. 樂趣 (= *amusement*)
I had so much *fun* at the party last night.
【片語】 *have fun* (玩得愉快)

* **function**[2] 〔'fʌŋkʃən〕 n. 功能
(= *use*)   v. 起作用；擔任
What is the *function* of the heart?
【記憶技巧】 *funct* (perform) + *ion* (n.)
(能執行某件事，就是有某種「功能」)

* **functional**[4] 〔'fʌŋkʃənl̩〕 adj. 功能的
(= *operative*)

F

*fund[3] 〔 fʌnd 〕 n. 資金 (= money)；
基金 (= money reserve)
【衍伸詞】 **fund raising** (募款)

*fundamental[4] 〔,fʌndə'mɛntḷ 〕
adj. 基本的 (= basic)
Good health care is one of the
fundamental needs of our society.
【記憶技巧】 **funda** (base) + **ment** (n.)
+ **al** (adj.)

*funeral[4] 〔'fjunərəl 〕 n. 葬禮

‡funny[1] 〔'fʌnɪ 〕 adj. 好笑的
(= comical)；有趣的

*fur[3] 〔 fɝ 〕 n. 毛皮 adj. 毛皮製的

*furious[4] 〔'fjʊrɪəs 〕 adj. 狂怒的
Father was furious when he saw
the scratch on his new car.
【記憶技巧】 **fur** + **ious** (adj.)
(被惹毛就會「狂怒的」)

【典型考題】
The angry passengers argued _____
with the airline staff because their flight
was cancelled without any explanation.
A. evidently B. furiously
C. obediently D. suspiciously [B]

*furnish[4] 〔'fɝnɪʃ 〕 v. 裝置家具
(= equip and decorate)
My landlord will furnish the room
with a sofa and two chairs.
【記憶技巧】 **furn** (備有) + **ish** (v.) (使
家裡擁有所需的裝備，就是「裝置家具」)
【衍伸詞】 furnished (附家具的)

*furniture[3] 〔'fɝnɪtʃɚ 〕 n. 傢俱
(= household property)
【片語】 **a piece of furniture** (一件
傢俱)

*further[2] 〔'fɝðɚ 〕 adj. 更進一步的
adv. 更進一步地 (= more)
He will need further help.

*furthermore[4] 〔'fɝðɚ,mor 〕 adv. 此外
(= moreover)
Ted is the most talented pianist we
have. Furthermore, he is very reliable.

‡future[2] 〔'fjutʃɚ 〕 n. 未來
adj. 未來的
【片語】 **in the future** (將來)

G g

‡gain[2] 〔 gen 〕 v. 獲得 (= get = obtain)；
增加 n. 增長；好處；利潤
He gained a bad reputation.

*gallery[4] 〔'gælərɪ 〕 n. 畫廊
The gallery is showing the work of
several local artists.

*gallon[3] 〔'gælən 〕 n. 加侖 (容量單位)

*gamble[3] 〔'gæmbḷ 〕 v. 賭博
They gambled at cards all night.

【典型考題】
Aside from playing the lottery, he
doesn't _____ at all.
A. gamble B. inquire
C. invent D. strive [A]

‡game[1] 〔 gem 〕 n. 遊戲

*__gang__[3]〔gæŋ〕 *n.* 幫派
（= *band of gangsters*）

*__gangster__[4]〔'gæŋstɚ〕 *n.* 歹徒
（= *bandit*）
【記憶技巧】 *gang*（幫派）+ *ster*（人）
（參加幫派者，即「歹徒」）

*__gap__[3]〔gæp〕 *n.* 裂縫；差距
Sunshine came in through a *gap* in
the curtains.
【衍伸詞】 *generation gap*（代溝）
【片語】 *bridge the gap*（彌補差距）

‡__garage__[2]〔gə'rɑʒ〕 *n.* 車庫
Tom's parents park their car in the
garage.
【記憶技巧】 *gar*（cover）+ *age*（表地點）
（「車庫」就是提供車子遮蔽的地方）

‡__garbage__[2]〔'gɑrbɪdʒ〕 *n.* 垃圾
（= *trash*）
We must take out the *garbage* at
9:00.

‡__garden__[1]〔'gɑrdṇ〕 *n.* 花園；庭園
Grandpa usually spends his free
time in the *garden*.

*__gardener__[2]〔'gɑrdnɚ〕 *n.* 園丁；園藝家

*__garlic__[3]〔'gɑrlɪk〕 *n.* 大蒜

‡__gas__[1]〔gæs〕 *n.* 瓦斯；汽油；氣體
【衍伸詞】 *gas station*（加油站）
【重要知識】「瓦斯」就是 gas 的音譯，
指「汽油」時則是 gasoline 的簡稱。

*__gasoline__[3]〔'gæsḷ,in〕 *n.* 汽油
（= *gas* = *petrol*【英式用法】）
Gasoline is necessary in our daily life.

‡__gate__[2]〔get〕 *n.* 大門
The castle's *gate* is very high.

‡__gather__[2]〔'gæðɚ〕 *v.* 聚集（= *assemble*）
A lot of people *gathered* to see the
parade.

*__gaze__[4]〔gez〕 *v. n.* 凝視；注視
（= *stare*）
The climbers *gazed* at the view from
the top of the mountain.

*__gear__[4]〔gɪr〕 *n.* 排檔
She changed *gear* to make the car
go up the hill faster.

*__gene__[4]〔dʒin〕 *n.* 基因
Scientists believe that certain *genes*
can determine everything from our
eye color to our personality.

‡__general__[1,2]〔'dʒɛnərəl〕 *adj.* 一般的
（= *common*） *n.* 將軍（= *commander*）
The book is intended for the *general*
reader.

*__generation__[4]〔,dʒɛnə'reʃən〕 *n.* 世代
【片語】 *from generation to generation*
（一代接一代）

*__generosity__[4]〔,dʒɛnə'rɑsətɪ〕 *n.* 慷慨
We were all impressed by the
generosity of Tim's large donation.

【典型考題】
We are grateful for his ＿＿＿＿ in
giving a large contribution to our
educational foundation.
A. generosity　　B. hypothesis
C. appreciation　D. experiment　　[A]

G

⁑**generous**² (ˈdʒɛnərəs) *adj.* 慷慨的
(= *liberal*)
【反義詞】 stingy (吝嗇的；小氣的)

⁑**genius**⁴ (ˈdʒinjəs) *n.* 天才；天賦
Mark is smart and he is thought of
as a *genius*.

⁑**gentle**² (ˈdʒɛntḷ) *adj.* 溫柔的
(= *mild and benign*)
Ricky is very *gentle*.

⁑**gentleman**² (ˈdʒɛntḷmən) *n.* 紳士
This *gentleman* wishes to see the
manager.
【記憶技巧】 *gentle* + *man*

***genuine**⁴ (ˈdʒɛnjuɪn) *adj.* 真正的
(= *real*)
Is this a *genuine* antique or a copy?
【記憶技巧】 *genu* (innate) + *ine* (*adj.*)
(天生未經加工的，就是「真正的」)
【反義詞】 counterfeit (偽造的；仿冒的)

┌─【典型考題】─────
│ Of course ——— gold jewelry is more
│ expensive than imitation gold.
│ A. truthful   B. artificial
│ C. simulated   D. genuine   [D]
└──────────────

***geography**² (dʒiˈɑgrəfɪ) *n.* 地理學
I am going to have an exam in
geography tomorrow.
【記憶技巧】 *geo* (earth) + *graph*
(write) + *y* (*n.*) (「地理學」記錄有關土
地的事情)

***germ**⁴ (dʒɝm) *n.* 病菌 (= *bacterium*)
Washing your hands frequently will
kill *germs* that might otherwise
make you sick.

***gesture**³ (ˈdʒɛstʃɚ) *n.* 手勢
The police officer indicated that we
should proceed with a *gesture*.
【記憶技巧】 *gest* (carry) + *ure* (*n.*)
(用「手勢」帶出自己想要表達的意思)
【比較】 congest (阻塞；擁擠)
digest (消化)

⁑⁑**get**¹ (gɛt) *v.* 得到

⁑**ghost**¹ (gost) *n.* 鬼
Do you believe in *ghosts*?

⁑⁑**giant**² (ˈdʒaɪənt) *n.* 巨人
The basketball players on this team
are all *giants*.
【注意】 giant 也可指「大公司」或「偉人」，
如 a scientific giant (偉大的科學家)。

⁑⁑⁑**gift**¹ (gɪft) *n.* 禮物

***gifted**⁴ (ˈgɪftɪd) *adj.* 有天份的
(= *talented*)
Rachel is a *gifted* pianist and it is a
pleasure to listen to her.
【記憶技巧】「天份」是上天所賦予的禮物
(gift)，所以 gifted 就是「有天份的」。

***gigantic**⁴ (dʒaɪˈgæntɪk) *adj.* 巨大的
(= *extremely huge* = *enormous*)
You can find anything you want in
this *gigantic* store.
【反義詞】 tiny (微小的)

***giggle**⁴ (ˈgɪgḷ) *v.* 咯咯地笑
(= *snicker*)
The children *giggled* when Danny
told a joke.
【記憶技巧】 這個字的發音聽起來就像笑聲。

***ginger**⁴ (ˈdʒɪndʒɚ) *n.* 薑

G

*giraffe[2] 〔 dʒə'ræf 〕 *n.* 長頸鹿

‡girl[1] 〔 gɜl 〕 *n.* 女孩

‡give[1] 〔 gɪv 〕 *v.* 給

‡glad[1] 〔 glæd 〕 *adj.* 高興的
(= *delightful*)
I'm *glad* to see you again.

*glance[3] 〔 glæns 〕 *n. v.* 看一眼
(= *glimpse*)
I just *glanced* at the paper because I didn't have time to sit down and read it.
【片語】 *take a glance* (看一眼)

‡glass[1] 〔 glæs 〕 *n.* 玻璃；玻璃杯

‡glasses[1] 〔 'glæsɪz 〕 *n. pl.* 眼鏡
I need *glasses* when I read.

*glide[4] 〔 glaɪd 〕 *v.* 滑行 (= *slide*)；
滑動；滑翔；悄悄地走
I threw the paper airplane and watched it *glide* around the room.

*glimpse[4] 〔 glɪmps 〕 *n. v.* 看一眼
(= *glance*)；瞥見
Janice was excited when she *glimpsed* her favorite singer in the hotel lobby.
【片語】 catch a glimpse of 看一眼
(= *take a glimpse at*)

*global[3] 〔 'globḷ 〕 *adj.* 全球的
(= *worldwide*)
Because it affects everyone, the environment is a *global* concern.
【衍伸詞】 *global warming* (全球暖化)

*globe[4] 〔 glob 〕 *n.* 地球 (= *earth*)

*glorious[4] 〔 'glorɪəs 〕 *adj.* 光榮的
(= *honorable*)
Winning a gold medal in the Olympics was a *glorious* achievement.

*glory[3] 〔 'glorɪ 〕 *n.* 光榮 (= *honor*)；
榮譽；輝煌

‡glove[2] 〔 glʌv 〕 *n.* 手套
Baseball players need to wear *gloves*.
【記憶技巧】 *g* + *love*

*glow[3] 〔 glo 〕 *v.* 發光
(= *radiate light*)
My new watch will *glow* in the dark.

‡glue[2] 〔 glu 〕 *n.* 膠水

‡go[1] 〔 go 〕 *v.* 去

*goal[2] 〔 gol 〕 *n.* 目標 (= *aim*)
Getting into university is my *goal*.

【典型考題】
The Bush Administration's _____ is to raise fifty million dollars for the hurricane victims in one month.
A. treatment　　B. goal
C. bargain　　　D. ability　　[B]

‡goat[2] 〔 got 〕 *n.* 山羊
Goats make funny sounds.
【比較】 sheep (綿羊)

*god[1] 〔 gɑd 〕 *n.* 神 (= *deity*)
【比較】 God (上帝)

G

*goddess[1] 〔'gɑdɪs〕 *n.* 女神
(= *female deity*)
【記憶技巧】 *godd* (神) + *ess* (女性名詞)
【比較】 host*ess* (女主人)
waitr*ess* (女服務生)
princ*ess* (公主)

*gold[1] 〔 gold 〕 *n.* 黃金
Gold is a shiny, yellow metal.

golden[2] 〔'goldn̩〕 *adj.* 金色的
(= *gold color*)；金製的
(= *made of gold*)
【記憶技巧】 *gold* + *en* (由～做成)
【比較】 wood*en* (木製的)
wool*en* (羊毛製的)

*golf[2] 〔 gɑlf , gɔlf 〕 *n.* 高爾夫球
Everyone in my family plays *golf*.
【衍伸詞】 *golf course* (高爾夫球場)

*good[1] 〔 gʊd 〕 *adj.* 好的 (= *great*)；
擅長的；有效的 *n.* 優勢；利益

*good-bye[1] 〔 gʊd'baɪ 〕 *interj.* 再見
(= *goodbye* ; *bye*)

*goods[4] 〔 gʊdz 〕 *n. pl.* 商品
(= *commodity* = *merchandise*)；
貨物；財物；動產
In a stationery store, one can easily
find writing *goods*, such as paper,
pens, pencils, ink, envelopes, etc.

*goose[1] 〔 gus 〕 *n.* 鵝
The farmer is running after the *goose*.
【注意】 複數型是 geese 〔 gis 〕。

*gossip[3] 〔'gɑsəp〕 *v.* 說閒話
(= *talk about others*) *n.* 閒話；八卦

It's not a good idea to *gossip* about
your friends, especially when you
are not sure whether the story is
true.

*govern[2] 〔'gʌvən〕 *v.* 統治 (= *rule*)
After *governing* the country for
twenty years, the ruler decided
to retire.

*government[2] 〔'gʌvənmənt〕 *n.*
政府
(= *administrative authority*)

*governor[3] 〔'gʌvənə〕 *n.* 州長
(= *highest administrator*)

*gown[3] 〔 gaʊn 〕 *n.* 禮服 (= *robe*)
Cheryl wore a beautiful *gown* to
the formal dance.
【衍伸詞】 *wedding gown* (結婚禮服)

*grab[3] 〔 græb 〕 *v. n.* 抓住 (= *grasp*)
The climber *grabbed* the rope and
pulled himself up.

*grace[4] 〔 gres 〕 *n.* 優雅 (= *elegance*)
Louise may not be the most beautiful
dancer, but no one has more *grace*
than she does.

*graceful[4] 〔'gresfəl〕 *adj.* 優雅的
(= *elegant*)

【典型考題】
The ballet dancers' _____ movements
delighted all the audience.
A. truthful   B. doubtful
C. graceful   D. helpful   [C]

G

*gracious[4] 〔'greʃəs 〕 *adj.* 親切的
(= *kind*)

‡grade[2] 〔 gred 〕 *n.* 成績
(= *score* = *mark*)
Mary always got high *grades* in school.

【典型考題】
We're so surprised that Tom always gets very good _____ in math.
A. grades   B. graduate
C. great   D. produce   [A]

*gradual[3] 〔'grædʒuəl 〕 *adj.* 逐漸的
No one noticed the *gradual* rise of the river until it was too late.
【記憶技巧】*gradu* (step) + *al* (*adj.*)
(一步一步來，即「逐漸的」)
【衍伸詞】gradually (逐漸地)

*graduate[3] 〔'grædʒu͵et 〕 *v.* 畢業
〔'grædʒuɪt 〕 *n.* 畢業生
We will all *graduate* from high school in June.
【記憶技巧】*gradu* (grade) + *ate* (*v.*)
(不斷升級，最後「畢業」)

*graduation[4] 〔͵grædʒu'eʃən 〕 *n.* 畢業

*grain[3] 〔 gren 〕 *n.* 穀物
These farmers grow *grains*, such as wheat, barley, and so on.

‡gram[3] 〔 græm 〕 *n.* 公克
Mom asked me to buy 200 *grams* of sugar.

*grammar[4] 〔'græmɚ 〕 *n.* 文法

*grammatical[4] 〔 grə'mætɪkḷ 〕
adj. 文法上的

*grand[1] 〔 grænd 〕 *adj.* 雄偉的
(= *magnificent*)；壯麗的
I was deeply impressed by the *grand* building.

*grandchild[1] 〔'grænd͵tʃaɪld 〕
n. 孫子；孫女
【記憶技巧】*grand-* 表較年長或較年幼的字首。

‡granddaughter[1] 〔'græn͵dɔtɚ 〕
n. 孫女
My father has five *granddaughters*.

‡grandfather[1] 〔'grænd͵fɑðɚ 〕 *n.* 祖父
(= *grandpa*)
My *grandfather* died when I was young.

‡grandmother[1] 〔'grænd͵mʌðɚ 〕
n. 祖母 (= *grandma*)
My *grandmother* is still alive.

‡grandson[1] 〔'græn͵sʌn 〕 *n.* 孫子
My mother wants to have a *grandson*.

‡grape[2] 〔 grep 〕 *n.* 葡萄
Wine is made from *grapes*.
【比較】raisin (葡萄乾)

*grapefruit[4] 〔'grep͵frut 〕 *n.* 葡萄柚
【注意】為什麼葡萄柚叫作 grapefruit？
其實是因為葡萄柚長在樹上的樣子，和葡萄一樣是成串的。

*grasp[3] 〔 græsp 〕 *v.* 抓住 (= *grip*)
Timmy *grasped* my hand tightly during the scary part of the movie.

‡grass[1] 〔 græs 〕 *n.* 草

G

* **grasshopper**[3] 〔'græs,hɑpɚ 〕 *n.* 蚱蜢 (= *locust*)

【記憶技巧】*grass* + *hop* (跳) + *per* （ 在草叢中跳來跳去的，就是「蚱蜢」 ）

grassy[2] 〔'græsɪ 〕 *adj.* 多草的

【記憶技巧】*-y* 表「多…的；有…的」字尾。

* **grateful**[4] 〔'gretfəl 〕 *adj.* 感激的 (= *appreciative*)

I am *grateful* for all your help and support.

* **gratitude**[4] 〔'grætə,tjud 〕 *n.* 感激 (= *appreciation*)

【記憶技巧】*grat* (grateful) + *itude* (表「狀態」)

* **grave**[4] 〔 grev 〕 *n.* 墳墓 (= *tomb*)

He was digging his own *grave* by taking such dangerous actions.

‡ **gray**[1] 〔 gre 〕 *adj.* 灰色的 (= *grey*)

The color of an elephant is *gray*.

* **greasy**[4] 〔'grisɪ 〕 *adj.* 油膩的

Betty felt ill after eating too many *greasy* French fries.

‡ **great**[1] 〔 gret 〕 *adj.* 很棒的；重大的 (= *important*)

‡ **greedy**[2] 〔'gridɪ 〕 *adj.* 貪心的；貪婪的 (= *eager*)

‡ **green**[1] 〔 grin 〕 *adj.* 綠色的；環保的

* **greenhouse**[3] 〔'grin,haʊs 〕 *n.* 溫室

If the climate becomes too hot because of the *greenhouse* effect, life on earth can not continue to exist.

【常考】*greenhouse effect* (溫室效應)

【重要知識】如果指 green house，重音在 house 上。形容詞加名詞，通常重音在名詞上。

* **greet**[2] 〔 grit 〕 *v.* 問候 (= *hail*)；迎接

Juniors should *greet* seniors.

* **greeting**[4] 〔'gritɪŋ 〕 *n.* 問候

* **grief**[4] 〔 grif 〕 *n.* 悲傷 (= *sadness*)

Albert was too mature to display his *grief* in public.

【記憶技巧】*gr* (gravity) + *ief* (心中有沉重的事，即「悲傷」)

* **grieve**[4] 〔 griv 〕 *v.* 悲傷 (= *mourn*)；使悲傷

* **grin**[3] 〔 grɪn 〕 *v.* 露齒而笑；咧嘴笑 *n.* 露齒而笑

Jack *grinned* when I told him the joke, but he didn't laugh out loud.

* **grind**[4] 〔 graɪnd 〕 *v.* 磨

The waiter asked if we wanted him to *grind* some pepper over our pasta.

* **grocery**[3] 〔'grosɚɪ 〕 *n.* 雜貨店 (= *grocer's shop*)

You can buy some vegetables at the *grocery* store.

【記憶技巧】*grocer* (雜貨商) + *y* (place)

ground[1] 〔 graʊnd 〕 *n.* 地面
（ = *land* ）；理由 (= *reason*) *v.* 禁足
She lay on the *ground*.
【衍伸詞】 *on the ground(s) of* (因為)

group[1] 〔 grup 〕 *n.* 群；團體；小組
In class, we form *groups* to do
different things.

【典型考題】
It was still too early to enter the
dining room, and the guests, hanging
about in _____ of two or three,
exchanged pleasantries.
A. teams   B. gangs
C. groups   D. herds   [C]

grow[1] 〔 gro 〕 *v.* 成長；變得
(= *become*)

growth[2] 〔 groθ 〕 *n.* 成長
(= *increase*)

guarantee[4] 〔ˌgærənˈti 〕 *v. n.* 保證
(= *promise* = *warrant*)
They *guarantee* this clock for a year.

guard[2] 〔 gɑrd 〕 *n.* 警戒 (= *caution*)；
警衛 (= *watchman*) *v.* 看守
【比較】 bodyguard (保鏢)

guardian[3] 〔ˈgɑrdɪən 〕 *n.* 監護人；
守護者
【記憶技巧】 *guard* (watch over) + *ian*
(人)（ 負責看管的人，就是「監護人」）

guava[2] 〔ˈgwɑvə 〕 *n.* 芭樂

guess[1] 〔 gɛs 〕 *v. n.* 猜
Can you *guess* my age?

guest[1] 〔 gɛst 〕 *n.* 客人

guidance[3] 〔ˈgaɪdn̩s 〕 *n.* 指導
(= *advice*)；方針

guide[1] 〔 gaɪd 〕 *v.* 引導；帶領
n. 引導；導遊；指標；指南
She *guided* the visitors around the
city.

guilt[4] 〔 gɪlt 〕 *n.* 罪；罪惡感
(= *bad conscience*)

guilty[4] 〔ˈgɪltɪ 〕 *adj.* 有罪的
Proved *guilty* of bribery, the official
was soon sent to jail.
【反義詞】 innocent (無罪的；清白的)

guitar[2] 〔 gɪˈtɑr 〕 *n.* 吉他
John plays the *guitar* very well.

gulf[4] 〔 gʌlf 〕 *n.* 海灣 (= *bay*)
The *Gulf* of Mexico stretches from
Mexico to Florida.
【記憶技巧】 海灣 (gulf) 的形狀，就像 u
字型；高爾夫球 (golf) 的形狀則像 o。

gum[3] 〔 gʌm 〕 *n.* 牙齦；膠水；樹膠；
口香糖 (= *chewing gum*)

gun[1] 〔 gʌn 〕 *n.* 槍 *v.* 用槍射擊
He taught Helen how to shoot a *gun*.

guy[2] 〔 gaɪ 〕 *n.* 人；傢伙
Mr. Johnson is a nice *guy*.

gym[3] 〔 dʒɪm 〕 *n.* 體育館；健身房
(= *gymnasium*)
We play basketball in a *gym*.

G

H h

‡**habit**[2] (ˈhæbɪt) *n.* 習慣

The boy has very good *habits*.

【片語】*acquire a habit* (養成習慣)

give up a habit (改掉習慣)

* **habitual**[4] (həˈbɪtʃuəl) *adj.* 習慣性的

(= *regular*)

‡**hair**[1] (hɛr) *n.* 頭髮

Rose has long black *hair*.

‡**haircut**[1] (ˈhɛr͵kʌt) *n.* 理髮

I had a *haircut* yesterday.

* **hairdresser**[3] (ˈhɛr͵drɛsə) *n.* 美髮師

I went to another *hairdresser*.

【比較】barber (理髮師)

‡**half**[1] (hæf) *n.* 一半【注意發音】

Half of the boys in this room are my friends.

‡**hall**[2] (hɔl) *n.* 大廳

Your father is waiting for you across the *hall*.

* **hallway**[3] (ˈhɔl͵we) *n.* 走廊

(= *passageway*)

* **halt**[4] (hɔlt) *n. v.* 停止 (= *stop*)

The dentist *halted* the procedure when his patient said he was in pain.

‡**ham**[1] (hæm) *n.* 火腿

I had *ham* and eggs for my breakfast.

‡**hamburger**[2] (ˈhæmbɝgə) *n.* 漢堡

(= *burger*)

I think I'll have a *hamburger*.

【重要知識】「漢堡」是沒有火腿的，它的名稱是源自德國城市「漢堡」(Hamburg)

‡**hammer**[2] (ˈhæmə) *n.* 鐵鎚

v. 擊打

‡**hand**[1] (hænd) *n.* 手

* **handful**[3] (ˈhænd͵ful) *n.* 一把

Alice picked up a *handful* of dirt and put it in the pot.

【片語】*a handful of* (一把；一些)

* **handkerchief**[2] (ˈhæŋkətʃɪf) *n.* 手帕

She dropped her *handkerchief*.

【記憶技巧】*hand* + *ker* (cover) + *chief* (head) (手帕可以拿來蓋住頭)

* **handle**[2] (ˈhændl̩) *v.* 處理

The court has many cases to *handle*.

‡**handsome**[2] (ˈhænsəm) *adj.* 英俊的

Todd is a *handsome* man.

【典型考題】
I think Brad Pitt is very _____. He is my favorite movie star.
A. black   B. crazy
C. handsome   D. interest   [C]

* **handwriting**[4] (ˈhænd͵raɪtɪŋ)

n. 筆跡

The doctor's *handwriting* is so difficult to read that I'm not sure what medicine he prescribed.

* **handy**³〔'hændɪ〕adj. 便利的
  (= convenient)；手邊的
  (= accessible)；附近的

  It's very *handy* to live next door to
  a convenience store.

  【典型考題】
  Everything is cheaper in the market,
  but 7-Eleven is so ＿＿＿ that I
  usually go there.
  A. various   B. ridiculous
  C. usable   D. handy   [D]

‡ **hang**²〔hæŋ〕v. 懸掛 (= suspend)；
  吊死 (= kill with rope)

  She *hung* the picture on the wall.

  【三態變化為：hang-hung-hung】
  【注意】hang 如作「吊死」解，三態變化
  為 hang-hanged-hanged。

‡ **hanger**²〔'hæŋɚ〕n. 衣架
  (= clothes hanger)

  How about that one on the *hanger*?

‡ **happen**¹〔'hæpən〕v. 發生

‡ **happy**¹〔'hæpɪ〕adj. 快樂的

* **harbor**³〔'hɑrbɚ〕n. 港口 (= port)
  Kaohsiung has a *harbor* and wide
  roads, so transportation is good.

‡ **hard**¹〔hɑrd〕adj. 困難的
  (= difficult)；硬的   adv. 努力地
  (= diligently)

  It is a *hard* question to answer.

* **harden**⁴〔'hɑrdn̩〕v. 變硬；使麻木

‡ **hardly**²〔'hɑrdlɪ〕adv. 幾乎不
  I can *hardly* believe it.

【典型考題】
The old man could ＿＿＿ swallow
because his throat was too dry.
A. actually   B. strictly
C. exactly   D. hardly   [D]

* **hardship**⁴〔'hɑrdʃɪp〕n. 艱難
  (= difficulty)

  【記憶技巧】-ship 表「樣子」的字尾。

* **hardware**⁴〔'hɑrd,wɛr〕n. 硬體；
  五金

  【比較】software (軟體)

* **harm**³〔hɑrm〕v. n. 傷害
  (= damage)

* **harmful**³〔'hɑrmfəl〕adj. 有害的
  (= damaging)

* **harmonica**⁴〔hɑr'mɑnɪkə〕n.
  口琴

  【記憶技巧】*har* + *monica* (女子名)

* **harmony**⁴〔'hɑrmənɪ〕n. 和諧
  (= accord)

  The choir sang in perfect *harmony*.

* **harsh**⁴〔hɑrʃ〕adj. 嚴厲的
  (= severe)；無情的 (= unpleasant)

  Barry was upset by the others' *harsh*
  criticism of his artwork.

* **harvest**³〔'hɑrvɪst〕n. 成果；收穫
  (= reaping)   v. 收穫 (= reap)

  Farmers are predicting a record
  harvest this year.

  【記憶技巧】*har* + *vest* (背心)

H

* **haste**[4] 〔 hest 〕 *n.* 匆忙 (= *hurry*)

When he realized he was late for work, Jeff left the house in great *haste*.

【片語】 ***in haste*** (匆忙地)

* **hasten**[4] 〔 'hesn̩ 〕 *v.* 催促；加速；趕快 (= *hurry*)

* **hasty**[3] 〔 'hestɪ 〕 *adj.* 匆忙的 (= *hurried*)

‡ **hat**[1] 〔 hæt 〕 *n.* 帽子

* **hatch**[3] 〔 hætʃ 〕 *v.* 孵化 (= *breed*)；孵出

Some birds have built a nest outside my window and I expect the eggs to *hatch* very soon.

【典型考題】
Baby whales are not _____ from eggs but are born alive.
A. hatched   B. drowned
C. trapped   D. blown   [A]

‡ **hate**[1] 〔 het 〕 *v.* 恨；討厭

My brother *hates* snakes.

hateful[2] 〔 'hetfəl 〕 *adj.* 可恨的

* **hatred**[4] 〔 'hetrɪd 〕 *n.* 憎恨

Ned's *hatred* for the city is a result of a bad experience he had there as a tourist.

【記憶技巧】 ***hat***(*e*) + ***red*** (憎恨別人，就會眼紅)

‡ **have**[1] 〔 hæv 〕 *v.* 有

* **hawk**[3] 〔 hɔk 〕 *n.* 老鷹

* **hay**[3] 〔 he 〕 *n.* 乾草

We store *hay* for the animals to eat during the winter.

‡ **head**[1] 〔 hɛd 〕 *n.* 頭

* **headline**[3] 〔 'hɛd,laɪn 〕 *n.* (報紙的) 標題

Did you see the *headlines* about the murder?

* **headphone**[4] 〔 'hɛd,fon 〕 *n.* 耳機 (= *earphone*)

* **headquarters**[3] 〔 'hɛd'kwɔrtɚz 〕 *n. pl.* 總部

This is just a branch office. Our *headquarters* are located in Hong Kong.

【記憶技巧】 ***head*** + ***quarters***

* **heal**[3] 〔 hil 〕 *v.* 痊癒 (= *get well*)；(使) 復原

If you keep the wound clean and dry, it will *heal* soon.

‡ **health**[1] 〔 hɛlθ 〕 *n.* 健康 (= *fitness*)

Nothing is better than having good *health*.

* **healthful**[4] 〔 'hɛlθfəl 〕 *adj.* 有益健康的

‡ **healthy**[2] 〔 'hɛlθɪ 〕 *adj.* 健康的 (= *fit*)；有益健康的

* **heap**[3] 〔 hip 〕 *n.* 一堆 (= *a large pile of sth.*)

Please hang up the towels instead of leaving them in a *heap* on the floor.

‡ **hear**[1] 〔 hɪr 〕 *v.* 聽到

‡ **heart**[1] 〔 hɑrt 〕 *n.* 心；心地

‡ **heat**[1] 〔 hit 〕 *n.* 熱 (= *hotness*) *v.* 加熱；變熱

The sun gives us *heat* and light.

heater[2] 〔ˈhitɚ〕 *n.* 暖氣機
【比較】*air conditioner*（冷氣機）

*heaven[3] 〔ˈhɛvən〕 *n.* 天堂
（= *paradise*）

**heavy[1] 〔ˈhɛvɪ〕 *adj.* 重的
（= *weighty*）；大量的
（= *considerable*）；嚴重的（= *severe*）
This box is very *heavy*.
【衍伸詞】*heavy rain*（大雨）

*heel[3] 〔hil〕 *n.* 腳跟；(*pl.*) 高跟鞋
The shoes look nice, but they are
too tight in the *heel*.
【衍伸詞】*Achilles*[ˈ]* heel*（致命傷）

**height[2] 〔haɪt〕 *n.* 高度（= *tallness*）；
身高；海拔；高峰 *pl.* 高處
The tree grows to a *height* of 20 feet.

**helicopter[4] 〔ˈhɛlɪˌkɑptɚ〕 *n.* 直昇機
A *helicopter* is an aircraft that can
go straight up into the air.
【記憶技巧】分音節背 he-li-cop-ter。

*hell[3] 〔hɛl〕 *n.* 地獄
（= *the underworld*）
【反義詞】heaven（天堂）

*helmet[3] 〔ˈhɛlmɪt〕 *n.* 安全帽
All motorcyclists are required to
wear *helmets* on the city streets.

**help[1] 〔hɛlp〕 *v.* 幫助；幫忙（= *aid*）
n. 有幫助的人或物；幫手

**helpful[2] 〔ˈhɛlpfəl〕 *adj.* 有幫助的

**hen[2] 〔hɛn〕 *n.* 母雞；雌禽 *adj.* 雌的
My grandfather raises *hens* in the
country.
【比較】cock（公雞）

*herd[4] 〔hɝd〕 *n.* （牛）群
The ranchers moved the *herd* from
one pasture to another.

**hero[2] 〔ˈhɪro〕 *n.* 英雄（= *great man*）；
偶像（= *idol*）；男主角
My father is my *hero*.

*heroine[2] 〔ˈhɛro·ɪn〕 *n.* 女英雄；
女主角
【注意】heroine（女英雄）和 heroin（海洛
因）是同音字，且拼法只差一個 e，如果不小
心拼錯，麻煩可大了！

*hesitate[3] 〔ˈhɛzəˌtet〕 *v.* 猶豫
When you see a good opportunity,
don't *hesitate* to take advantage
of it.
【記憶技巧】*hesit* (stick 黏住) + *ate*
(*v.*) (「猶豫」不決，就像被黏住)

【典型考題】
If I can help you with the project, don't
＿＿＿＿ to call me.
A. concern　　　 B. hesitate
C. notify　　　　 D. submit　　　 [B]

*hesitation[4] 〔ˌhɛzəˈteʃən〕 *n.* 猶豫

**hide[2] 〔haɪd〕 *v.* 隱藏（= *conceal*）；
遮掩；躲藏；隱瞞（真相等）
The girl *hides* herself from her
mother.

**high[1] 〔haɪ〕 *adj.* 高的（= *tall*）
adv. 高高地 *n.* 高點

*highly[4] 〔ˈhaɪlɪ〕 *adv.* 非常地
（= *very*）

‡ **highway** [2] ('haɪ,we) n. 公路
We're driving on the *highway*.

‡ **hike** [3] (haɪk) v. n. 健行
I go *hiking* every Sunday morning.

‡ **hill** [1] (hɪl) n. 山丘
We climbed a *hill* last Sunday.

* **hint** [3] (hɪnt) n. 暗示
I won't tell you where we're going,
but I'll give you a *hint*.

‡ **hip** [2] (hɪp) n. 屁股
The boy hurt his *hip*.
【衍伸詞】 hip-hop (饒舌歌；嘻哈風)

‡ **hippo** [2] ('hɪpo) n. 河馬
We can see a lot of *hippos* in the zoo.

* **hippopotamus** [2] (,hɪpə'patəməs)
n. 河馬 (= *hippo*)

‡ **hire** [2] (haɪr) v. 雇用 (= *employ*)；
租用；出租　n. 出租；出租費；雇用
He *hired* a workman to paint
the wall.

* **historian** [3] (hɪs'toriən) n. 歷史學家

* **historic** [3] (hɪs'tɔrɪk) adj. 歷史上重
要的

* **historical** [3] (hɪs'tɔrɪkl̩) adj. 歷史的；
歷史學的

‡ **history** [1] ('hɪstrɪ) n. 歷史
(= *the past*)
History is my favorite subject.

‡ **hit** [1] (hɪt) v. 打 (= *strike*)；達到
(= *reach*)　n. 成功的事物
(= *success*)
He was *hit* by the teacher because
he didn't do his homework.

* **hive** [3] (haɪv) n. 蜂巢 (= *beehive*)；
蜂房；群居一起的蜜蜂；嘈雜繁忙
The beekeeper carefully removed
the cover of the *hive*.

‡ **hobby** [2] ('habɪ) n. 嗜好 (= *pastime*)
My favorite *hobby* is collecting
stamps.

‡ **hold** [1] (hold) v. 握住
He *held* my hand softly.

holder [2] ('holdə) n. 保持者

* **hole** [1] (hol) n. 洞
There is a *hole* in this bowl.

‡ **holiday** [1] ('halə,de) n. 假日
People don't work or go to school
on a *holiday*.

* **hollow** [3] ('halo) adj. 中空的
(= *empty*)；虛假的
The squirrel built a nest in the
hollow trunk of the tree.
【反義詞】 solid (實心的)

* **holy** [3] ('holɪ) adj. 神聖的 (= *sacred*)
Easter is one of the *holy* days of the
Catholic church.

‡ **home** [1] (hom) n. 家

* **homeland** [4] ('hom,lænd) n. 祖國
(= *mother country*)
Although they liked their new
country, the immigrants still missed
their *homeland*.

‡ **homesick** [2] ('hom,sɪk) adj. 想家的
I became *homesick* after a week's
stay at my aunt's.

hometown[3] (ˈhomˈtaʊn) *n.* 家鄉

‡**homework**[1] (ˈhomˌwɜk) *n.* 功課
(= *schoolwork*)；準備作業

‡**honest**[2] (ˈɑnɪst) *adj.* 誠實的
(= *frank*)
You need to be *honest* with yourself.
【反義詞】 dishonest (不誠實的)

*#**honesty**[3] (ˈɑnɪstɪ) *n.* 誠實
(= *frankness*)

‡**honey**[2] (ˈhʌnɪ) *n.* 蜂蜜

*#**honeymoon**[4] (ˈhʌnɪˌmun) *n.* 蜜月旅行
The newlyweds will spend their *honeymoon* in Bali.
【記憶技巧】 *honey* + *moon* (month)

*#**honor**[3] (ˈɑnɚ) *n.* 光榮
(= *high respect*)
v. 表揚 (= *treat with honor*)
It is an *honor* for me to meet such a respected scientist.

*#**honorable**[4] (ˈɑnərəb!) *adj.* 值得尊敬的

*#**hook**[4] (huk) *n.* 鉤子 *v.* 鉤住
Ben hung his jacket on a *hook* behind the door.

‡**hop**[2] (hɑp) *v.* 跳 (= *jump*)；單腳跳躍 *n.* 跳躍；短程旅行
The children are *hopping* on the bed.

‡**hope**[1] (hop) *v. n.* 希望
I *hope* I will pass the exam.

*#**hopeful**[4] (ˈhopfəl) *adj.* 充滿希望的

*#**horizon**[4] (həˈraɪzṇ) *n.* 地平線
pl. 知識範圍；眼界
We watched until the sun sank below the *horizon*.
【衍伸詞】 horizons (知識範圍)
【重要片語】 *broaden* one's *horizons*
(拓展眼界；增廣見聞)

*#**horn**[3] (hɔrn) *n.* (牛、羊的) 角；喇叭

‡**horrible**[3] (ˈhɔrəb!,ˈhɑrəb!)
adj. 可怕的 (= *terrible*)
The food at the school was *horrible*.

*#**horrify**[4] (ˈhɔrəˌfaɪ,ˈhɑrəˌfaɪ) *v.*
使驚嚇 (= *terrify*)

*#**horror**[3] (ˈhɔrɚ,ˈhɑrɚ) *n.* 恐怖
(= *terror*)

‡**horse**[1] (hɔrs) *n.* 馬
【片語】 *eat like a horse* 食量很大
eat like a bird 食量很小

*#**hose**[4] (hoz) *n.* 軟管(= *a flexible pipe*)

‡**hospital**[2] (ˈhɑspɪt!) *n.* 醫院
Hospitals, doctors, and nurses provide medical care.

‡**host**[2,4] (host) *n.* 主人；主持人
v. 擔任…的主人；主辦
He was the *host* of the party.

【典型考題】
Many students like to watch that talk show because the _____ is brilliant at entertaining young people.
A. guest B. owner
C. player D. host 　　[D]

* **hostel**[4] 〔'hɑstḷ 〕 n. 青年旅館
The students decided to stay in *hostels* during the trip in order to save money.

* **hostess**[2] 〔'hostɪs 〕 n. 女主人

‡ **hot**[1] 〔 hɑt 〕 adj. 熱的 (= *heated*)；辣的；熱情的；最新的；活躍的

‡ **hotel**[2] 〔 ho'tɛl 〕 n. 旅館；飯店
He stayed in a *hotel* while he was in Spain.

‡ **hour**[1] 〔 aʊr 〕 n. 小時
【注意】複數型 hours 有時作「時間」解。

* **hourly**[3] 〔'aʊrlɪ 〕 adj. 每隔一小時的

‡ **house**[1] 〔 haʊs 〕 n. 房子

* **household**[4] 〔'haʊs,hold 〕 adj. 家庭的
(= *domestic*) n. 一家人；家庭
Jack never helps his mother with the *household* chores.
【片語】 *household chores* (家事)

* **housekeeper**[3] 〔'haʊs,kipɚ 〕 n.
女管家；家庭主婦 (= *housewife*)

‡ **housewife**[4] 〔'haʊs,waɪf 〕 n. 家庭主婦
(= *housekeeper* = *homemaker*)
My mother is a *housewife*.

‡ **housework**[4] 〔'haʊs,wɝk 〕 n. 家事
(= *household chores*)
My brother and I shared the *housework*.
【比較】 homework (家庭作業)

‡ **however**[2] 〔 haʊ'ɛvɚ 〕 adv. 然而
This, *however*, is not your fault.

* **hug**[3] 〔 hʌg 〕 v. n. 擁抱 (= *embrace*)
Nancy *hugged* her daughter goodbye when she dropped her off at kindergarten.

* **huge**[1] 〔 hjudʒ 〕 adj. 巨大的
(= *enormous*)
There is a *huge* rock on the road.

* **hum**[2] 〔 hʌm 〕 v. 哼唱；嗡嗡作響
(= *buzz*) n. 蜜蜂嗡嗡聲
As he couldn't remember the words, Dave just *hummed* the song.

** **human**[1] 〔'hjumən 〕 n. 人
(= *human being*) adj. 人 (類) 的
Wolves won't usually attack *humans*.
【常考】 *human beings* (人類)

* **humanity**[4] 〔 hju'mænətɪ 〕 n. 人類
(= *mankind*)；人性
(= *human nature*)
【記憶技巧】 *-ity* (抽象名詞字尾)

** **humble**[2] 〔'hʌmbḷ 〕 adj. 謙卑的
(= *modest*)；卑微的 (= *lowly*)
Many famous people are very *humble*.
【記憶技巧】 *hum* (ground) + *(a)ble*
(把自己的地位擺得比別人低，表示謙卑)
【反義詞】 arrogant (傲慢的；自大的)

┌─【典型考題】─────────
│ Jack is a _____ person. He never
│ talks about his background or boasts
│ about his wealth.
│ A. generous   B. compassionate
│ C. humble   D. reasonable   [C]
└──────────────────────

‡**humid**[2] 〔'hjumɪd 〕*adj.* 潮溼的
（ = *damp* = *wet* = *moist* ）
It will be *humid* tomorrow.

* **humidity**[4] 〔 hju'mɪdətɪ 〕*n.* 濕氣；
濕度（ = *dampness* ）

‡**humor**[2] 〔'hjumɚ 〕*n.* 幽默
（ = *humour*【英式用法】）
I don't see the *humor* of it.

‡**humorous**[3] 〔'hjumərəs 〕*adj.* 幽默的
（ = *funny* ）

‡**hundred**[1] 〔'hʌndrəd 〕*n.* 百

‡**hunger**[2] 〔'hʌŋgɚ 〕*n.* 飢餓
（ = *starvation* ）；渴望（ = *desire* ）
He died of *hunger*.

‡**hungry**[1] 〔'hʌŋgrɪ 〕*adj.* 飢餓的
（ = *starving* ）；渴望的（ = *eager* ）

‡**hunt**[2] 〔 hʌnt 〕*v.* 打獵；獵捕
n. 尋找（ = *search* ）
The hunters are *hunting* rabbits.

‡**hunter**[2] 〔'hʌntɚ 〕*n.* 獵人

* **hurricane**[4] 〔'hɝɪˏken 〕*n.* 颶風；
暴風雨
Every year *hurricanes* cause
thousands of dollars worth of
damage to property.

【注意】在太平洋地區形成的稱為 typhoon；
在大西洋地區形成的稱做 hurricane。

‡**hurry**[2] 〔'hɝɪ 〕*v.* 趕快（ = *rush* ）；催促
Hurry up, or you'll be late.
【片語】*hurry up*（趕快）

‡**hurt**[1] 〔 hɝt 〕*v.* 傷害（ = *injure* ）；
使痛苦；疼痛 *n.* 傷；損害；苦痛
My back was *hurt* in the accident.

‡**husband**[1] 〔'hʌzbənd 〕*n.* 丈夫
Her *husband* has been working in
France.

* **hush**[3] 〔 hʌʃ 〕*v.* 使安靜（ = *make
silent* ）；（叫人保持安靜）噓
The principal's words *hushed* the
students.
【衍伸詞】*hush money*（遮羞費；封口錢）

【重要知識】老一輩的美國人叫別人安靜時，手指
著嘴巴說 hush，現在人會說 shh…。

* **hut**[3] 〔 hʌt 〕*n.* 小木屋（ = *cabin* ）
There are several *huts* on the
mountain where hikers can spend
the night.

* **hydrogen**[4] 〔'haɪdrədʒən 〕*n.* 氫
【記憶技巧】*hydro*（water）+ *gen*
（produce）（水由氫和氧兩種元素組成）
【比較】<u>hydro</u>electric（水力發電的）

I i

‡**ice**[1] 〔 aɪs 〕*n.* 冰
Nancy put some *ice* in the drink.

* **iceberg**[4] 〔'aɪsˏbɝg 〕*n.* 冰山
【比較】glacier（冰河）

* **icy**[3] 〔'aɪsɪ 〕*adj.* 結冰的；冷漠的
（ = *indifferent* ）

‡**idea**[1] 〔 aɪ'diə 〕*n.* 想法（ = *opinion* ）；
主意（ = *plan* ）

H

*　**ideal**[3]〔aɪ'diəl〕*adj.* 理想的
（＝*highly satisfactory*）；完美的
n. 理想

The winter vacation is an *ideal* time
to go abroad because we have several
days off.

*　**identical**[4]〔aɪ'dɛntɪkl̩〕*adj.* 完全相
同的（＝*the same*）

After he broke his mother's vase,
Walter bought an *identical* one for
her.

┌─【典型考題】──────
│ The study of the characteristics of
│ these two plants shows that they are
│ _____ only in appearance.
│ A. identical　　B. superficial
│ C. potential　　D. eventual　　[A]
└──────────────

*　**identification**[4]〔aɪ,dɛntəfə'keʃən〕
n. 確認身分；身分證明（文件）

*　**identify**[4]〔aɪ'dɛntə,faɪ〕*v.* 辨認
（＝*recognize*）；指認；認同

The teacher can easily *identify* the
students if they are in uniform.

【記憶技巧】*identi*（the same）＋*fy*（*v.*）
（發現是一樣的，也就是「確認」）

┌─【典型考題】──────
│ People in this community tend to _____
│ with the group they belong to, and often
│ put group interests before personal ones.
│ A. appoint　　　B. eliminate
│ C. occupy　　　D. identify　　[D]
└──────────────

*　**identity**[3]〔aɪ'dɛntətɪ〕*n.* 身分；
身分證件

【衍伸詞】*identity card*（身分證）

*　**idiom**[4]〔'ɪdɪəm〕*n.* 成語（＝*phrase*）；
慣用語

*　**idle**[4]〔'aɪdl̩〕*adj.* 遊手好閒的
（＝*unemployed*）；懶惰的（＝*lazy*）

You should do something useful
instead of sitting here *idle* all day.

*　**idol**[4]〔'aɪdl̩〕*n.* 偶像

Teens will often go to great lengths
to get a glimpse of their *idols*.

【記憶技巧】id**o**l 是受崇敬的事物
（**o**bject）。

***　**if**[1]〔ɪf〕*conj.* 如果

*　**ignorance**[3]〔'ɪgnərəns〕*n.* 無知
Ignorance is bliss.

*　**ignorant**[4]〔'ɪgnərənt〕*adj.* 無知的
（＝*unaware*）

**　**ignore**[2]〔ɪg'nor〕*v.* 忽視
（＝*neglect*）

He *ignored* the traffic light and
caused an accident.

【記憶技巧】*i*（not）＋*gnore*（know）
（裝作不知道，就是「忽視」）

┌─【典型考題】──────
│ Mr. Chang never _____ any questions
│ from his students even if they sound
│ stupid.
│ A. reforms　　　B. depresses
│ C. ignores　　　D. confirms　　[C]
└──────────────

**　**ill**[2]〔ɪl〕*adj.* 生病的（＝*sick*）；壞的
n. 罪惡；*pl.* 不幸　*adv.* 惡意地

* **illustrate**[4] 〔'ɪləstret 〕 *v.* 圖解說明；
說明 (= *explain*)；畫插圖
【記憶技巧】 *il* (in) + *lustr* (bright)
+ *ate* (*v.*) (使變亮，就是用圖解說明，
使讀者一目了然)

* **illustration**[4] 〔,ɪləs'treʃən 〕 *n.* 插圖
(= *picture*)；實例 (= *example*)
Books with *illustrations* often give
the readers better ideas than those
without them.

【典型考題】
David's new book made it to the
best-seller list because of its beautiful
_____ and amusing stories.
A. operations   B. illustrations
C. engagements   D. accomplishments
           [B]

* **image**[3] 〔'ɪmɪdʒ 〕 *n.* 形象 (= *idea*)；
圖像 (= *picture*)
His behavior ruined his public *image*.

【典型考題】
The _____ I have of the principal
is that of a very kind and gentle
person.
A. aspect   B. effect
C. image   D. message   [C]

* **imaginable**[4] 〔 ɪ'mædʒɪnəbḷ 〕
adj. 想像得到的

* **imaginary**[4] 〔 ɪ'mædʒə,nɛrɪ 〕
adj. 虛構的 (= *made-up*)；想像的
【記憶技巧】 *-ary* 表「與…有關」的字尾。

* **imagination**[3] 〔 ɪ,mædʒə'neʃən 〕
n. 想像力 (= *creativity*)

* **imaginative**[4] 〔 ɪ'mædʒə,netɪv 〕
adj. 有想像力的 (= *creative*)

【典型考題】
This writer is very _____. His
original ideas are widely admired.
A. imaginative   B. representative
C. cooperative   D. persuasive   [A]

* **imagine**[2] 〔 ɪ'mædʒɪn 〕 *v.* 想像
You can *imagine* how nice the new
car is.

【典型考題】
There is serious pollution here. I
cannot _____ that there were fish
in the water before.
A. imagine   B. examine
C. link   D. criticize   [A]

* **imitate**[4] 〔'ɪmə,tet 〕 *v.* 模仿 (= *copy*)
My younger son likes to *imitate* his
older brother.

* **imitation**[4] 〔,ɪmə'teʃən 〕 *n.* 模仿
(= *copy*)；仿製品

* **immediate**[3] 〔 ɪ'midɪɪt 〕 *adj.* 立即的
(= *instant*)
The general has ordered an
immediate stop to the fighting.
【記憶技巧】 *im* (not) + *medi* (middle)
+ *ate* (*adj.*) (事情立刻做完，不中斷)

* **immigrant**[4] 〔'ɪməgrənt 〕 *n.* (從外
國來的)移民 (= *settler*)
As a recent *immigrant*, Jean still has
a lot to learn about her new home.

* **immigrate**[4] 〔'ɪmə,gret 〕 *v.* 移入
【記憶技巧】 *im* (into) + *migr* (move)
+ *ate* (*v.*) (把東西搬進去，就是「移入」)

I

* **immigration**[4] 〔 ˌɪmə'greʃən 〕
   n. 移入；出入境管理

* **impact**[4] 〔'ɪmpækt 〕 n. 影響
   (= effect)；衝擊；撞擊力
   〔 ɪm'pækt 〕 v. 影響；對…有衝擊
   The driver hit a fence and the *impact*
   crushed the front of his car.

* **imply**[4] 〔 ɪm'plaɪ 〕 v. 暗示
   (= suggest)；意味著 (= mean)
   Are you *implying* that I am not
   telling the truth?
   【記憶技巧】 *im* (in) + *ply* (fold)
      (話中有話，也就是「暗示」)

> 【典型考題】
> Sue didn't come right out and say that
> John was fired, but she _____ it.
> A. explained   B. announced
> C. quoted   D. implied   [D]

* **import**[3] 〔 ɪm'port 〕 v. 進口 (= bring
   in)   〔'ɪmport 〕 n. 進口
   Europe *imports* coal from America.
   【反義詞】 export (出口)

‡ **importance**[2] 〔 ɪm'pɔrtn̩s 〕 n. 重要性
   (= significance)
   The *importance* of using your time
   well is quite clear.

‡ **important**[1] 〔 ɪm'pɔrtn̩t 〕 adj. 重要的
   (= significant)

* **impress**[3] 〔 ɪm'prɛs 〕 v. 使印象深刻
   We were greatly *impressed* by
   his speech.
   【記憶技巧】 *im* (in) + *press* (壓)
      (壓進腦海裡，表示「使印象深刻」)

* **impression**[4] 〔 ɪm'prɛʃən 〕 n. 印象
   (= idea)

* **impressive**[3] 〔 ɪm'prɛsɪv 〕 adj. 令人
   印象深刻的 (= striking)；令人感動
   的；令人欽佩的

> 【典型考題】
> The professor's speech on environmental
> protection was really _____.
> A. impressive   B. insecure
> C. indeed   D. image   [A]

* **improve**[2] 〔 ɪm'pruv 〕 v. 改善
   To make something better is to
   improve it.
   【記憶技巧】 *im* (表「引起」的字首) +
      prove (profit) (「改善」會帶來好處)

* **improvement**[2] 〔 ɪm'pruvmənt 〕
   n. 改善

‡ **inch**[1] 〔 ɪntʃ 〕 n. 英吋
   (= 2.54 centimeters)
   She is three *inches* taller than me.

* **incident**[4] 〔'ɪnsədənt 〕 n. 事件
   (= event)
   There were 17 reported *incidents* of
   high radiation exposure at nuclear
   plants between 1957 and 1988.
   【比較】 accident (意外)

‡ **include**[2] 〔 ɪn'klud 〕 v. 包括
   (= contain)
   The price *includes* the service
   charge.
   【記憶技巧】 *in* (in) + *clude* (shut)
      (把東西關在裡面，就是「包括」)
   【反義詞】 exclude (排除)

*__including__ [4] 〔 ɪnˈkludɪŋ 〕 *prep.* 包括
Everyone had a lot of fun, *including* my father.

*__income__ [2] 〔ˈɪnˌkʌm 〕 *n.* 收入
She has an *income* of 2,000 dollars a week.

*__increase__ [2] 〔 ɪnˈkris 〕 *v.* 增加 (= *rise*)
〔 ˈɪnkris 〕 *n.* 增加
My weight has *increased* by ten pounds.

> 【典型考題】
> New schools have to be set up because the number of students is _____.
> A. increasing   B. clapping
> C. condemning   D. expressing   [A]

*__indeed__ [3] 〔 ɪnˈdid 〕 *adv.* 的確
(= *certainly*)；真正地 (= *really*)
A friend in need is a friend *indeed*.
【記憶技巧】 *in* + *deed* (行為)

*__independence__ [2] 〔ˌɪndɪˈpɛndəns 〕
n. 獨立 (= *self-reliance*)

*__independent__ [2] 〔ˌɪndɪˈpɛndənt 〕 *adj.*
獨立的 (= *self-reliant*)
He is *independent* of his parents.
【片語】 *be independent of* (不依賴)

*__indicate__ [2] 〔ˈɪndəˌket 〕 *v.* 指出；
顯示 (= *show*)
The flashing light *indicates* that there is some road construction ahead.
【記憶技巧】 *in* (towards) + *dic* (proclaim 宣稱) + *ate* (*v.*)

*__indication__ [4] 〔ˌɪndəˈkeʃən 〕 *n.* 跡象
(= *sign*)；指標

> 【典型考題】
> There are many _____ that the economy will recover from the recession.
> A. indications   B. organizations
> C. contributions   D. traditions   [A]

*__individual__ [3] 〔ˌɪndəˈvɪdʒʊəl 〕 *n.* 個人
(= *person*)   *adj.* 個別的
(= *separate*)
We use *individual* textbooks.
【記憶技巧】 *in* (not) + *divid* (divide) + *ual* (*adj.*) (不能再分割，表示已經是獨立的個體)

> 【典型考題】
> In team sports, how all members work as a group is more important than how they perform _____.
> A. frequently   B. typically
> C. individually   D. completely   [C]

*__indoor__ [3] 〔ˈɪnˌdor 〕 *adj.* 室內的
The club has both an *indoor* and an outdoor swimming pool.

*__indoors__ [3] 〔ˈɪnˈdorz 〕 *adv.* 在室內

*__industrial__ [3] 〔 ɪnˈdʌstrɪəl 〕 *adj.*
工業的
This is an *industrial* area; most people work in factories.
【記憶技巧】 industrial 字尾像工廠的煙囪，不要和 industrious (勤勉的) 搞混。

*__industrialize__ [4] 〔 ɪnˈdʌstrɪəlˌaɪz 〕 *v.*
使工業化

I

* **industry**[2] 〔'ɪndəstrɪ〕 n. 產業；
工業（= *production*）；勤勉
（= *diligence*）

【注意】industry 這個字有兩種形容詞的變
化：① industrious 勤勉的　② industrial
工業的

* **infant**[4] 〔'ɪnfənt〕 n. 嬰兒（= *baby*）；
幼兒　 adj. 初期的
A young couple with an *infant* have
moved in upstairs.

【記憶技巧】*in* (not) + *fant* (speak)
（「嬰兒」還不太會説話）

* **infect**[4] 〔ɪn'fɛkt〕 v. 感染；傳染
Cover your mouth when you cough
or you may *infect* other people.

【記憶技巧】*in* (in) + *fect* (make)
（使病菌進入體內，就是「傳染」）

* **infection**[4] 〔ɪn'fɛkʃən〕 n. 感染

* **inferior**[3] 〔ɪn'fɪrɪɚ〕 adj. 較差的
（= *worse*）
Although this television is more
expensive, it is *inferior* to that one.

【反義詞】 superior（較優秀的）

* **inflation**[4] 〔ɪn'fleʃən〕 n. 通貨膨脹
（= *rising prices*）；膨脹（= *swelling*）
With the high rate of *inflation*, people
are worried that they may not be able
to afford the necessities of life.

【記憶技巧】*in* (into) + *flat* (blow) +
ion (n.)（價格上升像對氣球吹氣一樣）

* **influence**[2] 〔'ɪnfluəns〕 n. 影響
（= *impact*）

Television has had a great *influence*
on young people.

【常考】*have an influence on*（對…有
影響）

* **influential**[4] 〔,ɪnflu'ɛnʃəl〕 adj. 有影
響力的

* **inform**[3] 〔ɪn'fɔrm〕 v. 通知
（= *notify*）
We should *inform* the committee of
the change of plans.

【片語】*inform* sb. *of* sth.（通知某人某事）
【記憶技巧】*in* (into) + *form* (form)
（事先的「通知」就是讓人心中有個底）

* **information**[4] 〔,ɪnfɚ'meʃən〕 n.
資訊（= *news*）；情報；消息

* **informative**[4] 〔ɪn'fɔrmətɪv〕
adj. 知識性的（= *instructive*）

【衍伸詞】*informative program*（知識
性的節目）

* **ingredient**[4] 〔ɪn'gridɪənt〕 n. 原料
（= *component*）；材料；要素
（= *factor*）
The main *ingredient* of this dish is
chicken.

【記憶技巧】*in* (in) + *gredi* (walk) +
ent (n.)（製作產品時加入的東西）

* **initial**[4] 〔ɪ'nɪʃəl〕 adj. 最初的
（= *beginning*）　 n.（字的）起首字母
The *initial* response to the proposal
surprised the government officials.

***injure**[3] 〔'ɪndʒɚ 〕*v.* 傷害 (= *harm*)

Don't hold the knife like that or you may *injure* yourself.

【記憶技巧】*in* (not) + *jure* (right)
　（「傷害」別人是不正當的行為）

injury[3] 〔'ɪndʒərɪ 〕*n.* 傷 (= *wound*)；
受傷 (= *harm*)

****ink**[2] 〔 ɪŋk 〕*n.* 墨水

My pen is running out of *ink*.

***inn**[3] 〔 ɪn 〕*n.* 小旅館 (= *hostel*)；
小酒館 (= *bar*)

We stayed at a small *inn* just outside the town.

***inner**[3] 〔'ɪnɚ 〕*adj.* 內部的
　(= *internal*)

Upon hearing that a tornado had been sighted, they moved to an *inner* room of the house.

【反義詞】 outer (外部的)

***innocence**[4] 〔'ɪnəsn̩s 〕*n.* 清白
　(= *guiltlessness*)；天真
　(= *ingenuousness*)

Convinced of the boy's *innocence*, the police let him go.

***innocent**[3] 〔'ɪnəsn̩t 〕*adj.* 清白的；
天真的

【記憶技巧】*in* (not) + *noc* (harm) +
　ent (*adj.*) (沒有傷害別人，表示這個人
　是「清白的」)

【反義詞】 guilty (有罪的)

***input**[4] 〔'ɪnˌpʊt 〕*n.* 輸入；投入；
輸入的資訊

We mustn't forget the sales department's *input*.

【反義詞】 output (輸出；產品)

****insect**[2] 〔'ɪnsɛkt 〕*n.* 昆蟲

A mosquito is an *insect*.

【記憶技巧】*in* (into) + *sect* (cut) (「昆
蟲」的身體看起來像是一節一節的)

***insert**[4] 〔 ɪn'sɝt 〕*v.* 插入 (= *put in*)

Mindy *inserted* the phone card and made a call.

【記憶技巧】*in* (into) + *sert* (join)
　（ 加在裡面，就是「插入」)

****inside**[1] 〔 ɪn'saɪd 〕*prep.* 在…裡面

No one is *inside* the school.

***insist**[2] 〔 ɪn'sɪst 〕*v.* 堅持 (= *persist*)；
堅持認為 (= *claim*)

I *insist* that he stay at home.

【記憶技巧】*in* (on) + *sist* (stand) (一直
　站在自己的立場，就是「堅持」自己的
　想法)

┌─【典型考題】──────
│ I didn't want to mow the lawn but my
│ brother ＿＿＿ that it was my turn.
│ A. offered　　　 B. allowed
│ C. conceded　　 D. insisted　　 **[D]**
└──────────────

***inspect**[3] 〔 ɪn'spɛkt 〕*v.* 檢查
　(= *examine*)

The factory employs someone to *inspect* the finished products for flaws.

【記憶技巧】*in* (into) + *spect* (look)
　（ 窺視內部，進行「檢查」)

***inspection**[4] 〔 ɪn'spɛkʃən 〕*n.* 檢查
　(= *examination*)；審查 (= *review*)

***inspector**[3] 〔 ɪn'spɛktə 〕 *n.* 檢查員
(= *examiner*)

***inspiration**[4] 〔 ˌɪnspə'reʃən 〕
n. 靈感；鼓舞 (= *motivation*)
The writer declared that his experiences during the war were the *inspiration* for his work.
【記憶技巧】*in* (into) + *spir* (breathe) + *ation* (*n.*) (多吸一點氧氣可讓腦袋保持清晰，有助於產生「靈感」)

┌─【典型考題】─────
│ To poets, the beautiful scenery of Sun Moon Lake is a great source of _____.
│
│ A. contribution　B. illusion
│ C. inspiration　D. distribution　[C]
└────────────

***inspire**[4] 〔 ɪn'spaɪr 〕 *v.* 激勵
(= *encourage*)；給予靈感

┌─【典型考題】─────
│ The story of his success _____ us to make more effort.
│ A. socialized　　B. demonstrated
│ C. inspired　　D. punished　[C]
└────────────

***install**[4] 〔 ɪn'stɔl 〕 *v.* 安裝
(= *set up for use*)；安置 (= *settle*)
We will have to *install* a new air conditioner.

***instance**[2] 〔 'ɪnstəns 〕 *n.* 實例
(= *example*)
I visited several countries, for *instance*, Japan, France, and Spain.
【片語】*for instance* (例如)

***instant**[2] 〔 'ɪnstənt 〕 *adj.* 立即的
n. 瞬間
The book was an *instant* best-seller, and the author became famous overnight.
【衍伸詞】*instant noodles* (速食麵)

***instead**[3] 〔 ɪn'stɛd 〕 *adv.* 作為代替
There was no Coke, so I had orange juice *instead*.
【衍伸詞】*instead of* (而不是)

***instinct**[4] 〔 'ɪnstɪŋkt 〕
n. 本能 (= *natural tendency*)；直覺 (= *intuition*)
Birds fly south in winter by *instinct*.
【記憶技巧】*in* (on) + *stinct* (prick)
(被刺激，才能發揮出「本能」)

instruct[4] 〔 ɪn'strʌkt 〕 *v.* 教導
(= *teach*)
My brother has promised to *instruct* me in how to use the machine.
【記憶技巧】*in* (in) + *struct* (build)
(透過「教導」，把所學的內容建構在心中)
【比較】con<u>struct</u> (建造)
　　　ob<u>struct</u> (阻礙)

instruction[3] 〔 ɪn'strʌkʃən 〕 *n.* 教導
(= *teaching*)　*pl.* 使用說明
(= *directions*)

***instructor**[4] 〔 ɪn'strʌktə 〕 *n.* 講師
(= *teacher*)

***instrument**[2] 〔 'ɪnstrəmənt 〕
n. 儀器；樂器
Pianos and violins are musical *instruments*.

***insult**[4]〔ɪnˈsʌlt〕v. 侮辱
〔ˈɪnsʌlt〕n. 侮辱
Ever since John *insulted* her, the teacher has had it in for him.
【記憶技巧】*in* (on) + *sult* (leap)
（跳到別人的身上，表示「侮辱」）
【比較】re<u>sult</u>（結果）
con<u>sult</u>（請教；查閱）

***insurance**[4]〔ɪnˈʃʊrəns〕n. 保險
（= *coverage*）
After the house burned down, we were very happy that we had fire *insurance*.

***intellectual**[4]〔ˌɪntḷˈɛktʃʊəl〕
adj. 智力的（= *mental*）；理解力的
n. 知識份子
Nutrition is important for children's *intellectual* development.

***intelligence**[4]〔ɪnˈtɛlədʒəns〕
n. 聰明才智（= *cleverness*）；情報
（= *information*）
The students were given an *intelligence* test.
【記憶技巧】*intel* (between) + *ligence* (read)（read between the lines 有智慧的人，才能讀出字裡行間的意思）

*intelligent**[4]〔ɪnˈtɛlədʒənt〕
adj. 聰明的（= *smart* = *clever*）

***intend**[4]〔ɪnˈtɛnd〕v. 打算（= *plan*）；意圖；打算作為…之用 <*for*>
I had *intended* to stay there for a week, but due to an accident, I stayed there more than a month.
【記憶技巧】*in* (towards) + *tend* (stretch)（把手伸過去，就是「打算」做某事）

***intense**[4]〔ɪnˈtɛns〕*adj.* 強烈的
（= *fierce*）
The *intense* heat made everyone feel tired and irritable.
【衍伸詞】*intense heat*（酷暑）

***intensify**[4]〔ɪnˈtɛnsəˌfaɪ〕v. 加強
（= *strengthen*）
┌【典型考題】
The weather bureau issued a warning when the storm began to _____.
A. notify B. intensify
C. personify D. signify [B]
└

***intensity**[4]〔ɪnˈtɛnsətɪ〕n. 強度
（= *force*）

***intensive**[4]〔ɪnˈtɛnsɪv〕*adj.* 密集的
（= *concentrated*）
The sales force received *intensive* training over the weekend.

***intention**[4]〔ɪnˈtɛnʃən〕n. 意圖
（= *plan*）
┌【典型考題】
The driver signaled his _____ to turn right at the corner.
A. passion B. intention
C. destination D. affection [B]
└

***interact**[4]〔ˌɪntɚˈækt〕v. 互動；相互作用
These two chemicals will *interact* and produce a gas with a terrible smell.
【記憶技巧】*inter* (between) + *act*（行動）
┌【典型考題】
John should _____ more often with his friends and family after work, instead of staying in his room to play computer games.
A. explore B. interact
C. negotiate D. participate [B]
└

I

*__interaction__[4]〔͵ɪntɚˋækʃən〕 *n.* 相互作用

‡__interest__[1]〔ˋɪntrɪst〕 *v.* 使感興趣
（＝ *fascinate* ）
n. 興趣；利息；利益
The story didn't *interest* me.
【片語】*be interested in* （對…感興趣）

*__interfere__[4]〔͵ɪntɚˋfɪr〕 *v.* 干涉
（＝ *meddle* ）；妨礙
I tried to help my friends resolve
their argument, but they told me not
to *interfere*.
【記憶技巧】*inter* (between) ＋ *fere*
(strike) （從中間打擊，表示「干涉」）

*__intermediate__[4]〔͵ɪntɚˋmidɪɪt〕
adj. 中級的 （＝ *average* ）
Daniel's English has improved to
an *intermediate* level.
【記憶技巧】*inter* (between) ＋ *mediate*
(middle) （在中間，就是「中級的」）

*__internal__[3]〔ɪnˋtɝnl̩〕 *adj.* 內部的
（＝ *inner* ）
The wage dispute is an *internal*
problem at the factory.
【反義詞】external （外部的）

‡__international__[2]〔͵ɪntɚˋnæʃənl̩〕
adj. 國際的
English has become a very
important *international* language.

‡__Internet__[4]〔ˋɪntɚ͵nɛt〕 *n.* 網際網路
（＝ *the Net* ＝ *the Web* ）

If you have a computer, you can use
the *Internet* to find information.

*__interpret__[4]〔ɪnˋtɝprɪt〕 *v.* 解釋
（＝ *explain* ）；口譯
（＝ *translate orally* ）
How do you *interpret* this dream?
【記憶技巧】*inter* (between) ＋
pret (price) （在兩者間確定價值）

【典型考題】
This poem may be ＿＿＿＿ in several
different ways and each of them
makes sense.
A. negotiated　　B. designated
C. interpreted　　D. substituted　　[C]

‡__interrupt__[3]〔͵ɪntɚˋrʌpt〕 *v.* 打斷
（＝ *disrupt* ）
I don't want to be *interrupted*.
【記憶技巧】*inter* (between) ＋ *rupt*
(break) （從中間破壞，就是「打斷」）

【典型考題】
A polite person never ＿＿＿＿ others
while they are discussing important
matters.
A. initiates　　B. instills
C. inhabits　　D. interrupts　　[D]

*__interruption__[4]〔͵ɪntɚˋrʌpʃən〕
n. 打斷 （＝ *disruption*〔dɪsˋrʌpʃən〕）

‡__interview__[2]〔ˋɪntɚ͵vju〕 *n.* 面試
Jim is going to ABC Company for
a job *interview*.
【記憶技巧】*inter* (between) ＋ *view*
(看) （「面試」的時候要互相看）

*__intimate__[4] 〔ˈɪntəmɪt〕 *adj.* 親密的
(= *close*)

Robert counts Mike among his
intimate friends.

【典型考題】
An open display of ____ behavior
between men and women, such as
hugging and kissing, is not allowed in
some conservative societies.
A. intimate   B. ashamed
C. earnest   D. urgent   [A]

***__into__[1] 〔ˈɪntu〕 *prep.* 到⋯之內

*__intonation__[4] 〔ˌɪntoˈneʃən〕 *n.* 語調

If one wants to speak English
without a foreign accent, one has
to learn correct *intonation*.

【記憶技巧】 *in* (into) + *ton* (tone)
+ *ation* (*n.*) (說話要融入腔調，才會有
「語調」產生)

【典型考題】
Even though they both speak Chinese,
their ____ is totally different.
A. intuition
B. institution
C. indication
D. intonation   [D]

*__introduce__[2] 〔ˌɪntrəˈdjus〕 *v.* 介紹；
引進

The teacher *introduced* Ted to the
class.

【記憶技巧】 *intro* (inward) + *duce*
(lead) (「介紹」別人的時候，通常會把
他帶領到人群中讓大家看清楚)

【典型考題】
It is the host's duty to ____ strangers
to each other at a party.
A. introduce   B. inform
C. immigrate   D. inspire   [A]

*__introduction__[3] 〔ˌɪntrəˈdʌkʃən〕
n. 介紹 (= *presentation*)；引進；
入門；序言

*__invade__[4] 〔ɪnˈved〕 *v.* 入侵

Ants *invaded* our kitchen so we
called an exterminator.

【記憶技巧】 *in* (into) + *vade* (go)
(走進別人的地盤，表示「入侵」)
【比較】 e<u>vade</u> (逃避；閃避)
per<u>vade</u> (遍布；瀰漫)

【典型考題】
The Normans ____ England in
1066.
A. interpreted   B. invaded
C. interfered   D. invested   [B]

*__invasion__[4] 〔ɪnˈveʒən〕 *n.* 侵略；
侵害

*__invent__[2] 〔ɪnˈvɛnt〕 *v.* 發明
(= *create*)

He *invented* the first electric clock.

【記憶技巧】 *in* (upon) + *vent* (come)
(「發明」東西，就是靈感突然跑來腦中)

*__invention__[4] 〔ɪnˈvɛnʃən〕 *n.* 發明
(= *creation*)

*__inventor__[3] 〔ɪnˈvɛntɚ〕 *n.* 發明者
(= *creator*)

I

*__invest__[4]〔ɪn'vɛst〕*v.* 投資（= *put in*）

Harvey spends only a portion of his income and *invests* the rest.

【記憶技巧】*in* (in) + *vest* (clothe)

（錢先放入別人的口袋，就是「投資」）

【片語】*invest in*（投資）

┌─【典型考題】─────

Our country has become hi-tech by ──── heavily in the electronics industry.
A. inspiring   B. invading
C. investing   D. inventing   [C]

└─────────────

*__investigate__[3]〔ɪn'vɛstə,get〕*v.* 調查（= *examine*）

We are *investigating* the cause of the accident.

【記憶技巧】*in* (in) + *vestig* (trace) + *ate*（往內追蹤，就是「調查」）

*__investigation__[4]〔ɪn,vɛstə'geʃən〕*n.* 調查（= *examination*）

*__investment__[4]〔ɪn'vɛstmənt〕*n.* 投資（= *investing*）；投入資本；投資項目

‡__invitation__[2]〔,ɪnvə'teʃən〕*n.* 邀請

‡__invite__[2]〔ɪn'vaɪt〕*v.* 邀請

I *invited* her to dinner.

*__involve__[4]〔ɪn'vɑlv〕*v.* 使牽涉 < *in* >（= *concern*）；包含；需要

Only Angie was not *involved* in the cheating, and only she will not be punished.

【記憶技巧】*in* (in) + *volve* (roll)

（捲入其中，也就是「牽涉」）

*__involvement__[4]〔ɪn'vɑlvmənt〕*n.* 牽涉（= *association*）；興趣；戀愛關係

‡__iron__[1]〔'aɪən〕*n.* 鐵；熨斗　*v.* 熨燙

This gun is made of *iron*.

‡__island__[2]〔'aɪlənd〕*n.* 島（= *isle*）

An *island* is a piece of land with water all around it.

【記憶技巧】*is* (是) + *land* (土地)

（「島」就是一塊地）

*__isolate__[4]〔'aɪsḷ,et〕*v.* 使隔離（= *insulate*〔'ɪnsə,let〕）

SARS patients must be *isolated* from others in the hospital.

【記憶技巧】*isol* (island) + *ate* (*v.*)

（病人像小島一樣被孤立，表示遭到隔離）

┌─【典型考題】─────

Doctors decided to ──── the patient until the nature of his illness could be determined.
A. alienate   B. violate
C. isolate   D. operate   [C]

└─────────────

*__isolation__[4]〔,aɪsḷ'eʃən〕*n.* 隔離（= *separation*）；分離；孤獨

*__itch__[4]〔ɪtʃ〕*v. n.* 癢（= *tickle*）；使發癢；渴望

Shortly after he touched the plant, Bart's hand began to *itch*.

*__item__[2]〔'aɪtəm〕*n.* 項目

We have many *items* to discuss today.

*__ivory__[3]〔'aɪvərɪ〕*n.* 象牙（= *tusk*）；象牙製品　*adj.* 象牙白的；乳白色的

【衍伸詞】*ivory tower*（象牙塔）

J j

‡jacket[2] 〔'dʒækɪt 〕 *n.* 夾克 (= *coat*)
The waiter in the white *jacket* is very polite.

*jail[3] 〔 dʒel 〕 *n.* 監獄 (= *prison*)
The suspect was kept in *jail* until his trial.

‡jam[1,2] 〔 dʒæm 〕 *n.* 果醬；阻塞
(= *congestion*)
Cathy loves toast with strawberry *jam*.
I got caught in a traffic *jam*.
【注意】jam 作「阻塞」解時，是可數名詞。

‡January[1] 〔'dʒænjʊ,ɛrɪ 〕 *n.* 一月

*jar[3] 〔 dʒɑr 〕 *n.* 廣口瓶；一罐的量
There is a *jar* of peanut butter on the shelf.

*jaw[3] 〔 dʒɔ 〕 *n.* 顎
【比較】jaws (動物的) 嘴

‡jazz[2] 〔 dʒæz 〕 *n.* 爵士樂
We went to a *jazz* concert last night.

‡jealous[3] 〔'dʒɛləs 〕 *adj.* 嫉妒的
(= *envious*)
Mary is *jealous* of Helen's beauty.

*jealousy[4] 〔'dʒɛləsɪ 〕 *n.* 嫉妒
(= *envy*)

‡jeans[2] 〔 dʒinz 〕 *n. pl.* 牛仔褲
Most teenagers like to wear *jeans*.

*jeep[2] 〔 dʒip 〕 *n.* 吉普車
A *jeep* is good as a family car.

*jelly[3] 〔'dʒɛlɪ 〕 *n.* 果凍

*jet[3] 〔 dʒɛt 〕 *n.* 噴射機
【衍伸詞】*jet lag* (時差)

*jewel[3] 〔'dʒuəl 〕 *n.* 珠寶【可數名詞】
【記憶技巧】*Jew* (猶太人) + *el*
(猶太人很會賺錢，身上總有「珠寶」)

*jewelry[3] 〔'dʒuəlrɪ 〕 *n.* 珠寶【集合名詞】
(= *jewels*)

‡job[1] 〔 dʒɑb 〕 *n.* 工作 (= *work*)

‡jog[2] 〔 dʒɑg 〕 *v.* 慢跑
I like to *jog* in the morning.

‡join[1] 〔 dʒɔɪn 〕 *v.* 加入
Scott *joined* the army last year.

*joint[2] 〔 dʒɔɪnt 〕 *n.* 關節　*adj.* 聯合的
I have a pain in my knee *joint*.

‡joke[1] 〔 dʒok 〕 *n.* 笑話；玩笑
Mr. Black told a *joke* to his children.

*journal[3] 〔'dʒɝnl̩ 〕 *n.* 期刊；雜誌；報紙；日誌；日記
My research paper was published in a famous *journal*.

*journey[3] 〔'dʒɝnɪ 〕 *n.* 旅程
(= *travel*)

‡joy[1] 〔 dʒɔɪ 〕 *n.* 喜悅 (= *pleasure*)

J

*joyful³ 〔'dʒɔɪfəl 〕 *adj.* 愉快的
(= *pleasing*)
The class reunion was a *joyful* event.

‡judge² 〔 dʒʌdʒ 〕 *v.* 判斷   *n.* 法官
You can't *judge* a person by his appearance.

*judgment² 〔'dʒʌdʒmənt 〕 *n.* 判斷

┌─【典型考題】─────
In order to make no mistake, be sure to think twice before you make a(n)

_____.
A. sentiment   B. equipment
C. achievement D. judgment   [D]
└──────────────

‡juice¹ 〔 dʒus 〕 *n.* 果汁
I drink a glass of orange *juice* every morning.

*juicy² 〔'dʒusɪ 〕 *adj.* 多汁的

‡July¹ 〔 dʒu'laɪ 〕 *n.* 七月

‡jump¹ 〔 dʒʌmp 〕 *v.* 跳 (= *leap*)
That big dog *jumped* over the fence.

‡June¹ 〔 dʒun 〕 *n.* 六月
【衍伸詞】*June bride* (六月新娘)

*jungle³ 〔'dʒʌŋḷ 〕 *n.* 叢林
It's not a good idea to venture into the *jungle* alone because you might get lost.

*junior⁴ 〔'dʒunjɚ 〕 *adj.* 年少的
(= *young*)
【反義詞】senior (年長的)

*junk³ 〔 dʒʌŋk 〕 *n.* 垃圾 (= *rubbish*)；
無價值的東西
【衍伸詞】*junk food* (垃圾食品)

‡just¹ 〔 dʒʌst 〕 *adv.* 剛剛；僅
(= *merely* = *only*)   *adj.* 公正的

*justice³ 〔'dʒʌstɪs 〕 *n.* 正義
(= *justness*)；公正；公平
When people go to court they hope to find *justice*.

K k

‡kangaroo³ 〔ˌkæŋgə'ru 〕 *n.* 袋鼠
The *kangaroo* is a symbol of Australia.
【比較】koala (無尾熊)

*keen⁴ 〔 kin 〕 *adj.* 渴望的 (= *eager*)；
強烈的；敏銳的；鋒利的
Betty is thrilled that she got into a good university and she is *keen* to start her courses.

‡keep¹ 〔 kip 〕 *v.* 保存 (= *preserve*)；
保持；持續；飼養

keeper¹ 〔'kipɚ 〕 *n.* 管理員；(動物園的) 飼養員；看守人 (= *overseer*)

‡ketchup² 〔'kɛtʃəp 〕 *n.* 蕃茄醬
Please pass me the *ketchup*.

*kettle³ 〔'kɛtḷ 〕 *n.* 茶壺

key[1] 〔 ki 〕 *n.* 鑰匙　*adj.* 非常重要的
　(= *significant*)；關鍵性的
　He held a *key* position in the firm.

*****keyboard**[3] 〔'ki,bord 〕 *n.* 鍵盤
　Ken is typing on the computer
　keyboard.

*****kick**[1] 〔 kɪk 〕 *v.* 踢
　The children *kicked* the ball for fun.

kid[1] 〔 kɪd 〕 *n.* 小孩 (= *child*)
　v. 開玩笑
　They've got three *kids*.

*****kidney**[3] 〔'kɪdnɪ 〕 *n.* 腎臟

kill[1] 〔 kɪl 〕 *v.* 殺死 (= *murder*)；
　止 (痛)；打發 (時間)
　Lions *kill* small animals for food.

kilogram[3] 〔'kɪlə,græm 〕 *n.* 公斤
　We measure weight in *kilograms*.
　【記憶技巧】*kilo* (thousand) + *gram*
　(公克)(一千公克，也就是一「公斤」)

*****kilometer**[3] 〔 kə'lamətə 〕 *n.* 公里
　(= *km* = *kilometre*【英式用法】)
　Kaohsiung is about 400 *kilometers*
　away from Taipei.
　【重要知識】現在美國知識份子只有 16% 的人唸
　〔'kɪlə,mitə 〕，84% 的人都唸〔 kə'lamətə 〕。
　另外，常用 kilo 代替 kilogram (公斤)，而
　不用來代替 kilometer。

kind[1] 〔 kaɪnd 〕 *adj.* 親切的
　(= *friendly*)；仁慈的　*n.* 種類
　It's very *kind* of you.

*****kindergarten**[2] 〔'kɪndə,gartn̩ 〕 *n.*
幼稚園
　My younger sister is studying in the
　kindergarten.
　【記憶技巧】*kinder* (小孩) + *garten*
　(garden) (注意是 ten，不要背錯)

king[1] 〔 kɪŋ 〕 *n.* 國王
　They made him *King* of England.

*****kingdom**[2] 〔'kɪŋdəm 〕 *n.* 王國
　Holland is a *kingdom*.
　【記憶技巧】*king* (國王) + *dom*
　(domain 領域) (「王國」是國王的領域)

kiss[1] 〔 kɪs 〕 *v. n.* 親吻
　She *kissed* the baby on the face.

*****kit**[3] 〔 kɪt 〕 *n.* 一套用具；工具箱
　There are some bandages in the
　medicine *kit*.

kitchen[1] 〔'kɪtʃɪn 〕 *n.* 廚房
　(= *cookhouse*)

kite[1] 〔 kaɪt 〕 *n.* 風箏

kitten[1] 〔'kɪtn̩ 〕 *n.* 小貓

knee[1] 〔 ni 〕 *n.* 膝蓋
　Tony fell and hurt his *knees*.

*****kneel**[3] 〔 nil 〕 *v.* 跪下
　The minister asked the congregation
　to *kneel* and pray.
　【記憶技巧】*knee* (膝蓋) + *l*

knife[1] 〔 naɪf 〕 *n.* 刀子 (= *blade*)
　Michelle used a *knife* to cut the
　apple.

K

* **knight**[3] 〔 naɪt 〕 *n.* 騎士
  【記憶技巧】*k* + *night* (夜晚)
  (「騎士」常在夜晚出動)

* **knit**[3] 〔 nɪt 〕 *v.* 編織
  My grandmother *knit* this sweater
  for me.

* **knob**[3] 〔 nɑb 〕 *n.* 圓形把手
  (= *a round handle*)
  The *knob* doesn't turn; the door
  must be locked.

‡ **knock**[2] 〔 nɑk 〕 *v.* 敲 (= *strike*)
  The kid *knocked* on the door.

* **knot**[3] 〔 nɑt 〕 *n.* 結

The child could not untie the *knot*
in his shoelace.
  【記憶技巧】*k* + *not* (打不開的東西，
    就是「結」)
  【片語】*tie the knot* (結婚)

‡ **know**[1] 〔 no 〕 *v.* 知道

‡ **knowledge**[2] 〔'nɑlɪdʒ 〕 *n.* 知識
  Knowledge is power.

* **knuckle**[4] 〔'nʌkḷ 〕 *n.* 指關節
  (= *a finger joint*)
  Gail knocked on the door with her
  knuckles.

‡ **koala**[2] 〔 kə'alə 〕 *n.* 無尾熊

L l

* **lab**[4] 〔 læb 〕 *n.* 實驗室 (= *laboratory*)
  The students performed the
  experiment in the *lab*.

* **label**[3] 〔'lebḷ 〕 *n.* 標籤 (= *tag*)；稱號
  v. 給…加標籤；看作
  According to the *label*, this shirt is
  made of cotton.

┌─【典型考題】─────────┐
When taking medicine, we should
read the instructions on the _____
carefully because they provide
important information such as how
and when to take it.
A. medal   B. quote
C. label   D. recipe   [C]
└─────────────────────┘

* **labor**[4] 〔'lebɚ 〕 *n.* 勞動；勞工；勞力
  (= *workforce*)
  Labor has the right to strike.

* **laboratory**[4] 〔'læbrə,torɪ 〕 *n.* 實驗室
  (= *lab*)

* **lace**[3] 〔 les 〕 *n.* 蕾絲；鞋帶 *v.* 把…
  繫緊

‡ **lack**[1] 〔 læk 〕 *v. n.* 缺乏
  I don't seem to *lack* anything.

* **ladder**[3] 〔'lædɚ 〕 *n.* 梯子
  【衍伸詞】*the social ladder* (立身成功
    的途徑)

‡ **lady**[1] 〔'ledɪ 〕 *n.* 女士 (= *madam*)
  You are quite a young *lady*.

* **ladybug**[2] 〔'ledɪ,bʌg 〕 *n.* 瓢蟲
  【記憶技巧】*lady* (女士) + *bug* (昆蟲)
  (「瓢蟲」的殼花樣眾多，像愛美的女士)

***lag**[4]〔læg〕*n.* 落後

A *lag* in technological development is one of the problems in the region.

【衍伸詞】*jet lag*（時差）

‡**lake**[1]〔lek〕*n.* 湖

Jim lives near a *lake*.

‡**lamb**[1]〔læm〕*n.* 羔羊

A *lamb* is a young sheep.

【記憶技巧】lam<u>b</u> 就是羊 <u>baby</u>，而 lam<u>e</u>（跛的）就是腳（<u>feet</u>）有問題。

‡**lamp**[1]〔læmp〕*n.* 燈；檯燈

Turn on the *lamp*, please.

‡**land**[1]〔lænd〕*n.* 陸地（= *earth*）
v. 降落

He traveled over *land* and sea.

***landmark**[4]〔'lænd,mark〕*n.* 地標

New York City has some famous *landmarks*.

【記憶技巧】*land* + *mark*（標誌）
（土地上的標誌，就是「地標」）

┌─【典型考題】─────────
As the tallest building in the world, Taipei 101 has become a new _____ of Taipei City.
A. incident   B. geography
C. skylight   D. landmark   **[D]**
└──────────────────────

***landscape**[4]〔'lænskep〕*n.* 風景
（= *scenery*）

We took several photographs of the beautiful *landscape* of southern France.

***landslide**[4]〔'lænd,slaɪd〕*n.* 山崩
（= *landslip*）

Continuous heavy rain for days brought about *landslides* in many areas.

【記憶技巧】*land* + *slide*（滑落）
（土地滑下來，就是「山崩」）

***lane**[2]〔len〕*n.* 巷子；車道

Because of road construction, traffic is restricted to one *lane* in each direction.

‡**language**[2]〔'læŋgwɪdʒ〕*n.* 語言

He can speak five *languages*.

‡**lantern**[2]〔'læntən〕*n.* 燈籠

***lap**[2]〔læp〕*n.* 膝上

The boy held the dog on his *lap*.

【衍伸詞】laptop（膝上型電腦）

‡**large**[1]〔lardʒ〕*adj.* 大的（= *big*）；
巨大的

***largely**[4]〔'lardʒlɪ〕*adv.* 大部分
（= *mainly*）；主要地；大致上；大多

‡**last**[1]〔læst〕*adj.* 最後的；最不可能的

The *last* game starts at seven o'clock.
He is the *last* person to betray you.

‡**late**[1]〔let〕*adj.* 遲到的；已故的

Jimmy was *late* for school this morning.

***lately**[4]〔'letlɪ〕*adv.* 最近（= *recently*）

‡**latest**[2]〔'letɪst〕*adj.* 最新的

┌─【典型考題】─────────
If you want to know the present trends, try to browse through the _____ issues of all the fashion magazines.
A. nearest   B. favorite
C. latest   D. trendiest   **[C]**
└──────────────────────

L

‡**latter**[3] 〔'lætɚ 〕 *pron.* 後者
　adj. 較後的
　I can speak English and Chinese, and the *latter* is my mother tongue.
　【比較】former（前者）

‡**laugh**[1] 〔 læf 〕 *v.* 笑（= *chuckle* ）
　【片語】*laugh at*（嘲笑）

***laughter**[3] 〔'læftɚ 〕 *n.* 笑
　（= *chuckling* ）
　Laughter is the best medicine.

***launch**[4] 〔 lɔntʃ 〕 *v.* 發射；發動
　The rocket will be *launched* on Friday. They *launched* an attack.

***laundry**[3] 〔'lɔndrɪ 〕 *n.* 洗衣服；待洗的衣物
　We always do the *laundry* on Tuesday and the shopping on Wednesday.
　【片語】*do the laundry*（洗衣服）
　【記憶技巧】*laun* (wash) + *dry*（烘乾）

‡**law**[1] 〔 lɔ 〕 *n.* 法律；定律

***lawful**[4] 〔'lɔfəl 〕 *adj.* 合法的（= *legal* ）

***lawn**[3] 〔 lɔn 〕 *n.* 草地
　┌─【典型考題】─────
　│ The _____ in front of the house is kept very neat.
　│ A. plug　　　　B. lawn
　│ C. reward　　　D. shore　　　**[B]**
　└──────────────

‡**lawyer**[2] 〔'lɔjɚ 〕 *n.* 律師
　（= *attorney* 〔 ə'tɝnɪ 〕）

‡**lay**[1] 〔 le 〕 *v.* 放置（= *put* ）；下（蛋）；奠定
　This hen *lays* an egg every day.
　【片語】*lay emphasis on*（重視）
　　　　　lay the foundation（奠定基礎）

【比較】lay-laid-laid（下蛋；放置；奠定）
　　　　lie-lay-lain（躺）
　　　　lie-lied-lied（說謊）

‡**lazy**[1] 〔'lezɪ 〕 *adj.* 懶惰的
　My brother is very *lazy*.
　【反義詞】diligent（勤勉的）

‡**lead**[1,4] 〔 lid 〕 *v.* 帶領　*n.* 率先
　〔 lɛd 〕 *n.* 鉛
　The teacher *leads* students to the playground.
　【片語】*lead to*（導致）

‡**leader**[1] 〔'lidɚ 〕 *n.* 領導者

***leadership**[2] 〔'lidɚʃɪp 〕 *n.* 領導能力

‡**leaf**[1] 〔 lif 〕 *n.* 葉子
　It's fall, and the *leaves* on the trees are falling.

***leak**[3] 〔 lik 〕 *v.* 漏出　*n.* 漏洞；漏水；小便
　There was a hole in my cup and the coffee *leaked* all over the table.

***lean**[4] 〔 lin 〕 *v.* 倚靠（= *incline* ）；傾斜
　adj. 瘦的；收穫少的
　He *leaned* against the wall.
　【片語】*lean against*（倚靠）

***leap**[3] 〔 lip 〕 *v.* 跳（= *jump* ）；突然而迅速地移動；猛漲　*n.* 跳；激增
　Not wanting to get our feet wet, we *leaped* across the puddle.

‡**learn**[1] 〔 lɝn 〕 *v.* 學習（= *pick up* ）；知道；熟記

***learned**[4] 〔'lɝnɪd 〕 *adj.* 有學問的（= *scholarly* ）；學術性的；學而得的
　【注意】learned 中的 ed，唸 / ɪd /。

L

learning[4]〔ˈlɜnɪŋ〕*n.* 學問
(= *knowledge*)；學習
There is no royal road to *learning*.

least[1]〔list〕*adj.* 最少的
He has the *least* experience of them all.
【衍伸詞】*at least* (至少)

leather[3]〔ˈlɛðɚ〕*n.* 皮革
【衍伸詞】*genuine leather* (眞皮)

leave[1]〔liv〕*v.* 遺留；使處於（某種狀態）；離開 (= *go away from*)
n. 允許；休假
The bus will *leave* the station in ten minutes.

lecture[4]〔ˈlɛktʃɚ〕*n.* 講課；說敎；教訓；演講 (= *speech*)   *v.* 演講；講課；訓誡
Please turn your cell phones off before the *lecture* begins.
【記憶技巧】*lect* (read) + *ure* (*n.*)
(準備「演講」都會先讀自己寫的稿子)

lecturer[4]〔ˈlɛktʃərɚ〕*n.* 講師；講者

left[1]〔lɛft〕*n.* 左邊

leg[1]〔lɛg〕*n.* 腿 (= *limb*)
【衍伸詞】*pull one's leg* (開某人玩笑)

legal[2]〔ˈligḷ〕*adj.* 合法的；法律的
(= *lawful* = *legitimate*)
Mr. Chen owns a company. All his *legal* business is handled by a law firm in Taipei.
【反義詞】illegal (非法的)

legend[4]〔ˈlɛdʒənd〕*n.* 傳說
The adventures of the explorer are the basis of many popular *legends*.

【典型考題】
King Arthur is the hero of an old
＿＿＿＿.
A. legend   B. laboratory
C. mercy   D. loyalty   [A]

leisure[3]〔ˈliʒɚ〕*n.* 空閒；悠閒
This relaxing trip is good for the man who loves *leisure*.

leisurely[4]〔ˈliʒɚlɪ〕*adv.* 悠閒地

lemon[2]〔ˈlɛmən〕*n.* 檸檬

lemonade[2]〔ˌlɛmənˈed〕*n.* 檸檬水

lend[2]〔lɛnd〕*v.* 借（出）
Can you *lend* me your car?
【反義詞】borrow 借（入）

length[2]〔lɛŋθ〕*n.* 長度 (= *distance*)
The river has a *length* of 100 kilometers.
【記憶技巧】*leng* (long) + *th* (抽象名詞字尾)
【片語】*at length* (最後；終於)

lengthen[3]〔ˈlɛŋθən〕*v.* 加長；(使) 變長；延長 (= *make longer*) *v.* 笑

【典型考題】
We added two songs in order to ＿＿＿
the music program.
A. legalize   B. sacrifice
C. lengthen   D. export   [C]

L

*lens³ 〔 lɛnz 〕 n. 鏡頭；鏡片；(眼球的)水晶體

I dropped my glasses and broke one *lens*.

【衍伸詞】 *contact lenses* (隱形眼鏡)

*leopard² 〔 'lɛpəd 〕 n. 豹【注意發音】

【記憶技巧】 *leo* (獅子) + *pard*

‡‡less¹ 〔 lɛs 〕 adj. 較少的

*lesson¹ 〔 'lɛsn̩ 〕 n. 課 (= *class*)；教訓；訓誡

‡‡let¹ 〔 lɛt 〕 v. 讓

My father won't *let* me go to the concert.

‡‡letter¹ 〔'lɛtə 〕 n. 信；字母

‡‡lettuce² 〔'lɛtɪs 〕 n. 萵苣

Lettuce is a plant with large green leaves.

‡‡level¹ 〔'lɛvl̩ 〕 n. 水平線；水平面；水準；地位；層級；程度 (= *degree*)

Robert is a man with a high *level* of education.

*liar³ 〔'laɪə 〕 n. 說謊者

Nina is such a *liar* that you should never believe what she says.

【記憶技巧】 *-ar* 表「人」的名詞字尾。

*liberal³ 〔'lɪbərəl 〕 adj. 開明的 (= *open-minded*)；大量的；慷慨的

Jenny's parents are quite *liberal* and give her a lot of freedom.

*liberty³ 〔'lɪbətɪ 〕 n. 自由 (= *freedom*)

【衍伸詞】 *the Statue of Liberty* (自由女神像)

*librarian³ 〔 laɪ'brɛrɪən 〕 n. 圖書館員

‡library² 〔'laɪ,brɛrɪ 〕 n. 圖書館

A *library* has a collection of books.

*license⁴ 〔'laɪsn̩s 〕 n. 執照

Don't drive without a *license* or you could get a big ticket.

【記憶技巧】 *lic* (be permitted) + *ense* (表動作的名詞字尾)(擁有「執照」，就是被允許做某件事)

【衍伸詞】 *driver's license* (駕照)

‡lick² 〔 lɪk 〕 v. 舔

Many pets like to *lick* their owners to show their love.

‡lid² 〔 lɪd 〕 n. 蓋子

Take the *lid* off the pot.

‡‡lie¹ 〔 laɪ 〕 v. 躺；說謊；位於；在於 n. 謊言

He went to *lie* down on the bed.

【比較】 lie-lied-lied (說謊)
　　　　lie-lay-lain (躺)
　　　　lay-laid-laid (下蛋；放置；奠定)

‡‡life¹ 〔 laɪf 〕 n. 生活；生命

Life is full of surprises.

*lifeboat³ 〔'laɪf,bot 〕 n. 救生艇

【比較】 *life vest* (救生衣)

*lifeguard³ 〔'laɪf,gɑrd 〕 n. 救生員 (= *lifesaver*)

【記憶技巧】 *life* + *guard* (守護)(「救生員」是守護生命的人)

【比較】 bodyguard (保鑣)

*lifetime³ 〔'laɪf,taɪm 〕 n. 一生

My grandmother never saw such a thing in her *lifetime*.

‡lift[1] 〔 lɪft 〕 v. 舉起;抱起 (= *raise*)
The mother *lifts* her baby up gently.

【典型考題】
I _____ the chairs carefully and placed them in order.
A. rised　　　B. left
C. handed　　D. lifted　　[D]

‡light[1] 〔 laɪt 〕 n. 燈;光　v. 點燃;照亮;變亮　adj. 輕的;淡的
When it's dark, we cannot see without *light*.

*lighten[4] 〔'laɪtn̩ 〕 v. 照亮 (= *brighten*);變亮;減輕

*lighthouse[3] 〔'laɪt,haʊs 〕 n. 燈塔

‡lightning[2] 〔'laɪtnɪŋ 〕 n. 閃電
During the storm, we saw *lightning* in the sky.

‡like[1] 〔 laɪk 〕 v. 喜歡　prep. 像
I *like* this bag so much.
【注意】dislike 是「不喜歡」,unlike 是「不像」。

*likely[1] 〔'laɪklɪ 〕 adj. adv. 可能的 (地)
It is *likely* to rain soon.
【注意】likely 可用於「人」和「非人」,而 possible 原則上只可用於「非人」。

【典型考題】
Since we are short of manpower in the factory, it is very _____ we will hire some people next month.
A. badly　　　B. nearly
C. mostly　　　D. likely　　[D]

*lily[1] 〔'lɪlɪ 〕 n. 百合
【衍伸詞】*water lily* (睡蓮;荷花)

*limb[3] 〔 lɪm 〕 n. 四肢;大樹枝
Many people lost their *limbs* when they unknowingly stepped on a landmine.
【記憶技巧】lamb (羔羊) 是 animal (動物),不要搞混。

*limit[2] 〔'lɪmɪt 〕 v. 限制 (= *restrict* = *confine*)　n. 限制
Limit your answer to yes or no.

*limitation[4] 〔,lɪmə'teʃən 〕 n. 限制 (= *restriction*)

【典型考題】
The small size of the hall is a(n) _____ when you are planning big events.
A. advantage　　B. limitation
C. exaggeration　D. description　　[B]

‡line[1] 〔 laɪn 〕 n. 線;行;一排;(貨品)種類　v. 給 (衣服或容器)安襯裡;沿…排列

*linen[3] 〔'lɪnɪn 〕 n. 亞麻布

*link[2] 〔 lɪŋk 〕 v. 連結 (= *connect*)
The new canal will *link* the two rivers.

‡lion[1] 〔'laɪən 〕 n. 獅子

‡lip[1] 〔 lɪp 〕 n. 嘴唇
We move our *lips* when we speak.

*lipstick[3] 〔'lɪp,stɪk 〕 n. 口紅
【記憶技巧】*lip* (嘴唇) + *stick* (棒狀物) (用來擦嘴唇的棒狀物,即「口紅」)

‡liquid[2] 〔'lɪkwɪd 〕 n. 液體
Oil, milk, and water are all *liquids*.
【衍伸詞】*liquid paper* (立可白)
【比較】solid (固體),fluid (流體)

L

*liquor[4] 〔'lɪkɚ〕 *n.* 烈酒

The bartender recycled all the empty *liquor* bottles.

‡‡list[1] 〔lɪst〕 *n.* 名單

There were ten names on the *list*.

【衍伸詞】 *waiting list* (候補名單)

‡‡listen[1] 〔'lɪsn̩〕 *v.* 聽

*listener[2] 〔'lɪsnɚ〕 *n.* 聽眾

*literary[4] 〔'lɪtə,rɛrɪ〕 *adj.* 文學的

The author's new novel was featured in a *literary* review.

【記憶技巧】 *liter* (letter 字母) + *ary* (adj.) (有關文字的，就是「文學的」)

*literature[4] 〔'lɪtərətʃɚ〕 *n.* 文學

*litter[3] 〔'lɪtɚ〕 *v.* 亂丟垃圾 (= *discard rubbish*) *n.* 垃圾

The sign said, "No *littering* in the park."

‡‡little[1] 〔'lɪtl̩〕 *adj.* 小的 (= *small*)；很少的；幾乎沒有的

‡‡live[1] 〔lɪv〕 *v.* 住 〔laɪv〕 *adj.* 活的；現場的

*lively[3] 〔'laɪvlɪ〕 *adj.* 活潑的 (= *active*)；有活力的；熱烈的

My daughter is a *lively* girl.

*liver[3] 〔'lɪvɚ〕 *n.* 肝臟

*load[3] 〔lod〕 *n.* 裝載；負擔 *v.* 裝載

Finishing the report is a heavy *load* for her.

‡loaf[2] 〔lof〕 *n.* 一條 (麵包) *v.* 閒混

My mother puts a *loaf* in the basket.

*loan[4] 〔lon〕 *n.* 貸款；借出 *v.* 借出；借給

Not being able to afford the cost of the car, they asked the bank for a *loan*.

*lobby[3] 〔'labɪ〕 *n.* 大廳 (= *entrance hall*)

*lobster[3] 〔'labstɚ〕 *n.* 龍蝦

【比較】 shrimp (蝦子)

‡local[2] 〔'lokl̩〕 *adj.* 當地的 *n.* 當地人；本地居民

I'm not used to the *local* customs yet.

【記憶技巧】 *loc* (place) + *al* (adj.) (地方性的，也就是「當地的」)

*locate[2] 〔lo'ket, 'loket〕 *v.* 使位於 (= *situate*)；找出；查出 (位置)

The house is *located* by the river.

*location[4] 〔lo'keʃən〕 *n.* 位置 (= *position*)

‡lock[2] 〔lak〕 *v.* 鎖 *n.* 鎖

Don't forget to *lock* the door.

‡locker[4] 〔'lakɚ〕 *n.* 置物櫃

*log[2] 〔lɔg〕 *n.* 圓木；航海日誌 *v.* 記載；伐木

In the summer camp, we lived in a cabin built of *logs*.

*logic[4] 〔'ladʒɪk〕 *n.* 邏輯

【記憶技巧】 *log* (speak) + *ic* (學術用語字尾) (說話的學術，說話顯示一個人的思考是否有「邏輯」)

* **logical**[4] 〔'lɑdʒɪkḷ 〕 *adj.* 合乎邏輯的
  When Francine said she was going
  to the doctor, John made the *logical*
  conclusion that she did not feel well.

* **lollipop**[3] 〔'lɑlɪˌpɑp 〕 *n.* 棒棒糖

  lone[2] 〔 lon 〕 *adj.* 孤單的 (= *solitary*)
  【衍伸詞】 loner (獨行俠)

‡ **lonely**[2] 〔'lonlɪ 〕 *adj.* 寂寞的
  (= *lonesome*)
  Jimmy is a *lonely* boy.

  ┌─【典型考題】─────────────
  │ Did you feel _____ while your parents
  │ were away from home?
  │ A. outstanding   B. missing
  │ C. lonely   D. disgusted   [C]
  └──────────────────────────

‡ **long**[1] 〔 lɔŋ 〕 *adj.* 長的 *adv.* 長時間地
  n. 長時間   *v.* 渴望

‡ **look**[1] 〔 luk 〕 *v. n.* 看
  I'm *looking* at a small dog.

* **loose**[3] 〔 lus 〕 *adj.* 鬆的
  Please make the belt tighter; it is
  too *loose* for comfort.
  【反義詞】 tight (緊的)

* **loosen**[3] 〔'lusṇ 〕 *v.* 鬆開
  【比較】 tighten (使變緊)

  ┌─【典型考題】─────────────
  │ These warm-up exercises are designed
  │ to help people _____ their muscles
  │ and prevent injuries.
  │ A. produce   B. connect
  │ C. broaden   D. loosen   [D]
  └──────────────────────────

* **lord**[3] 〔 lɔrd 〕 *n.* (封建時代的) 領主；
  君主；主人；支配者；(大寫) 上帝
  Sir James is the *lord* of the manor.

‡ **lose**[2] 〔 luz 〕 *v.* 遺失
  Nancy *loses* her pens very often.

* **loser**[2] 〔'luzɚ 〕 *n.* 失敗者
  He is not a bad *loser*; he takes
  defeat well.

* **loss**[2] 〔 lɔs 〕 *n.* 損失
  It's a great *loss* to me.

* **lot**[1] 〔 lɑt 〕 *n.* 很多
  We always have a *lot* of rain in May.

* **lotion**[4] 〔'loʃən 〕 *n.* 乳液
  【比較】 toner (化粧水)

‡ **loud**[1] 〔 laud 〕 *adj.* 大聲的   *adv.* 大聲地
  The man speaks in a *loud* voice.

* **loudspeaker**[3] 〔'laud'spikɚ 〕 *n.* 擴音
  器；喇叭
  The results of the contest were
  announced over the *loudspeaker*.

  【重要知識】 loudspeaker 是整組擴音器的「喇
  叭」；microphone 是對著嘴巴的「麥克風」。

* **lousy**[4] 〔'lauzɪ 〕 *adj.* 差勁的
  Grace did such a *lousy* job on the
  assignment that her teacher told her
  to do it over again.

‡ **love**[1] 〔 lʌv 〕 *n. v.* 愛

‡ **lovely**[2] 〔'lʌvlɪ 〕 *adj.* 可愛的

* **lover**[2] 〔'lʌvɚ 〕 *n.* 情人

‡ **low**[1] 〔 lo 〕 *adj.* 低的
  This chair is too *low* for Rose.

L

***lower**² 〔′loæ 〕 *v.* 降低   *adj.* 較低的

***loyal**⁴ 〔′lɔɪəl 〕 *adj.* 忠實的 (= *faithful*)
He wanted to be *loyal* to his family.
【比較】royal (皇家的)

***loyalty**⁴ 〔′lɔɪəltɪ 〕 *n.* 忠實
(= *faithfulness*)；忠誠；忠心

***luck**² 〔 lʌk 〕 *n.* 運氣；幸運

‡**lucky**¹ 〔′lʌkɪ 〕 *adj.* 幸運的
(= *fortunate*)
You are a *lucky* girl to have so many good friends.

***luggage**³ 〔′lʌgɪdʒ 〕 *n.* 行李【集合名詞】
(= *baggage*)
【重要知識】美國人多用 bag 代替 luggage。

┌─【典型考題】─────────
Remember to bring all your _____
with you when you get off the train.
A. booth   B. laboratory
C. beam   D. luggage   **[D]**
└──────────────────

***lullaby**³ 〔′lʌlə,baɪ 〕 *n.* 搖籃曲
(= *cradlesong* 〔′kredl̩,sɔŋ 〕)
The mother sang a *lullaby* as she put the baby to bed.

【記憶技巧】*lull* (使入睡) + *a* + *by*
(bye) (哄小孩說再見就唱「搖籃曲」)

***lunar**⁴ 〔′lunæ 〕 *adj.* 月亮的
Neil Armstrong was the first astronaut to walk on the *lunar* surface.
【衍伸詞】*lunar calendar* (陰曆；農曆)
【比較】solar (太陽的)

‡**lunch**¹ 〔 lʌntʃ 〕 *n.* 午餐

***luncheon**¹ 〔′lʌntʃən 〕 *n.* 午餐
The *luncheon* will begin at twelve o'clock

***lung**³ 〔 lʌŋ 〕 *n.* 肺
Smoking causes air pollution and harms our *lungs*.
【衍伸詞】*lung cancer* (肺癌)

***luxurious**⁴ 〔 lʌg′ʒurɪəs , lʌk′ʃurɪəs 〕
adj. 奢侈的；豪華的
We decided to pay a little more and upgrade to a more *luxurious* cabin.
【重要知識】79% 的美國人唸成〔 lʌg′ʒurɪəs 〕，21% 的人唸成〔 lʌk′ʃurɪəs 〕。

***luxury**⁴ 〔′lʌkʃərɪ ,′lʌgʒərɪ 〕 *n.* 奢侈
【記憶技巧】*lux* (洗髮精品牌) + *ury*

M m

‡**ma'am**⁴ 〔 mæm,mɑm 〕 *n.* 女士
Yes, *ma'am*?

‡**machine**¹ 〔 mə′ʃin 〕 *n.* 機器
Machines help us to do things more easily.

***machinery**⁴ 〔 mə′ʃinərɪ 〕 *n.* 機器
【集合名詞】

【記憶技巧】*-ery* 表「…類事物」的字尾。

‡**mad**¹ 〔 mæd 〕 *adj.* 發瘋的 (= *crazy*)
He behaves as if he were *mad*.

***madam**⁴ 〔′mædəm 〕 *n.* 女士
"*Madam*, would you care for tea or coffee?"

****magazine**[2] 〔ˈmægəˌzin〕 n. 雜誌
Children's *magazines* are full of interesting pictures.
【比較】journal（期刊）
【重要知識】現在，新一代的美國人多唸〔ˈmægəˌzin〕，較少人唸〔ˌmægəˈzin〕。

****magic**[2] 〔ˈmædʒɪk〕 n. 魔術；魔法
The girl was turned by *magic* into a swan.

***magical**[3] 〔ˈmædʒɪkḷ〕 adj. 神奇的

****magician**[2] 〔məˈdʒɪʃən〕 n. 魔術師

***magnet**[3] 〔ˈmægnɪt〕 n. 磁鐵

***magnetic**[4] 〔mægˈnɛtɪk〕 adj. 有磁性的
【衍伸詞】*magnetic field*（磁場）
【典型考題】
Agnes seems to have a _____ personality. Almost everyone is immediately attracted to her when they first see her.
A. clumsy　　　B. durable
C. furious　　　D. magnetic　　[D]

***magnificent**[4] 〔mægˈnɪfəsṇt〕 adj. 壯麗的；很棒的（=*splendid*）
Switzerland is a country with *magnificent* scenery.
【記憶技巧】*magn*（great）+ *ific*（do）+ *ent*（adj.）
【典型考題】
In Iraq Saddam Hussein owned several _____ palaces.
A. magnificent　B. maximum
C. multiple　　　D. moderate　　[A]

***maid**[3] 〔med〕 n. 女傭

****mail**[1] 〔mel〕 v. 郵寄　n. 信件

***main**[2] 〔men〕 adj. 主要的（=*primary*）
This is the *main* building of our college.

***maintain**[2] 〔menˈten〕 v. 維持（=*keep*）；維修
The increase in sales is being *maintained*.
【記憶技巧】*main*（hand）+ *tain*（hold）
（把東西握在手中，表示「維持」）
【典型考題】
The Browns spend a great deal of time _____ their beautiful yard.
A. containing　　B. restraining
C. remaining　　D. maintaining　[D]

***major**[3] 〔ˈmedʒɚ〕 adj. 主要的（=*main*）　v. 主修　n. 主修科目；主修學生
The *major* problem of this artist is a lack of creativity.

***majority**[3] 〔məˈdʒɔrətɪ〕 n. 大多數
A *majority* of the voters approved of the candidate and he won the election.
【反義詞】minority（少數）

****make**[1] 〔mek〕 v. 製作；製造

***makeup**[4] 〔ˈmekˌʌp〕 n. 化妝品（=*make-up* = *cosmetics*）；化妝
Some girls in my junior high school have started wearing *makeup*.
【片語】*wear makeup*（化妝）

****male**[2] 〔mel〕 n. 男性（=*man*）　adj. 男性的（=*masculine*）
Boys are *males* and girls are females.
【反義詞】female（女性；女性的）

M

‡**mall**³〔mɔl〕*n.* 購物中心
（= *shopping center*）

‡**man**¹〔mæn〕*n.* 男人（= *male*）；
人類（= *mankind*）

***manage**³〔'mænɪdʒ〕*v.* 管理
（= *control*）；設法
Mr. Wang has *managed* this
apartment for two years.

manageable³〔'mænɪdʒəbḷ〕*adj.*
可管理的

【典型考題】
This company, with its serious financial
problems, is no longer _____.
A. achievable   B. stretchable
C. repeatable   D. manageable   **[D]**

***management**³〔'mænɪdʒmənt〕*n.*
管理

‡**manager**³〔'mænɪdʒɚ〕*n.* 經理

***Mandarin**²〔'mændərɪn〕*n.* 國語；
北京話
My grandmother can't speak
Mandarin.

‡**mango**²〔'mæŋgo〕*n.* 芒果

***mankind**³〔mæn'kaɪnd〕*n.* 人類
（= *human beings*）
Mankind did not exist ten million
years ago.

‡**manner**²〔'mænɚ〕*n.* 方式；樣子
（= *way*）
Fold the paper in this *manner*.

***manners**³〔'mænɚz〕*n. pl.* 禮貌
Eleanor praised her son for his good
table *manners*.

【典型考題】
The man offered the lady his seat out
of politeness; he must be a gentleman
with good _____.
A. manners   B. conversations
C. genes   D. departures   **[A]**

***manual**⁴〔'mænjʊəl〕*n.* 手冊
（= *handbook*）；說明書
adj. 手工的；用手的
I have read the *manual*, but I still
don't understand how to operate
this machine.

***manufacture**⁴〔ˌmænjə'fæktʃɚ〕*v.*
製造（= *make*）
This factory *manufactures* cars.
【記憶技巧】*manu* (hand) + *fact*
(make) + *ure*（動手做，就是「製造」）

***manufacturer**⁴〔ˌmænjə'fæktʃərɚ〕
n. 製造業者（= *maker*）

‡**map**¹〔mæp〕*n.* 地圖
Have you got the *map* of Paris?

***marathon**⁴〔'mærəˌθɑn〕*n.* 馬拉松
Thousands of runners participated
in the *marathon*.

***marble**³〔'mɑrbḷ〕*n.* 大理石；彈珠
There is a *marble* statue of the
general in the park.

‡**March**¹〔mɑrtʃ〕*n.* 三月

***march**³〔mɑrtʃ〕*v.* 行軍；行進
n. 行進；行軍；進行曲
The soldiers had to *march* twenty
kilometers to the next camp.

* **margin**[4] 〔'mɑrdʒɪn 〕 *n.* 邊緣
（ = *edge*)；差距；頁邊的空白
The teacher wrote some comments
in the *margin* of my paper.
【片語】 *by a narrow margin* (差一點點)

‡ **mark**[2] 〔 mɑrk 〕 *n.* 記號；分數
v. 作記號；標示

‡ **market**[1] 〔'mɑrkɪt 〕 *n.* 市場
She sold vegetables in the *market*.

* **marriage**[2] 〔'mærɪdʒ 〕 *n.* 婚姻
Her first *marriage* was not very
happy.

* **marry**[1] 〔'mærɪ 〕 *v.* 結婚

* **marvelous**[3] 〔'mɑrvḷəs 〕 *adj.* 令人
驚嘆的 (= *amazing*)；很棒的

┌─【典型考題】─────────
This exhibition of Chinese paintings
is _____. Indeed, it's the best in
ten years.
A. marvelous　　B. potential
C. artificial　　D. populous　　[A]
└────────────────

‡ **mask**[2] 〔 mæsk 〕 *n.* 面具
Tom has to wear a *mask* in the school
play.

‡ **mass**[2] 〔 mæs 〕 *adj.* 大量的；大衆的
The assembly line allowed *mass*
production to develop.
Paul is studying *mass* communication.
【重要知識】我們熟悉的捷運（ *MRT* ）全名
是 Mass Rapid Transit。

‡ **master**[1] 〔'mæstə 〕 *v.* 精通 (= *become*
skilled in)　 *n.* 主人；大師；碩士
If you study hard, you can *master*
English.

‡ **mat**[2] 〔 mæt 〕 *n.* 墊子

‡ **match**[2,1] 〔 mætʃ 〕 *v.* 搭配(= *go with*)；
與…匹敵　 *n.* 火柴；配偶
This tie doesn't *match* your suit.

* **mate**[2] 〔 met 〕 *n.* 伴侶 (= *partner*)
The female bird went in search of
food while its *mate* guarded the nest.

* **material**[2,6] 〔 mə'tɪrɪəl 〕 *n.* 物質
(= *substance*)；材料　 *adj.* 物質的
Plastic is a widely used *material*.

‡ **math**[3] 〔 mæθ 〕 *n.* 數學
They were doing *math* exercises
when I left.

* **mathematical**[3] 〔,mæθə'mætɪkḷ 〕
adj. 數學的

‡ **mathematics**[3] 〔,mæθə'mætɪks 〕 *n.*
數學 (= *math*)

‡ **matter**[1] 〔'mætə 〕 *n.* 事情 (= *affair*)；
物質(= *substance*)　 *v.* 重要
(= *count*)
That's another *matter*.
It doesn't *matter* how you do it.

* **mature**[3] 〔 mə'tʃʊr 〕 *adj.* 成熟的
v. 變成熟
Years later, May has grown up to be
a *mature* and elegant lady.
【反義詞】 childish (幼稚的)

┌─【典型考題】─────────
According to recent research, children
under the age of 12 are generally not
_____ enough to recognize risk and
deal with dangerous situations.
A. diligent　　B. mature
C. familiar　　D. sincere　　[B]
└────────────────

M

* **maturity** [4] 〔 məˈtʃʊrətɪ 〕 *n.* 成熟

【典型考題】
This job calls for a man with a great deal of _____ .
A. literature　　B. investigation
C. maturity　　D. maximum　[C]

* **maximum** [4] 〔 ˈmæksəməm 〕 *n.* 最大量　*adj.* 最大的
She types a *maximum* of seventy words per minute.
【反義詞】 minimum（最小量）

【典型考題】
The _____ capacity of this elevator is 400 kilograms. For safety reasons, it shouldn't be overloaded.
A. delicate　　B. automatic
C. essential　　D. maximum　[D]

‡ **May** [1] 〔 me 〕 *n.* 五月

‡ **maybe** [1] 〔 ˈmebɪ 〕 *adv.* 也許
Maybe my mother will come here next month.

* **mayor** [3] 〔 ˈmeə 〕 *n.* 市長
Most people in this city approve of the job our *mayor* is doing.

* **meadow** [3] 〔 ˈmɛdo 〕 *n.* 草地

‡ **meal** [2] 〔 mil 〕 *n.* 一餐
Breakfast is our morning *meal*.

‡ **mean** [1] 〔 min 〕 *v.* 意思是（ = *signify* ）　*adj.* 卑鄙的；惡劣的

* **meaning** [2] 〔 ˈminɪŋ 〕 *n.* 意義

* **meaningful** [3] 〔 ˈminɪŋfəl 〕 *adj.* 有意義的（ = *significant* ）

* **means** [2] 〔 minz 〕 *n.* 方法；手段
【單複數同型】
Do you know of any *means* to get there?

【典型考題】
A search engine is a new _____ of getting information.
A. merchandise　B. university
C. revolution　　D. means　[D]

* **meanwhile** [3] 〔 ˈminˌhwaɪl 〕 *adv.* 同時（ = *at the same time* ）
You look in the shoe store and *meanwhile* I'll find the book I want in the bookstore.

measurable [2] 〔 ˈmɛʒərəbḷ 〕 *adj.* 可測量的

* **measure** [2,4] 〔 ˈmɛʒə 〕 *v.* 測量（ = *quantify* ）　*n.* 措施（ = *means* ）
Harvey *measured* the window carefully before buying new curtains.
【片語】 *take measures*（採取措施）

* **measurement** [2] 〔 ˈmɛʒəmənt 〕 *n.* 測量
【比較】 measurements（尺寸）

‡ **meat** [1] 〔 mit 〕 *n.* 肉
【比較】 flesh（活的動物的）肉

* **mechanic** [4] 〔 məˈkænɪk 〕 *n.* 技工
Mr. Brown is a good *mechanic*.
【記憶技巧】 *mechan* (machine) + *ic*
【重要知識】字尾 ic 可表「人」，例如：critic（批評家）, lunatic（瘋子）。

* **mechanical** [4] 〔 məˈkænɪkḷ 〕 *adj.* 機械的

M

* **medal**[3] 〔'mɛdḷ 〕 *n.* 獎牌

The swimmer won a gold *medal* in the Olympics.

【記憶技巧】背 med**al** 想到 award(頒發)。

‡ **media**[3] 〔'midɪə 〕 *n.pl.* 媒體

You can know the news through the mass *media*.

【常考】*the mass media*（大眾傳播媒體）

* **medical**[3] 〔'mɛdɪkḷ 〕 *adj.* 醫學的；醫療的

Dr. Peterson has a Ph.D. in history; he is not a *medical* doctor.

【記憶技巧】*med* (heal) + *ical* (*adj.*)
（醫學就是在教導大家如何治療疾病）

‡ **medicine**[2] 〔'mɛdəsn̩ 〕 *n.* 藥（= *drug*）；醫學

┌─【典型考題】────────
Mary was sick. She had to take some _____.

A. time   B. money
C. medicine   D. drink   [C]
└─────────────────

‡ **medium**[3] 〔'midɪəm 〕 *adj.* 中等的（= *middle*） *n.* 媒體；媒介

The man is of *medium* height.

‡ **meet**[1] 〔 mit 〕 *v.* 遇見；認識

It's nice to *meet* you.

‡ **meeting**[2] 〔'mitɪŋ 〕 *n.* 會議（= *conference*）

* **melody**[2] 〔'mɛlədɪ 〕 *n.* 旋律（= *tune*）

I hear that *melody* everywhere; it must be a very popular song.

* **melon**[2] 〔'mɛlən 〕 *n.* 甜瓜；(各種的) 瓜【尤指西瓜、香瓜】

Would you like a slice of *melon*?

【比較】watermelon（西瓜）

* **melt**[3] 〔 mɛlt 〕 *v.* 融化

In the spring when the snow *melts* there may be flooding.

【比較】dissolve（溶解）

‡ **member**[2] 〔'mɛmbɚ 〕 *n.* 成員

Jack is a *member* of a football team.

* **membership**[3] 〔'mɛmbɚ͵ʃɪp 〕 *n.* 會員資格

* **memorable**[4] 〔'mɛmərəbḷ 〕 *adj.* 難忘的（= *unforgettable*）

Our trip to China was a really *memorable* experience.

* **memorial**[4] 〔 mə'morɪəl 〕 *adj.* 紀念的

【衍伸詞】*memorial hall*（紀念堂）

* **memorize**[3] 〔'mɛmə͵raɪz 〕 *v.* 背誦

* **memory**[2] 〔'mɛmərɪ 〕 *n.* 回憶

The picture brings back many *memories*.

【記憶技巧】*memor* (remember) + *y*

* **mend**[3] 〔 mɛnd 〕 *v.* 修補；改正（= *correct*）

It is never too late to *mend*.

┌─【典型考題】────────
When we were poor, my mother used to _____ my clothes for me when they were worn out.

A. merge   B. memorize
C. mend   D. wore   [C]
└─────────────────

* **mental**[3] 〔'mɛntḷ 〕 *adj.* 心理的；精神的

Although he is not strong physically, Ned has amazing *mental* powers.

【記憶技巧】*ment* (mind) + *al* (*adj.*)

【衍伸詞】*mental and physical health*（身心健康）

M

* **mention**[3] 〔'mɛnʃən〕 v. 提到
  (= *refer to*)
  Did you *mention* the party to Jill?
  She seems to know all about it.

** **menu**[2] 〔'mɛnju〕 n. 菜單

* **merchant**[3] 〔'mɝtʃənt〕 n. 商人
  (= *trader*)

* **mercy**[4] 〔'mɝsɪ〕 n. 慈悲；仁慈
  The convicted robber begged the
  judge for *mercy* because he did not
  want to go to jail.
  【重要知識】乞丐向人要錢常説：Have **mercy**
  (on me). 意思是「可憐可憐我吧！」

* **mere**[4] 〔mɪr〕 adj. 不過；僅僅
  (= *no more than*)
  Don't be so impatient. We've been
  waiting a *mere* five minutes.

* **merit**[4] 〔'mɛrɪt〕 n. 價值；優點
  (= *advantage*) v. 值得 (= *deserve*)
  Bryan's *merits* outnumber his flaws.
  【反義詞】 shortcoming (缺點)
           drawback (缺點)
  【重要知識】一般美國中學，學生表現優良，學
  校會記「優點」，稱爲 a merit point，「缺點」
  則稱爲 a demerit point。

* **merry**[3] 〔'mɛrɪ〕 adj. 歡樂的
  (= *cheerful*)
  It was a *merry* party and everyone
  had a good time.
  【衍伸詞】 *Merry Christmas*! (聖誕快樂!)

* **mess**[3] 〔mɛs〕 n. 雜亂 (= *disorder*)
  v. 使雜亂；搞砸

Father told me to clean up the *mess* in
the living room before I watched TV.
【片語】 *in a mess* (亂七八糟)

* **message**[2] 〔'mɛsɪdʒ〕 n. 訊息
  Will you take this *message* to my
  grandparents?

  【典型考題】
  Using and understanding abbreviated
  _____ like "AFIK" (as far as I know)
  is considered fashionable among
  younger cell phone users.
  A. emotions   B. names
  C. messages   D. data   [C]

* **messenger**[4] 〔'mɛsṇdʒɚ〕 n. 送信的人
  A *messenger* just arrived with a
  package for Mr. Philips.

  【典型考題】
  A person who carries a message is a
  _____.
  A. monitor   B. manager
  C. messenger   D. passenger   [C]

* **messy**[4] 〔'mɛsɪ〕 adj. 雜亂的
  (= *disorderly*)

** **metal**[2] 〔'mɛtḷ〕 n. 金屬
  Iron is a kind of *metal*.

** **meter**[2] 〔'mitɚ〕 n. 公尺；儀；錶

** **method**[2] 〔'mɛθəd〕 n. 方法 (= *way*)
  I want to know a good *method* for
  learning English.

* **microphone**[3] 〔'maɪkrə,fon〕 n.
  麥克風
  【記憶技巧】 *micro* (small) + *phone*
  (sound) (「麥克風」是給聲音小的人用)

M

* **microscope**[4] 〔'maɪkrə,skop 〕 *n.* 顯微鏡

【記憶技巧】 *micro* (small) + *scope* (look)（觀察細小的東西要用「顯微鏡」）

【典型考題】
Germs can only be seen with the aid of a _____.
A. microscope   B. liquor
C. minister   D. mechanic   [A]

‡ **microwave**[3] 〔'maɪkrə,wev 〕 *adj.* 微波的   *n.* 微波爐（= *microwave oven*）
I bought a new *microwave* oven for my mother.

‡ **middle**[1] 〔'mɪdḷ 〕 *adj.* 中間的
Most Westerners' names consist of three parts, the first name, the *middle* name, and the last name.

‡ **might**[3] 〔 maɪt 〕 *aux.* may 的過去式 *n.* 力量
He *might* not be back until tonight.

* **mighty**[3] 〔'maɪtɪ 〕 *adj.* 強有力的（= *powerful*）
The boxer looked worried when he saw his *mighty* opponent.

* **mild**[4] 〔 maɪld 〕 *adj.* 溫和的（= *moderate*）
The weather this winter is so *mild* that I haven't even worn my winter coat.

‡ **mile**[1] 〔 maɪl 〕 *n.* 英哩
Wendy walks two *miles* to school every day.

* **military**[2] 〔'mɪlə,tɛrɪ 〕 *adj.* 軍事的
Henry plans to attend a *military* academy.

【記憶技巧】 *milit* (soldier) + *ary* (adj.)（有關於軍人的）

‡ **milk**[1] 〔 mɪlk 〕 *n.* 牛奶

* **mill**[3] 〔 mɪl 〕 *n.* 磨坊；磨粉機；工廠
The old *mill* was once used by all the farmers in the village.

‡ **million**[2] 〔'mɪljən 〕 *n.* 百萬

* **millionaire**[3] 〔,mɪljən'ɛr 〕 *n.* 百萬富翁
Oscar became a *millionaire* overnight when he won the grand prize.
【記憶技巧】 *-aire* 表「人」的字尾。

‡ **mind**[1] 〔 maɪnd 〕 *n.* 心；精神
You are always on my *mind*.

‡ **mine**[2] 〔 maɪn 〕 *pron.* I 的所有格代名詞   *n.* 礦坑   *v.* 開採
That wasn't his fault; it was *mine*.

* **miner**[3] 〔'maɪnɚ 〕 *n.* 礦工

* **mineral**[4] 〔'mɪnərəl 〕 *n.* 礦物；礦物質
【衍伸詞】 *mineral water*（礦泉水）

* **minimum**[4] 〔'mɪnəməm 〕 *n.* 最小量 *adj.* 最小的
We need a *minimum* of three people to play this card game.
【記憶技巧】 *mini* (small) + *mum*（拉丁文的最高級字尾）
【反義詞】 maximum（最大量）

【典型考題】
The restaurant has a _____ charge of NT $ 250 per person. So the four of us need to pay at least NT $ 1,000 to eat there.
A. definite   B. minimum
C. flexible   D. numerous   [B]

M

* **minister** [4] 〔'mɪnɪstɚ〕 n. 部長

The *minister* is responsible for the treasury department of the government.

【記憶技巧】 *mini* (small) + *ster* (人)

（「部長」也是人民的僕人）

* **ministry** [4] 〔'mɪnɪstrɪ〕 n. 部

(= *a governmental department*)

【衍伸詞】 *the Ministry of Education*

（教育部）

‡ **minor** [3] 〔'maɪnɚ〕 adj. 次要的

(= *secondary*)　v. 副修　n. 副修

That's only a *minor* problem.

┌─【典型考題】─────────┐
They have made some ＿＿＿ changes to the schedule. You have to read it again; otherwise, you might miss them.
A. gathering　　B. responsible
C. complaint　　D. minor　　　[D]
└────────────────┘

* **minority** [3] 〔mə'nɔrətɪ,maɪ-〕 n. 少數

【反義詞】 majority（大多數）

‡ **minus** [2] 〔'maɪnəs〕 prep. 減

One *minus* one is zero.

【反義詞】 plus（加）

【重要知識】加減乘除的説法:(5+5-4)×2÷3=4
Five *plus* five *minus* four *times* two *divided by* three equals four.

‡ **minute** [1] 〔'mɪnɪt〕 n. 分鐘

〔maɪ'njut〕 adj. 微小的

* **miracle** [3] 〔'mɪrəkḷ〕 n. 奇蹟(= *wonder*)

When the blind man regained his sight, many people called it a *miracle*.

【記憶技巧】 *mira* (wonder) + *cle* (n.)

（「奇蹟」的出現，總是讓人感到驚訝）

‡ **mirror** [2] 〔'mɪrɚ〕 n. 鏡子　v. 反映

(= *reflect*)

* **mischief** [4] 〔'mɪstʃɪf〕 n. 惡作劇

(= *trouble*)；頑皮 (= *naughtiness*)

The teacher warned the children not to get into *mischief* while she was out of the room.

【片語】 *get into mischief*（開始惡作劇）

【記憶技巧】 *mis* (badly) + *chief*（長官）

（對長官不敬，就是「惡作劇」）

* **miserable** [4] 〔'mɪzərəbḷ〕 adj. 悲慘的

(= *poor*)

Lucy was *miserable* when her boyfriend went overseas to study.

* **misery** [3] 〔'mɪzərɪ〕 n. 悲慘

(= *misfortune*)

* **misfortune** [4] 〔mɪs'fɔrtʃən〕 n. 不幸

(= *bad luck*)

Will was not discouraged by his great *misfortune*.

【記憶技巧】 *mis* (badly) + *fortune*

（運氣）（運氣不好就會「不幸」）

* **mislead** [4] 〔mɪs'lid〕 v. 誤導

Some advertisements are carefully worded to *mislead* consumers without actually lying.

‡ **Miss** [1] 〔mɪs〕 n. 小姐

‡ **miss** [1] 〔mɪs〕 v. 錯過 (= *skip*)；想念

(= *long for*)

John *missed* the train to Tainan.

* **missile** [3] 〔'mɪsḷ〕 n. 飛彈

(= *projectile* 〔prə'dʒɛktḷ〕)

The North threatened to launch its *missiles* at the South if war broke out.

【記憶技巧】 *miss* (throw) + *ile*

（可以投擲的武器，就是「飛彈」）

M

* **missing**[3] 〔'mɪsɪŋ〕 *adj.* 失蹤的

Our dog has been *missing* for two days and we are very worried about it.

* **mission**[3] 〔'mɪʃən〕 *n.* 任務 (= *task*)

To finish all this work by the end of the month seems to be an impossible *mission*.

* **mist**[3] 〔mɪst〕 *n.* 薄霧

The top of the building was covered in *mist*.

【比較】fog (濃霧)

‡ **mistake**[1] 〔mə'stek〕 *n.* 錯誤

Jill has made a *mistake*.

mister[1] 〔'mɪstɚ〕 *n.* 先生 (= *Mr.*)

* **misunderstand**[4] 〔,mɪsʌndɚ'stænd〕 *v.* 誤會

I think you *misunderstood* Peter when he told us the time of the meeting.

‡ **mix**[2] 〔mɪks〕 *v.* 混合

Helen *mixes* flour, eggs and sugar to bake a cake.

* **mixture**[3] 〔'mɪkstʃɚ〕 *n.* 混合物

* **mob**[3] 〔mab〕 *n.* 暴民;亂民; 烏合之衆【集合名詞】

An angry *mob* formed outside the factory when the layoff was announced.

【記憶技巧】*mob* (move) (「暴民」會動手動腳,以暴力解決事情)

* **mobile**[3] 〔'mobḷ〕 *adj.* 可移動的; 活動的

The *mobile* library travels to different neighborhoods in a van.

【衍伸詞】*mobile phone* (行動電話)

‡ **model**[2] 〔'madḷ〕 *n.* 模型;模範; 模特兒

He made a *model* of his new house.

* **moderate**[4] 〔'madərɪt〕 *adj.* 適度的 (= *reasonable*);溫和的 (= *mild*)

My father eats a *moderate* amount of meat, not too much and not too little.

【記憶技巧】*-ate* 形容詞字尾。

‡ **modern**[2] 〔'madɚn〕 *adj.* 現代的 (= *current*)

There are a lot of *modern* buildings in New York.

* **modest**[4] 〔'madɪst〕 *adj.* 謙虛的 (= *humble*);樸素的 (= *simple*)

When she says that her success is due to good luck, she's being *modest*.

【記憶技巧】*mode* (模式) + *st* (不超出一定的模式,表「謙虛的」)

* **modesty**[4] 〔'madəstɪ〕 *n.* 謙虛 (= *humility*);樸素 (= *simplicity*)

【典型考題】

The young scientist showed great
_____. He attributed his success to good luck.
A. industry   B. modesty
C. intensity   D. identity   **[B]**

* **moist**[3] 〔mɔɪst〕 *adj.* 潮濕的 (= *humid* = *wet*);(眼睛) 淚汪汪的

Tea grows best in a cool, *moist* climate.

* **moisture**[3] 〔'mɔɪstʃɚ〕 *n.* 濕氣 (= *humidity*);水分

M

‡ **moment**[1] 〔'momənt 〕 *n.* 時刻
（= *point*)；片刻（= *minute*)
The *moment* the child was run down
by a car, he was sent to a hospital.

‡ **mommy**[1] 〔'mɑmɪ 〕 *n.* 媽媽（= *mom*)
【比較】mummy（木乃伊）

‡ **Monday**[1] 〔'mʌndɪ 〕 *n.* 星期一

‡ **money**[1] 〔'mʌnɪ 〕 *n.* 錢

* **monitor**[4] 〔'mɑnətɚ 〕 *n.* 螢幕 *v.* 監視
【記憶技巧】 *monit* (advise) + *or* (n.)
【典型考題】
When you write with your computer,
the words will appear on the _____.
A. browser   B. scanner
C. modem   D. monitor   [D]

* **monk**[3] 〔 mʌŋk 〕 *n.* 修道士；和尚
Michael decided to devote his life to
the church and he became a *monk*.
【比較】nun（修女；尼姑）

‡ **monkey**[1] 〔'mʌŋkɪ 〕 *n.* 猴子（= *ape*)
Monkeys like to climb trees.

* **monster**[2] 〔'mɑnstɚ 〕 *n.* 怪物
The film is about a *monster*.
【記憶技巧】分音節背 mon-ster。
【典型考題】
Fairy tales often feature terrible
creatures such as _____.
A. diplomats   B. fairies
C. monsters   D. princesses   [C]

‡ **month**[1] 〔 mʌnθ 〕 *n.* 月份
She has been here for a *month*.

* **monthly**[4] 〔'mʌnθlɪ 〕 *adj.* 每月的

* **monument**[4] 〔'mɑnjəmənt 〕 *n.* 紀念碑
（= *memorial*)

The government will build a
monument to the soldiers.
【記憶技巧】 *monu* (remind) + *ment*
(n.)（「紀念碑」會讓人想起過去發生的事）

* **mood**[3] 〔 mud 〕 *n.* 心情
Gary has been in a bad *mood* since
he lost the game this morning.
【典型考題】
I'm not in the _____ to play the
piano.
A. mood   B. idea
C. taste   D. heart   [A]

‡ **moon**[1] 〔 mun 〕 *n.* 月亮
I love the light of a full *moon*.
【片語】 *full moon*（滿月）

‡ **mop**[3] 〔 mɑp 〕 *n.* 拖把 *v.* 用拖把拖
（地板）
I *mopped* the floor every day.
【比較】sweep（掃）
vacuum（用吸塵器打掃）
【典型考題】
When the floor is dirty, my brother is
always the first one to _____ it.
A. finish   B. solve
C. remove   D. mop   [D]

* **moral**[3] 〔'mɔrəl 〕 *adj.* 道德的
n. 道德教訓（= *lesson*)；寓意
Nate feels he has a *moral* obligation
to take care of his old aunt.
【記憶技巧】 *mor* (custom) + *al* (adj.)
（道德標準會因風俗習慣不同而產生差異）
【反義詞】immoral（不道德的）
【比較】mortal（必死的；難逃一死的）
【典型考題】
It is both legally and _____ wrong
to spread rumors about other people
on the Internet.
A. morally   B. physically
C. literarily   D. commercially [A]

* **moreover** [4] ﹝ mor'ovɚ ﹞ *adv.* 此外
(= *besides* = *in addition*
= *furthermore*)
Jessica isn't interested in learning to
drive a car. *Moreover*, she is too
young to learn.

‡ **morning** [1] ﹝'mɔrnɪŋ ﹞ *n.* 早晨

‡ **mosquito** [2] ﹝ mə'skito ﹞ *n.* 蚊子
Mosquitoes are small insects which
can carry diseases.
【比較】fly (蒼蠅)

‡ **most** [1] ﹝ most ﹞ *adj.* 最多的；大多數的
Most people like Taiwanese food.

* **mostly** [4] ﹝'mostlɪ ﹞ *adv.* 大多

* **motel** [3] ﹝ mo'tɛl ﹞ *n.* 汽車旅館
As it was late and he was tired, the
driver decided to stop for the night
at a *motel*.

* **moth** [2] ﹝ mɔθ ﹞ *n.* 蛾
After we lit the candle, several *moths*
circled the flame.

‡ **mother** [1] ﹝'mʌðɚ ﹞ *n.* 母親 (= *mom*)

* **motion** [2] ﹝'moʃən ﹞ *n.* 動作
(= *action*)；移動 (= *movement*)
All her *motions* were graceful.
【衍伸詞】 *motion picture* (動畫；電影)

* **motivate** [4] ﹝'motə,vet ﹞ *v.* 激勵
(= *inspire*)；使有動機；激起 (行動)
In order to *motivate* him, Dan's
parents promised to buy him a new
bike if he improved his grades.
【記憶技巧】 *motiv* (move) + *ate* (*v.*)
(叫人動起來，就是「激勵」)

* **motivation** [4] ﹝,motə'veʃən ﹞ *n.* 動機

* **motor** [3] ﹝'motɚ ﹞ *n.* 馬達 (= *engine*)
I turned the key, but the *motor* just
won't start.

‡ **motorcycle** [2] ﹝'motɚ,saɪkḷ ﹞ *n.* 摩托車
There are more and more *motorcycles*
on the streets.
【重要知識】美國人常用 bike 來代替
「腳踏車」和「摩托車」。

‡ **mountain** [1] ﹝'maʊntṇ ﹞ *n.* 山；大量
(= *a large amount*)
Alex is walking to the top of the
mountain.

* **mountainous** [4] ﹝'maʊntṇəs ﹞ *adj.*
多山的 (= *rocky*)

‡ **mouse** [1] ﹝ maʊs ﹞ *n.* 老鼠；滑鼠
【比較】rat (老鼠) 的體型比 mouse 大。

‡ **mouth** [1] ﹝ maʊθ ﹞ *n.* 嘴巴
His *mouth* is full of rice.

* **movable** [2] ﹝'muvəbḷ ﹞ *adj.* 可移動的
(= *portable*)

‡ **move** [1] ﹝ muv ﹞ *v.* 移動；搬家；
使感動   *n.* 行動
She *moved* away from the window.
┌─【典型考題】────
│ After hearing her sad story, I was
│ _____ to tears.
│ A. impressed   B. embarrassed
│ C. relaxed   D. moved   [D]

‡ **movement** [1] ﹝'muvmənt ﹞ *n.* 動作
(= *act*)；運動 (= *campaign*)

‡ **movie** [1] ﹝'muvɪ ﹞ *n.* 電影 (= *film*)
I want to see a *movie* with her.

M

mow[4] 〔mo〕 *v.* 割（草）

You should *mow* your lawn tomorrow.

Mr.[1] 〔'mɪstɚ〕 *n.* 先生

Mr. White teaches us music.

Mrs.[1] 〔'mɪsɪz〕 *n.* 太太

Mrs. Brown is our math teacher.

MRT[2] *n.* 捷運（= *Mass Rapid Transit*）

I take the *MRT* to school every day.

MTV[4] *n.* 音樂電視節目（= *Music Television*）

My sister likes to watch *MTV* very much.

much[1] 〔mʌtʃ〕 *adj.* 很多的 *adv.* 非常地 *n.* 大量；許多

【修飾不可數名詞】

Don't eat too *much* cake.

mud[1] 〔mʌd〕 *n.* 泥巴

When it rains, the ground is covered with *mud*.

muddy[4] 〔'mʌdɪ〕 *adj.* 泥濘的

mug[1] 〔mʌg〕 *n.* 馬克杯

Alice poured the coffee into a *mug* and then added cream and sugar.

mule[2] 〔mjul〕 *n.* 騾

【比較】donkey（驢子）

multiple[4] 〔'mʌltəpḷ〕 *adj.* 多重的（= *many*）

There are *multiple* benefits to a university education.

【記憶技巧】*multi*（many）+ *ple*（fold）
（摺疊多次的，就是「多重的」）

multiply[2] 〔'mʌltə͵plaɪ〕 *v.* 繁殖（= *reproduce*）；大量增加；乘

Some insects reproduce very fast. They *multiply* rapidly.

murder[3] 〔'mɝdɚ〕 *v.* 謀殺（= *kill*）；徹底擊敗（= *defeat*） *n.* 謀殺（= *killing*）

He admitted killing the man but claimed it was an accident and not *murder*.

murderer[4] 〔'mɝdərɚ〕 *n.* 兇手（= *killer*）

The *murderer* received a life sentence.

murmur[4] 〔'mɝmɚ〕 *n.* 低語 *v.* 小聲地說；喃喃自語

Not wanting to disturb anyone else, John *murmured* an excuse and quietly left the room.

【典型考題】
The chairperson of the meeting asked everyone to speak up instead of ＿＿＿ their opinions among themselves.
A. reciting　　B. giggling
C. murmuring　D. whistling　[C]

muscle[3] 〔'mʌsḷ〕 *n.* 肌肉

museum[2] 〔mju'ziəm〕 *n.* 博物館

mushroom[3] 〔'mʌʃrum〕 *n.* 蘑菇 *v.* 迅速增加

♣music[1] 〔'mjuzɪk 〕 *n.* 音樂

*** musical**[3] 〔'mjuzɪkḷ 〕 *adj.* 音樂的
   n. 音樂劇
   【衍伸詞】*a Broadway musical*（百老匯音樂劇）

♣musician[2] 〔 mju'zɪʃən 〕 *n.* 音樂家

♣must[1] 〔 mʌst 〕 *aux.* 必須；一定
   (= *have to*)   *n.* 必備之物

*** mustache**[4] 〔 mə'stæʃ , 'mʌstæʃ 〕 *n.* 八字鬍
   The man had a lot of facial hair—both a *mustache* and a beard.
   【記憶技巧】*must* + *ache* (疼痛)

*** mutual**[4] 〔'mjutʃʊəl 〕 *adj.* 互相的
   (= *shared*)

Bob and I have a *mutual* agreement. I water his plants when he goes on vacation, and he does the same for me.
   【記憶技巧】*mut* (change) + *ual* (*adj.*)

*** mysterious**[4] 〔 mɪs'tɪrɪəs 〕 *adj.* 神秘的
   Bill is investigating the *mysterious* noise in the attic.

*** mystery**[3] 〔'mɪstrɪ 〕 *n.* 神祕；神祕的事物；謎 (= *puzzle*)
   【記憶技巧】*my* + *stery* (story) (每個人都有故事，我的故事就是個「謎」)
   【典型考題】
   The detective did his best to solve the _____ of the missing painting.
   A. liberty   B. mystery
   C. suspect   D. inquiry   [B]

N n

♣nail[2] 〔 nel 〕 *n.* 指甲；釘子
   Henry put a *nail* in the wall to hang a picture.
   【衍伸詞】*nail clippers* (指甲剪)

*** naked**[2] 〔'nekɪd 〕 *adj.* 赤裸的
   (= *nude*)；無覆蓋的；無掩飾的
   The baby ran through the house *naked* after his bath.

♣name[1] 〔 nem 〕 *n.* 名字   *v.* 命名
   【片語】*name* A *after* B (以 B 的名字爲 A 命名)

*** namely**[4] 〔'nemlɪ 〕 *adv.* 也就是說
   (= *specifically* = *that is to say*)

Six percent of the fifty students in this class are absent today; *namely*, Mary, Joe and Jack are absent today.
   【典型考題】
   The teacher said that one of the students was responsible for the broken window, _____ Joe.
   A. accordingly   B. essentially
   C. totally   D. namely   [D]

nanny[3] 〔'nænɪ 〕 *n.* 奶媽；褓姆

*** nap**[3] 〔 næp 〕 *n.* 小睡 (= *a short sleep*)
   My brother always takes a *nap* at noon.
   【片語】*take a nap* (小睡片刻)

♣napkin[2] 〔'næpkɪn 〕 *n.* 餐巾
   【比較】pumpkin (南瓜)

N

‡**narrow**² 〔ˈnæro 〕 *adj.* 窄的；勉強的
The road is very *narrow*.
【衍伸詞】 narrowly（狹窄地；勉強地）
【片語】 *have a narrow escape*（死裡逃生）

┌─【典型考題】──────
│ In the keen competition of this
│ international tennis tournament, she
│ _____ won the championship.
│ A. privately   B. distantly
│ C. locally   D. narrowly   [D]
└─────────────────

‡**nation**¹ 〔ˈneʃən 〕 *n.* 國家（= *country*）
There are many *nations* in the world.

‡**national**² 〔ˈnæʃənḷ 〕 *adj.* 全國的
（= *nationwide*）

*****nationality**⁴ 〔ˌnæʃənˈælətɪ 〕 *n.* 國籍
（= *citizenship*）

*****native**³ 〔ˈnetɪv 〕 *adj.* 本國的；本地的
（= *local*）；天生的   *n.* 當地人
For most people living in the U.S.,
English is their *native* language.

‡**natural**² 〔ˈnætʃərəl 〕 *adj.* 自然的；
天生的
Jimmy is interested in animals and
wild flowers, so I'm sure he would
enjoy this book on the *natural*
history of Taiwan.

┌─【典型考題】──────
│ Although many people think Sue's
│ blonde hair is _____, she actually
│ dyes it.
│ A. feverish   B. imitated
│ C. valid   D. natural   [D]
└─────────────────

‡**nature**¹ 〔ˈnetʃɚ 〕 *n.* 自然；本質
（= *quality*）

‡**naughty**² 〔ˈnɔtɪ 〕 *adj.* 頑皮的
（= *mischievous*）
These two brothers are really
naughty.

*****navy**³ 〔ˈnevɪ 〕 *n.* 海軍
（= *naval forces*）
Rick chose to do his military service
in the *navy*.
【比較】 army（陸軍）；*air force*（空軍）

‡**near**¹ 〔 nɪr 〕 *prep.* 在⋯附近
My house is *near* the school.

*****nearby**² 〔ˈnɪrˈbaɪ 〕 *adv.* 在附近
（= *not far away*）

‡**nearly**² 〔ˈnɪrlɪ 〕 *adv.* 幾乎（= *almost*）

*****nearsighted**⁴ 〔ˌnɪrˈsaɪtɪd 〕 *adj.*
近視的；短視近利的
Dave has to wear glasses because
he is *nearsighted*.
【反義詞】 farsighted（遠視的）
【重要知識】這個字以前唸成〔ˈnɪrˈsaɪtɪd 〕，
現在都唸成〔ˌnɪrˈsaɪtɪd 〕。

*****neat**² 〔 nit 〕 *adj.* 整潔的（= *tidy*）
Tanya always keeps her room *neat*
so that she can find things easily.

‡**necessary**² 〔ˈnɛsəˌsɛrɪ 〕 *adj.* 必要的
Sleep is *necessary* for good health.
【記憶技巧】 *ne*（not）+ *cess*（go away）
+ *ary*（不可或缺的東西，就是「必要的」）

*****necessity**³ 〔 nəˈsɛsətɪ 〕 *n.* 必要；需要
Necessity is the mother of invention.

‡**neck**¹ 〔 nɛk 〕 *n.* 脖子
She has a long *neck*.

necklace[2] 〔'nɛklɪs 〕 *n.* 項鍊
　【記憶技巧】*neck* + *lace*（細帶子）
　　（掛在脖子上的細帶子，即「項鍊」）
　【重要知識】necklace 可唸成〔'nɛklɪs 〕或
　〔'nɛkləs 〕，但不能唸成〔'nɛk‚les 〕，與 lace
　〔 les 〕、shoelace〔'ʃu‚les 〕比較。

necktie[3] 〔'nɛk‚taɪ 〕 *n.* 領帶（ = *tie*）
　【記憶技巧】*neck* + *tie*（綁）
　　（綁在脖子上的東西，即「領帶」）

need[1] 〔 nid 〕 *v.* 需要（ = *want*）
　n. 需要（ = *demand*）

needle[2] 〔'nidḷ 〕 *n.* 針；針頭

needy[4] 〔'nidɪ 〕 *adj.* 窮困的（ = *poor*）
　We collect old clothes to give to
　needy families.

negative[2] 〔'nɛgətɪv 〕 *adj.* 否定的；
　負面的
　Instead of being so *negative*, why
　don't you try thinking about the
　advantages of the situation?
　【記憶技巧】*neg*（deny）+ *ative*（adj.）
　　（對任何事情都抱持否定態度）
　【反義詞】positive（肯定的；正面的）

neglect[4] 〔 nɪ'glɛkt 〕 *v.* 忽略
　（ = *ignore*）　*n.* 忽略（ = *disregard*）
　Heidi *neglected* the houseplants
　and they all died.
　【記憶技巧】*neg*（not）+ *lect*（select）
　　（沒有選擇，即是「忽略」）

　【典型考題】
　He was dismissed for _____ his duty.
　A. motivating　　B. nourishing
　C. monitoring　　D. neglecting　　[D]

negotiate[4] 〔 nɪ'goʃɪ‚et 〕 *v.* 談判
　（ = *discuss*）；協商
　We were able to *negotiate* a fair
　price with the seller of the house.

　【記憶技巧】諧音法，談判破裂就會說「你
　　狗屎耶（negotiate）」。

　【典型考題】
　His personality makes it very
　difficult to _____ and reach an
　agreement with him.
　A. negotiate　　B. liberate
　C. decorate　　D. imitate　　[A]

neighbor[2] 〔'nebɚ 〕 *n.* 鄰居
　（ = *neighbour*【英式用法】）
　I'm lucky to have you as my *neighbor*.
　【記憶技巧】*nei*（near）+ *ghbor*
　　（dweller）（住在附近的人，就是「鄰居」）

neighborhood[3] 〔'nebɚ‚hud 〕 *n.*
　鄰近地區（ = *a nearby region*）

　【典型考題】
　After the earthquake, everyone in our
　_____ moved to the school next to my
　house.
　A. childhood　　B. neighborhood
　C. direction　　D. position　　[B]

neither[2] 〔'niðɚ 〕 *conj.* 也不
　If you cannot go, *neither* can I.
　I love *neither* James nor his brother.
　【片語】*neither* A *nor* B（既不是 A，
　　也不是 B）

nephew[2] 〔'nɛfju 〕 *n.* 姪兒；外甥
　【比較】niece（姪女；外甥女）

nerve[3] 〔 nɝv 〕 *n.* 神經；勇氣
　The brain sends signals to the body
　through *nerves*.

nervous[3] 〔'nɝvəs 〕 *adj.* 緊張的
　（ = *tense*）；神經的

nest[2] 〔 nɛst 〕 *n.* 巢
　There are six birds in the *nest*.

N

* **net**[2] 〔 nɛt 〕 n. 網 (= *web*)
adj. 淨餘的 (= *final*)；純的
The fishermen pulled in the *net* and
threw their catch on the deck of the
boat.
【衍伸詞】 *the Net* (網際網路)

* **network**[3] 〔'nɛt,wɜk 〕 n. (電腦)網路；
網路系統 (= *system*)；網狀組織
The *network* of roads around the city
can be confusing to people who are
unfamiliar with the area.
【記憶技巧】 *net* + *work*

‡ **never**[1] 〔'nɛvɚ 〕 adv. 從未
She has *never* been to a nightclub.
【記憶技巧】 *n* (not) + *ever* (曾經)

* **nevertheless**[4] 〔,nɛvɚðə'lɛs 〕 adv.
然而；仍然
John is short but he is a good
basketball player *nevertheless*.
【記憶技巧】 *never* + *the* + *less*

‡ **new**[1] 〔 nju 〕 adj. 新的

‡ **news**[1] 〔 njuz 〕 n. 新聞；消息
That man was on the *news* for killing
someone.

【典型考題】
The poor man's wife was very sick.
We did not know how to tell him the
bad _____.
A. example   B. health
C. idea   D. news   [D]

‡ **newspaper**[1] 〔'njuz,pepɚ 〕 n. 報紙
I read *newspapers* every day to know
what is happening in the world.

‡ **next**[1] 〔 nɛkst 〕 adj. 下一個
Linda is the *next* person to give a
speech.

‡ **nice**[1] 〔 naɪs 〕 adj. 好的
Julie is a very *nice* person.

* **nickname**[3] 〔'nɪk,nem 〕 n. 綽號
(= *informal name*)   v. 給…取綽號
My name is Theodore, but most of my
friends call me by my *nickname*, Mr. T.

* **niece**[2] 〔 nis 〕 n. 姪女；外甥女
Mrs. Black is going to visit her *niece*.
【比較】 nephew (姪兒；外甥)

‡ **night**[1] 〔 naɪt 〕 n. 晚上

* **nightmare**[4] 〔'naɪt,mɛr 〕 n. 惡夢
(= *bad dream*)；可怕的情景
Francine had a terrible *nightmare*
and was afraid to go back to sleep.
【記憶技巧】 *night* + *mare* (母馬)
(晚上做「惡夢」，夢見母馬)

* **noble**[3] 〔'nobḷ 〕 adj. 高貴的
Giving your place in the lifeboat to
that man was a *noble* act.

‡ **nobody**[2] 〔'no,badɪ 〕 pron. 沒有人
There is *nobody* inside the room.

‡ **nod**[2] 〔 nad 〕 v. 點頭
She *nodded* to me on the street.
【衍伸詞】 *a nodding acquaintance*
(點頭之交)

‡ **noise**[1] 〔 nɔɪz 〕 n. 噪音
I hate that *noise* because it drives
me crazy.

【典型考題】
When the teacher was not in the
classroom, the students talked loudly
and made a lot of _____.
A. excuses   B. heat
C. languages   D. noise   [D]

N

‡**noisy**[1] 〔ˋnɔɪzɪ〕 *adj.* 吵鬧的

‡**none**[2] 〔nʌn〕 *pron.* 沒有人
None of us are Americans.

***nonsense**[4] 〔ˋnɑnsɛns〕 *n.* 胡鬧；
胡說 (= *foolish words*)；無意義的話
The man was so drunk that he was
speaking *nonsense*.
【記憶技巧】 *non* (none) + *sense* (意義)
(沒有意義的話，就是「胡說」)

‡**noodle**[2] 〔ˋnudḷ〕 *n.* 麵
Chinese food is often served with
rice or *noodles*.
【衍伸詞】 *instant noodles* (速食麵)

‡**noon**[1] 〔nun〕 *n.* 正午
Lunch will be served at *noon*.

***nope**[1] 〔nop〕 *adv.* 不 (= *no*)
"*Nope*, I have no idea what time the
train leaves."

‡**nor**[1] 〔nɔr〕 *conj.* 也不
He can neither read *nor* write.
【片語】 *neither* A *nor* B (既不 A，也不 B)

***normal**[3] 〔ˋnɔrmḷ〕 *adj.* 正常的
(= *common*)
Thirty degrees is a *normal*
temperature for this time of year.
【反義詞】 abnormal (不正常的)

‡**north**[1] 〔nɔrθ〕 *n.* 北方
The wind is blowing from the
north.

***northern**[2] 〔ˋnɔrðən〕 *adj.* 北方的

‡**nose**[1] 〔noz〕 *n.* 鼻子 (= *snout*)
The clown has painted his *nose*
red.

‡**note**[1] 〔not〕 *n.* 筆記 (= *record*)
v. 注意
She never takes *notes* in class.
【片語】 *take notes* (做筆記)

‡**notebook**[2] 〔ˋnotˌbʊk〕 *n.* 筆記本；
筆記型電腦
I've written all the new words in
my *notebook*.

‡**nothing**[1] 〔ˋnʌθɪŋ〕 *pron.* 什麼也沒有
I will have *nothing* if I have to live
without you.

‡**notice**[1] 〔ˋnotɪs〕 *v.* 注意到 (= *note*)
n. 通知
Did you *notice* her new dress?

┌─【典型考題】─────────
│ Yuki loves wearing strange hats
│ because she wants people to _____
│ her.
│ A. believe   B. control
│ C. notice   D. visit   [C]
└──────────────────

***noun**[4] 〔naʊn〕 *n.* 名詞
【比較】 pronoun (代名詞)

***novel**[2] 〔ˋnɑvḷ〕 *n.* 小說 (= *fiction*)
adj. 新奇的 (= *new*)
He has written two *novels*, but
neither has been published yet.
【記憶技巧】 *nov* (new) + *el* (n.)
(「小說」的內容要新奇才會讓人想看)
【比較】 fiction (小說) 則是集合名詞。

***novelist**[3] 〔ˋnɑvḷɪst〕 *n.* 小說家

‡**November**[1] 〔noˋvɛmbə〕 *n.* 十一月

***nowadays**[4] 〔ˋnaʊəˌdez〕 *adv.* 現今
Air pollution is one of the most
important problems in Taiwan
nowadays.

* **nuclear**[4] 〔ˈnjuklɪ⋗〕 *adj.* 核子的
Nuclear energy can be used to
produce electricity.
【衍伸詞】 *nuclear weapon*（核子武器）

‡ **number**[1] 〔ˈnʌmb⋗〕 *n.* 數字；數量；
號碼
Each house has a *number*.

* **numerous**[4] 〔ˈnjumərəs〕 *adj.* 非常多
的【注意發音】（= *many*）
There are *numerous* advantages to
completing high school.
【記憶技巧】 *numer* (number) + *ous*
（數量眾多，也就是「非常多的」）

* **nun**[3] 〔nʌn〕 *n.* 修女；尼姑
【比較】 monk（修道士；和尚）

‡ **nurse**[1] 〔nɝs〕 *n.* 護士   *v.* 照顧
（= *take care of*）

* **nursery**[4] 〔ˈnɝsərɪ〕 *n.* 育兒室；
托兒所
There are several children in the
nursery.
【記憶技巧】 *nurs* (nurse) + *ery*（表「地
點」的字尾）
【衍伸詞】 *nursery rhyme*（兒歌；童謠）

‡ **nut**[2] 〔nʌt〕 *n.* 堅果
Henry likes to eat *nuts*.
【衍伸詞】 *go nuts*（發瘋）

* **nylon**[4] 〔ˈnaɪlɑn〕 *n.* 尼龍
Sarah wore a light *nylon* jacket to
protect herself from the wind.

O o

* **oak**[3] 〔ok〕 *n.* 橡樹
We sat in the shade of the *oak* tree.

* **obedience**[4] 〔əˈbidɪəns〕 *n.* 服從
（= *compliance*）
The commander demanded complete
obedience.
【記憶技巧】 *ob* (to) + *edi* (hear) + *ence*
（聽從命令，表示「服從」）

* **obedient**[4] 〔əˈbidɪənt〕 *adj.* 服從的
（= *compliant*）

‡ **obey**[2] 〔əˈbe〕 *v.* 服從（= *give in*）；
遵守（= *follow* = *observe*）
Students are supposed to *obey* school
regulations.

‡ **object**[2] 〔ˈɑbdʒɪkt〕 *n.* 物體
〔əbˈdʒɛkt〕 *v.* 反對

I can see a shining *object* in the sky.
The boss wouldn't *object* if you
smoked in his office.
【記憶技巧】 *ob* (against) + *ject* (throw)
（把東西丟向某人，就是「反對」）

* **objection**[4] 〔əbˈdʒɛkʃən〕 *n.* 反對
（= *opposition*）

* **objective**[4] 〔əbˈdʒɛktɪv〕 *adj.* 客觀的
（= *neutral*）   *n.* 目標（= *purpose*）
Newspaper articles should be as
objective as possible.
【反義詞】 subjective（主觀的）
【重要知識】 objection 和 objective 無詞類
變化的關係，objection 沒有形容詞，可用
oppositional 〔ˌɑpəˈzɪʃənl〕 *adj.* 反對的。

* **observation**[4] 〔ˌɑbzⱥˈveʃən〕 *n.* 觀察
（= *watching*）；遵守

O

** **observe**[3] 〔əbˋzɝv〕 v.* 觀察（= *watch carefully* ）；遵守（= *obey* ）

It is interesting to *observe* how students act on the first day at school.

【記憶技巧】 *ob* (eye) + *serve* (keep)（眼睛不停地看，即是「觀察」、「遵守」）

【典型考題】

In order to write a report on stars, we decided to ＿＿＿＿ the stars in the sky every night.

A. design   B. seize

C. quote   D. observe   **[D]**

** **obstacle**[4] 〔ˋɑbstəkḷ〕 n.* 阻礙；障礙（= *barrier* ）

The computer programmer discovered an *obstacle* that had to be overcome.

【記憶技巧】 *ob* (near) + *sta* (stand) + *cle* (*n.*)（站在反對立場，是一種「阻礙」）

【典型考題】

His reluctance to compromise is an ＿＿＿＿ to his political success.

A. obstacle   B. orchestra

C. objective   D. occupation   **[A]**

** **obtain**[4] 〔əbˋten〕 v.* 獲得

We won't be able to fix your car today because we couldn't *obtain* the part we need.

【記憶技巧】 *ob* (to) + *tain* (hold)（擁有就是「獲得」）

【比較】 con*tain* （包含）

sus*tain* （支撐；維持）

** **obvious**[3] 〔ˋɑbvɪəs〕 adj.* 明顯的（= *apparent* = *evident* ）

It's *obvious* that there are still some disadvantages to the plan he presented.

【記憶技巧】 *ob* (near) + *vi* (way) + *ous* (*adj.*)（靠近馬路的東西，看起來是非常「明顯的」）

** **occasion**[3] 〔əˋkeʒən〕 n.* 場合；特別的大事（= *a significant event* ）

Your graduation is an important *occasion* for you and your family.

【片語】 *on occasion* （偶爾）

【重要知識】美國人常說 What's the *occasion*?（有什麼特別的事？），如果你看到某人盛裝打扮，就可以說這句話。

** **occasional**[4] 〔əˋkeʒənḷ〕 adj.* 偶爾的（= *infrequent* ）

【衍伸詞】 occasionally （偶爾）

** **occupation**[4] 〔͵ɑkjəˋpeʃən〕 n.* 職業（= *job* = *vocation* ）；佔領

If you confine your choice to a certain *occupation*, your chance of getting a job may become smaller.

** **occupy**[4] 〔ˋɑkjə͵paɪ〕 v.* 使忙碌；佔領（= *take over* ）；居住（= *live in* ）

My club activities *occupy* most of my free time.

【記憶技巧】 *oc* (over) + *cupy* (seize)（奪取，也就是「佔據」）

【典型考題】

The U.S. Armed Forces tried to ＿＿＿＿ Baghdad and remove Saddam from power in a very short time.

A. protest   B. polish

C. offend   D. occupy   **[D]**

** **occur**[2] 〔əˋkɝ〕 v.* 發生（= *happen* ）

When a plane accident *occurs*, most people are killed.

*** **ocean**[1] 〔ˋoʃən〕 n.* 海洋；大量（= *a lot* ）

Oceans are very deep seas.

*** **o'clock**[1] 〔əˋklɑk〕 adv.* …點鐘

**** **October**[1] 〔ɑkˋtobɚ〕 n.* 十月

O

* **odd**[3] 〔 ɑd 〕 *adj.* 古怪的（ = *strange* ）；奇數的；零星的

I cannot understand Joan's *odd* behavior.

【注意】 這個字也作「奇數的」解，如 odd number（奇數）。

* **offend**[4] 〔 əˈfɛnd 〕 *v.* 得罪；觸怒；冒犯（ = *irritate* ）

Debbie was *offended* when I said she looked as though she had put on weight.

【記憶技巧】 *of*（against）+ *fend*（strike）

（所做的事讓人反感，表示「冒犯」到他人）

【典型考題】

Peter got fired because he said something that ＿＿＿＿ his boss.
A. beat   B. constructed
C. offended   D. against   [C]

* **offense**[4] 〔 əˈfɛns 〕 *n.* 攻擊；生氣

The best defense is *offense*.

【反義詞】 defense（防禦）

【片語】 *take offense*（生氣）

* **offensive**[4] 〔 əˈfɛnsɪv 〕 *adj.* 無禮的（ = *insulting* ）

‡ **offer**[2] 〔ˈɔfə 〕 *v.* 提供（ = *give* ）；提議 *n.* 提供

He *offered* me a better job.

【記憶技巧】 *of*（to）+ *fer*（carry）

（把東西帶來，也就是「提供」）

‡ **office**[1] 〔ˈɔfɪs 〕 *n.* 辦公室

‡ **officer**[1] 〔ˈɔfəsə 〕 *n.* 警官；軍官

The police *officer* stopped the car.

* **official**[2] 〔 əˈfɪʃəl 〕 *adj.* 官方的；正式的（ = *formal* ） *n.* 公務員；高級職員

An *official* from the Ministry of Health came to the hospital to explain the new regulations.

【重要知識】officer 是武官，official 是文官。

‡ **often**[1] 〔ˈɔfən 〕 *adv.* 常常

‡ **oil**[1] 〔 ɔɪl 〕 *n.* 油

Pat puts *oil* in the pan to fry an egg.

‡ **old**[1] 〔 old 〕 *adj.* 老的；舊的

* **omit**[2] 〔 oˈmɪt 〕 *v.* 遺漏（ = *leave out* ）

Don't *omit* his name from the list.

【記憶技巧】 *o*（away）+ *mit*（send）

（把東西送走，忘了帶，就是「遺漏」）

‡ **once**[1] 〔 wʌns 〕 *adv.* 一次 *conj.* 一旦

Henry has been to Paris *once*.

* **onion**[2] 〔ˈʌnjən 〕 *n.* 洋蔥

Do not put the *onion* in the soup.

‡ **only**[1] 〔ˈonlɪ 〕 *adj.* 唯一的 *adv.* 只有

* **onto**[3] 〔ˈɑntə ,ˈɑntu 〕 *prep.* 到…之上

The cat jumped *onto* the counter while I was preparing dinner.

‡ **open**[1] 〔ˈopən 〕 *v.* 打開 *adj.* 開放的

* **opera**[4] 〔ˈɑpərə 〕 *n.* 歌劇

Do you like to listen to Chinese *opera*?

【記憶技巧】 *oper*（work）+ *a*

（「歌劇」就是一件作品）

【衍伸詞】 *soap opera*（肥皂劇；連續劇）

* **operate**[2] 〔ˈɑpə,ret 〕 *v.* 操作（ = *run* ）；動手術（ = *perform surgery* ）

He can't make this machine work; he doesn't know how to *operate* it.

【記憶技巧】 *oper*（work）+ *ate*（v.）

（工作就是需要動手「操作」）

‡ **operation**[4] 〔,ɑpəˈreʃən 〕 *n.* 手術（ = *surgery* ）；運作（ = *action* ）；操作

I had an *operation* on my heart.

O

* **operator** [3] 〔'ɑpə,retɚ〕 *n.* 接線生；
操作員
I asked the telephone *operator*
to look up the number for me.

** **opinion** [2] 〔ə'pɪnjən〕 *n.* 意見
（= *idea*）；看法（= *view*）
Mary has no *opinion* at all.
【片語】 *in one's opinion*（依某人之見）

┌─【典型考題】──────
│ Helen's doctor suggested that she
│ undergo heart surgery. But she
│ decided to ask for a second _____
│ from another doctor.
│ A. purpose   B. statement
│ C. opinion   D. excuse   [C]
└────────────────

* **opportunity** [3] 〔,ɑpɚ'tjunətɪ〕 *n.* 機會
（= *chance*）
Traveling abroad will give you the
opportunity to learn about other
cultures.
【記憶技巧】 *op* (toward) + *portun*
(harbor) + *ity* (*n.*)（風吹進港口，就是
「機會」來了）

┌─【典型考題】──────
│ If you are not afraid of talking to
│ strangers, you'll have more _____
│ to make friends.
│ A. languages   B. opportunities
│ C. prescriptions D. problems   [B]
└────────────────

* **oppose** [4] 〔ə'poz〕 *v.* 反對（= *object to*）
They *opposed* the plan by mounting
a public protest.
【記憶技巧】 *op* (against) + *pose* (put)

┌─【典型考題】──────
│ We _____ the building of the bridge
│ here. We are against it.
│ A. manage   B. force
│ C. capture   D. oppose   [D]
└────────────────

* **opposite** [3] 〔'ɑpəzɪt〕 *adj.* 相反的
（= *contrary*）；對面的　*n.* 相反
Sandra turned and ran in the
opposite direction.

* **optimistic** [3] 〔,ɑptə'mɪstɪk〕 *adj.* 樂觀
的（= *hopeful*）
【反義詞】 pessimistic（悲觀的）
【記憶技巧】 optimistic 唸起來就有
高興的感覺，所以是「樂觀的」，而
pessimistic 就正好相反。

┌─【典型考題】──────
│ A person who thinks there is no need
│ to worry about tomorrow and that
│ everything will turn out fine is _____.
│ A. energetic   B. creative
│ C. optimistic   D. ambitious   [C]
└────────────────

oral [4] 〔'orəl , 'ɔrəl〕 *adj.* 口頭的
（= *spoken*）；口部的
Students will have to take an *oral*
exam as well as a written one.
【衍伸詞】 *oral exam*（口試）
【重要知識】 這個字也可唸〔'orəl〕，但美國人
現在多唸〔'ɔrəl〕。

** **orange** [1] 〔'ɔrɪndʒ〕 *n.* 柳橙
Sarah bought some *oranges* at the
supermarket.

* **orbit** [4] 〔'ɔrbɪt〕 *n.* 軌道；勢力範圍
v. 繞軌道運行
The satellite was launched into
orbit around the moon.

┌─【典型考題】──────
│ Each of the planets in the solar system
│ circles around the sun in its own
│ _____, and this prevents them from
│ colliding with each other.
│ A. entry   B. haste
│ C. orbit   D. range   [C]
└────────────────

O

* **orchestra**[4] 〔'ɔrkɪstrə 〕 n. 管絃樂團
The dancers were accompanied by a full *orchestra*.

‡ **order**[1] 〔'ɔrdɚ 〕 n. 命令
(= *command*)；順序　v. 命令
You have to learn to obey *orders*.

‡ **ordinary**[2] 〔'ɔrdṇ,ɛrɪ 〕 adj. 普通的
(= *usual*)；平淡的
We just want an *ordinary* lunch.
【記憶技巧】 *ordin* (order) + *ary* (adj.)
（ 按照順序，就是「普通的」）
【反義詞】 extraordinary (特別的)

┌─【典型考題】────────
We are _____ people. We can't be
as famous as Brad Pitt.
A. dependable　　B. terrified
C. genuine　　　　D. ordinary　　**[D]**
└──────────────────

* **organ**[2] 〔'ɔrgən 〕 n. 器官
(= *body part*)；機構 (= *organization*)
An unhealthy lifestyle can cause
damage to *organs* such as the heart
and lungs.
【記憶技巧】 organ 和 organize 一起背。

* **organic**[4] 〔 ɔr'gænɪk 〕 adj. 有機的；
天然的 (= *natural*)；器官的
The residents were asked to separate
organic and inorganic materials
when sorting their garbage.

* **organization**[2] 〔,ɔrgənə'zeʃən 〕 n.
組織；機構

* **organize**[2] 〔'ɔrgən,aɪz 〕 v. 組織
(= *form*)；安排；籌辦
They want to *organize* a political party.

* **origin**[3] 〔'ɔrədʒɪn 〕 n. 起源
(= *beginning*)；出身 【常用複數】

No one knows the exact *origin* of
the tribe, but most people think
they came from the northern plains.

* **original**[3] 〔 ə'rɪdʒənḷ 〕 adj. 最初的
(= *first*)；原本的；新穎的；有創意
的　 n. 原物；原文
【衍伸詞】 originally (本來；最初)

┌─【典型考題】────────
My _____ offer was turned down
politely. But when I tried again in my
most sincere manner, it was gladly
accepted.
A. numerous　　B. original
C. responsible　　D. talented　　**[B]**
└──────────────────

* **orphan**[3] 〔'ɔrfən 〕 n. 孤兒
The *orphan* was sent to live with
his grandparents after his parents
were killed.

* **otherwise**[4] 〔'ʌðɚ,waɪz 〕 adv. 否則
You had better hurry up; *otherwise*,
you are going to be late for school.
【記憶技巧】 *other* + *wise* (方式)
（ 除非有其他方式，「否則」就要按照原來
的方式做 ）

* **ought to**[3] 　 aux. 應該 (= *should*)
You *ought to* take an umbrella
because it might rain.

‡ **out**[1] 〔 aʊt 〕 adv. 向外；外出
v. 暴露；公開

* **outcome**[4] 〔'aʊt,kʌm 〕 n. 結果
(= *result*)
The *outcome* of the election was
announced two weeks ago.
【比較】 income (收入)

┌─【典型考題】────────
On the basis of the clues, can you
predict the _____ of the story?
A. outcome　　B. performance
C. cause　　　　D. headline　　**[A]**
└──────────────────

* **outdoor** [3] (ˈaʊtˌdor) *adj.* 戶外的
(= *open-air*)
It was an *outdoor* party, held beside the lake.

* **outdoors** [3] (ˈaʊtˈdorz) *adv.* 在戶外

* **outer** [3] (ˈaʊtɚ) *adj.* 外部的
(= *external*)
When he became too warm, Ted took off an *outer* layer of clothing.

* **outline** [3] (ˈaʊtˌlaɪn) *n.* 輪廓；大綱
(= *summary*)　*v.* 畫…的輪廓
After doing some research, I was able to write an *outline* of my term paper.
【記憶技巧】 *out* + *line* (線條)
(寫「大綱」就像畫出外部的線條)

‡ **outside** [1] (ˈaʊtˈsaɪd) *adv.* 在外面
(= *outdoors*)

* **outstanding** [4] (ˈaʊtˈstændɪŋ) *adj.* 傑出的 (= *excellent*)；出眾的；顯著的
Michael was awarded a medal for his *outstanding* performance.

* **oval** [4] (ˈovl̩) *adj.* 橢圓形的
(= *egg-shaped*)

‡ **oven** [2] (ˈʌvən) *n.* 烤箱
【衍伸詞】 *microwave oven* (微波爐)

* **overcoat** [3] (ˈovɚˌkot) *n.* 大衣
(= *heavy coat*)
Eric wears his *overcoat* only on the coldest days.

* **overcome** [4] (ˌovɚˈkʌm) *v.* 克服
(= *beat*)；戰勝 (= *defeat*)
A friendly smile helps us make friends quickly and *overcomes* differences in customs.

【典型考題】
Many students don't know how to
———— their stage fright.
A. conquest　　B. overcome
C. respond　　D. succumb　　**[B]**

* **overlook** [4] (ˌovɚˈluk) *v.* 忽視
(= *neglect* = *ignore*)；俯瞰 (= *look down on*)
The study has either been forgotten or *overlooked*, because no one mentioned it at the meeting.

* **overnight** [4] (ˈovɚˈnaɪt) *adv.* 一夜之間 (= *within one night*)；突然
He became famous *overnight*.

‡ **overpass** [2] (ˈovɚˌpæs) *n.* 天橋
(= *footbridge*)；高架橋；高架道路
It's safe for pedestrians to use the *overpass*.
【比較】 underpass (地下道)

‡ **overseas** [2] (ˈovɚˈsiz) *adv.* 在海外
adj. 海外的
This is my first *overseas* trip.
【衍伸詞】 *overseas Chinese* (華僑)

* **overtake** [4] (ˌovɚˈtek) *v.* 趕上
(= *catch up with*)；超越；超車
Ben ran as fast as he could but was not able to *overtake* the front-runner, so he came in second.

* **overthrow** [4] (ˌovɚˈθro) *v.* 打翻；推翻 (= *overturn*)
It is no surprise that there is a movement to *overthrow* the corrupt leader.
【記憶技巧】 *over* + *throw* (丟)

* **owe**[3] 〔 o 〕 *v.* 欠 (= *be in debt to*)
  You *owe* me four hundred dollars for the book I bought for you.

* **owl**[2] 〔 aʊl 〕 *n.* 貓頭鷹

‡ **own**[1] 〔 on 〕 *v.* 擁有 (= *possess*)
  adj. 自己的

‡ **owner**[2] 〔 'onɚ 〕 *n.* 擁有者
  (= *possessor*)

* **ownership**[3] 〔 'onɚˌʃɪp 〕 *n.* 所有權
  (= *right of possession*)
  The *ownership* of the land is uncertain.

‡ **ox**[2] 〔 ɑks 〕 *n.* 公牛 (= *bull*)
  【反義詞】 cow (母牛)

* **oxygen**[4] 〔 'ɑksədʒən 〕 *n.* 氧 (= O_2)
  【記憶技巧】 *oxy* (acid) + *gen* (produce)
  (「氧」被視爲構成酸的必要成分)

P p

* **pace**[4] 〔 pes 〕 *n.* 步調
  (= *tempo of motion*)
  Becky walked through the store at such a fast *pace* that I couldn't keep up with her.
  【注意】 表「以…步調」，介系詞用 at。

  ┌─【典型考題】─────
  If we walk at this slow ————, we'll never get to our destination on time.
  A. mood   B. pace
  C. tide   D. access   [B]
  └──────────────

‡ **pack**[2] 〔 pæk 〕 *v.* 包裝；打包   *n.* 小包
  All clothes will be *packed* into the bag.

‡ **package**[2] 〔 'pækɪdʒ 〕 *n.* 包裹
  (= *parcel*)；包裝好的商品；一套方案；套裝軟體
  Here is a *package* for you.
  【記憶技巧】 *pack* (包裝) + *age* (表「一組」的字尾)

* **pad**[3] 〔 pæd 〕 *n.* 墊子；便條紙；襯墊
  【重要知識】 pad 是種「片狀物」，像 iPad，i 代表 Internet，iPad 字面意思就是「可以上網的片狀物」。

‡ **page**[1] 〔 pedʒ 〕 *n.* 頁
  How many *pages* are there in this book?

* **pail**[3] 〔 pel 〕 *n.* 桶 (= *bucket*)
  Diane carried a *pail* of water to the garden.

‡ **pain**[2] 〔 pen 〕 *n.* 疼痛 (= *ache*)；痛苦
  She was in *pain* after she broke her leg.

‡ **painful**[2] 〔 'penfəl 〕 *adj.* 疼痛的
  (= *agonizing*)；痛苦的

‡ **paint**[1] 〔 pent 〕 *v.* 畫；油漆   *n.* 油漆
  I *painted* my house blue.
  【重要知識】 用鉛筆、原子筆等劃出線條，稱爲 draw，用水彩筆畫，就像刷油漆一樣的畫，才稱爲 paint。

* **painter**[2] 〔 'pentɚ 〕 *n.* 畫家；油漆工
  He wishes to be a *painter* in the future.

* **painting**[2] 〔 'pentɪŋ 〕 *n.* 畫

‡ **pair**[1] 〔 pɛr 〕 *n.* 一雙
  This *pair* of shoes is not on sale.

‡**pajamas**[2]〔pə'dʒæməz〕*n.pl.* 睡衣
I bought a new pair of *pajamas* today.
【記憶技巧】分音節背 pa-ja-mas。

***pal**[3]〔pæl〕*n.* 朋友（= *friend*）；夥伴
（= *companion*）；同志
Derek is one of my old *pals* from
junior high.

***palace**[3]〔'pælɪs〕*n.* 宮殿
（= *royal mansion*）
【記憶技巧】place 多加個 a，就是「宮殿」。
【衍伸詞】*the Palace Museum*（故宮博物院）

‡**pale**[3]〔pel〕*adj.* 蒼白的
She was *pale* with fear.

***palm**[2]〔pɑm〕*n.* 手掌；棕櫚樹
The fortune teller looked at the
palm of my hand and told me I
would have a happy life.

‡**pan**[2]〔pæn〕*n.* 平底鍋

***pancake**[3]〔'pæn,kek〕*n.* 薄煎餅；
鬆餅

‡**panda**[2]〔'pændə〕*n.* 貓熊；熊貓

***panel**[4]〔'pænḷ〕*n.* 面板；專門小組
The control *panel* in the cockpit is
crowded with instruments.
【片語】*control panel*（儀表板）

***panic**[3]〔'pænɪk〕*v.n.* 恐慌（= *fright*）
The passengers *panicked* when the
ship began to sink.
【panic的過去式及過去分詞為 panicked】

‡**pants**[1]〔pænts〕*n.pl.* 褲子
（= *trousers*〔'trauzɚz〕【英式用法】）
I saw him in a white shirt and black
pants.

***papa**[1]〔'pɑpə〕*n.* 爸爸

‡**papaya**[2]〔pə'paɪə〕*n.* 木瓜
Rose bought a *papaya* at the market.

‡**paper**[1]〔'pepɚ〕*n.* 紙；報告

***parachute**[4]〔'pærə,ʃut〕*n.* 降落傘
The skydivers have a backup
parachute in case the first one
doesn't open.
【記憶技巧】*para* (against) + *chute*
(fall)（防止掉落的東西，就是「降落傘」）

***parade**[3]〔pə'red〕*n.v.* 遊行
The townspeople celebrate the
festival with a *parade*.

***paradise**[3]〔'pærə,daɪs〕*n.* 天堂
（= *heaven*）；樂園（= *wonderland*）
Chris didn't like the beach, but I
thought it was *paradise*.

***paragraph**[4]〔'pærə,græf〕*n.* 段落
（= *passage*）
Our assignment is to write a
five-*paragraph* essay.
【記憶技巧】*para* (beside) + *graph*
(write)（不相關的內容寫在不同「段落」）

***parcel**[3]〔'pɑrsḷ〕*n.* 包裹
Would you like to send this *parcel*
by air or sea?

***pardon**[2]〔'pɑrdṇ〕*n.v.* 原諒
（= *forgive*）
I beg your *pardon*.
【記憶技巧】*par* (thoroughly) + *don*
(give)（願意全心付出，表示「原諒」）

‡**parents**[1]〔'pɛrənts〕*n.pl.* 父母
Linda stays with her *parents*.
【記憶技巧】*par* (give birth to) + *ents*
(persons)（生小孩的人，也就是「父母」）

P

‡**park**[1] 〔 pɑrk 〕 n. 公園　 v. 停車

‡**parrot**[2] 〔'pærət 〕 n. 鸚鵡
Parrots are birds of very bright colors.

‡**part**[1] 〔 pɑrt 〕 n. 部分 (= *portion*)
v. 分開 (= *separate*)
The best of friends must *part*.

***partial**[4] 〔'pɑrʃəl 〕 *adj.* 部分的；局部的；不完全的 (= *incomplete*)

┌─【典型考題】────────┐
Jack made a(n) ＿＿＿＿ payment on
the new computer because he did not
have enough money for it.
A. partial　　　B. original
C. effective　　D. courteous　　[A]
└──────────────┘

***participate**[3] 〔 pɑr'tɪsə,pet 〕 *v.* 參加
(= *take part in*)
In a modern democracy people
want to *participate* more fully.
【記憶技巧】 *parti* (part) + *cip* (take) +
ate (*v.*) (take part in，就是「參加」)

***participation**[4] 〔 pə,tɪsə'peʃən 〕 *n.*
參與

┌─【典型考題】────────┐
They wanted more direct ＿＿＿＿ in
the steel production programs.
A. phenomenon　B. participation
C. panels　　　　D. parachutes　　[B]
└──────────────┘

***participle**[4] 〔'pɑrtəsəpl̩ 〕 *n.* 分詞
【衍伸詞】 *past participle* (過去分詞)

***particular**[2] 〔 pə'tɪkjələ 〕 *adj.* 特別的
(= *special*)
I have nothing *particular* to do today.
【片語】 *in particular* (特別地；尤其)
【衍伸詞】 particularly (特別是；尤其)

***partner**[2] 〔'pɑrtnə 〕 n. 夥伴
(= *companion*)
They were *partners* in business.

***partnership**[4] 〔'pɑrtnə,ʃɪp 〕 n. 合夥
關係 (= *cooperation*)

‡**party**[1] 〔'pɑrtɪ 〕 n. 宴會
(= *celebration*)；政黨 (= *political
group*)
【衍伸詞】 *party politics* (政黨政治)

‡**pass**[1] 〔 pæs 〕 v. 經過 (= *go by*)；
通過；及格　 n. 通行證；通道

***passage**[3] 〔'pæsɪdʒ 〕 n. 一段 (文章)
(= *paragraph*)

***passenger**[2] 〔'pæsn̩dʒə 〕 n. 乘客

┌─【典型考題】────────┐
It is the bus driver's job to make sure
that every ＿＿＿＿ is safe.
A. maid　　　　B. passenger
C. stranger　　 D. vendor　　　[B]
└──────────────┘

***passion**[3] 〔'pæʃən 〕 n. 熱情
(= *affection*)
Young people often have more
passion for politics than their elders.

***passive**[4] 〔'pæsɪv 〕 *adj.* 被動的
(= *inactive*)
You should stand up for yourself
instead of taking such a *passive*
attitude.
【反義詞】 active (主動的)

┌─【典型考題】────────┐
The child was ＿＿＿＿. He just sat there
and waited for something to happen.
A. passive　　　B. expressive
C. extensive　　D. persuasive　　[A]
└──────────────┘

* **passport**[3] 〔'pæs,port 〕 *n.* 護照
When you cross the border of a country, you usually have to show your *passport*.
【記憶技巧】 *pass* (通過) + *port* (港口)
(通過港口要出示「護照」)

* **password**[3] 〔'pæs,wɜd 〕 *n.* 密碼
In order to log on, you have to enter your *password*.

‡ **past**[1] 〔 pæst 〕 *adj.* 過去的 (= *previous*)
n. 過去   *prep.* 超過；經過
┌─【典型考題】─
│ Life in Taiwan has changed a lot in
│ the _____ 20 years.
│ A. past   B. passed
│ C. passive   D. pass   [A]
└─────

* **pasta**[4] 〔'pɑstɑ , 'pæstə 〕 *n.* 義大利麵【總稱】
【比較】 spaghetti 〔 spə'gɛtɪ 〕 *n.* 義大利麵

‡ **paste**[2] 〔 pest 〕 *n.* 漿糊 (= *glue*)；糊狀物；糊；醬；膏；麵糰
Please use *paste* to stick your picture at the top of the application form.
【衍伸詞】 toothpaste (牙膏)

* **pat**[2] 〔 pæt 〕 *v. n.* 輕拍 (= *tap*)
The nurse *patted* my arm and told me not to worry.

‡ **path**[2] 〔 pæθ 〕 *n.* 小徑 (= *lane*)
Harry likes to walk down this *path* to get to the lake.

* **patience**[3] 〔'peʃəns 〕 *n.* 耐心
I have no *patience* with such an arrogant man.
【記憶技巧】 *pati* (endure) + *ence* (*n.*)

‡ **patient**[2] 〔'peʃənt 〕 *adj.* 有耐心的
n. 病人
【反義詞】 impatient (不耐煩的)
┌─【典型考題】─
│ One of the requirements of being
│ either a good teacher or a good nurse
│ is to be _____.
│ A. patient   B. artificial
│ C. familiar   D. original   [A]
└─────

* **pattern**[2] 〔'pætən 〕 *n.* 模式 (= *order*)；圖案；典範   *v.* 繪製圖案；仿照
Their movements all followed the same *pattern*.

‡ **pause**[3] 〔 pɔz 〕 *n.v.* 暫停
After a short *pause*, Lori kept on working.

* **pave**[3] 〔 pev 〕 *v.* 鋪 (路)
The residents have asked the city to *pave* the dirt road.

* **pavement**[3] 〔'pevmənt 〕 *n.* 人行道 (= *sidewalk*)；路面
Bobby fell off his bicycle and scraped his knee on the *pavement*.

* **paw**[3] 〔 pɔ 〕 *n.* (貓、狗的) 腳掌

‡ **pay**[1,3] 〔 pe 〕 *v.* 支付；付錢   *n.* 薪水
I'll *pay* for the meal.

* **payment**[1] 〔'pemənt 〕 *n.* 付款 (= *expense*)

* **pea**[3] 〔 pi 〕 *n.* 豌豆 (= *bean*)

‡ **peace**[2] 〔 pis 〕 *n.* 和平 (= *calmness*)
Both warring nations longed for *peace*.

* **peaceful**[2] 〔'pisfəl 〕 *adj.* 和平的 (= *at peace*)；平靜的；寧靜的 (= *serene*)

‡‡peach[2] 〔 pitʃ 〕 *n.* 桃子

*peak[3] 〔 pik 〕 *n.* 山頂（＝*top*）；
最高峰　*adj.* 旺季的；高峰時期的
v. 達到高峰；達到最高值
This is a high mountain and it will take
two days of hiking to reach the *peak*.

*peanut[2] 〔ˈpiˌnʌt 〕 *n.* 花生
【衍伸詞】*peanut butter*（花生醬）

‡‡pear[2] 〔 pɛr 〕 *n.* 西洋梨【注意發音】
A *pear* is a sweet and juicy fruit.

【重要知識】有則謎語：What fruit is never
alone? 答案就是 pear，因爲它和 pair（一對）
發音相同，如此就不會唸成〔 pɪr 〕（誤）。

*pearl[3] 〔 pɝl 〕 *n.* 珍珠

*pebble[4] 〔ˈpɛbḷ 〕 *n.* 小圓石；鵝卵石
Calvin walked along the lakeshore,
picking up *pebbles* and throwing
them into the water.

*peculiar[4] 〔 pɪˈkjuljɚ 〕 *adj.* 獨特的
（＝*special*）；特有的
John has a *peculiar* way of speaking
because he is not from around here.

【典型考題】
The native greeted the travelers in a
_____ language which was strange
to them.
A. contrary　　B. relative
C. peculiar　　D. spiral　　　[C]

*pedal[4] 〔ˈpɛdḷ 〕 *n.* 踏板；腳踏板
Marty bought some new parts for his
bike, including handlebars and *pedals*.
【比較】petal（花瓣）

【重要知識】字根 ped 意爲「腳；步」。「踏板」
就是腳踩的工具，如腳踏車、汽車油門、煞車，
還有鋼琴等的「踏板」。

【典型考題】
He pushed hard on the brake _____
to avoid a collision.
A. pebble　　　B. pasta
C. perfume　　D. pedal　　　[D]

*peel[3] 〔 pil 〕 *v.* 剝（皮）（＝*skin*）；
剝；脫落　*n.* 外皮
You need to *peel* that fruit before
eating it.

*peep[3] 〔 pip 〕 *v.* 偷窺
The little girl *peeped* through the
curtains at the visitors.
【衍伸詞】*peeping Tom*（偷窺者）

*peer[4] 〔 pɪr 〕 *n.* 同儕；同輩；相匹敵
的人　*v.* 凝視；仔細看；費力地看
The boy *peered* at the notice.
【衍伸詞】*peer pressure*（同儕壓力）

‡‡pen[1] 〔 pɛn 〕 *n.* 筆

*penalty[4] 〔ˈpɛnḷtɪ 〕 *n.* 處罰；刑罰；
懲罰
The *penalty* for robbery is death.
There can be no exception to the law.
【記憶技巧】*pen* (punish)＋*al* (adj.)
＋*ty* (n.)（處罰罪犯就是給予「刑罰」）

‡‡pencil[1] 〔ˈpɛnsḷ 〕 *n.* 鉛筆

*penguin[2] 〔ˈpɛngwɪn 〕 *n.* 企鵝

*penny[3] 〔ˈpɛnɪ 〕 *n.* 一分硬幣
（＝*cent*）；便士（英國貨幣單位）

‡‡people[1] 〔ˈpipḷ 〕 *n. pl.* 人
Many *people* ride the MRT at rush
hour.

‡‡pepper[2] 〔ˈpɛpɚ 〕 *n.* 胡椒；胡椒粉
I put *pepper* on the pizza.

***per**[2] 〔 pɚ 〕 *prep.* 每… (= *every*)
Gas prices have risen by three dollars *per* liter.

***percent**[4] 〔 pɚˈsɛnt 〕 *n.* 百分之…
Twenty is twenty *percent* of one hundred.
【記憶技巧】 *per* (每) + *cent* (hundred)

***percentage**[4] 〔 pɚˈsɛntɪdʒ 〕 *n.* 百分比 (= *rate*)

****perfect**[2] 〔 ˈpɝfɪkt 〕 *adj.* 完美的 (= *flawless*)；最適當的
【記憶技巧】 *per* (thoroughly) + *fect* (make) (把一件事完整做完，就是「完美的」)

***perfection**[4] 〔 pɚˈfɛkʃən 〕 *n.* 完美 (= *flawlessness*)

***perform**[3] 〔 pɚˈfɔrm 〕 *v.* 表演 (= *appear on stage*)；執行 (= *do*)
【記憶技巧】 背這個字要先背 form (形成)。

***performance**[3] 〔 pɚˈfɔrməns 〕 *n.* 表演 (= *public presentation*)；表現
The musician gave a wonderful *performance* at the concert hall.
【記憶技巧】 *per* (thoroughly) + *form* (provide) + *ance* (*n.*) (完整地呈現出來，就是「表演」)

***perfume**[4] 〔 pɚˈfjum 〕 *v.* 灑香水
〔 ˈpɝfjum 〕 *n.* 香水 (= *fragrance*)
Many department stores offer customers free samples of *perfume*.
【記憶技巧】 *per* (through) + *fume* (smoke) (噴灑「香水」時，看起來煙霧瀰漫)

*****perhaps**[1] 〔 pɚˈhæps 〕 *adv.* 也許
Perhaps your book is on your desk.

【記憶技巧】 *per* (by) + *haps* (chance)
(要憑運氣，就是也許有，也許沒有)

***period**[2] 〔 ˈpɪrɪəd 〕 *n.* 期間；時期；句點
This was the most difficult *period* of his life.
【記憶技巧】 *peri* (round) + *od* (way)
(繞一圈的時間，表示「期間」)

***permanent**[4] 〔 ˈpɝmənənt 〕 *adj.* 永久的 (= *eternal*)
After a series of temporary jobs, John found a *permanent* position in a big company.
【記憶技巧】 *per* (through) + *man* (stay) + *ent* (*adj.*) (一直停留，就是「永久的」)

***permission**[3] 〔 pɚˈmɪʃən 〕 *n.* 許可 (= *approval*)
Without special *permission*, no one can visit the castle.
【記憶技巧】 背這個字要先背 mission (任務)。

***permit**[3] 〔 pɚˈmɪt 〕 *v.* 允許 (= *allow*)
【記憶技巧】 *per* (through) + *mit* (send) (「允許」就是答應把你送過去)
【比較】 e<u>mit</u> (發射)；ad<u>mit</u> (承認)；sub<u>mit</u> (提出)；o<u>mit</u> (省略)

****person**[1] 〔 ˈpɝsn̩ 〕 *n.* 人
"VIP" means Very Important *Person*.

***personal**[2] 〔 ˈpɝsn̩l̩ 〕 *adj.* 個人的 (= *individual*)

***personality**[3] 〔 ˌpɝsn̩ˈælətɪ 〕 *n.* 個性 (= *individuality* = *character*)
Diana has such a wonderful *personality* that everyone likes her.

P

* **persuade**[3] 〔pɚˈswed〕 v. 說服
(= *convince*)
She *persuaded* her friend to go
camping with her.
【記憶技巧】 *per* (thoroughly) + *suade*
(advise) (徹底地勸告，就是「說服」)
【反義詞】 dissuade (勸阻)

* **persuasion**[4] 〔pɚˈsweʒən〕 n. 說服力

* **persuasive**[4] 〔pɚˈswesɪv〕 adj. 有說
服力的 (= *convincing*)
┌─【典型考題】──────
│ Mr. Wang's arguments were very
│ _____, and the committee finally
│ accepted his proposal.
│ A. artificial   B. inappropriate
│ C. persuasive   D. descriptive   [C]
└──────────────────

* **pessimistic**[4] 〔ˌpɛsəˈmɪstɪk〕 adj.
悲觀的 (= *gloomy*)
【反義詞】 optimistic (樂觀的)

* **pest**[3] 〔pɛst〕 n. 害蟲 (= *blight*)；
討厭的人或物 (= *annoyance*)
My little brother is a *pest*, following
me everywhere and doing anything
he can to get my attention.

* **pet**[1] 〔pɛt〕 n. 寵物

* **petal**[4] 〔ˈpɛtḷ〕 n. 花瓣

* **phenomenon**[4] 〔fəˈnaməˌnan〕 n.
現象 (= *happening*)
A tornado is an interesting weather
phenomenon.
【複數型為 phenomena】
【記憶技巧】 *phe* + *no* + *men* + *on*

* **philosopher**[4] 〔fəˈlasəfɚ〕 n.
哲學家

* **philosophical**[4] 〔ˌfɪləˈsafɪkəl〕 adj.
哲學的

* **philosophy**[4] 〔fəˈlasəfɪ〕 n. 哲學；
人生觀
"There's no such thing as a free
lunch" is his father's *philosophy*.
【記憶技巧】 *philo* (love) + *soph*
(wisdom) + *y* (n.) (「哲學」就是愛好
智慧者研究的學問)

* **photo**[2] 〔ˈfoto〕 n. 照片 (= *photograph*)
I took a lot of *photos* on my trip.

* **photograph**[2] 〔ˈfotəˌgræf〕 n. 照片
(= *snapshot*)

* **photographer**[2] 〔fəˈtagrəfɚ〕 n.
攝影師

* **photography**[4] 〔fəˈtagrəfɪ〕 n. 攝影

* **phrase**[2] 〔frez〕 n. 片語
【比較】 phase (階段)

* **physical**[4] 〔ˈfɪzɪkḷ〕 adj. 身體的
Stress can affect both our *physical*
and mental health.
【記憶技巧】 *phys*-表「身體」的字首。

* **physician**[4] 〔fəˈzɪʃən〕 n. 內科醫生
(= *medical doctor*)
The *physician* gave the patient a
complete checkup but could find
nothing wrong with him.
【比較】 surgeon (外科醫生)

* **physicist**[4] 〔ˈfɪzəsɪst〕 n. 物理學家

* **physics**[4] 〔ˈfɪzɪks〕 n. 物理學
Physics is my favorite subject.

***pianist**[4] 〔 pɪˋænɪst 〕 *n.* 鋼琴家
【記憶技巧】 *-ist* 表「人」的字尾。

‡**piano**[1] 〔 pɪˋæno 〕 *n.* 鋼琴

‡**pick**[2] 〔 pɪk 〕 *v.* 挑選 (*=choose*)；摘
Frank *picked* a ball from the box.

***pickle**[3] 〔ˋpɪkḷ 〕 *n.* 酸黃瓜；泡菜

***pickpocket**[4] 〔ˋpɪkͺpɑkɪt 〕 *n.* 扒手
(*=thief*)
A *pickpocket* stole my wallet while
I was in the crowded market.
【記憶技巧】 *pick* + *pocket* (口袋)
【衍伸詞】 *Beware of pickpockets*!
(小心扒手！)

‡**picnic**[2] 〔ˋpɪknɪk 〕 *n.* 野餐
(*=outdoor meal*)　 *v.* 去野餐
【片語】 *go on a picnic* (去野餐)

‡**picture**[1] 〔ˋpɪktʃɚ 〕 *n.* 圖畫
(*=drawing*)；照片 (*=photo*)
An artist is painting a *picture*.
【記憶技巧】 *pict* (paint) + *ure* (*n.*)

‡**pie**[1] 〔 paɪ 〕 *n.* 派 (*=pastry*)；餡餅
Elsa made a cherry *pie* by herself.

‡**piece**[1] 〔 pis 〕 *n.* 片 (*=slice*)；一件；
一項　 *v.* 拼湊
I gave him a *piece* of paper.

‡**pig**[1] 〔 pɪg 〕 *n.* 豬 (*=swine*)

***pigeon**[2] 〔ˋpɪdʒɪn 〕 *n.* 鴿子 (*=dove*)

***pile**[2] 〔 paɪl 〕 *n.* 堆　 *v.* 堆積
He puts the fruits in *piles* under
the tree.

***pilgrim**[4] 〔ˋpɪlgrɪm 〕 *n.* 朝聖者
(*=palmer*)

This is a sacred mountain and many
pilgrims visit it every year.
【記憶技巧】 *pil* (beyond) + *grim*
(country) (出國去尋找東西的人，就是
「朝聖者」)
【比較】 grim (嚴厲的)

***pill**[3] 〔 pɪl 〕 *n.* 藥丸
The doctor gave me some *pills* for
my headache.
【比較】 tablet (藥片)；capsule (膠囊)

‡**pillow**[2] 〔ˋpɪlo 〕 *n.* 枕頭 (*=cushion*)
This *pillow* is so hard that I can't
sleep.

─【典型考題】─────────
I bought two ＿＿＿＿ in a bedding
store yesterday.
A. pillars　　　　B. pets
C. pillows　　　　D. pickles　　[C]
─────────────────

***pilot**[3] 〔ˋpaɪlət 〕 *n.* 飛行員
The *pilot* announced that we would
be landing in Taipei shortly.

‡**pin**[2] 〔 pɪn 〕 *n.* 別針 (*=tack*)；大頭針
Lisa used *pins* to hold pieces of
cloth together.

***pine**[3] 〔 paɪn 〕 *n.* 松樹
We decided not to fell the *pine* in
the front yard.

‡**pineapple**[2] 〔ˋpaɪnͺæpḷ 〕 *n.* 鳳梨
A *pineapple* has a sweet taste.

***ping-pong**[2] 〔ˋpɪŋͺpɑŋ 〕 *n.* 乒乓球
(*=table tennis*)
I learned to play *ping-pong* when I
was in elementary school.

‡**pink**[2] 〔 pɪŋk 〕 *adj.* 粉紅色的

pint³ 〔paɪnt〕 n. 品脫（液體的衡量
單位，1 品脫約 0.473 公升）

* **pioneer**⁴ 〔ˌpaɪə'nɪr〕 n. 先驅
   （= starter）；先鋒（= forerunner）
   Henry Ford was a pioneer in the
   automobile industry.

‡ **pipe**² 〔paɪp〕 n. 管子（= tube）；煙斗
   （= smoking tool）；笛子（= flute）

* **pirate**⁴ 〔'paɪrət〕 n. 海盜　v. 盜版
   （= copy）
   Pirates attacked the ship and stole
   its cargo.
   【記憶技巧】背這個字要先背 rate（比率）。
   【衍伸詞】 piracy（盜版）

* **pit**³ 〔pɪt〕 n. 洞（= hole）；坑；礦坑
   The thieves dug a pit in the woods
   and buried the stolen money in it.

* **pitch**² 〔pɪtʃ〕 v. 投擲（= throw）
   n. 投擲；音調（= tone）
   She speaks in a high pitch.
   Ryan pitched the ball and the
   batter swung.

* **pity**³ 〔'pɪtɪ〕 n. 同情；可惜的事
   We felt pity for the poor people
   begging on the street.
   It is a pity that you missed the party.

‡ **pizza**² 〔'pitsə〕 n. 披薩

‡ **place**¹ 〔ples〕 n. 地方　v. 放置

‡ **plain**² 〔plen〕 n. 平原　adj. 平凡的
   （= ordinary）；淺顯易懂的；樸素的；
   坦白的
   Isabel likes to wear plain clothes and
   she is not interested in fashion at all.

‡ **plan**¹ 〔plæn〕 n.v. 計劃（= design）
   Eve planned to study abroad.

‡ **planet**² 〔'plænɪt〕 n. 行星
   Our earth is one of the planets in the
   solar system.

‡ **plant**¹ 〔plænt〕 n. 植物；工廠
   v. 種植（= cultivate）
   The mango is a tropical plant.

* **plastic**³ 〔'plæstɪk〕 adj. 塑膠的
   The cup is plastic, so it won't break
   if you drop it.

‡ **plate**² 〔plet〕 n. 盤子

‡ **platform**² 〔'plæt,fɔrm〕 n. 月台
   We are waiting for him on the
   platform.
   【記憶技巧】 plat (flat) + form
   （「月台」是一塊平坦的地方）

‡ **play**¹ 〔ple〕 v. 玩　n. 戲劇

‡ **player**¹ 〔'pleɚ〕 n. 運動員；演奏者；
   播放器；選手（= contestant）

   playful² 〔'plefəl〕 adj. 愛玩的；頑皮
   的；開玩笑的；鬧著玩的

‡ **playground**¹ 〔'ple,graʊnd〕 n.
   運動場（= schoolyard）；遊樂場

‡ **pleasant**² 〔'plɛznt〕 adj. 令人愉快的
   （= agreeable）
   I spent a pleasant afternoon at the
   seaside.

‡ **please**¹ 〔pliz〕 v. 取悅（= entertain）
   adv. 請
   Nothing pleased him.

‡**pleasure**² 〔ˈplɛʒɚ 〕 *n.* 樂趣
(= *enjoyment*)

┌─【典型考題】────────────┐
│ Playing piano gives me great _____.
│ I want to be a pianist in the future.
│ A. pleasure   B. jewelry
│ C. furniture   D. scrape   [A]
└────────────────────────┘

*plentiful⁴ 〔ˈplɛntɪfəl 〕 *adj.* 豐富的
(= *abundant*)
There will be *plentiful* food and
drink at the party.
【記憶技巧】 *plen* (full) + *ti* (*n.*) + *ful*
(*adj.*) (充滿資源的，表示「豐富的」)

*plenty³ 〔ˈplɛntɪ 〕 *n.* 豐富
(= *abundance*)
【片語】 *plenty of* (很多)

*plot⁴ 〔 plɑt 〕 *n.* 情節 (= *story*)；策略
v. 密謀；構思
The movie is so complicated that I
cannot follow the *plot*.

*plug³ 〔 plʌg 〕 *n.* 插頭   *v.* 插插頭
【比較】 outlet (插座)

*plum³ 〔 plʌm 〕 *n.* 梅子
【衍伸詞】 *plum blossom* (梅花)

*plumber³ 〔ˈplʌmɚ 〕 *n.* 水管工人
(= *pipe fitter*)
The *plumber* was able to fix the
leak in the pipe.

*plural⁴ 〔ˈplʊrəl 〕 *n.* 複數
Make sure you use the *plural* of the
verb when you are talking about two
people.
【反義詞】 singular (單數)

*plus² 〔 plʌs 〕 *prep.* 加上 (= *added to*)
Three *plus* five is eight.

‡**p.m.**⁴ 〔ˈpiˈɛm 〕 下午(= *pm* = *P.M.* = *PM*)
It's 5:30 *p.m.*
【比較】 a.m. (上午)

‡**pocket**¹ 〔ˈpɑkɪt 〕 *n.* 口袋 (= *pouch*)
There are two *pockets* on my pants.
【衍伸詞】 *pocket money* (零用錢)

*poem² 〔ˈpo‧ɪm 〕 *n.* 詩 (= *verse*)

*poet² 〔ˈpo‧ɪt 〕 *n.* 詩人
【重要知識】 poet (詩人) 和 pickpocket
(扒手)，都是 et 結尾，代表「人」。

*poetry¹ 〔ˈpo‧ɪtrɪ 〕 *n.* 詩【集合名詞】
(= *rhyme*)

‡**point**¹ 〔 pɔɪnt 〕 *n.* 點 (= *spot*)
What do these *points* on the map
stand for?

‡**poison**² 〔ˈpɔɪzn̩ 〕 *n.* 毒藥 (= *toxin*)
There is *poison* in the bottle.

*poisonous⁴ 〔ˈpɔɪznəs 〕 *adj.* 有毒的
(= *toxic*)

*pole³ 〔 pol 〕 *n.* (南、北) 極；竿；
極端；電池極點；(大寫) 波蘭人
Both the North and South *Poles* are
covered by ice.

‡**police**¹ 〔 pəˈlis 〕 *n.* 警察；警方
The *police* caught the robbers.
【衍伸詞】 *police station* (警察局)

*policeman¹ 〔 pəˈlismən 〕 *n.* 警察
(= *cop*)

*policy² 〔ˈpɑləsɪ 〕 *n.* 政策 (= *plan*)
Honesty is the best *policy*.

* **polish**[4] 〔'palɪʃ〕 *v.* 擦亮（= *shine*）；
加強；潤飾　*n.* 亮光劑；擦亮；
光澤；完美
We will *polish* all the silverware
before the party.

‡ **polite**[2] 〔pə'laɪt〕 *adj.* 有禮貌的
You have to be *polite* when speaking
to the teacher.
【反義詞】 impolite（不禮貌的）

┌─【典型考題】─────────
│ Be _____ to people when you talk
│ to them.
│ A. stupid　　　B. bump
│ C. convenient　D. polite　　[D]
└──────────────────────

* **political**[3] 〔pə'lɪtɪkḷ〕 *adj.* 政治的
Political decisions have a widespread
impact on economic development.
【記憶技巧】 *polit* (state) + *ical* (adj.)
（政治方面的事，就是關於國家的事）

* **politician**[3] 〔,palə'tɪʃən〕 *n.* 政治人物
（= *statesman*）；政客
【比較】 statesman（政治家）

* **politics**[3] 〔'palə,tɪks〕 *n.* 政治學

* **poll**[3] 〔pol〕 *n.* 民意調查；（選舉的）
投票　*v.* 對…進行民意調查；得到
（票數）
The most recent *poll* told the
candidate that he was losing support.

‡ **pollute**[3] 〔pə'lut〕 *v.* 污染
（= *contaminate*）
The rivers have been *polluted*.

‡ **pollution**[4] 〔pə'luʃən〕 *n.* 污染
（= *contamination*）

┌─【典型考題】─────────
│ Is air _____ very serious in Taipei?
│ A. semester　　　B. pollution
│ C. system　　　　D. future　　[B]
└──────────────────────

‡ **pond**[1] 〔pand〕 *n.* 池塘（= *pool*）
There were two dogs drinking from
the *pond*.

* **pony**[3] 〔'ponɪ〕 *n.* 小馬（= *little horse*）
The children rode *ponies* around the
farm.
【衍伸詞】 ponytail（馬尾）

‡ **pool**[1] 〔pul〕 *n.* 水池；游泳池
There is a swimming *pool* in the
front yard.

‡ **poor**[1] 〔pʊr〕 *adj.* 窮的
【反義詞】 rich（有錢的）

* **pop**[3] 〔pap〕 *adj.* 流行的（= *popular*）
Most young people are interested in
pop culture.
【衍伸詞】 *pop music*（流行音樂）

‡ **popcorn**[1] 〔'pap,kɔrn〕 *n.* 爆米花
（= *popped corn*）
I love to eat *popcorn* when watching
TV.
【記憶技巧】 *pop* + *corn*（玉米）

‡ **popular**[2,3] 〔'papjələ˞〕 *adj.* 受歡迎的
（= *liked*）；流行的
"Snow White" is a very *popular* story.
【記憶技巧】 *popul* (people) + *ar* (adj.)
（大家都能接受的，表示「受歡迎的」）

* **popularity**[4] 〔,papjə'lærətɪ〕 *n.* 受歡
迎（= *being popular*）；流行；普遍

‡population[2] 〔͵pɑpjəˈleʃən〕 *n.* 人口
　（= *inhabitant*）；（動物的）群體
　China has a large *population*.

‡pork[2] 〔pork〕 *n.* 豬肉
　I hate eating *pork*.

*port[2] 〔port〕 *n.* 港口（= *harbor*）；
　港市

*portable[4] 〔ˈportəbl̩〕 *adj.* 手提的
　Lucy's parents gave her a *portable*
　CD player for her birthday.

┌─【典型考題】──────────────┐
│ Julie wants to buy a _____ computer
│ so that she can carry it around when
│ she travels.
│ A. memorable　　B. portable
│ C. predictable　　D. readable　　[B]
└────────────────────────┘

*porter[4] 〔ˈportɚ〕 *n.* （行李）搬運員
　（= *bearer*）
　We asked a *porter* to help us with
　our luggage.

*portion[3] 〔ˈporʃən〕 *n.* 部分（= *part*）
　As it was my birthday, Mother gave
　me the largest *portion* of the cake.
　【記憶技巧】*port* (part) + *ion* (*n.*)

*portrait[3] 〔ˈportret〕 *n.* 肖像
　（= *image*）
　I had my *portrait* painted last year.

*portray[4] 〔porˈtre〕 *v.* 描繪；描寫
　【記憶技巧】*por* (forward) + *tray*
　(draw)（用筆畫出線條，就是「描繪」）

*pose[2] 〔poz〕 *n.* 姿勢　*v.* 擺姿勢
　（= *posture*）
　The model sat in a relaxed *pose*.

*position[1] 〔pəˈzɪʃən〕 *n.* 位置
　（= *location*）
　Someone removed the book from its
　position on the shelf.

*positive[2] 〔ˈpɑzətɪv〕 *adj.* 肯定的
　（= *certain*）；樂觀的（= *optimistic*）；
　正面的
　Be *positive*! You still have a chance
　to pass the exam.
　【反義詞】negative（否定的；消極的）

┌─【典型考題】──────────────┐
│ Don't be sad. Be _____ and believe
│ the door of opportunity will always
│ open to you.
│ A. positive　　　B. well-mannered
│ C. original　　　D. hospitable　　[A]
└────────────────────────┘

possess[4] 〔pəˈzɛs〕 *v.* 擁有
　（= *have* = *own*）
　He *possessed* great wisdom.
　【記憶技巧】*po* + *ssess*

*possession[4] 〔pəˈzɛʃən〕 *n.* 擁有
　（= *hold*）
　Those paintings are in my father's
　possession.
　【片語】*in* one's *possession*（為某人所有）

*possibility[2] 〔͵pɑsəˈbɪlətɪ〕 *n.* 可能性
　（= *probability*）

┌─【典型考題】──────────────┐
│ Is there much _____ of his winning
│ the election?
│ A. collection　　B. plastics
│ C. garbage　　　D. possibility　　[D]
└────────────────────────┘

‡‡possible[1] 〔ˈpɑsəbl̩〕 *adj.* 可能的
　If *possible*, send it to my office
　tomorrow.
　【反義詞】impossible（不可能的）

P

P

****post**[2] 〔 post 〕 *n.* 郵政（ = *mail service*）; 柱子; 崗位;（網路）貼文 *v.* 郵寄（ = *mail*）; 把（最近的）消息告訴（某人）

Send the package by *post*.

【片語】 *by post*（以郵寄）

****postage**[3] 〔'postɪdʒ 〕 *n.* 郵資（ = *postal fees*）

Our government has decided to raise the *postage* on July 20th.

【記憶技巧】 *post*（郵件）+ *age* (*n.*)

（寄發郵件須支付的費用，就是「郵資」）

*‡‡***postcard**[2] 〔'post,kɑrd 〕 *n.* 明信片

****poster**[3] 〔'postɚ 〕 *n.* 海報（ = *placard*）

I saw a *poster* advertising the new movie.

【記憶技巧】 *post*（柱子）+ *er* (*n.*)

（以前「海報」都是貼在柱子上）

****postpone**[3] 〔 post'pon 〕 *v.* 延期（ = *delay* = *put off*）; 延後

We will *postpone* the meeting until next week.

【記憶技巧】 *post* (after) + *pone* (put)

（將時間往後挪，就是「延期」）

┌─【典型考題】─────────┐
The young couple decided to _____
their wedding until all the details
were well taken care of.
A. announce　　B. maintain
C. postpone　　D. simplify　　[C]
└────────────────┘

****postponement**[3] 〔 post'ponmənt 〕 *n.* 延期（ = *delay*）; 延後

*‡‡***pot**[2] 〔 pɑt 〕 *n.* 鍋子（ = *pan*）; 壺; 陶罐

****potato**[2] 〔 pə'teto 〕 *n.* 馬鈴薯

【衍伸詞】 *potato chips*（洋芋片）

****pottery**[3] 〔'pɑtɚɪ 〕 *n.* 陶器（ = *ceramic*）; 陶藝

****poultry**[4] 〔'poltrɪ 〕 *n.* 家禽（ = *domesticated birds*）

The *poultry* farmer has over twenty thousand chickens.

*‡***pound**[2] 〔 paʊnd 〕 *n.* 磅

The tomato weighs four *pounds*.

****pour**[3] 〔 por 〕 *v.* 傾倒（ = *drain*）; 下傾盆大雨

Can I *pour* some more coffee for you?

****poverty**[3] 〔'pɑvɚtɪ 〕 *n.* 貧窮（ = *scarcity*）

After both parents lost their jobs, the family lived in *poverty*.

****powder**[3] 〔'paʊdɚ 〕 *n.* 粉末

He doesn't like this brand of milk *powder*.

【記憶技巧】 背這個字要先背 power, 在字中加 d。

*‡‡***power**[1] 〔'paʊɚ 〕 *n.* 力量（ = *ability*）

Carrying this heavy box requires a lot of *power*.

****powerful**[2] 〔'paʊɚfəl 〕 *adj.* 強有力的（ = *strong*）

Lucas gave that thief a *powerful* blow.

****practical**[3] 〔'præktɪkḷ 〕 *adj.* 實際的（ = *realistic*）

Although he studied management in college, John does not have any *practical* experience.

【衍伸詞】 practically（實際上; 幾乎）

‡practice[1] (ˈpræktɪs) v. 練習
(= *exercise*)   n. 實踐；慣例；做法
My younger sister *practices* playing
piano every day.

﹡praise[2] (prez) v. n. 稱讚
(= v. *applaud*; n. *applause*)
My teacher always *praises* me.
【記憶技巧】 *praise* (price)
    (給予好的評價，就表示「稱讚」)

┌─【典型考題】────────
│ Since he is jealous of my success, his
│ words of ＿＿＿ don't sound sincere.
│ They ring hollow.
│ A. command   B. praise
│ C. gratitude   D. empathy   [B]
└─────────────────

‡pray[2] (pre) v. 祈禱
John *prays* before he goes to bed.

﹡prayer[3] (ˈpreɚ) n. 祈禱者
(prɛr) n. 祈禱 (文)

﹡precious[3] (ˈprɛʃəs) adj. 珍貴的
(= *valuable*)
Diamonds are *precious* stones.
【記憶技巧】 *preci* (price) + *ous* (adj.)

﹡precise[4] (prɪˈsaɪs) adj. 精確的
(= *accurate*)
Please tell me the *precise* cost of
the tour.
【記憶技巧】 *pre* (before) + *cise* (cut)
   (為了追求精確，會先把多餘的東西切掉)

﹡predict[4] (prɪˈdɪkt) v. 預測
(= *forecast*)
It is impossible to *predict* an
earthquake.
【記憶技巧】 *pre* (before) + *dict* (say)
   (在事情發生前先說出來，也就是「預測」)

﹡prefer[2] (prɪˈfɝ) v. 比較喜歡
(= *favor*)
He *prefers* a new house to a
remodeled one.
【記憶技巧】 *pre* (before) + *fer* (carry)
   (擺在前面的位置，表示「比較喜歡」)

﹡preferable[4] (ˈprɛfərəbḷ) adj. 比較
好的 (= *favored*)；較合人意的

┌─【典型考題】────────
│ Emma and Joe are looking for a live-in
│ babysitter for their three-year-old twins,
│ ＿＿＿ one who knows how to cook.
│ A. initially   B. apparently
│ C. preferably   D. considerably   [C]
└─────────────────

﹡pregnancy[4] (ˈprɛgnənsɪ) n. 懷孕
(= *child-bearing*)

﹡pregnant[4] (ˈprɛgnənt) adj. 懷孕的
The *pregnant* woman said that she
would soon have twins.
【記憶技巧】 *pre* (before) + *gnant*
(be born) (生產前的狀態就是「懷孕」)

﹡preparation[3] (ˌprɛpəˈreʃən) n.
準備 (= *arrangement*)

┌─【典型考題】────────
│ John's part-time experience at the
│ cafeteria is good ＿＿＿ for running
│ his own restaurant.
│ A. preparation   B. recognition
│ C. formationt   D. calculation   [A]
└─────────────────

‡prepare[1] (prɪˈpɛr) v. 準備
(= *get ready*)
Fred *prepares* his own breakfast in
the morning.
【記憶技巧】 *pre* (before) + *pare* (get
ready)

P

* **preposition**⁴ 〔ˌprɛpə'zɪʃən〕 *n.*
介系詞

* **presence**² 〔'prɛzn̩s〕 *n.* 出席
(= *attendance*)

‡‡ **present**² 〔'prɛzn̩t〕 *adj.* 現在的；出席
的 (= *appear*)　　*n.* 禮物 (= *gift*)；
現在　〔prɪ'zɛnt〕 *v.* 展示；呈現
A lot of students were *present* at
the meeting.
【反義詞】 absent (缺席的)

【重要知識】美國人常說："Today is the
present." 句中 the present 可當「現在」，
也可當「禮物」，表示「要珍惜今天」。

【典型考題】
My son's birthday is coming. I want
to buy him a computer as a birthday
_____ .
A. place　　　B. party
C. poster　　　D. present　　　**[D]**

* **presentation**⁴ 〔ˌprɛzn̩'teʃən〕 *n.*
報告；演出；贈送；呈現；提出；
引見；介紹；出席；被贈送或提出之物
A well-written *presentation* can
create a strong impression that will
help you a lot in getting a good job.

* **preservation**⁴ 〔ˌprɛzɚ'veʃən〕 *n.*
保存；維持

【典型考題】
The police are in charge of the _____
of law and order.
A. presentation　B. preservation
C. preposition　D. possession　**[B]**

* **preserve**⁴ 〔prɪ'zɜv〕 *v.* 保存
(= *protect*)
Drying is one of the oldest known
ways of *preserving* fruits.

【記憶技巧】 *pre* (before) + *serve* (keep)
(保持在以前的狀態，就是「保存」)
【比較】 ob<u>serve</u> (觀察；遵守)
de<u>serve</u> (應得)
re<u>serve</u> (預訂；保留)
con<u>serve</u> (節省)

‡‡ **president**² 〔'prɛzədənt〕 *n.* 總統；
總裁
The *president* gave a speech on TV.

* **press**² 〔prɛs〕 *v.* 壓；按
Please *press* this button.
【衍伸詞】 *the press* (新聞界)

* **pressure**³ 〔'prɛʃɚ〕 *n.* 壓力
(= *force* = *stress* = *tension*)

【典型考題】
Many businessmen are under great
_____ to gain the largest market
share possible.
A. pressure　　　B. fame
C. stage　　　　D. greed　　　**[A]**

* **pretend**³ 〔prɪ'tɛnd〕 *v.* 假裝
(= *make believe*)；謊稱；裝扮
Steven *pretended* to be ill so that he
could stay home from school.
【記憶技巧】 *pre* (before) + *tend*
(stretch) (在別人面前展開另一種面貌，
就是「假裝」)

【典型考題】
When you make a mistake, you have
to face it. You just can't _____
nothing has happened.
A. prevent　　　B. preview
C. pretend　　　D. prepare　　　**[C]**

‡‡ **pretty**¹ 〔'prɪtɪ〕 *adj.* 漂亮的
adv. 相當
Emma is a *pretty* girl.

* **prevent**[3] 〔 prɪˋvɛnt 〕 *v.* 預防；阻止
Washing your hands frequently is
one way to *prevent* illness.
【記憶技巧】 *pre* (before) + *vent*
(come) (事情來臨前所做的，即「預防」)

* **prevention**[4] 〔 prɪˋvɛnʃən 〕 *n.* 預防
(= *avoidance*)
Prevention is better than cure.

* **previous**[3] 〔ˋprivɪəs 〕 *adj.* 先前的
(= *earlier*)；以前的；預先的
First we reviewed what we had
learned in the *previous* lesson.
【衍伸詞】 previously (以前)

‡ **price**[1] 〔 praɪs 〕 *n.* 價格；代價
┌─【典型考題】────────────
The _____ of the house is too high.
My parents do not have enough
money to buy it.
A. price   B. size
C. space   D. wall   [A]
└──────────────────────

* **pride**[2] 〔 praɪd 〕 *n.* 驕傲(= *self-esteem*)
He took *pride* in his daughter's
achievements.
【片語】 *take pride in* (以～為榮)
┌─【典型考題】────────────
Peter's parents felt great _____ when
he won the speech contest.
A. talent   B. pride
C. personality   D. friendship   [B]
└──────────────────────

‡ **priest**[3] 〔 prist 〕 *n.* 神職人員；神父
(= *clergyman*)
That man is a *priest*, isn't he?

‡ **primary**[3] 〔ˋpraɪˏmɛrɪ 〕 *adj.* 主要的
(= *main*)；基本的 (= *basic*)
I don't know the *primary* purpose
of his visit.

【記憶技巧】 *prim* (first) + *ary* (*adj.*)
(排在第一順位，表示「主要的」)
【衍伸詞】 *primary school* (小學)

* **prime**[4] 〔 praɪm 〕 *adj.* 主要的
(= *chief*)；上等的 (= *best*)
Immigration is the *prime* factor in
the increase of the state's population.
【衍伸詞】 *prime minister* (首相)
           prime beef (上等牛肉)

* **primitive**[4] 〔ˋprɪmətɪv 〕 *adj.* 原始的
(= *original*)
Primitive man used fire to drive
away dangerous animals.
┌─【典型考題】────────────
_____ people often lived in caves.
A. Primitive   B. Pregnant
C. Precise   D. Poisonous   [A]
└──────────────────────

‡ **prince**[2] 〔 prɪns 〕 *n.* 王子；親王
A *prince* is the son of a king and
a queen.

‡ **princess**[2] 〔ˋprɪnsɪs 〕 *n.* 公主
A *princess* is the daughter of a king
and a queen.

‡ **principal**[2] 〔ˋprɪnsəpḷ 〕 *n.* 校長
adj. 主要的 (= *chief*)
Mr. Brown is the *principal* of our
school.
【比較】 principle (原則)
┌─【記憶技巧】 principal 和 principle 容易
搞混，只要記住 pal 是「朋友；夥伴」，
當校長 (princi**pal**)要把老師和學生當作
朋友 (**pal**)。

* **principle**[2] 〔ˋprɪnsəpḷ 〕 *n.* 原則
(= *basic rule*)
The *principle* was established that
the chairman should change yearly.

P

P

***print**[1]〔 prɪnt 〕*v. n.* 印刷（ = *v.* *publish*）；列印

Many books are *printed* for use in schools.

***printer**[2]〔'prɪntɚ〕*n.* 印表機（ = *printing machine*）

***prison**[2]〔'prɪzn̩〕*n.* 監獄（ = *jail*）

The robber was sent to *prison*.

【記憶技巧】*pris* (seize) + *on* (n.)
（抓到人關進「監獄」）

┌─【典型考題】─────────
It is said that three men escaped from _____ but were soon captured.
A. safety   B. audience
C. appearance   D. prison   **[D]**
└────────────────────

***prisoner**[2]〔'prɪznɚ〕*n.* 囚犯（ = *captive*）；俘虜

***privacy**[4]〔'praɪvəsɪ〕*n.* 隱私權（ = *secrecy*）

Reporters sometimes invade superstars' *privacy*.

***private**[2]〔'praɪvɪt〕*adj.* 私人的（ = *personal*）

This is my *private* room.

【反義詞】public（公眾的）

***privilege**[4]〔'prɪvl̩ɪdʒ〕*n.* 特權（ = *special right*）

Club members enjoy special *privileges* that ordinary visitors do not.

【記憶技巧】*privi* (private) + *lege* (law)（限於一個人的法律，表示「特權」）

┌─【典型考題】─────────
First class passengers have special _____ when flying.
A. baggage   B. flights
C. privileges   D. context   **[C]**
└────────────────────

***prize**[2]〔 praɪz 〕*n.* 獎；獎品

He won first *prize*.

***probable**[3]〔'prɑbəbl̩〕*adj.* 可能的

Bad weather is the *probable* cause of the delay.

【記憶技巧】*prob* (test) + *able* (adj.)
（經過測試才知道可能的結果）

***problem**[1]〔'prɑbləm〕*n.* 問題

***procedure**[4]〔 prə'sidʒɚ 〕*n.* 程序

In the event of a fire, just follow the *procedure* we have practiced.

┌─【典型考題】─────────
His application for citizenship was not accepted because he did not follow the correct _____.
A. miracle   B. calculation
C. interaction   D. procedure   **[D]**
└────────────────────

***proceed**[4]〔 prə'sid 〕*v.* 前進（ = *advance*）

The store will close in ten minutes, so all customers should *proceed* to the checkout line.

【記憶技巧】*pro* (forward) + *ceed* (go)（往前走，就是「前進」）

***process**[3]〔'prɑsɛs〕*n.* 過程 *v.* 加工；處理

In the *process* of learning to write, one has to learn to think at the same time.

【記憶技巧】*pro* (forward) + *cess* (go)

┌─【典型考題】─────────
Applying in college means sending in applications, writing study plan, and so on. It's a long _____, and it makes students nervous.
A. errand   B. operation
C. process   D. display   **[C]**
└────────────────────

*produce² 〔 prə'djus 〕 v. 生產
（ = *manufacture* ）；製造
The fickle behavior of nature both
produces life and destroys it.
【記憶技巧】 *pro* (forth) + *duce*
(lead) (向前引出，表示「生產」)

【典型考題】
The country is unable to ＿＿＿＿ enough
food for its growing population.
A. construct　　B. produce
C. consume　　D. establish　　[B]

*producer² 〔 prə'djusə 〕 n. 生產者；
製造者 (= *manufacturer*)；製作人

*product³ 〔'pradəkt 〕 n. 產品

【典型考題】
Cheese, powdered milk, and yogurt
are common milk ＿＿＿＿.
A. produces　　B. productivities
C. productions　D. products　　[D]

*production⁴ 〔 prə'dʌkʃən 〕 n. 生產

*productive⁴ 〔 prə'dʌktɪv 〕 adj. 有
生產力的；多產的

【典型考題】
The piece of land near the valley is so
fertile that it has been very ＿＿＿＿
every year.
A. dynamic　　B. productive
C. marvelous　D. critical　　[B]

*profession⁴ 〔 prə'fɛʃən 〕 n. 職業
(= *occupation*)
My uncle is a musician by *profession*.
【片語】 *by profession* (就職業而言)

*professional⁴ 〔 prə'fɛʃənḷ 〕 adj.
職業的；專業的；內行的；高水準的
【反義詞】 amateur (業餘的)

*professor⁴ 〔 prə'fɛsə 〕 n. 教授
She is a *professor* of physics at my
university.

*profit³ 〔'prafɪt 〕 n. 利潤 (= *benefit*)；
利益
Although business was slow, we still
made a small *profit*.

*profitable⁴ 〔'prafɪtəbḷ 〕 adj. 有利
可圖的 (= *beneficial*)；盈利的

*program³ 〔'progræm 〕 n. 節目；
課程；程式
There are *programs* on television
that explain how to do things.

*progress² 〔'pragrɛs 〕 n. 進步
He has made great *progress* in math.
【記憶技巧】 *pro* (forward) + *gress*
(walk) (往前邁進，表示「進步」)

*project² 〔'pradʒɛkt 〕 n. 計劃
〔 prə'dʒɛkt 〕 v. 投射
The bridge is a Japanese *project*.
【記憶技巧】 *pro* (forward) + *ject*
(throw) (決定動作前，要先拿出企劃案)

*prominent⁴ 〔'pramənənt 〕 adj.
卓越的 (= *outstanding*)；突出的；
著名的
The scandal involved several
prominent business leaders.
【記憶技巧】 *pro* (forth) + *min* (jut 突出)
+ *ent* (adj.) (卓越人士的表現都很突出)

*promise² 〔'pramɪs 〕 v. n. 保證
(= *guarantee*)；答應；承諾
He *promised* to wait till I came back.

*promising⁴ 〔'pramɪsɪŋ 〕 adj. 有前
途的
He has a *promising* future as a scientist.

P

* **promote**[3] 〔 prəˊmot 〕 *v.* 使升遷；
推銷；提倡；促銷

I hear that the company plans on *promoting* him soon because of his good work.

【記憶技巧】*pro* (forward) + *mote* (move)（職位向前移動，就是「使升遷」）

【典型考題】
To ＿＿＿＿ the new product, the company offered some free samples before they officially launched it.
A. contribute   B. impress
C. promote   D. estimate   [C]

* **promotion**[4] 〔 prəˊmoʃən 〕 *n.* 升遷；
促銷；提倡

【典型考題】
The car company is planning a big ＿＿＿＿ for their new car.
A. procedure   B. promotion
C. profession   D. protection   [B]

* **prompt**[4] 〔 prɑmpt 〕 *adj.* 迅速的
(= *immediate*)；即時的；及時的；
敏捷的

We were warned to be *prompt* for the meeting as it always starts on time.

【典型考題】
The bank tries its best to attract more customers. Its staff members are always available to provide ＿＿＿＿ service
A. singular   B. prompt
C. expensive   D. probable   [B]

* **pronoun**[4] 〔ˊpronaʊn 〕 *n.* 代名詞
【記憶技巧】*pro* (in place of) + *noun* (名詞)

⁑ **pronounce**[2] 〔 prəˊnaʊns 〕 *v.* 發音
How do you *pronounce* this word?

【記憶技巧】*pro* (out) + *nounce* (announce)（向外宣佈，就是「發音」）

* **pronunciation**[4] 〔 prəˏnʌnsɪˊeʃən 〕 *n.* 發音

* **proof**[3] 〔 pruf 〕 *n.* 證據 (= *evidence*)

* **proper**[3] 〔ˊprɑpɚ 〕 *adj.* 適當的
(= *suitable*)

What would be a *proper* gift for my hostess?

* **property**[3] 〔ˊprɑpɚtɪ 〕 *n.* 財產
(= *assets*)；特性 (= *quality*)

They lost a lot of money and they are considering selling their *property*.

【衍伸詞】*the properties of iron*
(鐵的特性)

* **proposal**[3] 〔 prəˊpozl̩ 〕 *n.* 提議；求婚

* **propose**[2] 〔 prəˊpoz 〕 *v.* 提議
(= *suggest*)；求婚

At the conclusion of the meal, the host rose and *proposed* a toast.

【記憶技巧】*pro* (forward) + *pose* (put)（將自己的想法放在大家面前，就是「提議」）

【典型考題】
We ＿＿＿＿ three dates for the conference and they chose the first one.
A. proposed   B. anticipated
C. decided   D. served   [A]

* **prosper**[4] 〔ˊprɑspɚ 〕 *v.* 繁榮
(= *thrive*)；興盛

The business did not *prosper* and it soon closed.

【記憶技巧】背這個字要先背 proper (適當的)，中間再加 s。

P

* **prosperity**[4] 〔 prɑsˈpɛrətɪ 〕 *n.* 繁榮

【典型考題】
The country's vast oil fields have
meant ＿＿＿ for most of its citizens.
A. prosperity　　B. community
C. investment　　D. economics　　[A]

* **prosperous**[4] 〔ˈprɑspərəs 〕 *adj.* 繁榮
的 (= *thriving* = *flourishing*)

* **protect**[2] 〔 prəˈtɛkt 〕 *v.* 保護
(= *defend*)；防護
Parents try their best to *protect* their
children from getting hurt.

【典型考題】
The president is ＿＿＿ by special
agents 24 hours a day.
A. offended　　B. protected
C. acquired　　D. enclosed　　[B]

* **protection**[3] 〔 prəˈtɛkʃən 〕 *n.* 保護
(= *defense*)

* **protective**[3] 〔 prəˈtɛktɪv 〕 *adj.* 保護的
(= *defensive*)

* **protein**[4] 〔ˈprotiɪn 〕 *n.* 蛋白質
Foods such as eggs are high in *protein*.

* **protest**[4] 〔ˈprotɛst 〕 *n.* 抗議
(= *objection*)　〔 prəˈtɛst 〕 *v.*
The residents *protested* when the
park was closed.
【記憶技巧】 *pro* + *test* (測驗)

* **proud**[2] 〔 praʊd 〕 *adj.* 驕傲的
(= *arrogant*)；得意的；自豪的
They are *proud* that she is doing
well at school.
【片語】 *be proud of* (以～為榮)

* **prove**[1] 〔 pruv 〕 *v.* 證明；證明是；
結果是
I can *prove* his innocence.

* **proverb**[4] 〔ˈprɑvɝb 〕 *n.* 諺語
(= *saying*)；格言
My father often quotes a *proverb* to
make his point.
【記憶技巧】 *pro* (before) + *verb*
(word) (「諺語」是以前的人說的話)

* **provide**[2] 〔 prəˈvaɪd 〕 *v.* 提供
They didn't *provide* me with any
details.
【片語】 *provide sb. with sth.* (提供某
物給某人)

* **psychological**[4] 〔ˌsaɪkəˈlɑdʒɪkl̩ 〕 *adj.*
心理的

* **psychologist**[4] 〔 saɪˈkɑlədʒɪst 〕 *n.*
心理學家

* **psychology**[4] 〔 saɪˈkɑlədʒɪ 〕 *n.* 心理學
【記憶技巧】 *psycho* (soul) + *logy*
(study) (關於心靈的研究，就是「心理學」)

* **pub**[3] 〔 pʌb 〕 *n.* 酒吧 (= *bar*)

* **public**[1] 〔ˈpʌblɪk 〕 *adj.* 公共的；
公開的
You mustn't do that in a *public*
place.

* **publication**[4] 〔ˌpʌblɪˈkeʃən 〕 *n.*
出版 (品)
Harry Potter fans eagerly await the
publication of the seventh book in
the series.

P

* **publicity**[4] 〔 pʌbˈlɪsətɪ 〕 *n.* 出名；知名度

Neil's restaurant was mentioned in the newspaper and the *publicity* brought him several new customers.

【典型考題】

To gain more _____, some legislators would get into violent physical fights so that they might appear in TV news reports.
A. publicity   B. communication
C. symbol   D. reputation   [A]

* **publish**[4] 〔ˈpʌblɪʃ 〕 *v.* 出版
(= *issue* = *print*)

Ethan has written three books, but none of them have been *published*.
【記憶技巧】 *publ* (public) + *ish* (*v.*)
(「出版」就是把文章公開)

* **publisher**[4] 〔ˈpʌblɪʃɚ 〕 *n.* 出版商

* **pudding**[2] 〔ˈpʊdɪŋ 〕 *n.* 布丁

For dessert we had a simple chocolate *pudding*.

‡ **pull**[1] 〔 pʊl 〕 *v.* 拉

I *pulled* her up from the river.
【反義詞】 push (推)

‡ **pump**[2] 〔 pʌmp 〕 *n.* 抽水機

We use a *pump* to draw water.

‡ **pumpkin**[2] 〔ˈpʌmpkɪn 〕 *n.* 南瓜
【記憶技巧】 *pump* (large melon) + *kin* (small)
【比較】 napkin (餐巾)

* **punch**[3] 〔 pʌntʃ 〕 *v.* 用拳頭打
(= *strike*)

Arthur was winning the fight until the other boy *punched* him in the nose.

* **punish**[2] 〔ˈpʌnɪʃ 〕 *v.* 處罰
(= *discipline*)

Sam's parents *punished* him for being bad.
【記憶技巧】 *pun* (penalty) + *ish* (*v.*)
(給予懲罰，也就是「處罰」)

* **punishment**[2] 〔ˈpʌnɪʃmənt 〕 *n.* 處罰
(= *discipline*)

Most people are against physical *punishment* today.

* **pupil**[2] 〔ˈpjupḷ 〕 *n.* 學生 (= *student*)；瞳孔

Mrs. Clark taught her *pupils* a new song in music class today.

* **puppet**[2] 〔ˈpʌpɪt 〕 *n.* 木偶；傀儡

The *puppet* is controlled by strings attached to its arms and legs.

‡ **puppy**[2] 〔ˈpʌpɪ 〕 *n.* 小狗

A lot of *puppies* were sold at the night market.
【衍伸詞】 *puppy love* (初戀)

* **pure**[3] 〔 pjʊr 〕 *adj.* 純粹的
(= *unmixed*)

The piece of old jewelry was found to be made of *pure* gold.

‡ **purple**[1] 〔ˈpɝpḷ 〕 *adj.* 紫色的
n. 紫色

‡ **purpose**[1] 〔ˈpɝpəs 〕 *n.* 目的
(= *intention*)

The *purpose* of going to school is to learn.
【記憶技巧】 *pur* (before) + *pose* (put)
(置於每件事的前方，表示做事的「目的」)
【片語】 *on purpose* (故意地)

P

‡**purse**[2] 〔 pɜs 〕 *n.* 錢包；手提包；
財力 *v.* 噘（嘴）
A *purse* is a very small bag.
【比較】wallet（皮夾）

***pursue**[3] 〔 pəˈsu 〕 *v.* 追求（= *chase*）；
從事；追查
She *pursued* the goal of perfection
in her works.
【記憶技巧】*pur* (forth) + *sue* (follow)
（跟隨自己的目標前進，就是「追求」）
【比較】sue（控告）；ensue（跟著發生）

***pursuit**[4] 〔 pəˈsut 〕 *n.* 尋求；追求
（= *seeking*）；嗜好
【片語】*in pursuit of*（追求）

‡**push**[1] 〔 puʃ 〕 *v.* 推
They *pushed* him into the car.
【反義詞】pull（拉）

‡**put**[1] 〔 put 〕 *v.* 放

***puzzle**[2] 〔ˈpʌzl̩ 〕 *v.* 使困惑（= *confuse*）
He was *puzzled* and couldn't answer
the question.

Q q

***quake**[4] 〔 kwek 〕 *n.* 地震
（= *earthquake*）
The strong *quake* caused extensive
damage to the downtown area.

***quality**[2] 〔ˈkwɑlətɪ 〕 *n.* 品質；特質

***quantity**[2] 〔ˈkwɑntətɪ 〕 *n.* 量
（= *amount*）
The products of this company are
cheaper if you order them in large
quantities.

***quarrel**[3] 〔ˈkwɔrəl 〕 *n. v.* 爭吵
（= *argue*）
The children often *quarrel* over
what to watch on TV.

‡**quarter**[2] 〔ˈkwɔrtɚ 〕 *n.* 四分之一；
二角五分硬幣；一刻鐘；十五分鐘；
一季（三個月）
He has walked a *quarter* of a mile.

‡**queen**[1] 〔 kwin 〕 *n.* 女王；皇后

***queer**[3] 〔 kwɪr 〕 *adj.* 奇怪的
（= *strange*）
I find it *queer* that John never talks
about his past.

‡**question**[1] 〔ˈkwɛstʃən 〕 *n.* 問題
v. 質問；詢問

‡**quick**[1] 〔 kwɪk 〕 *adj.* 快的
I'm not a *quick* runner.

‡**quiet**[1] 〔ˈkwaɪət 〕 *adj.* 安靜的
Sally is a *quiet* child.

【典型考題】
Be _____ when you enter the
classroom.
A. easy   B. quiet
C. handsome   D. quite   [B]

***quilt**[4] 〔 kwɪlt 〕 *n.* 棉被；被子

***quit**[2] 〔 kwɪt 〕 *v.* 停止（= *stop*）；辭職
（= *resign*）
He has to *quit* smoking.

‡**quite**[1] 〔kwaɪt〕*adv.* 非常（= *very*）；
相當；十分

He is *quite* sick, so he can't go to
school today.

‡**quiz**[2] 〔kwɪz〕*n.* 小考

We'll have a *quiz* in math class
tomorrow.

***quotation**[4] 〔kwoˈteʃən〕*n.* 引用的
文句

The article contains several
quotations from the Bible.

***quote**[3] 〔kwot〕*v.* 引用（= *cite*）

Our teacher always *quotes* from
the Bible.

【典型考題】
To impress the audience, speakers
often ＿＿＿＿ traditional sayings in
their speech.
A. betray　　　　B. quote
C. adapt　　　　D. attain　　　[B]

R r

‡**rabbit**[2] 〔ˈræbɪt〕*n.* 兔子

【比較】hare（野兔）

‡**race**[1] 〔res〕*n.* 種族（= *people*）；
賽跑

He came in second in the *race*.

***racial**[3] 〔ˈreʃəl〕*adj.* 種族的

The company was accused of *racial*
discrimination when it did not give
the job to the best candidate, who
was black.

***radar**[3] 〔ˈredɑr〕*n.* 雷達

‡**radio**[1] 〔ˈredɪˌo〕*n.* 收音機；無線電

***rag**[3] 〔ræg〕*n.* 破布
（= *a piece of cloth*）

【片語】*in rags*（衣衫襤褸）

rage[4] 〔redʒ〕*n.* 憤怒（= *anger*）

My parents flew into a *rage* when
they saw my bad grades.

【片語】*fly into a rage*（勃然大怒）

***railroad**[1] 〔ˈrelˌrod〕*n.* 鐵路
（= *railway*【英式用法】）

A new *railroad* is being built.

‡**rain**[1] 〔ren〕*n.* 雨　*v.* 下雨

‡**rainbow**[1] 〔ˈrenˌbo〕*n.* 彩虹

There are seven colors in the *rainbow*.

【記憶技巧】*rain* + *bow*（弓）
（雨後的彩虹是弓型的）

***rainfall**[4] 〔ˈrenˌfɔl〕*n.* 降雨（量）；
下雨

Since there has been almost no
rainfall, the farmers won't have good
harvests.

【比較】water<u>fall</u>（瀑布）

rainy[2] 〔ˈrenɪ〕*adj.* 下雨的

‡**raise**[1] 〔rez〕*v.* 提高（= *lift*）；舉起；
養育

Jennifer is the first to *raise* her hand.

***raisin**[3] ﹝'rezn̩﹞ *n.* 葡萄乾
（＝*dried grape*）
【比較】grape（葡萄）

***range**[2] ﹝rendʒ﹞ *n.* 範圍（＝*scope*）；
種類；牧場 *v.*（範圍）包括
There is a wide price *range* for books.
【片語】*range from* A *to* B（範圍）從
A 到 B 都有

***rank**[3] ﹝ræŋk﹞ *n.* 階級（＝*class*）；
地位；排；橫列 *v.* 排列；（使）位居
If you are promoted, you will move
up in *rank*.

***rapid**[2] ﹝'ræpɪd﹞ *adj.* 迅速的；快速的
（＝*quick*）
He took a *rapid* glance at me.

***rare**[2] ﹝rɛr﹞ *adj.* 罕見的（＝*scarce*）
These flowers are very *rare* in this
country.

***rat**[1] ﹝ræt﹞ *n.* 老鼠（＝*large mouse*）
The *rats* have made holes in those
bags of rice.
【比較】mouse（老鼠），體型較 rat 小。

***rate**[3] ﹝ret﹞ *n.* 速度（＝*speed*）；
速率；比率；費用；價格
We will never get there at this *rate*
of speed.

***rather**[2] ﹝'ræðɚ﹞ *adv.* 相當地
It was *rather* a cool day.
【片語】*would rather⋯than*～（寧願⋯，
也不願～）

***raw**[3] ﹝rɔ﹞ *adj.* 生的
Put that *raw* meat into the refrigerator
until we are ready to cook it.

***ray**[3] ﹝re﹞ *n.* 光線
A *ray* of sunshine came through the
curtains and woke me up.

***razor**[3] ﹝'rezɚ﹞ *n.* 刮鬍刀；剃刀

***reach**[1] ﹝ritʃ﹞ *v.* 抵達（＝*arrive at*）；
伸出
We *reached* the airport in time.
【衍伸詞】*reach out for*（伸手去拿）

***react**[3] ﹝rɪ'ækt﹞ *v.* 反應
When someone yelled fire, the
audience *reacted* by running for
the exits.
【記憶技巧】*re*（back）＋*act*
（做動作回覆，也就是「反應」）

┌─【典型考題】─────────
│ Smart children always ＿＿＿＿ to their
│ parents' facial expressions. When
│ their parents look angry, they behave
│ themselves.
│ A. rely   B. react
│ C. refuse   D. resort   **[B]**
└──────────────────────

***reaction**[3] ﹝rɪ'ækʃən﹞ *n.* 反應

***read**[1] ﹝rid﹞ *v.* 讀
Dad *reads* the newspaper every
morning.

***ready**[1] ﹝'rɛdɪ﹞ *adj.* 準備好的
Karen is not *ready* for the exam.

***real**[1] ﹝'riəl﹞ *adj.* 真的（＝*actual*）
This apple is not *real*.

***realistic**[4] ﹝ˌriə'lɪstɪk﹞ *adj.* 寫實的

***reality**[2] ﹝rɪ'ælətɪ﹞ *n.* 真實
（＝*actuality*）
【片語】*in reality*（事實上）

‡**realize**[2] 〔ˈriəˌlaɪz〕 v. 了解
(= *understand*)；實現

Penny didn't *realize* that it was already Saturday.

【典型考題】
Only when we lose our health can we _____ how much it means to us. Before that, we always take it for granted.
A. realize   B. ignore
C. swear   D. attract   [A]

‡**reason**[1] 〔ˈrizn̩〕 n. 理由 (= *cause*)

We have *reason* to believe that he is right.

***reasonable**[3] 〔ˈriznəbl̩〕 adj. 合理的
(= *sensible*)

【典型考題】
The prices of some products in outlet stores are more _____ than those in supermarkets.
A. reasoning   B. reasonable
C. beneficial   D. personal   [B]

***rebel**[4] 〔rɪˈbɛl〕 v. 反叛 (= *revolt*)
〔ˈrɛbl̩〕 n. 叛徒
【記憶技巧】 *re* (again) + *bel* (war)
（因為敵軍「反叛」，而再次引起戰爭）

***recall**[4] 〔rɪˈkɔl〕 v. 回想
(= *remember*)；召回

Although I had memorized the formulas, I could not *recall* any of them during the test.
【記憶技巧】 *re* (back) + *call* (叫)

【典型考題】
How can you expect me to _____ exactly what happened twelve years ago?
A. remind   B. recall
C. refill   D. reserve   [B]

***receipt**[3] 〔rɪˈsit〕 n. 收據【注意發音】
(= *proof of purchase*)

Don't forget to ask the store for a *receipt* when you buy something.

‡**receive**[1] 〔rɪˈsiv〕 v. 收到 (= *get*)

Andrew *received* a bicycle from his uncle yesterday.
【記憶技巧】 *re* (back) + *ceive* (take)
（拿到自己這邊，表示「收到」）

***receiver**[3] 〔rɪˈsivɚ〕 n. 聽筒
(= *handset*)

Carrie picked up the *receiver* and dialed 119.

***recent**[2] 〔ˈrisn̩t〕 adj. 最近的

That is my experience of *recent* years.
【衍伸詞】 recently (最近)

***reception**[4] 〔rɪˈsɛpʃən〕 n. 歡迎
(會)；接待

I was given a warm *reception* when I first joined the company.

***recipe**[4] 〔ˈrɛsəpɪ〕 n. 食譜；祕訣；
竅門；方法

This is my grandmother's *recipe* for apple pie.

【典型考題】
Could you give me the _____ for that wonderful dessert? I'd like to try making it myself.
A. rehearsal   B. recipe
C. recipient   D. reflection   [B]

***recite**[4] 〔rɪˈsaɪt〕 v. 背誦 (= *repeat*)；
朗誦

I was asked to *recite* the poem in front of the class.
【記憶技巧】 *re* (again) + *cite* (call)
（把之前記的內容再說一次，就是「背誦」）

* **recognition** [4] 〔 ˌrɛkəg'nɪʃən 〕 *n.* 承認
（ = *acknowledgment* ）；認得

* **recognize** [3] 〔 'rɛkəgˌnaɪz 〕 *v.* 認得
（ = *know* ）
My English teacher had changed so
much that I almost did not *recognize*
her.
【記憶技巧】 *re* (again) + *cogn* (know)
+ *ize* (*v.*)（再看一次仍知道，表示「認得」）

┌─【典型考題】
│ I hadn't seen her for ages, so I didn't
│ ＿＿＿＿ her at first.
│ A. identify　　　　B. realize
│ C. recognize　　　D. prove　　　**[C]**
└────────────────

* **record** [2] 〔 rɪ'kɔrd 〕 *v.* 記錄
（ = *set down* ）；錄（音）；錄（影）
〔 'rɛkɚd 〕 *n.* 紀錄
She *recorded* everything in her
notebook.
【記憶技巧】 *re* (again) + *cord* (heart)
（將東西「記錄」下來，就像把事情再度
放在心上）

** **recorder** [3] 〔 rɪ'kɔrdɚ 〕 *n.* 錄音機

* **recover** [3] 〔 rɪ'kʌvɚ 〕 *v.* 恢復；復原
Mary has *recovered* from her illness.

* **recovery** [4] 〔 rɪ'kʌvərɪ 〕 *n.* 恢復；復原

┌─【典型考題】
│ Having received good care, she made
│ a quick ＿＿＿＿ from her illness.
│ A. input　　　　　B. entertainment
│ C. recovery　　　 D. focus　　　**[C]**
└────────────────

* **recreation** [4] 〔 ˌrɛkrɪ'eʃən 〕 *n.* 娛樂
（ = *pastime* ）〔 ˌrikrɪ'eʃən 〕 *n.* 再創造
It is important to set aside some time
for *recreation*, even when you are
very busy.

【記憶技巧】 *re* (again) + *creat*(*e*)
(produce) + *ion* (*n.*)（「娛樂」是要
讓人再度產生活力）

** **rectangle** [2] 〔 'rɛkˌtæŋgl̩ 〕 *n.* 長方形
This table is a *rectangle*.
【記憶技巧】 *rect* (right) + *angle*（角）
（「長方形」有四個直角）
【比較】 triangle（三角形）
　　　　square（正方形）

** **recycle** [4] 〔 ri'saɪkl̩ 〕 *v.* 回收；再利用
The glass from bottles can be
recycled.
【記憶技巧】 *re* (again) + *cycle*（循環）
（循環再利用，就是「回收」）

┌─【典型考題】
│ Irene does not throw away used
│ envelopes. She ＿＿＿＿ them by
│ using them for taking telephone
│ messages.
│ A. designs　　　　B. manufactures
│ C. disguises　　　D. recycles　　 **[D]**
└────────────────

*** **red** [1] 〔 rɛd 〕 *adj.* 紅色的

* **reduce** [3] 〔 rɪ'djus 〕 *v.* 減少（ = *decrease* ）
We should *reduce* the number of
plastic bags used.
【記憶技巧】 *re* (back) + *duce* (lead)
（導致數量往後跑，表示「減少」）

* **reduction** [4] 〔 rɪ'dʌkʃən 〕 *n.* 減少

* **refer** [4] 〔 rɪ'fɝ 〕 *v.* 提到（ = *mention* ）；
參考；委託；指
When John was talking about the
department's best professor, he was
referring to his own father.
【片語】 *refer to*（指的是；涉及）

* **reference** [4] 〔 'rɛfərəns 〕 *n.* 參考
【衍伸詞】 *reference book*（參考書）

R

R

*reflect[4] 〔 rɪ'flɛkt 〕 v. 反射
(= send back)；反映
The water of the lake was so still
that it reflected the clouds above.
【記憶技巧】 re (back) + flect (bend)
　　（曲折而回，也就是「反射」）

【典型考題】
My poor test score does not ＿＿＿＿＿
how much I know about this subject.
A. reflect　　　B. vanish
C. adapt　　　D. contain　　　[A]

*reflection[4] 〔 rɪ'flɛkʃən 〕 n. 反射

*reform[4] 〔 rɪ'fɔrm 〕 v. 改革
(= improve)
As the program has not been
successful, I think we should
reform it.
【記憶技巧】 re (again) + form (形成)

*refresh[4] 〔 rɪ'frɛʃ 〕 v. 使提神
(= revive)
A cold drink will refresh you after
your long walk.

*refrigerator[2] 〔 rɪ'frɪdʒə,retə 〕 n.
冰箱 (= fridge 〔 frɪdʒ 〕)
My sister-in-law usually goes
shopping once a week, and during
the week she depends upon her
refrigerator to keep the food fresh.
【記憶技巧】 re (again) + friger (cool)
+ at(e) (v.) + or (n.)
　　（「冰箱」使東西冷卻）

*refugee[4] 〔 ,rɛfjʊ'dʒi 〕 n. 難民
The refugees have been relocated to
homes in other countries.

*refusal[4] 〔 rɪ'fjuzl 〕 n. 拒絕

*refuse[2] 〔 rɪ'fjuz 〕 v. 拒絕 (= decline)
〔'rɛfjus 〕 n. 垃圾；廢物
If you refuse to help others, they
may not help you.
【記憶技巧】 re (back) + fuse (pour)
　　（把水倒回去，表示「拒絕」）

【典型考題】
The soldier was put on trial for
＿＿＿＿＿ to obey his commanding
officer's order.
A. refusing　　　B. regretting
C. resigning　　　D. restricting　　　[A]

*regard[2] 〔 rɪ'gɑrd 〕 v. 認為 (= view)；
尊重　 n. 尊重；關心　 pl. 問候
My father regards computer games
as a waste of time.
【片語】 regard A as B (認為 A 是 B)

*regarding[4] 〔 rɪ'gɑrdɪŋ 〕 adj. 關於
(= about = respecting = concerning)
I spoke to Marie regarding the
meeting.

*region[2] 〔'ridʒən 〕 n. 地區 (= area)
Africa is in a tropical region.
【記憶技巧】 reg (rule) + ion (n.)
　　（統治的地方，就是「地區」）

*regional[3] 〔'ridʒənl 〕 adj. 區域性的

*register[4] 〔'rɛdʒɪstə 〕 v. 登記
(= enroll)；註冊
If you move to a new district, you
are expected to register with local
authorities.
【記憶技巧】 re (back) + gister (carry)
　　（「登記」時，要把資料再帶過去）

*registration[4] 〔 ,rɛdʒɪ'streʃən 〕 n.
登記 (= enrollment)；註冊

＊regret[3] 〔rɪˈgrɛt〕 v. n. 後悔
(= *repent* 〔rɪˈpɛnt〕 v.)
Randy *regretted* making his dog so hungry.

＊＊regular[2] 〔ˈrɛgjələ〕 adj. 規律的
(= *steady*)；定期的
He is a *regular* customer of ours.
【片語】*regular customer* (老主顧)

┌─【典型考題】─────────
In order to stay healthy and fit, John exercises ——. He works out twice a week in a gym.
A. regularly   B. directly
C. hardly   D. gradually   [A]
└──────────────────

＊regulate[4] 〔ˈrɛgjəˌlet〕 v. 管制
(= *control*)
The price of gas is *regulated* by the government, so it does not vary from town to town.
【記憶技巧】*regul* (rule) + *ate* (v.)
(用規則來「管制」)

＊regulation[4] 〔ˌrɛgjəˈleʃən〕 n. 規定
(= *rule*)；管制
【衍伸詞】*traffic regulations* (交通規則)

┌─【典型考題】─────────
The recent cooking oil scandals have led to calls for tougher —— of sales of food products.
A. tolerance   B. guarantee
C. regulation   D. distribution   [C]
└──────────────────

＊rehearsal[4] 〔rɪˈhɝsḷ〕 n. 預演
The final *rehearsal* of the play went well and all the cast members felt confident about their performance.

＊rehearse[4] 〔rɪˈhɝs〕 v. 預演；排練
The singer was *rehearsing* until eight o'clock.
【記憶技巧】*re* (again) + *hearse* (harrow) (反覆耙平土壤，表示公演前反覆練習，把突出來的缺點去掉)

＊＊reject[2] 〔rɪˈdʒɛkt〕 v. 拒絕 (= *refuse*)
Unfortunately, the novelist's book has been *rejected* by three publishers.
【記憶技巧】*re* (back) + *ject* (throw)
(將別人的請求丟回去，表示「拒絕」)

＊rejection[4] 〔rɪˈdʒɛkʃən〕 n. 拒絕
(= *refusal*)

＊relate[3] 〔rɪˈlet〕 v. 使有關聯
(= *associate*)；有關聯
【片語】*be related to* (與…有關)

＊relation[2] 〔rɪˈleʃən〕 n. 關係
(= *association*)
The researchers are studying the *relation* between weather and mood.

＊relationship[2] 〔rɪˈleʃənˌʃɪp〕 n. 關係
(= *association*)

＊＊relative[4] 〔ˈrɛlətɪv〕 n. 親戚 (= *kin*)
adj. 相對的
You can choose your friends, but you can't choose your *relatives*.

＊relax[3] 〔rɪˈlæks〕 v. 放鬆 (= *ease*)
After we had shopped all day, it was nice to sit down in a coffee shop and *relax*.
【記憶技巧】*re* (back) + *lax* (loosen)
(把緊繃的神經鬆開，也就是「放鬆」)

＊relaxation[4] 〔ˌrilæksˈeʃən〕 n. 放鬆
I play tennis for *relaxation*.

R

*release³〔rɪ'lis〕v. 釋放（= set free）
The sun *releases* large amounts of solar energy toward the earth every minute.

【典型考題】
When I opened the box, it _____ a terrible odor.
A. released   B. recovered
C. hardened   D. faking   [A]

*reliable³〔rɪ'laɪəbl̩〕adj. 可靠的（= dependable）
Many employers have discovered that elderly persons are very *reliable* workers.

【典型考題】
The majority of the class decided to vote for that candidate, for he is honest, open-minded and _____.
A. passive   B. reliable
C. ignorant   D. desperate   [B]

*relief³〔rɪ'lif〕n. 放心（= ease）；鬆了一口氣；減輕
We all felt a sense of *relief* after the big exam.

【典型考題】
It was a great _____ for his family to hear that he had survived the cold weather in the mountains.
A. moral   B. promise
C. relief   D. success   [C]

*relieve⁴〔rɪ'liv〕v. 減輕（= soothe〔suð〕）；使放心
【記憶技巧】 re (again) + lieve (lift)
（再拿起來，表示負擔「減輕」了）

*religion³〔rɪ'lɪdʒən〕n. 宗教
Christianity is a popular *religion* in the Western world.

【記憶技巧】 re (back) + lig (bind) + ion (n.)（將自己綁回神的身邊）

*religious³〔rɪ'lɪdʒəs〕adj. 宗教的；虔誠的

*reluctant⁴〔rɪ'lʌktənt〕adj. 不情願的（= unwilling）；勉強的
My teacher was *reluctant* to let me take the test again, but I finally persuaded her.
【記憶技巧】 re (against) + luct (struggle) + ant (adj.)

【典型考題】
Betty was _____ to accept her friend's suggestion because she thought she could come up with a better idea herself.
A. tolerable   B. sensitive
C. reluctant   D. modest   [C]

*rely³〔rɪ'laɪ〕v. 信賴（= depend）；依靠
Samantha has broken her word so many times that I feel I can no longer *rely* on her.
【片語】 rely on（信賴；依靠）

*remain³〔rɪ'men〕v. 仍然；保持不變；留下（= stay）；剩下
She *remained* at home to look after her children.
The situation *remains* unchanged.
【記憶技巧】 re (again) + main (stay)（待在原地，表示仍然在做同樣的事）

【典型考題】
Henry, my old classmate, has _____ a true friend of mine all through the years.
A. retained   B. remained
C. regained   D. refrained   [B]

* **remark** [4] 〔 rɪ'mark 〕 *n.* 話；評論
  （ = *comment* ）
  Dennis made an unkind *remark* about Ellen's dress.
  【記憶技巧】 *re* (again) + *mark* (記號)
  （ 在別人身上留下記號，表示給予「評論」）

* **remarkable** [4] 〔 rɪ'markəbḷ 〕 *adj.* 出色的 (= *outstanding*)；值得注意的；顯著的；非凡的
  He is really a *remarkable* baseball player and stands out from the rest of the team.

* **remedy** [4] 〔'rɛmədɪ 〕 *n.* 治療法
  （ = *cure* ）
  The tea is a good *remedy* for a sore throat.
  【記憶技巧】 *re* (加強語氣的字首) + *med* (heal) + *y* (*n.*)

* **remember** [1] 〔 rɪ'mɛmbɚ 〕 *v.* 記得
  I can't *remember* where I put the pen.

* **remind** [3] 〔 rɪ'maɪnd 〕 *v.* 使想起；提醒
  The story *reminds* me of an experience I had.
  【片語】 *remind sb. of sth.* (使某人想起某事)

* **remote** [3] 〔 rɪ'mot 〕 *adj.* 遙遠的；偏僻的
  We don't often see Darrell because he lives in a *remote* town.
  【記憶技巧】 *re* (back) + *mote* (move)
  （ 退到遠處的，也就是「遙遠的」）
  【片語】 *remote control* (遙控器)

* **remove** [3] 〔 rɪ'muv 〕 *v.* 除去
  （ = *get rid of* ）

Scientists are trying to turn seawater into drinking water by *removing* the salt.
  ┌─【典型考題】
  │ Your desk is crowded with too many unnecessary things. You have to
  │ _____ some of them.
  │ A. remain   B. resist
  │ C. remove   D. renew   [C]
  └─

* **renew** [3] 〔 rɪ'nju 〕 *v.* 更新；將…延期；恢復
  I called a friend that I had not seen in many years and told him that I wanted to *renew* our friendship.

* **rent** [3] 〔 rɛnt 〕 *v.* 租　*n.* 租金
  Martin *rented* a boat to go out fishing.

* **repair** [3] 〔 rɪ'pɛr 〕 *v.* 修理 (= *fix*)
  The radio has to be *repaired*.
  【記憶技巧】 *re* (again) + *pair* (prepare)

* **repeat** [2] 〔 rɪ'pit 〕 *v.* 重複
  The teacher *repeated* his words to the class.

* **repetition** [4] 〔ˌrɛpɪ'tɪʃən 〕 *n.* 重複
  We were impressed by Danny's card trick and asked for a *repetition* of it.

* **replace** [3] 〔 rɪ'ples 〕 *v.* 取代
  （ = *substitute* ）
  Nothing can *replace* a mother's love and care.
  ┌─【典型考題】
  │ As more people rely on the Internet for information, it has _____
  │ newspapers as the most important source of news.
  │ A. distributed   B. subtracted
  │ C. replaced   D. transferred   [C]
  └─

R

R

* **replacement**³ 〔 rɪ'plesmənt 〕 *n.*
取代 (= *substitution*)

* **reply**² 〔 rɪ'plaɪ 〕 *v.* 回答 (= *answer*);
回覆
I sent Mary a letter last week, but
she has not *replied*.

* **report**¹ 〔 rɪ'port 〕 *v.* 報導 (= *tell*);
報告
It is *reported* that the general
election will be held soon.

* **reporter**² 〔 rɪ'portɚ 〕 *n.* 記者
(= *journalist*)

* **represent**³ 〔 ˌrɛprɪ'zɛnt 〕 *v.* 代表
(= *stand for*)
Each charm on her bracelet
represents a place she has visited.
【記憶技巧】先背 present (呈現)。
┌─【典型考題】──────────
│ The winner of this contest will _____
│ our school in the city finals.
│ A. claim   B. symbolize
│ C. indicate   D. represent   [D]
└─────────────────────────

* **representation**⁴ 〔 ˌrɛprɪzɛn'teʃən 〕
n. 代表

* **representative**³ 〔 ˌrɛprɪ'zɛntətɪv 〕
n. 代表人

* **republic**³ 〔 rɪ'pʌblɪk 〕 *n.* 共和國
As the country has become a *republic*,
the king is no longer the head of state.

* **reputation**⁴ 〔 ˌrɛpjə'teʃən 〕 *n.* 名聲
Neil has a *reputation* as a careful
and honest accountant.
【記憶技巧】*re* (again) + *put* (think)
+ *ation* (*n.*) (「名聲」打響後,就會讓人
一再地想起這個名號)

┌─【典型考題】──────────
│ The professor has a _____ for giving
│ extremely difficult exams.
│ A. character   B. history
│ C. sympathy   D. reputation   [D]
└─────────────────────────

* **request**³ 〔 rɪ'kwɛst 〕 *v. n.* 請求
(= *ask*)
He *requested* us to keep silent.
【片語】 *on request* (一經要求)

* **require**² 〔 rɪ'kwaɪr 〕 *v.* 需要
(= *need*)
An employer usually *requires* an
interview before hiring a job seeker.
【記憶技巧】 *re* (again) + *quire* (seek)
(一再地尋求,就表示很「需要」)
【比較】 ac*quire* (獲得); in*quire* (詢問)

* **requirement**² 〔 rɪ'kwaɪrmənt 〕 *n.*
必備條件 (= *necessity*);要求

┌─【典型考題】──────────
│ One of the _____ for the job is a
│ good knowledge of Japanese.
│ A. goals   B. requirements
│ C. fames   D. orphanages   [B]
└─────────────────────────

* **rescue**⁴ 〔 'rɛskju 〕 *v.* 拯救 (= *save*);
解救   *n.* 解救;援救
It was too late to *rescue* the animal.
【記憶技巧】 *re* (加強語氣的字首) + *(e)s*
(out) + *cue* (shake)

* **research**⁴ 〔 rɪ'sɝtʃ , 'risɝtʃ 〕 *v. n.*
研究 (= *study*)
The doctor is *researching* the link
between eating habits and diabetes.
【記憶技巧】 *re* (again) + *search* (尋找)
(不停地尋找答案,就是「研究」)

* **researcher**⁴ 〔 rɪ'sɝtʃɚ 〕 *n.* 研究人員

* **resemble**[4] 〔 rɪˈzɛmbḷ 〕 v. 像
  (= *take after*)
  Mark *resembles* his grandfather more than his father.
  【記憶技巧】 *re* (again) + *semble* (same) (再次出現相似的東西)

  【典型考題】
  It's amazing that make-up and costumes can make an actor closely _____ a government official.
  A. recover   B. regulate
  C. reform   D. resemble   [**D**]

* **reservation**[4] 〔ˌrɛzɚˈveʃən 〕 n. 預訂

* **reserve**[3] 〔 rɪˈzɝv 〕 v. 預訂 (= *book*)；保留 (= *keep*)
  We are *reserving* this bottle of champagne for New Year's Eve.
  【記憶技巧】 *re* (back) + *serve* (keep) (「預訂」就是先把東西保留在後面)

* **resign**[4] 〔 rɪˈzaɪn 〕 v. 辭職 (= *leave*)
  After the serious argument, he *resigned* from the post and left the company.
  【記憶技巧】 *re* (again) + *sign* (簽名) (離開公司要再次簽名，表示「辭職」)
  【比較】 as<u>sign</u> (指派)；de<u>sign</u> (設計)

* **resignation**[4] 〔ˌrɛzɪgˈneʃən 〕 n. 辭職

* **resist**[3] 〔 rɪˈzɪst 〕 v. 抵抗 (= *oppose*)；抗拒
  I couldn't *resist* another slice of cake even though I was supposed to be on a diet.
  【記憶技巧】 *re* (against) + *sist* (stand) (站在對立的立場，表示「抵抗」)

【典型考題】
Most children find it difficult to _____ the temptation of ice cream, especially in summer.
A. purchase   B. resist
C. stare at   D. accustom to   [**B**]

resistance[4] 〔 rɪˈzɪstəns 〕 n. 抵抗
  (= *opposition*)

* **resolution**[4] 〔ˌrɛzəˈluʃən 〕 n. 解決；決心 (= *determination*)；決定做的事
  Abby made a *resolution* to give up smoking once and for all.

【典型考題】
A person who hesitates a lot cannot make _____ even about trivial matters.
A. distributions   B. celebrations
C. institutions   D. resolutions   [**D**]

* **resolve**[4] 〔 rɪˈzɑlv 〕 v. 決定 (= *decide*)；決心；解決 (= *solve*)
  Greg *resolved* to speak to his boss about a promotion.
  【記憶技巧】 *re* (back) + *solve* (loosen) (把緊張情緒放鬆，表示「決定」好了)

* **resource**[3] 〔 rɪˈsors 〕 n. 才智；資源 (= *supply*)   *pl.* 處理問題的能力
  Students today have many *resources* available to them, including the Internet and the school library.
  【衍伸詞】 *natural resources* (天然資源)
  【比較】 source (來源)

* **respect**[2] 〔 rɪˈspɛkt 〕 v. n. 尊敬 (= *regard*)；方面；重視
  We *respect* our parents very much.
  【記憶技巧】 *re* (again) + *spect* (look) (再看一眼，表示重視，引申為「尊敬」)

* **respectable**[4] 〔 rɪˋspɛktəb!〕 *adj.*
可敬的

* **respectful**[4] 〔 rɪˋspɛktfəl〕 *adj.* 恭敬的
(= *regardful*)

【典型考題】

The spoilt child is so rude that he's
never ——— to his elders and teachers.
A. respected   B. respect
C. respectable   D. respectful   [D]

* **respond**[3] 〔 rɪˋspɑnd〕 *v.* 回答
(= *answer*)；反應
He *responded* to the question
without thinking.
【記憶技巧】 *re* (back) + *spond* (answer)

* **response**[3] 〔 rɪˋspɑns〕 *n.* 回答
(= *answer*)；回應

【典型考題】

The magician asked for a volunteer but
he got no ——— from the audience.
A. donation   B. response
C. insistence   D. applause   [B]

* **responsibility**[3] 〔 rɪ͵spɑnsəˋbɪlətɪ〕
n. 責任 (= *duty*)
John had to take on the *responsibility*
of educating his brother's children.

‡ **responsible**[2] 〔 rɪˋspɑnsəb!〕 *adj.*
應負責任的
【片語】 *be responsible for* (應對…負責)

‡ **rest**[1] 〔 rɛst〕 *v. n.* 休息 (= *ease*)
After running for half an hour, Joe
sat down to *rest*.
【片語】 *take a rest* (休息一下)

‡ **restaurant**[2] 〔ˋrɛstərənt〕 *n.* 餐廳

* **restore**[4] 〔 rɪˋstor〕 *v.* 恢復 (= *revive*)

The old building was *restored* to its
original condition and opened as a
museum.

* **restrict**[3] 〔 rɪˋstrɪkt〕 *v.* 限制
(= *limit*)；限定
The speed is *restricted* to 40
kilometers an hour here.

【典型考題】

The drug problem is universal. It is
not ——— to one country.
A. protected   B. detected
C. admitted   D. restricted   [D]

* **restriction**[4] 〔 rɪˋstrɪkʃən〕 *n.* 限制
(= *limitation*)

‡ **rest room**[2] *n.* 洗手間 (= *restroom*)；
廁所 (= *lavatory; bathroom*)
【重要知識】restroom 也寫成：rest room
或 rest-room。

‡ **result**[2] 〔 rɪˋzʌlt〕 *n.* 結果
(= *consequence* = *outcome*)
v. 導致 < *in* >
What was the *result* of the game?
Continuous heavy rains *resulted* in
a big landslide.

* **retain**[4] 〔 rɪˋten〕 *v.* 保留 (= *keep*)；
抑制；約束
China dishes *retain* heat longer
than metal pans do.
【片語】 *retain heat* (保溫)
【記憶技巧】 *re* (back) + *tain* (hold)
 (把東西拿到後面，就是「保留」)

【典型考題】

Many countries make an effort to
——— their traditions of the past.
A. patrol   B. inform
C. command   D. retain   [D]

* **retire**[4] 〔 rɪˈtaɪr 〕 v. 退休

Mr. Goodman hopes to *retire* early, at the age of fifty.

【記憶技巧】先背 tire (使疲倦)。

* **retirement**[4] 〔 rɪˈtaɪrmənt 〕 n. 退休

* **retreat**[4] 〔 rɪˈtrit 〕 v. 撤退(= *withdraw*)

I waved a stick at the growling dog and it *retreated*.

【記憶技巧】先背 treat (對待)。

* **return**[1] 〔 rɪˈtɜn 〕 v. 返回;歸還

Please *return* these books to the library.

* **reunion**[4] 〔 riˈjunjən 〕 n. 團聚

We had a family *reunion* where I saw relatives I hadn't seen for ten years.

【記憶技巧】*re* (again) + *union* (聯合)
(再聯合,就是「團聚」)

* **reveal**[3] 〔 rɪˈvil 〕 v. 透露;顯示
(= *show*)

An X-ray *revealed* a tumor in his brain.

【記憶技巧】*re* (opposite of) + *veal*
(to veil) (取下面紗,表示將隱藏在下面 的東西「顯示」出來)

┌─【典型考題】─────────────
│ Recent studies on whales have _____
│ that they, like humans, have
│ emotions.
│ A. revealed   B. remained
│ C. reviewed   D. rewarded   [A]
└──────────────────────────

* **revenge**[4] 〔 rɪˈvɛndʒ 〕 n. 報復
(= *retaliation*)

When Marsha told Gordon's secret to her girlfriends, Gordon took *revenge* by telling everyone Marsha's secret.

【片語】 *take revenge* (報復)

* **review**[2] 〔 rɪˈvju 〕 v. 復習

She spent the summer *reviewing* Taiwanese history as she was to teach that in the fall.

┌─【典型考題】─────────────
│ Our teacher _____ the old lessons
│ before starting a new one.
│ A. reviewed   B. noticed
│ C. previewed   D. remembered   [A]
└──────────────────────────

* **revise**[4] 〔 rɪˈvaɪz 〕 v. 修訂

The writer *revised* his story.

【比較】 ad<u>vise</u> (建議);de<u>vise</u> (設計)

* **revision**[4] 〔 rɪˈvɪʒən 〕 n. 修訂

* **revolution**[4] 〔 ˌrɛvəˈluʃən 〕 n. 革命;
重大改革

The *revolution* freed the city from its rulers.

┌─【典型考題】─────────────
│ Credit cards have brought a(n)
│ _____ in people's spending habits.
│ A. connection   B. communication
│ C. immigration   D. revolution   [D]
└──────────────────────────

* **revolutionary**[4] 〔 ˌrɛvəˈluʃənˌɛrɪ 〕
adj. 革命性的

* **reward**[4] 〔 rɪˈwɔrd 〕 n. 報酬
(= *return*);獎賞   v. 獎賞

I gave the boy a *reward* for running an errand for me.

┌─【典型考題】─────────────
│ To teach children right from wrong,
│ some parents will _____ their
│ children when they behave well and
│ punish them when they misbehave.
│ A. settle   B. declare
│ C. reward   D. neglect   [C]
└──────────────────────────

R

* **rhyme**[4] 〔raɪm〕 *n.* 押韻詩（＝*poem*）；
同韻字；押韻；童詩　*v.* 押韻
Not all poems *rhyme*.

* **rhythm**[4] 〔'rɪðəm〕 *n.* 節奏
Dennis was not successful as a
drummer because he couldn't match
the *rhythm* of the rest of the band.

* **ribbon**[3] 〔'rɪbən〕 *n.* 絲帶

‡ **rice**[1] 〔raɪs〕 *n.* 稻米；飯
The children like to eat *rice* more
than noodles.

‡ **rich**[1] 〔rɪtʃ〕 *adj.* 有錢的（＝*wealthy*）；
豐富的
【衍伸詞】 *be rich in*（有豐富的…）

* **riches**[2] 〔'rɪtʃɪz〕 *n. pl.* 財富；資源
Patty dreamed of the *riches* she
would enjoy if she won the lottery.

* **rid**[3] 〔rɪd〕 *v.* 除去
It took us all day to *rid* the garden
of weeds.
【片語】 *rid* A *of* B（除去 A 中的 B）
get rid of（除去；擺脫）

* **riddle**[3] 〔'rɪdl̩〕 *n.* 謎語（＝*puzzle*）
We could not solve the *riddle* and
asked Clara to tell us the answer.

‡ **ride**[1] 〔raɪd〕 *v.* 騎；搭乘

‡ **right**[1] 〔raɪt〕 *adj.* 對的；右邊的
n. 權利；右邊
You have no *right* to choose.

‡ **ring**[1] 〔rɪŋ〕 *n.* 戒指；電話鈴聲；鐘聲；
拳擊場；性質　*v.* 按（鈴）；發出聲響
He bought her a *ring*.
The telephone is *ringing*.

* **ripe**[3] 〔raɪp〕 *adj.* 成熟的（＝*mature*）
I can't eat this mango because it is
not *ripe* yet.

‡ **rise**[1] 〔raɪz〕 *v.* 上升
People demand higher wages all the
time because prices are always *rising*.
【片語】 *give rise to*（導致）

【典型考題】
Whales usually ———— to breathe
every five or ten minutes.
A. hang   B. rise
C. shoot   D. float   [B]

* **risk**[3] 〔rɪsk〕 *n.* 風險　*v.* 冒…的危險
Businessmen recognize the
convenience of being protected from
running certain *risks*.
I'm willing to *risk* losing everything.

‡ **river**[1] 〔'rɪvɚ〕 *n.* 河流

‡ **road**[1] 〔rod〕 *n.* 道路

* **roar**[3] 〔ror〕 *v.* 吼叫（＝*shout*）；大叫；
大笑；咆哮　*n.* 吼叫；隆隆聲
The crowd *roared* when the winning
goal was made.
【記憶技巧】 roar 這個字唸起來就像在怒吼。

* **roast**[3] 〔rost〕 *v.* 烤；烘焙　*n.* 大塊
烤肉　*adj.* 烘烤的；火烤的
We *roasted* the meat on an open fire.

‡ **rob**[3] 〔rab〕 *v.* 搶劫（＝*sack*）
Farmers were *robbed* of their rice.
【片語】 *rob* sb. *of* sth.（搶走某人的某物）

* **robber**[3] 〔'rabɚ〕 *n.* 強盜（＝*bandit*）

* **robbery**[3] 〔'rabərɪ〕 *n.* 搶劫
（＝*looting*）；搶案

* **robe**[3] 〔 rob 〕 *n.* 長袍（= *gown*）
Rachel put on a *robe* after her shower.

‡ **robot**[1] 〔'robət 〕 *n.* 機器人
（= *automaton*）
A *robot* can do things like a human being.

‡ **rock**[1,2] 〔 rɑk 〕 *n.* 岩石（= *stone*）
v. 搖動（= *shake*）

* **rocket**[3] 〔'rɑkɪt 〕 *n.* 火箭

 rocky[2] 〔'rɑkɪ 〕 *adj.* 多岩石的
（= *stony*）

‡ **role**[2] 〔 rol 〕 *n.* 角色（= *character*）
She played the *role* of Snow White.
【片語】 *play ~ role*（扮演 ~ 角色）

‡ **roll**[1] 〔 rol 〕 *v.* 滾動（= *turn*）
The ball *rolled* over and over.
【衍伸詞】 rock'n'roll（搖滾樂）

* **romance**[4] 〔 ro'mæns 〕 *n.* 愛情故事
（= *romantic story*）；羅曼史；戀愛
Sandy had a *romance* with a dancer.

* **romantic**[3] 〔 ro'mæntɪk 〕 *adj.* 浪漫的
Ellen and Dave enjoyed a *romantic* dinner on Valentine's Day.

‡ **roof**[1] 〔 ruf 〕 *n.* 屋頂
There is a kitten on the *roof* of the house.
【比較】 proof（證據）

‡ **room**[1] 〔 rum 〕 *n.* 房間；空間
（= *space*）

* **rooster**[1] 〔'rustɚ 〕 *n.* 公雞（= *cock*）
【比較】 hen（母雞）

‡ **root**[1] 〔 rut 〕 *n.* 根（= *radix*）；根源
Roots hold the plant in the soil.
【片語】 *be rooted in*（在…根深蒂固）

‡ **rope**[1] 〔 rop 〕 *n.* 繩子
Edward uses a *rope* to tie the boat.

‡ **rose**[1] 〔 roz 〕 *n.* 玫瑰

* **rot**[3] 〔 rɑt 〕 *v.* 腐爛（= *decay*）
If you leave the wood out in the rain, it will eventually *rot*.

* **rotten**[3] 〔'rɑtn̩ 〕 *adj.* 腐爛的
（= *decayed*）；討厭的；差勁的
【重要知識】rotten 這字和中文的「爛」一樣，美國人常用，如：What a ***rotten*** day!

* **rough**[3] 〔 rʌf 〕 *adj.* 粗糙的
（= *rugged* = *coarse*）
This *rough* material irritates my skin.

 roughly[4] 〔'rʌflɪ 〕 *adv.* 大約
（= *about* = *approximately*）
Roughly 60 people came to the party.

‡ **round**[1] 〔 raʊnd 〕 *adj.* 圓的 *n.* 回合
He was knocked out in the second *round*.

* **route**[4] 〔 rut 〕 *n.* 路線（= *way*）
There are several stops along this *route*.

* **routine**[3] 〔 ru'tin 〕 *n.* 例行公事
Ted decided to change his *routine* and take a walk after dinner rather than watch TV.

‡ **row**[1] 〔 ro 〕 *n.* 排（= *line*）
v. 划（船）〔 raʊ 〕 *v. n.* 吵鬧
We have two *rows* of teeth.

* **royal**[2] 〔'rɔɪəl 〕 *adj.* 皇家的
The prince lives in a *royal* palace.
【比較】 loyal（忠實的）

---

rub[1] 〔rʌb〕 v. 摩擦 (= graze)
The cat *rubbed* its back against my leg.
【片語】*rub sb. the wrong way* (激怒某人)

rubber[1] 〔'rʌbɚ〕 n. 橡膠；橡皮擦
Balloons are made of *rubber*.

rude[2] 〔rud〕 adj. 無禮的 (= bold = impolite)
It's *rude* to eat and talk at the same time.

rug[3] 〔rʌg〕 n. (小塊) 地毯 (= small carpet)
The dog prefers to lie on the *rug* rather than the cold floor.
【比較】carpet (整片) 地毯

ruin[4] 〔'ruɪn〕 v. 毀滅 (= destroy)
The typhoon *ruined* the city.

rule[1] 〔rul〕 n. 規則 v. 統治
Traffic *rules* should be observed by anyone using the road.

ruler[2] 〔'rulɚ〕 n. 統治者 (= lord)；尺

rumor[3] 〔'rumɚ〕 n. 謠言 (= hearsay)
Rumor has it that Marty is going to get married.

run[1] 〔rʌn〕 v. 跑；經營
My father *runs* a store.

runner[2] 〔'rʌnɚ〕 n. 跑者

rural[4] 〔'rʊrəl〕 adj. 鄉村的 (= country)
There are few convenience stores in this *rural* area.
【記憶技巧】*rur* (country) + *al* (adj.)
【反義詞】urban (都市的)

rush[2] 〔rʌʃ〕 v. 衝 n. 匆忙
The police immediately *rushed* to the scene.
【衍伸詞】*rush hour* (尖峰時間)
【片語】*in a rush* (匆忙地)

rust[3] 〔rʌst〕 v. 生銹 (= oxidize)
If you leave your bicycle outside, it may *rust*.

rusty[3] 〔'rʌstɪ〕 adj. 生銹的 (= corroded)

S s

sack[3] 〔sæk〕 n. 一大袋 (= bag)
I went to the supermarket for some milk and a *sack* of potatoes.
【片語】*give sb. the sack* (把某人開除)

sacrifice[4] 〔'sækrə,faɪs〕 v. n. 犧牲
Joe had to *sacrifice* much of his free time to get the work done on time.
【記憶技巧】*sacr* (sacred) + *ifice* (make) (「犧牲」是一種神聖的行為)

【典型考題】
Young people always _____ their health for wealth.
A. divide   B. complete
C. sacrifice   D. appreciate   [C]

sad[1] 〔sæd〕 adj. 悲傷的 (= gloomy)

safe[1] 〔sef〕 adj. 安全的 (= secure)
n. 保險箱 (= strongbox)

‡**safety**[2] 〔'seftɪ 〕 *n.* 安全（ = *security* ）
adj. 安全的
We put money in a bank for *safety*.

┌─【典型考題】────────
For your own _____, please don't
open the door until the train fully stops.
A. humanity   B. safety
C. liberty   D. vanity   **[B]**
└──────────────────

‡**sail**[1] 〔 sel 〕 *v.* 航行（ = *navigate* ）
n. （船的）帆；帆船
The ship *sails* slowly into the harbor.

‡**sailor**[2] 〔'selɚ 〕 *n.* 水手（ = *seaman* ）
I saw a *sailor* walking near the port.

*＊**sake**[3] 〔 sek 〕 *n.* 緣故（ = *reason* ）
For your mother's *sake*, please
apologize to your sister.
【片語】*for one's sake*（為了某人）
        for God's sake（看在老天的份上）

‡**salad**[2] 〔'sæləd 〕 *n.* 沙拉
【重要知識】沙拉醬是 salad dressing，注
意「沙拉醬」由上淋下，用 dressing 而不是
sauce（沾醬）。

*＊**salary**[4] 〔'sælərɪ 〕 *n.* 薪水
（ = *earnings* ）
【記憶技巧】*sal* (salt) + *ary* (*n.*)
（源於古羅馬發鹽給士兵當作「薪水」）

‡**sale**[1] 〔 sel 〕 *n.* 出售
Mr. Dawson's car is for *sale*.

‡**salesman**[4] 〔'selzmən 〕 *n.* 售貨員
（ = *salesperson* ）；推銷員；業務員

‡**salt**[1] 〔 sɔlt 〕 *n.* 鹽
【片語】*take…with a grain of salt*
（對…持保留的態度）

salty[2] 〔'sɔltɪ 〕 *adj.* 鹹的
Tears are *salty*.

‡**same**[1] 〔 sem 〕 *adj.* 相同的
We always go to the *same* place after
work.

‡**sample**[2] 〔'sæmpḷ 〕 *n.* 範例；樣品
（ = *example* ）
They distributed free *samples* of
shampoo to passers-by in the street.

‡**sand**[1] 〔 sænd 〕 *n.* 沙子
She got some *sand* in her eye.

‡**sandwich**[2] 〔'sændwɪtʃ 〕 *n.* 三明治

*＊**satellite**[4] 〔'sætḷ͵aɪt 〕 *n.* 衛星
Communication *satellites* enable
people to watch live broadcasts from
anywhere in the world.
【記憶技巧】*sate* (full) + *llite* (go)
（「衛星」就是環繞行星運行的物體）

*＊**satisfaction**[4] 〔͵sætɪs'fækʃən 〕 *n.*
滿足（ = *contentment* ）
Jerry felt a sense of *satisfaction* when
he finally finished painting the porch.

*＊**satisfactory**[3] 〔͵sætɪs'fæktərɪ 〕 *adj.*
令人滿意的（ = *satisfying* ）
What he has done is *satisfactory* to me.
【重要知識】北美系統的成績評等描述分為：
Outstanding > Good > Satisfactory >
Inferior > Failed。

‡**satisfy**[2] 〔'sætɪs͵faɪ 〕 *v.* 滿足
（ = *gratify* ）；使滿意
The government can't fully *satisfy*
people's needs.

‡‡**Saturday**[1] 〔'sætɚ͵dɪ 〕 *n.* 星期六（ = *Sat.* ）

S

* **sauce**[2] 〔 sɔs 〕 *n.* 醬汁

Two *sauces* are served with the meat course.

【衍伸詞】 *soy sauce* (醬油)

** **saucer**[3] 〔 'sɔsɚ 〕 *n.* 碟子

(= *small dish*)

She offered me tea in her best cup and *saucer*.

【衍伸詞】 *flying saucer* (飛碟) (= *UFO*)

* **sausage**[3] 〔 'sɔsɪdʒ 〕 *n.* 香腸

【記憶技巧】 *sa* + *usage* (用法)

** **save**[1] 〔 sev 〕 *v.* 節省；拯救

* **saving**[3] 〔 'sevɪŋ 〕 *n.* 節省

With the discount coupon, you will enjoy a *saving* of fifty dollars.

* **saw**[1] 〔 sɔ 〕 *n.* 鋸子

** **say**[1] 〔 se 〕 *v.* 說

* **scale**[3] 〔 skel 〕 *n.* 規模；程度；刻度；比例；音階；鱗　*pl.* 天平　*v.* 爬；調整；刮鱗

The business is large in *scale*.

【片語】 *on a large scale* (大規模地)

* **scarce**[3] 〔 skɛrs 〕 *adj.* 稀少的

(= *lacking*)

The endangered animal has become *scarce* in its natural habitat.

* **scarcely**[4] 〔 'skɛrslɪ 〕 *adv.* 幾乎不

(= *hardly* = *barely*)

He was so embarrassed that he *scarcely* knew what to say.

* **scare**[1] 〔 skɛr 〕 *v.* 驚嚇

Rex tried to *scare* the children by telling them ghost stories.

* **scarecrow**[3] 〔 'skɛr,kro 〕 *n.* 稻草人

(= *straw man*)

We put a *scarecrow* in the cornfield to frighten the birds away.

【重要知識】 從前在美國，田裡烏鴉 (crow) 很多，「稻草人」(scarecrow) 是用來嚇烏鴉的。

* **scarf**[3] 〔 skɑrf 〕 *n.* 圍巾

【記憶技巧】 car-scar (疤痕) -scarf (圍巾)

* **scary**[3] 〔 'skɛrɪ 〕 *adj.* 可怕的

(= *fearful*)；嚇人的

* **scatter**[3] 〔 'skætɚ 〕 *v.* 撒；散開；散播

(= *throw about* = *spread*)

After you have prepared the soil, *scatter* the seeds and then water the field.

** **scene**[1] 〔 sin 〕 *n.* 場景 (= *setting*)；風景 (= *view*)

The boats in the harbor make a beautiful *scene*.

【片語】 *on the scene* (當場)

** **scenery**[4] 〔 'sinərɪ 〕 *n.* 風景 【集合名詞】

We stopped to admire the *scenery*.

* **schedule**[3] 〔 'skɛdʒul 〕 *n.* 時間表

(= *time plan*)

I have to check my *schedule*.

* **scholar**[3] 〔 'skɑlɚ 〕 *n.* 學者

He is a *scholar* of ancient history.

【記憶技巧】 一般說來，字尾是 ar，都不是什麼好人，像 liar (說謊者)，burglar (竊賊)，beggar (乞丐)。而 scholar (學者)，讀書人壞起來，更可怕。

* **scholarship**[3] 〔 'skɑlɚ,ʃɪp 〕 *n.* 獎學金

‡school[1] 〔 skul 〕 *n.* 學校；(魚) 群
We go to *school* five days a week.
We saw a *school* of whales.

‡science[2] 〔'saɪəns 〕 *n.* 科學

【典型考題】

Today, ＿＿＿＿＿＿ gives us different
explanations of how things happen.
A. infant　　　　　B. orbit
C. shadow　　　　D. science　　　[D]

*scientific[3] 〔,saɪən'tɪfɪk 〕 *adj.* 科學的
Eugene does not believe in
superstitions because they are not
based on *scientific* facts.

‡scientist[2] 〔'saɪəntɪst 〕 *n.* 科學家

*scissors[2] 〔'sɪzɚz 〕 *n.pl.* 剪刀
I need a pair of *scissors* to cut this
string.
【片語】*a pair of scissors* (一把剪刀)

*scold[4] 〔 skold 〕 *v.* 責罵 (= *blame*)；
責備
Lucy was *scolded* by her mother
because she forgot to take out the trash.
【記憶技巧】先背 cold (寒冷的)，因為被罵
的人會感到心寒。

*scoop[3] 〔 skup 〕 *v.* 舀取；挖起；賺得
(= *earn*)　　*n.* 一杓 (量)；獨家新聞
Maggie *scooped* the ice cream from
the carton into the bowls.

‡score[2] 〔 skor 〕 *n.* 分數 (= *grade*)
The teacher blamed her for her low
score.

*scout[3] 〔 skaʊt 〕 *v.* 偵察；搜索；物色
人才　　*n.* 偵查員；星探；童子軍
One soldier was sent ahead to *scout*
the terrain.

【記憶技巧】*sc* + *out* (到外面去看看，
就是「偵察」)

*scratch[4] 〔 skrætʃ 〕 *v.* 抓 (癢)
(= *scrape*)；搔 (頭)　　*n.* 抓痕；
刮痕；擦傷；【牌】零分
If you *scratch* the mosquito bite, it
will only itch more.

*scream[3] 〔 skrim 〕 *v.* 尖叫 (= *cry*)
n. 尖叫 (聲)

‡screen[2] 〔 skrin 〕 *n.* 螢幕；銀幕；幕；
簾；紗窗 (門)　　*v.* 遮蔽；篩檢；
審查；放映
There is a spot on the TV *screen*.

【典型考題】

To prevent the spread of the Ebola
virus from West Africa to the rest of
the world, many airports have begun
Ebola ＿＿＿＿＿＿ for passengers from the
infected areas.
A. screenings　　B. listings
C. clippings　　　D. blockings　　[A]

*screw[3] 〔 skru 〕 *n.* 螺絲
The cover of the DVD player is held
in place with four *screws*.

*screwdriver[4] 〔'skru,draɪvɚ 〕 *n.*
螺絲起子

*scrub[3] 〔 skrʌb 〕 *v.* 刷洗；用力擦洗；
擦掉；刷掉
No matter how hard she *scrubbed*,
Alice could not get the stain out of
the carpet.
【記憶技巧】*sc* + *rub* (摩擦)

*sculpture[4] 〔'skʌlptʃɚ 〕 *n.* 雕刻
(= *carved artwork*)；雕刻術；雕像
The sculptor worked on the outdoor
sculpture garden for over twenty years.

S

‡**sea**[1] 〔 si 〕 *n.* 海（＝*marine*）
Is the *sea* here warm enough for swimming?

***seagull**[4] 〔'si͵gʌl 〕 *n.* 海鷗（＝*gull*）

***seal**[3] 〔 sil 〕 *v.* 密封（＝*shut airtight*）
n. 印章；海豹
The letter was *sealed* with wax.

‡**search**[2] 〔 sɝtʃ 〕 *v.* 尋找；搜尋
Peter is *searching* for his watch.

【典型考題】
The policemen have _____ the whole area but haven't found the criminal yet.
A. looked　　B. improved
C. searched　　D. discovered　[C]

‡**season**[1] 〔'sizn̩ 〕 *n.* 季節
There are four *seasons* in a year.

‡**seat**[1] 〔 sit 〕 *n.* 座位　*v.* 使就座
Alisa gave her *seat* on the bus to an old woman.
Please be *seated*.

【典型考題】
This _____ is taken. You can't sit here.
A. sweater　　B. pants
C. dialogue　　D. seat　[D]

‡**second**[1] 〔'sɛkənd 〕 *adj.* 第二的　*n.* 秒

‡**secondary**[3] 〔'sɛkən͵dɛrɪ 〕 *adj.* 次要的
This thing is *secondary* to that.

‡**secret**[2] 〔'sikrɪt 〕 *n.* 祕密（＝*secrecy*）
adj. 祕密的
She can't keep a *secret*.
【記憶技巧】 *se* (apart) + *cret* (separate)
（與平常能講的話區隔開來，也就是不能說的「祕密」）

‡**secretary**[2] 〔'sɛkrə͵tɛrɪ 〕 *n.* 秘書（＝*special assistant*）
She is the private *secretary* of my boss.
【記憶技巧】 *secret*（秘密）+ *ary*（人）
（「秘書」是幫主管處理機密事項的人）

***section**[2] 〔'sɛkʃən 〕 *n.* 部分（＝*part*）
Mother cut the pie into eight equal *sections*.
【記憶技巧】 *sect* (cut) + *ion* (*n.*)
（經過切割，分成很多「部分」）

***security**[3] 〔 sɪ'kjurətɪ 〕 *n.* 安全（＝*safety*）；防護措施
The *security* at most airports has been very tight since the terrorist attacks.

‡**see**[1] 〔 si 〕 *v.* 看見

‡**seed**[1] 〔 sid 〕 *n.* 種子
We sowed vegetable *seeds* in the garden.

***seek**[3] 〔 sik 〕 *v.* 尋找（＝*look for*＝*search for*）
【三態變化為：seek-sought-sought】
He is *seeking* a new job.

***seem**[1] 〔 sim 〕 *v.* 似乎（＝*appear*）
This exam *seems* hard to her.

‡**seesaw**[1] 〔'si͵sɔ 〕 *n.* 蹺蹺板
The kids are playing on a *seesaw* at the playground.

***seize**[3] 〔 siz 〕 *v.* 抓住（＝*grab*）
The police *seized* the robber's arm.
【衍伸詞】 *seize the day*（把握時機）

‡**seldom**[3] 〔'sɛldəm 〕 *adv.* 很少（＝*rarely*）
I *seldom* go out at night.

*select² 〔 sə'lɛkt 〕 v. 挑選 (= *pick*)
John *selected* a present for his girlfriend.
【記憶技巧】 *se* (apart) + *lect* (choose)

*selection² 〔 sə'lɛkʃən 〕 n. 選擇 (= *choice*)；精選集

*self¹ 〔 sɛlf 〕 n. 自己
Jack has changed so much that he is nothing like his former *self*.

*selfish¹ 〔'sɛlfɪʃ 〕 adj. 自私的
After he went bankrupt, he became *selfish*.
【反義詞】 selfless (無私的)

*sell¹ 〔 sɛl 〕 v. 賣

*semester² 〔 sə'mɛstə 〕 n. 學期
I want to take a French class next *semester*.
【記憶技巧】 *se* (six) + *mester* (month) (一學期是六個月)

【典型考題】
In Taiwan, the first _____ of a school year usually begins in September.
A. example   B. rule
C. semester   D. system   [C]

*send¹ 〔 sɛnd 〕 v. 寄；送
I *sent* a greeting card to my sister.

*senior⁴ 〔'sinjə 〕 adj. 年長的；資深的
Ms. Lin is the *senior* flight attendant, so if you have any questions, you can consult her.
【反義詞】 junior (年幼的；資淺的)

*sense¹ 〔 sɛns 〕 n. 感覺 (= *feeling*)；判斷力；道理；意義；見識；智慧
Our five *senses* are sight, hearing, taste, smell, and touch.

*sensible³ 〔'sɛnsəbl̩ 〕 adj. 明智的；理智的；合理的 (= *reasonable*)
Realizing she had a bad cold, Dana did the *sensible* thing and stayed at home.

*sensitive³ 〔'sɛnsətɪv 〕 adj. 敏感的 (= *touchy*)
The microphone is very *sensitive* and can pick up even the slightest sound.
【片語】 *be sensitive to* (對…敏感)

【典型考題】
Most earthquakes are too small to be noticed; they can only be detected by _____ instruments.
A. manual   B. sensitve
C. portable   D. dominant   [B]

*sentence¹ 〔'sɛntəns 〕 n. 句子；刑罰 v. 宣判；處以…的刑
The death *sentence* has been abolished in Britain.

*separate² 〔'sɛpə,ret 〕 v. 使分開 (= *make apart*)；區別；分離
The two towns are *separated* by a river.
【片語】 *separate* A *from* B (區別 A 與 B)

*separation³ 〔,sɛpə'reʃən 〕 n. 分開 (= *division*)

*September¹ 〔 sɛp'tɛmbə 〕 n. 九月 (= *Sept.*)

S

serious[2] 〔'sɪrɪəs 〕 *adj.* 嚴重的；
嚴肅的
Tom had a *serious* car accident
yesterday.

【典型考題】
Air pollution has become more and
more _____ in Taiwan.
A. popular   B. impossible
C. serious   D. interesting   [C]

servant[2] 〔'sɜvənt 〕 *n.* 僕人
Policemen are public *servants*.
【重要知識】字尾 ant 指「人」，如：giant（巨人）、
merchant（商人）等。

serve[1] 〔 sɜv 〕 *v.* 服務；供應
（= *supply* ）
The cook *served* the Brown family
for one year.

service[1] 〔'sɜvɪs 〕 *n.* 服務；（郵電、
電話等的）（公共）事業；設施
The *service* in this restaurant is very
good.

【典型考題】
I am sorry that I went to a restaurant
with such dreadful _____ .
A. bill   B. service
C. politeness   D. complaint   [B]

set[1] 〔 sɛt 〕 *v.* 設定（= *arrange* ）；
創（紀錄）   *n.* 一套
We must *set* the time for the meeting.

settle[2] 〔'sɛtl̩ 〕 *v.* 定居；解決
（= *solve* ）
After moving from one city to
another for several years, Mike
decided to *settle* in Chicago.
【片語】 *settle down* （定居；安定下來）

settlement[2] 〔'sɛtl̩mənt 〕 *n.* 定居；
解決；殖民
The whole country is hoping for the
settlement of this strike.

settler[4] 〔'sɛtlɚ 〕 *n.* 殖民者
（= *colonist* ）；移民（= *immigrant* ）

several[1] 〔'sɛvərəl 〕 *adj.* 好幾個
Several boys took part in the race.

severe[4] 〔 sə'vɪr 〕 *adj.* 嚴格的
（= *strict* ）；嚴重的（= *serious* ）；
惡劣的（= *harsh* ）
He is very *severe* with his children.

sew[3] 〔 so 〕 *v.* 縫紉（= *stitch* ）；縫製；
縫補
Rather than buy her son a Halloween
costume, Betty decided to *sew* one
herself.

sex[3] 〔 sɛks 〕 *n.* 性（= *gender* ）

sexual[3] 〔'sɛkʃuəl 〕 *adj.* 性的
【衍伸詞】 *sexual harassment* （性騷擾）

sexy[3] 〔'sɛksɪ 〕 *adj.* 性感的
（= *sexually attractive* ）

shade[3] 〔 ʃed 〕 *n.* 陰影（= *shadow* ）；
樹蔭（= *tree shadow* ）
The sun was so hot that we decided
to sit in the *shade* of this tree.

shadow[3] 〔'ʃædo 〕 *n.* 影子

shady[3] 〔'ʃedɪ 〕 *adj.* 陰涼的（= *shaded* ）

shake[1] 〔 ʃek 〕 *v.* 搖動；抖動
You should *shake* the can before
drinking.
【片語】 *shake hands with* sb. （和某人
握手）

‡shall[1] 〔 ʃæl 〕 *aux.* 將會
After 10:00 p.m., Nancy *shall* call you again.

*shallow[3] 〔 'ʃælo 〕 *adj.* 淺的；膚淺的
Children are restricted to the *shallow* end of the swimming pool.

【典型考題】
"Superficial knowledge" means knowledge that is _____.
A. thorough   B. deep
C. unnecessary   D. shallow   **[D]**

*shame[3] 〔 ʃem 〕 *n.* 羞恥 (= *guilt*)；
可惜的事 (= *pity*)
Evan found it difficult to bear the *shame* of bankruptcy.
【衍伸詞】 ashamed (感到羞恥的)

*shameful[4] 〔 'ʃemfʊl 〕 *adj.* 可恥的
(= *guilty*)
Ms. Lin always tells her students that it's not *shameful* to ask questions in class.

*shampoo[3] 〔 ʃæm'pu 〕 *n.* 洗髮精
【比較】 rinse (潤絲精)

‡shape[1] 〔 ʃep 〕 *n.* 形狀
The shell has a strange *shape*.

‡share[2] 〔 ʃɛr 〕 *v.* 分享
My friend *shares* a cake with me.

‡shark[1] 〔 ʃɑrk 〕 *n.* 鯊魚
No one can catch the *shark*.
【衍伸詞】 *great white shark* (大白鯊)

‡sharp[1] 〔 ʃɑrp 〕 *adj.* 銳利的；急轉的；
鮮明的
The knife is very *sharp*.

【反義詞】 dull (鈍的)

*shave[3] 〔 ʃev 〕 *v.* 刮 (鬍子)
n. 刮鬍子
Lenny asked the barber to *shave* off his beard.

*shaver[4] 〔 'ʃevɚ 〕 *n.* 電動刮鬍刀
(= *electric razor*)
【比較】 razor (剃刀；刮鬍刀)

‡sheep[1] 〔 ʃip 〕 *n.* 綿羊；盲從的人
【單複數同型】
John keeps a lot of *sheep*.
【比較】 lamb (羔羊)；goat (山羊)；
mutton (羊肉)
【片語】 *a flock of sheep* (一群羊)

*sheet[1] 〔 ʃit 〕 *n.* 床單 (= *bedding*)；
一張 (紙)；薄板；廣大一片

*shelf[2] 〔 ʃɛlf 〕 *n.* 架子 (= *ledge*)
I took some books off the *shelf*.

*shell[2] 〔 ʃɛl 〕 *n.* 貝殼；(烏龜、蝦、
螃蟹等的) 甲殼

*shelter[4] 〔 'ʃɛltɚ 〕 *n.* 避難所
The original meaning of home is the best *shelter* where one can go for help.
【記憶技巧】 *shel* (shield 盾牌) + *ter*
(strong) (軍隊用盾牌圍成堅固的避難所)

【典型考題】
In the desert, a huge mall with art galleries, theaters, and museums will be constructed to _____ visitors from the heat outside.
A. convert   B. defend
C. shelter   D. vacuum   **[C]**

*shepherd[3] 〔 'ʃɛpɚd 〕 *n.* 牧羊人
v. 帶領；指引【注意發音】

S

*shift[4] 〔 ʃɪft 〕 v. 改變 (= change)；
換檔；轉移　n. 改變；輪班
The candidate was constantly *shifting*
his position on the issues.
【片語】 ***shift gears*** (換檔)
work in three shifts (三班輪流工作)

‡shine[1] 〔 ʃaɪn 〕 v. 照耀
The sun was *shining* brightly.

*shiny[3] 〔 'ʃaɪnɪ 〕 adj. 閃亮的

‡ship[1] 〔 ʃɪp 〕 n. 船

‡shirt[1] 〔 ʃɜt 〕 n. 襯衫

*shock[2] 〔 ʃɑk 〕 v. n. 震驚
His behavior *shocked* me.
Her death was a great *shock* to me.

‡shoes[1] 〔 ʃuz 〕 n. pl. 鞋子

‡shoot[2] 〔 ʃut 〕 v. 射擊
He was *shot* in the arm.

‡shop[1] 〔 ʃɑp 〕 n. 商店 (= store)；
店鋪；工廠　v. 購物；買東西

*shore[1] 〔 ʃor 〕 n. 海岸
The waves washed over the *shore*.

‡short[1] 〔 ʃɔrt 〕 adj. 短的；矮的；
缺乏的
【片語】 ***be short of*** (缺乏)

shorten[3] 〔 'ʃɔrtn̩ 〕 v. 縮短

*shortly[3] 〔 'ʃɔrtlɪ 〕 adv. 不久
(= soon = before long)
We will be landing *shortly*, so please
return to your seats and fasten your
seatbelts.

【典型考題】
The town is five kilometers away; we
will be there _____.
A. temporarily　B. virtually
C. shortly　　　D. abruptly　[C]

‡shorts[2] 〔 ʃɔrts 〕 n. pl. 短褲
(= short trousers)
She wore *shorts* to play volleyball.

*shortsighted[4] 〔 'ʃɔrt'saɪtɪd 〕 adj.
近視的 (= nearsighted)；短視近利的

*shot[1] 〔 ʃɑt 〕 n. 射擊；子彈
He fired five *shots*.

‡shoulder[1] 〔 'ʃoldɚ 〕 n. 肩膀
His *shoulder* was hurt in an accident.

‡shout[1] 〔 ʃaʊt 〕 v. 吼叫
My friend *shouted* at me yesterday.

*shovel[3] 〔 'ʃʌvl̩ 〕 n. 鏟子 (= spade)

‡show[1] 〔 ʃo 〕 v. 顯示；給…看
He *showed* me his album.

*shower[2] 〔 'ʃaʊɚ 〕 n. 淋浴；陣雨
I take a *shower* every morning.

*shrimp[2] 〔 ʃrɪmp 〕 n. 蝦子
There are a lot of *shrimps* in the river.
【比較】 lobster (龍蝦)

*shrink[3] 〔 ʃrɪŋk 〕 v. 收縮；減少；縮水
(= become smaller)；退縮；逃避
If you put this sweater in the dryer,
it will probably *shrink*.

*shrug[4] 〔 ʃrʌg 〕 v. n. 聳 (肩)
Peter *shrugged* his shoulders to
indicate that he didn't know.

shut[1]〔ʃʌt〕v. 關；閉（= close）
Strong wind *shut* the door.

shuttle[4]〔'ʃʌtḷ〕n. 來回行駛；太空梭
There is a *shuttle* bus to the airport
every half hour.
【衍伸詞】*space shuttle*（太空梭）

shy[1]〔ʃaɪ〕adj. 害羞的
I'm too *shy* to speak to strangers.

sick[1]〔sɪk〕adj. 生病的

side[1]〔saɪd〕n. 邊
You must walk on one *side* of the
road.

sidewalk[2]〔'saɪd,wɔk〕n. 人行道
（= pavement）
She fell on the icy *sidewalk*.

sigh[3]〔saɪ〕v. 嘆息；（風）呼嘯
n. 嘆息
After a long day of shopping, the
girls sat down with a *sigh*.

sight[1]〔saɪt〕n. 景象（= spectacle）；
看見；視力（= vision）

sightseeing[4]〔'saɪt,siɪŋ〕n. 觀光
We would like to do some
sightseeing while we are in Paris.
【記憶技巧】*sight*（風景）+ *seeing*
（「觀光」就是到處去看風景）

sign[2]〔saɪn〕n. 告示牌；信號；符號
v. 簽名
The *sign* says, "No Smoking."
Helen *signed* her name.

signal[3]〔'sɪgnḷ〕n. 信號
He gave me a *signal* to make a right
turn here.

signature[4]〔'sɪgnətʃɚ〕n. 簽名
The manager put his *signature* on
the last page of the document.
【比較】autograph（親筆簽名）

significance[4]〔sɪg'nɪfəkəns〕n.
意義；重要性
Having the first phase done is of
great *significance* to the whole
project.
【記憶技巧】*sign*（mark）+ *ifi*（v.）+
cance（n.）

significant[3]〔sɪg'nɪfəkənt〕adj.
意義重大的
May 5 is a *significant* date to this
couple.

silence[2]〔'saɪləns〕n. 沉默
Speech is silver, *silence* is golden.

silent[2]〔'saɪlənt〕adj. 沉默的；安靜的
The teacher told the students to be
silent.

┌─【典型考題】─────
The prisoner remained _____ when
he was questioned by police. He was
speechless.
A. unsteady　　B. smooth
C. silent　　　D. rake　　　[C]
└─────────────

silk[2]〔sɪlk〕n. 絲　adj. 絲（製）的

silly[1]〔'sɪlɪ〕adj. 愚蠢的（= foolish）；
荒謬的；無聊的
Mother lets me play a *silly* game.

S

silver[1] 〔'sɪlvɚ 〕 n. 銀　adj. 銀色的
That ring is made of *silver*.

similar[2] 〔'sɪmələ 〕adj. 相似的
(= *alike*)
Her dress is *similar* to yours in style.
【片語】 *be similar to* (和…相似)

【典型考題】
I sometimes take John's coat for my own because the two of them look so _____.
A. original　　B. cheerful
C. curious　　D. similar　　[D]

similarity[3] 〔,sɪmə'lærətɪ 〕n. 相似之處 (= *resemblance*)
There are some *similarities* between Arenia and me.

simple[1] 〔'sɪmpḷ 〕 adj. 簡單的
This book is written in *simple* English.

simply[2] 〔'sɪmplɪ 〕 adv. 僅僅
(= *merely*)
He worked *simply* to get money.

sin[3] 〔 sɪn 〕 n. 罪 (= *guilt*)
Not all religions agree on what is a *sin* and what isn't.
【注意】 sin 是指宗教、道德上的「罪」；而 crime 是指法律上的「罪」。

since[1] 〔 sɪns 〕conj. 因為；自從；既然 (= *now that*)
I've been very busy *since* I came back from my vacation.

sincere[3] 〔 sɪn'sɪr 〕 adj. 真誠的
(= *earnest*)
I accepted a *sincere* apology.

【重要知識】副詞 sincerely，常用於書信最後，相當於中文的「敬上」。英國人寫成 Yours sincerely，美國人寫成 Sincerely (yours).

sincerity[4] 〔 sɪn'sɛrətɪ 〕 n. 真誠；誠意 (= *earnestness*)

sing[1] 〔 sɪŋ 〕 v. 唱歌

singer[1] 〔'sɪŋɚ 〕 n. 歌手；唱歌的人

single[2] 〔'sɪŋgḷ 〕 adj. 單一的；單身的
John is still *single*.

singular[4] 〔'sɪŋgjələ 〕 adj. 單數的
The *singular* form of "media" is "medium".
【反義詞】 plural (複數的)

sink[2] 〔 sɪŋk 〕 v. 下沉 (= *immerse*)
n. 水槽
The ship *sank*.
Sinks are used for washing dishes.

sip[3] 〔 sɪp 〕 v. n. 啜飲；小口喝
He *sipped* his brandy.

sir[1] 〔 sɚ , sɝ 〕 n. 先生

sister[1] 〔'sɪstɚ 〕 n. 姊妹

sit[1] 〔 sɪt 〕 v. 坐；位於；坐落於
(= *lie* = *be situated* = *be located*)
The house *sits* on a hill.

site[4] 〔 saɪt 〕 n. 地點；網站 (= *website*)
This is the *site* of the new airport, which is expected to be built within three years.

situation[3] 〔,sɪtʃu'eʃən 〕 n. 情況
When Clara realized she had no money with which to pay the bill, she had no idea how to handle the *situation*.

‡**size**[1] 〔saɪz〕*n.* 尺寸
What *size* do you wear?

【典型考題】
I'm going to buy a new pair of shoes for Mother. But I don't remember the _____ of her feet.
A. age   B. size
C. space   D. price   [B]

‡**skate**[3] 〔sket〕*v.* 溜冰
Most young people enjoy *skating*.

***sketch**[4] 〔skɛtʃ〕*n.* 素描
My art teacher suggested that I make a *sketch* before beginning to paint.

‡**ski**[3] 〔ski〕*v.* 滑雪
He likes *skiing* very much.

‡**skill**[1] 〔skɪl〕*n.* 技巧；技能
Zoe showed us her *skill* at cooking.

skilled[2] 〔skɪld〕*adj.* 熟練的
Robert is a *skilled* mechanic.

‡**skillful**[2] 〔'skɪlfəl〕*adj.* 熟練的
(= *adept*)；擅長的
She is *skillful* at drawing.

‡**skin**[1] 〔skɪn〕*n.* 皮膚
She has beautiful *skin*.

‡**skinny**[2] 〔'skɪnɪ〕*adj.* 皮包骨的
(= *very thin*)
Tony is a *skinny* boy.

***skip**[3] 〔skɪp〕*v.* 跳過；跳繩；蹺（課）；不做；不吃
Since chapter three in your book is not relevant to this course, we are going to *skip* it.
【片語】*skip classes* (蹺課)

‡**skirt**[2] 〔skɝt〕*n.* 裙子
【比較】outskirts (郊區)

‡**sky**[1] 〔skaɪ〕*n.* 天空
Birds fly across the *sky*.

【典型考題】
When it is going to rain, the _____ gets dark.
A. sky   B. air
C. wind   D. weather   [A]

***skyscraper**[3] 〔'skaɪˏskrepɚ〕*n.* 摩天大樓
【記憶技巧】*sky* + *scrap(e)* (刮；擦) + *er* (*n.*) (「摩天大樓」就是高到會刮到天空)

***slave**[3] 〔slev〕*n.* 奴隸

‡**sleep**[1] 〔slip〕*v.* 睡   *n.* 睡眠

***sleepy**[2] 〔'slipɪ〕*adj.* 想睡的
(= *drowsy*)
I feel very *sleepy*.

***sleeve**[3] 〔sliv〕*n.* 袖子

***slender**[2] 〔'slɛndɚ〕*adj.* 苗條的
My mother is a *slender* woman.

***slice**[3] 〔slaɪs〕*n.* （一）片
With some meat, vegetables and two *slices* of bread, you can make a sandwich.

‡**slide**[2] 〔slaɪd〕*v.* 滑 (= *glide*)
A car *slides* along the road.

***slight**[4] 〔slaɪt〕*adj.* 輕微的
I'm not really ill, but I have a *slight* headache.

S

‡**slim**[2] 〔 slɪm 〕 *adj.* 苗條的（= *slender*）；
狹窄的；微小的   *v.* 減重；瘦身
She is very *slim* because she swims
every week.

***slip**[2] 〔 slɪp 〕 *v.* 滑倒；滑落
I *slipped* on a banana peel.

‡**slipper**[2] 〔'slɪpɚ 〕 *n.* 拖鞋
Joy wears *slippers* for a comfortable
walk.

***slippery**[3] 〔'slɪpərɪ 〕 *adj.* 滑的；
滑溜的
After the rain, the sidewalk becomes
slippery. You had better watch
your step.

***slogan**[4] 〔'slogən 〕 *n.* 口號；標語
The advertising agency has thought
up a new *slogan* for our product.

***slope**[3] 〔 slop 〕 *n.* 斜坡（= *slant*）
Although he is just a beginner, Keith
was able to ski down the *slope*
without falling.

‡**slow**[1] 〔 slo 〕 *adj.* 慢的

‡**small**[1] 〔 smɔl 〕 *adj.* 小的

‡**smart**[1] 〔 smɑrt 〕 *adj.* 聰明的
Victor is explaining his *smart* idea.

‡**smell**[1] 〔 smɛl 〕 *v.* 聞   *n.* 味道
Jenny *smelled* the rose with her
nose.

‡**smile**[1] 〔 smaɪl 〕 *v. n.* 微笑
Remember to *smile* when I take
your picture.

***smog**[4] 〔 smɑg 〕 *n.* 煙霧
The factory is one of the main
contributors to the *smog* that
always hangs over the city.

‡**smoke**[1] 〔 smok 〕 *v.* 抽煙

***smooth**[3] 〔 smuð 〕 *adj.* 平滑的
【反義詞】 rough（粗糙的）

‡**snack**[2] 〔 snæk 〕 *n.* 點心
Sam wants to eat a *snack* before
dinner.
【衍伸詞】 *midnight snack*（宵夜）

***snail**[2] 〔 snel 〕 *n.* 蝸牛
【記憶技巧】 *s* + *nail*（指甲）

‡**snake**[1] 〔 snek 〕 *n.* 蛇
Snakes have long and thin bodies.

***snap**[3] 〔 snæp 〕 *v.* 啪的一聲折斷
Damian pressed down so hard with
his pencil that it *snapped*.

***sneeze**[4] 〔 sniz 〕 *v.* 打噴嚏
I think Jerry has a cold because he is
coughing and *sneezing*.

‡**snow**[1] 〔 sno 〕 *n.* 雪   *v.* 下雪

‡**snowy**[2] 〔'snoɪ 〕 *adj.* 多雪的
We are going to have a *snowy* winter
this year.

***soap**[1] 〔 sop 〕 *n.* 肥皂
She washed her hands with *soap*.
【片語】 *soap opera*（肥皂劇；連續劇）

【重要知識】爲什麼要稱作 soap opera？是因
第一個在美國廣播電台播出的連續劇有「肥皂」
（soap）的廣告。

***sob**[4] 〔sɑb〕 *v.* 啜泣；哭訴
n. 啜泣；抽噎
Melissa *sobbed* when her pet dog
disappeared.

‡**soccer**[2] 〔'sɑkɚ〕 *n.* 足球
A lot of boys love playing *soccer*.

***social**[2] 〔'soʃəl〕 *adj.* 社會的；社交的
Unemployment is a *social* problem.

***society**[2] 〔sə'saɪətɪ〕 *n.* 社會
Chinese *society* is now changing.

> 【典型考題】
> Money and power are too important in
> our _____. Everyone is pursuing them.
> A. furniture   B. society
> C. gossip   D. realization   [B]

‡**socks**[2] 〔sɑks〕 *n. pl.* 短襪
(= *short stockings*)
We put on our *socks* before putting
on our shoes.

***socket**[4] 〔'sɑkɪt〕 *n.* 插座 (= *outlet*)
Maggie forgot to put the electric plug
of the radio into the *socket*.
【比較】plug (插頭)

***soda**[1] 〔'sodə〕 *n.* 汽水；氣泡水；
蘇打水 (= *soda water*)
I would like a glass of *soda*.

> 【重要知識】soda 是氣泡飲料的總稱，如 Coke
> (可口可樂)、Pepsi (百事可樂)、7-up (七
> 喜) 等。

‡**sofa**[1] 〔'sofə〕 *n.* 沙發 (= *couch*)

***soft**[1] 〔sɔft〕 *adj.* 柔軟的 (= *tender*)
Which would you like better? A
soft mattress or a hard one?

***software**[4] 〔'sɔft,wɛr〕 *n.* 軟體
It took the *software* company one month
to figure out how to fight the PC virus.
【反義詞】hardware (硬體)

***soil**[1] 〔sɔɪl〕 *n.* 土壤
Plants need sun, water, and good *soil*.

***solar**[4] 〔'solɚ〕 *adj.* 太陽的
Solar energy released from the sun
does not cause any pollution.
【記憶技巧】*sol* (sun) + *ar* (adj.)
【比較】lunar (月亮的)

‡**soldier**[2] 〔'soldʒɚ〕 *n.* 軍人
Peter is a *soldier*.

***solid**[3] 〔'sɑlɪd〕 *adj.* 堅固的
(= *hard* = *firm*)；固體的
A *solid* foundation is required
before building a skyscraper.
【記憶技巧】*sol* (sole) + *id* (adj.)
(結合成一體，表示堅固的)

***solution**[2] 〔sə'luʃən〕 *n.* 解決之道
We have to find a *solution* as soon
as possible.

***solve**[2] 〔sɑlv〕 *v.* 解決；解答
Michael is trying to *solve* the problem.
【比較】re<u>solve</u> (決心)；dis<u>solve</u> (溶解)

> 【典型考題】
> After spending one hour on this math
> problem, John still could not _____ it.
> A. count   B. figure
> C. add   D. solve   [D]

‡**some**[1] 〔sʌm〕 *adj.* 一些；某個
My sister wants to drink *some* milk.
He went to *some* place in Africa.
【注意】some 後接數字時，可作「大約」解。

S

‡**somebody**[2] 〔'sʌm,badɪ 〕 *pron.* 某人
Somebody wants to see you.

***someday**[3] 〔'sʌm,de 〕 *adv.* (將來)
有一天
If you keep trying, you are bound to
succeed *someday*.

***somehow**[3] 〔'sʌm,haʊ 〕 *adv.* 以某種
方法
The buses are not running today, but
Jill still got to the office *somehow*.

‡**someone**[1] 〔'sʌm,wʌn 〕 *pron.* 某人
(= *somebody*)

‡**something**[1] 〔'sʌmθɪŋ 〕 *pron.* 某物

***sometime**[3] 〔'sʌm,taɪm 〕 *adv.* 某時
I'll call Joe *sometime* tomorrow.

‡**sometimes**[1] 〔'sʌm,taɪmz 〕 *adv.*
有時候
Sometimes it rains in the morning.

***somewhat**[3] 〔'sʌm,hwɑt 〕 *adv.* 有一點
(= *sort of* = *kind of* = *a little*)
Gloria was *somewhat* disappointed
with the meal and decided not to go
to that restaurant again.

‡**somewhere**[2] 〔'sʌm,hwɛr 〕 *adv.*
在某處
Fred has left his books *somewhere*
in the school.

‡**son**[1] 〔 sʌn 〕 *n.* 兒子
She has two *sons* and one daughter.

‡**song**[1] 〔 sɔŋ 〕 *n.* 歌曲
Karen really loves to write *songs*.

‡**soon**[1] 〔 sun 〕 *adv.* 不久
I hope we will get there *soon*.

***sophomore**[4] 〔'sɑfm̩,or 〕 *n.* 大二學生
【記憶技巧】 *sopho* (wise) + *more*
(foolish) (「大二學生」所學的還不多，
算是一半聰明一半愚笨)
【比較】 freshman (大一學生)；junior
(大三學生)；senior (大四學生)

‡**sore**[3] 〔 sor , sɔr 〕 *adj.* 疼痛的
(= *painful*)
I have a *sore* throat.
【片語】 *have a sore throat* (喉嚨痛)

***sorrow**[3] 〔'saro 〕 *n.* 悲傷
(= *great sadness* = *grief*)
To our great *sorrow*, old Mr. Wang
passed away last night.

***sorrowful**[4] 〔'sɑrofəl 〕 *adj.* 悲傷的
(= *sad*)

‡**sorry**[1] 〔'sɑrɪ 〕 *adj.* 難過的 (= *sad*)；
抱歉的；遺憾的
I'm *sorry* to hurt you.
【重要知識】這個字以前都唸〔'sɔrɪ 〕，現在，
68% 的美國人都唸〔'sɑrɪ 〕。

***sort**[2] 〔 sɔrt 〕 *n.* 種類 (= *kind*)
v. 分類
I like this *sort* of house.
【衍伸詞】 *sort of* (有一點)

***soul**[1] 〔 sol 〕 *n.* 靈魂
Many people believe that a man's
soul never dies.

‡**sound**[1] 〔 saʊnd 〕 *n.* 聲音 *v.* 聽起來
I heard a strange *sound*.

‡**soup**[1] 〔 sup 〕 *n.* 湯
Henry asked for a bowl of *soup*.

***sour**[1] 〔 saʊr 〕 *adj.* 酸的
This lemon is very *sour*.

* **source**[2] 〔 sors 〕 *n.* 來源

I don't know the *source* of the information.

【記憶技巧】這個字要和 resource (資源) 一起背。

‡‡ **south**[1] 〔 sauθ 〕 *n.* 南方

Mexico is to the *south* of the United States.

【片語】 *to the south of* (在…以南)

* **southern**[2] 〔 'sʌðən 〕 *adj.* 南方的

We went to *southern* Taiwan last month.

* **souvenir**[4] 〔 ˌsuvə'nɪr 〕 *n.* 紀念品

She brought back lots of little *souvenirs* from Bali for her co-workers.

【記憶技巧】 *sou* (up) + *venir* (come) (「紀念品」會使你的回憶出現在腦中)

* **soybean**[2] 〔 'sɔɪˌbin 〕 *n.* 大豆

【衍伸詞】 *soybean milk* (豆漿)

‡‡ **space**[1] 〔 spes 〕 *n.* 空間；太空

Our new house has more *space*.

【典型考題】

It's very difficult to find a parking ＿＿＿＿ in Taipei.

A. space   B. street
C. way   D. fact   [A]

* **spade**[3] 〔 sped 〕 *n.* 鏟子 (= *shovel*)；(撲克牌的) 黑桃

【片語】 call a spade a spade (直言不諱)
【算命時抽到「黑桃」表示惡運，如果是黑桃就說是黑桃，也就是「直言不諱」。】

‡‡ **spaghetti**[2] 〔 spə'gɛtɪ 〕 *n.* 義大利麵

* **spare**[4] 〔 spɛr 〕 *adj.* 空閒的
     v. 騰出 (時間)；吝惜

Glen spent most of his *spare* time reading books.

【片語】 *spare time* (空閒時間)
       spare some time (騰出一些時間)
       spare no efforts (不遺餘力)

* **spark**[4] 〔 spɑrk 〕 *n.* 火花

A *spark* from the fireplace landed on the carpet.

* **sparkle**[4] 〔 'spɑrkḷ 〕 *n. v.* 閃耀

The black watch is nice, but this one has more *sparkle*.

* **sparrow**[4] 〔 'spæro 〕 *n.* 麻雀

【記憶技巧】 *sp* + *arrow* (箭)

‡‡ **speak**[1] 〔 spik 〕 *v.* 說

‡ **speaker**[2] 〔 'spikə 〕 *n.* 說話者

* **spear**[4] 〔 spɪr 〕 *n.* 矛

【比較】 shield (盾)

‡‡ **special**[1] 〔 'spɛʃəl 〕 *adj.* 特別的
     (= *different*)   *n.* 特製；特別節日

* **species**[4] 〔 'spiʃɪz 〕 *n.* 物種；種

The rhinoceros is an endangered *species*.

【片語】 *endangered species* (瀕臨絕種的動物)

【典型考題】

Whales are hunted for their meat and oil, and have become an endangered ＿＿＿＿.

A. cure   B. species
C. technology   D. substitute   [B]

* **specific**[3] 〔 spɪ'sɪfɪk 〕 *adj.* 特定的
     (= *particular*)

This coupon is to be used in *specific* shops.

‡ **speech**[1] 〔 spitʃ 〕 *n.* 演講
(= *speaking*)
【片語】*deliver a speech* (發表演說)

‡ **speed**[2] 〔 spid 〕 *n.* 速度
The *speed* of this train is 200
kilometers an hour.
【片語】*speed up* (加速)
【衍伸詞】speeding (超速)

‡ **spell**[1] 〔 spɛl 〕 *v.* 拼 (字)
He *spells* his name for me.

* **spelling**[2] 〔'spɛlɪŋ 〕 *n.* 拼字
Her *spelling* has improved.

‡ **spend**[1] 〔 spɛnd 〕 *v.* 花費
Nick *spends* so much money on
traveling.

* **spice**[3] 〔 spaɪs 〕 *n.* 香料 (= *flavor*)；
趣味
Variety is the *spice* of life.

* **spicy**[4] 〔'spaɪsɪ 〕 *adj.* 辣的
Lucy likes *spicy* food.

‡ **spider**[2] 〔'spaɪdɚ 〕 *n.* 蜘蛛

* **spill**[3] 〔 spɪl 〕 *v.* 灑出
Someone *spilled* some water on the
floor, so be careful.

* **spin**[3] 〔 spɪn 〕 *v.* 旋轉 (= *rotate*)；
紡織 (= *weave*)
The skater *spun* round and round.

* **spinach**[2] 〔'spɪnɪdʒ 〕 *n.* 菠菜

‡ **spirit**[2] 〔'spɪrɪt 〕 *n.* 精神 (= *mood*)
She lost her *spirit* after his death.
【片語】*in high spirits* (興高采烈)

* **spiritual**[4] 〔'spɪrɪtʃuəl 〕 *adj.* 精神上的

Liz saw a doctor for her physical health
and a priest for her *spiritual* health.
【反義詞】physical (身體的)

* **spit**[3] 〔 spɪt 〕 *v.* 吐出；吐口水
Oscar didn't like the food so he *spit*
it out.

* **spite**[3] 〔 spaɪt 〕 *n.* 惡意；怨恨
v. 故意激怒；存心刁難
Martha told Alice about the party,
ruining the surprise out of *spite*.
【片語】*in spite of* (儘管) (= *despite*)

* **splash**[3] 〔 splæʃ 〕 *v.* 濺起
n. 水濺起的聲音
The passing car *splashed* mud on my
coat.

* **splendid**[4] 〔'splɛndɪd 〕 *adj.* 壯麗的
(= *magnificent*)
We visited a *splendid* palace in
mainland China.
【記憶技巧】*splend* (shine) + *id* (adj.)
(閃著光輝的，表示「壯麗的」)

* **split**[4] 〔 splɪt 〕 *v.* 使分裂 (= *divide*)；
分攤
The dispute *split* the political party
into two.
【片語】*split the cost* (分攤費用)

* **spoil**[3] 〔 spɔɪl 〕 *v.* 破壞
(= *make worse*)；寵壞；腐壞
The bad weather *spoiled* our plans
to go hiking today.

┌─【典型考題】─────────────
The weather was so hot that the food
in the picnic basket ———— before we
had a chance to eat it.
A. evaporated   B. fled
C. spoiled   D. shattered   [C]

‡spoon[1] 〔spun〕 *n.* 湯匙（= *scoop* ）

People use *spoons* for eating.

*sport[1] 〔sport〕 *n.* 運動

（= *physical activity* ）

Soccer is the favorite *sport* of English people.

【注意】形容詞是 sports（運動的）。

*sportsman[4] 〔'sportsmən〕 *n.* 運動家；運動

*sportsmanship[4] 〔'sportsmən,ʃɪp〕 *n.* 運動家精神

It is important to show good *sportsmanship* whether you win the game or not.

*spot[2] 〔spɑt〕 *n.* 地點 *v.* 發現

Don't go to the dangerous *spot*.

【片語】***on the spot***（當場）

（= *on the scene* ）

*sprain[3] 〔spren〕 *v.* 扭傷

The doctor said my ankle is not broken, only *sprained*.

*spray[3] 〔spre〕 *v.* 噴灑

Nicole *sprayed* herself with perfume before she went out.

*spread[2] 〔sprɛd〕 *v.* 散播

The news *spread* quickly.

【注意】spread 三態同型。

【典型考題】

The rumor of the scandal involving the candidate _____ quickly during the election campaign.

A. explored   B. departed

C. breezed   D. spread   **[D]**

‡spring[1,2] 〔sprɪŋ〕 *n.* 春天 *v.* 跳躍

Mandy will come back home in *spring*.

*sprinkle[3] 〔'sprɪŋkḷ〕 *v.* 撒；下小雨；灑（= *scatter* = *spray* = *spread* ）

n. 少量；一點點

I already *sprinkled* some salt on the popcorn, so you don't need to add any more.

【典型考題】

I like to _____ some pepper on my steak to make it taste even better.

A. sprinkle   B. stress

C. stance   D. smooth   **[A]**

sprinkler[3] 〔'sprɪŋklɚ〕 *n.* 灑水裝置；自動灑水滅火器

*spy[3] 〔spaɪ〕 *n.* 間諜

Sandy was discovered to be a military *spy*.

‡square[2] 〔skwɛr〕 *n.* 正方形；廣場 *adj.* 方形的；平方的

The paper was cut into *squares*.

【比較】cubic（立方的）

*squeeze[3] 〔skwiz〕 *v.* 擠壓（= *press* ）；擠；塞

I had to *squeeze* ten oranges to make this pitcher of juice.

【典型考題】

To make fresh lemonade, cut the lemon in half, _____ the juice into a bowl, and then add as much water and sugar as you like.

A. decrease   B. squeeze

C. freeze   D. cease   **[B]**

*squirrel[2] 〔'skwɝəl , skwɝl〕 *n.* 松鼠

S

S

* **stab**³ 〔 stæb 〕 v. 刺 (= *pierce*)；戳
  n. 刺；刺痛 (= *prick*)
  The killer tried to *stab* Tom with a
  knife, but he missed.

* **stable**³ 〔'stebl 〕 adj. 穩定的 (= *steady*)
  Prices have been *stable* for a year.

* **stadium**³ 〔'stedɪəm 〕 n. 體育館

* **staff**³ 〔 stæf 〕 n. 職員【集合名詞】
  (= *employees*)
  The executive has a *staff* of four to
  help him with research.

* **stage**² 〔 stedʒ 〕 n. 舞台；階段
  (= *phase*)；發生的場所 v. 舉辦；
  上演；舉行
  He doesn't like to stand on the *stage*.
  【衍伸詞】 *stage fright* (怯場)

‡‡ **stairs**¹ 〔 stɛrz 〕 n. pl. 樓梯
  Tom is going down the *stairs*.

  stale³ 〔 stel 〕 adj. 腐壞的；陳腐的；
  膩煩的；不新鮮的 (= *not fresh*)
  I threw out that loaf of *stale* bread.
  【記憶技巧】 先背 tale (故事)，字首加 S
    (死)，死掉的故事就表示故事內容不新鮮。

‡‡ **stamp**² 〔 stæmp 〕 n. 郵票

‡‡ **stand**¹ 〔 stænd 〕 v. 站立；忍受
  (= *bear*)；位於 n. 立場 (= *opinion*)
  I can't *stand* it any more.
  The church *stands* on a hill.

* **standard**² 〔'stændəd 〕 n. 標準
  (= *criterion*) adj. 標準的；普通的
  His work was below the required
  standard.
  【片語】 *standard of living* (生活水準)

‡‡ **star**¹ 〔 star 〕 n. 星星；明星 v. 主演
  There are many *stars* in the sky
  tonight.
  【衍伸詞】 *movie star* (電影明星)

* **stare**³ 〔 stɛr 〕 v. n. 凝視 (= *gaze*)；
  瞪眼看
  Joan could not help but *stare* at the
  seven-foot-tall man.

‡‡ **start**¹ 〔 start 〕 v. 開始 (= *begin*)；
  啟動；引起 n. 開始 (= *beginning*)
  The bank machine will *start*
  working next Monday.

* **starve**³ 〔 starv 〕 v. 飢餓；餓死；
  使挨餓
  If we don't send some food to that
  poor country, many people there
  may *starve*.
  【衍伸詞】 starving (很餓的)

‡‡ **state**¹ 〔 stet 〕 n. 州；狀態 v. 敘述
  The house was in a *state* of disarray
  after the party.

* **statement**¹ 〔'stetmənt 〕 n. (銀行)
  對帳單；月結單；敘述 (= *account*)；
  聲明 (= *announcement*)
  The witness made a *statement* to
  the police.

‡‡ **station**¹ 〔'steʃən 〕 n. 車站 (= *stop*)；
  所；局

* **statue**³ 〔'stætʃʊ 〕 n. 雕像
  (= *a sculpted figure*)
  There is a *statue* of the famous
  poet in the park.
  【衍伸詞】 *the Statue of Liberty* (自由
    女神像)

***status**[4] 〔'stetəs 〕 *n.* 狀況；地位
（＝*standing*）；身份（＝*position*）
It used to be a *status* symbol to
have a Mercedes Benz.
【記憶技巧】*stat* (stand) + *us* (*n.*)
（佔有一席之地，表示有身分「地位」）

‡**stay**[1] 〔 ste 〕 *v.* 停留；保持

***steady**[3] 〔'stɛdɪ 〕 *adj.* 穩定的
┌─【典型考題】────────
│ A human body usually has a _____
│ temperature of about 37 degrees C.
│ A. steady   B. various
│ C. gradual   D. precious   [A]
└─────────────────────

‡**steak**[2] 〔 stek 〕 *n.* 牛排
The waiter is serving me *steak*.

‡**steal**[2] 〔 stil 〕 *v.* 偷
Jimmy has *stolen* my car.

‡**steam**[2] 〔 stim 〕 *n.* 蒸氣（＝*vapor*）
v. 冒蒸氣；蒸煮
Boiled water becomes *steam*.
┌─【典型考題】────────
│ The first car was powered by _____,
│ not by gasoline.
│ A. steam   B. distance
│ C. speed   D. spy   [A]
└─────────────────────

***steel**[2] 〔 stil 〕 *n.* 鋼
【衍伸詞】*stainless steel*（不銹鋼）

***steep**[3] 〔 stip 〕 *adj.* 陡峭的；急遽的
Jason fell when he tried to ski
down a very *steep* hill.
【反義詞】gentle（平緩的）

***stem**[4] 〔 stɛm 〕 *n.*（樹）幹（＝*trunk*）；
莖 *v.* 源自於
【衍伸詞】*stem cell*（幹細胞）

***step**[1] 〔 stɛp 〕 *n.* 一步（＝*pace*）；步驟
v. 走；邁步
We should take *steps* to stop it.
【片語】*take steps*（採取步驟）

stepchild[3] 〔'stɛp,tʃaɪld 〕 *n.* 夫或妻
以前婚姻所生之子女

***stepfather**[3] 〔'stɛp,faðə 〕 *n.* 繼父

***stepmother**[3] 〔'stɛp,mʌðə 〕 *n.* 繼母

***stereo**[3] 〔'stɛrɪo 〕 *n.* 立體音響；鉛版
印刷 *adj.* 立體聲的
Don't play your *stereo* too loud or
you will disturb the neighbors.

***stick**[2] 〔 stɪk 〕 *n.* 棍子（＝*rod*）
v. 把…插入；黏貼
Don't forget to *stick* a stamp on the
letter.
【片語】*stick to*（堅持）

***sticky**[3] 〔'stɪkɪ 〕 *adj.* 濕熱的
（＝*humid*）；黏的（＝*adhesive*
〔 əd'hisɪv 〕）
The table is *sticky* where I spilled
honey on it.

***stiff**[3] 〔 stɪf 〕 *adj.* 僵硬的
Doug pulled a muscle and now he
has a *stiff* neck.
┌─【典型考題】────────
│ After working in front of my computer
│ for the entire day, my neck and
│ shoulders got so _____ that I couldn't
│ even turn my head.
│ A. dense   B. harsh
│ C. stiff   D. concrete   [C]
└─────────────────────

‡**still**[1] 〔 stɪl 〕 *adv.* 仍然   *adj.* 靜止的

* **sting**[3] 〔 stɪŋ 〕 v. 叮咬 (= *bite*)
    n. 刺痛
    Don't bother that bee or it may *sting*
    you.

* **stingy**[4] 〔'stɪndʒɪ 〕 adj. 吝嗇的；小氣
    的 (= *mean*)
    He is too *stingy* to give money to
    charity.
    【反義詞】 generous (慷慨的；大方的)

> 【典型考題】
> Although Mr. Chen is rich, he is a very
> ——— person and is never willing to
> spend any money to help those who
> are in need.
> A. absolute   B. precise
> C. economic   D. stingy   **[D]**

* **stir**[3] 〔 stɝ 〕 v. 攪動；喚起；引發
    n. 攪動；騷動
    You had better *stir* the soup or it may burn.

* **stitch**[3] 〔 stɪtʃ 〕 n. 一針；一縫
    Melinda cut her finger and had to get
    three *stitches* to close the cut.
    A *stitch* in time saves nine.

* **stocking**[3] 〔'stɑkɪŋ 〕 n. 長襪

* **stomach**[2] 〔'stʌmək 〕 n. 胃；腹；嗜好
    The food we eat goes into our
    stomachs.

* **stone**[1] 〔 ston 〕 n. 石頭 (= *rock*)
    v. 用石頭砸

* **stool**[3] 〔 stul 〕 n. 凳子
    Duncan sat on a *stool* and changed
    his shoes.
    【記憶技巧】 *s + tool* (工具)

* **stop**[1] 〔 stɑp 〕 v. 停止；阻止
    The car *stops* at the red light.

* **store**[1] 〔 stor 〕 n. 商店 (= *shop*)
    v. 儲存 (= *keep*)
    Mother took us to the shoe *store*
    to buy shoes.

* **storm**[2] 〔 stɔrm 〕 n. 暴風雨
    v. 氣沖沖地離去
    The *storm* caused great damage.
    【衍伸詞】 thunderstorm (雷雨)

* **stormy**[3] 〔'stɔrmɪ 〕 adj. 暴風雨的
    (= *turbulent*)；激烈的；多風波的
    It was a *stormy* night.

* **story**[1] 〔'storɪ 〕 n. 故事；短篇小說
    "Harry Potter" is the *story* of a
    little wizard.
    【衍伸詞】 *detective story* (偵探小說)
            news story (新聞報導)

* **stove**[2] 〔 stov 〕 n. 爐子
    An old man was making a fire in
    the *stove*.

* **straight**[2] 〔 stret 〕 adj. 坦率的；直的
    (= *direct*)   adv. 筆直地；直接地
    She has beautiful long *straight* hair.

> 【典型考題】
> Residents are told not ot dump all
> household waste ——— into the trash
> can; reusable materials should first be
> sorted out and recycled.
> A. shortly   B. straight
> C. forward   D. namely   **[B]**

* **strange**[1] 〔 strendʒ 〕 adj. 奇怪的
    (= *odd*)；不熟悉的；不習慣的

S

stranger[2] (ˈstrendʒɚ) *n.* 陌生人
His dog barks at *strangers*.

【典型考題】
It could be dangerous for children to talk with ＿＿＿＿.
A. teachers　　　B. doctors
C. strangers　　D. classmates　　[C]

strategy[3] (ˈstrætədʒɪ) *n.* 策略
(= *scheme*)；戰略
We won the contest by *strategy*.

straw[2] (strɔ) *n.* 稻草；吸管
The last *straw* breaks the camel's back.

strawberry[2] (ˈstrɔ͵bɛrɪ) *n.* 草莓

stream[2] (strim) *n.* 溪流
A small *stream* runs in front of our garden.

street[1] (strit) *n.* 街

strength[3] (strɛŋθ) *n.* 力量
(= *physical power*)；長處
Rex doesn't have the *strength* to lift that heavy box by himself.

strengthen[4] (ˈstrɛŋθən) *v.* 加強
(= *reinforce*)
A person who thinks he is incapable tends to fail. Moreover, failure will *strengthen* his belief in his incompetence.
【記憶技巧】 **strength** (力量) + **en** (*v.*)

【典型考題】
We are more than willing to ＿＿＿＿ our ties with those countries that are friendly to us.
A. appeal　　　B. strengthen
C. expect　　　D. connect　　[B]

stress[2] (strɛs) *n.* 重音；強調；壓力
(= *pressure* = *tension*)　*v.* 強調
(= *emphasize*)
The exam put a lot of *stress* on him.

stretch[2] (strɛtʃ) *v.* 拉長；伸展
Joe *stretched* a rubber band and aimed it at me.

【典型考題】
My arm hurts when I ＿＿＿＿ it straight out.
A. pull　　　B. widen
C. stretch　　D. remove　　[C]

strict[2] (strɪkt) *adj.* 嚴格的
Psychologists have found that *strict* regulations do not always make a child behave better.

strike[2] (straɪk) *v.* 打擊；(災難) 侵襲　*n.* 罷工 (= *a work stoppage*)
The small boy tried to *strike* me with a stick.
【片語】 *go on strike* (進行罷工)

string[2] (strɪŋ) *n.* 細繩
(= *cord* = *line*)；一連串
The *string* broke and the kite was lost.
【比較】 rope (粗繩)

strip[3] (strɪp) *v.* 剝去 (= *remove*)；剝奪；脫掉 (= *undress* = *take off*)
Tom *strips* off his clothes and jumps into the swimming pool.

strive[4] (straɪv) *v.* 努力
(= *try very hard*)
【三態變化為：strive-strove-striven】
They *strove* to change the society's perception of homosexuals.

S

*stroke⁴ 〔 strok 〕 n. 打擊；中風；划水；
一筆；一劃；一撇；一擊　v. 撫摸
Little *strokes* fell great oaks.
【片語】 *have a stroke* (中風)

‡strong¹ 〔 strɔŋ 〕 adj. 有力的；強壯的
(= *powerful*)；穩固的；強效的

*structure³ 〔'strʌktʃɚ 〕 n. 結構；組織
(= *organization*)；建築物
The Shin Kong tower is one of the
largest *structures* in the city.
【記憶技巧】 *struct* (build) + *ure* (n.)

*struggle² 〔'strʌgl̩ 〕 v. 奮鬥；掙扎
(= *twist violently*)　　n. 奮鬥；抗爭
The cat *struggled* in his arms.

*stubborn³ 〔'stʌbɚn 〕 adj. 頑固的
(= *obstinate*)
The child is too *stubborn* to be
reasoned with.

‡student¹ 〔'stjudn̩t 〕 n. 學生
(= *pupil*)

*studio³ 〔'stjudɪ͵o 〕 n. 工作室
The artist's *studio* is very bright.

‡study¹ 〔'stʌdɪ 〕 v. 讀書 (= *learn*)；
研究　n. 研究；書房　pl. 學業
Andrew *studies* English by himself.

*stuff³ 〔 stʌf 〕 n. 東西 (= *things*)
v. 填塞；裝滿；填滿
What's this *stuff*?

‡stupid¹ 〔'stjupɪd 〕 adj. 愚笨的
Laura gave me a *stupid* idea.

*style³ 〔 staɪl 〕 n. 風格；方式

You'd better change your *style* of
living.

‡subject² 〔'sʌbdʒɪkt 〕 n. 科目；主題
(= *topic* = *theme*)　adj. 受制於 < *to* >
English is my favorite *subject*.

*submarine³ 〔'sʌbmə͵rin 〕 n. 潛水艇
adj. 海底的；海中的
【記憶技巧】 *sub* (under) + *marine*
(sea) (在海面下的東西，就是「潛水艇」)

*substance³ 〔'sʌbstəns 〕 n. 物質
(= *material*)；毒品；內容
Don't touch that *substance* with your
bare hands because it is toxic.
【記憶技巧】 *sub* (under) + *stan* (stand)
+ *ce* (n.) (立於表象之下的是「物質」)
┌─【典型考題】───────
│ Water, ice, and snow are the same
│ _____ in different forms.
│ A. effect　　　B. electron
│ C. substance　D. toilet　　　　[C]
└────────────────────

*subtract² 〔 səb'trækt 〕 v. 減去；減掉
(= *take away* = *deduct*)
Subtract 5 from 7, and you have 2.
【記憶技巧】 *sub* (under) + *tract*
(draw) (從底下抽出來，也就是「減掉」)

*suburbs³ 〔'sʌbɝbz 〕 n. pl. 郊區
(= *outskirts*)
After twenty years in the city, the
Millers have moved to the *suburbs*.
【比較】 outskirts (郊區)

*subway² 〔'sʌb͵we 〕 n. 地下鐵
(= *underground* = *MRT* = *metro*
〔'mɛtro 〕 = *tube* 〔 tjub 〕【英式用法】)
I take the *subway* to school every day.

*succeed[2] 〔sək'sid〕 v. 成功 < in > ;
繼承 < to > ; 接著發生
Our plan has *succeeded*.
He *succeeded* to his father's estate.
【記憶技巧】 *suc* (under) + *ceed* (go)

*success[2] 〔sək'sɛs〕 n. 成功
(= *victory*) ; 成功的人或事
His life is full of *success*.
【重要知識】有句諺語「一事成功,事事成功。」
Nothing succeeds like *success*. 字面的意
思是「沒有一件事像成功一樣,會接著發生。」句
中的 succeed 是指「接著發生」。

‡successful[2] 〔sək'sɛsfəl〕 adj. 成功的
(= *triumphant*)
【典型考題】
The restaurant wasn't _____ and
was forced to close down.
A. decreasing   B. unlucky
C. total   D. successful   [D]

*such[1] 〔sʌtʃ〕 adj. 那樣的

*suck[3] 〔sʌk〕 v. 吸
The girl *sucked* the lemonade
through a straw.

*sudden[2] 〔'sʌdn̩〕 adj. 突然的
Judy made a *sudden* decision about
going abroad.
【片語】 *all of a sudden* (突然地)
【衍伸詞】 suddenly (突然地)

*suffer[3] 〔'sʌfɚ〕 v. 罹患; 受苦
(= *be in pain*)
This poor boy is *suffering* from a
bad cold.
【片語】 *suffer from* (罹患)

*sufficient[3] 〔sə'fɪʃənt〕 adj. 足夠的
(= *enough*)

No one in the shelter has *sufficient* food.
【記憶技巧】 efficient (有效率的) -
sufficient-deficient (不足的) 這三個
字要一起背。
【典型考題】
We need your help in order to have
_____ funds to promote this social
welfare program.
A. efficient   B. sufficient
C. proficient   D. deficient   [B]

‡sugar[1] 〔'ʃʊgɚ〕 n. 糖
【片語】 *a lump of sugar* (一塊糖)

‡suggest[3] 〔səg'dʒɛst〕 v. 暗示; 建議
(= *advise*) ; 顯示 (= *indicate*)
He *suggested* that we should go home.
【記憶技巧】 *sug* (up) + *gest* (carry)
(「建議」就是把意見搬上檯面)

*suggestion[4] 〔səg'dʒɛstʃən〕 n. 建議
(= *proposal*) ; 暗示; 跡象 (= *sign*)
When planning the party, our class
leader asked us for *suggestions*.
【典型考題】
He made a _____ about how the
project should be done.
A. suggestion   B. situation
C. tradition   D. realization   [A]

*suicide[3] 〔'suə,saɪd〕 n. 自殺
(= *self-murder*)
John felt such despair that he even
contemplated *suicide*.
【記憶技巧】 *sui* (self) + *cide* (cut)
(切自己,也就是「自殺」)
【片語】 *commit suicide* (自殺)

*suit[2] 〔sut〕 v. 適合 (= *fit*)   n. 西裝;
訴訟 (= *lawsuit*)
The dress *suits* you.

S

* **suitable**[3] 〔'sutəbḷ 〕 *adj.* 適合的
  (= *appropriate*)
  There are several books *suitable* for children.

* **sum**[3] 〔 sʌm 〕 *n.* 金額；總額　*v.* 總結
  He spent a large *sum* of money.
  【片語】 *to sum up* (總之)

* **summarize**[4] 〔'sʌmə,raɪz 〕 *v.* 總結；扼要說明
  Headlines usually briefly *summarize* the news stories, so they can help the reader decide quickly what to read, skim, or ignore.

* **summary**[3] 〔'sʌmərɪ 〕 *n.* 摘要
  (= *outline*)　　*adj.* 概括的；簡要的
  The newscaster gave the viewers a *summary* of the day's events.
  【記憶技巧】 *summ* (sum) + *ary* (n.)
  　(「摘要」是總合了文章大意)

‡ **summer**[1] 〔'sʌmə 〕 *n.* 夏天

* **summit**[3] 〔'sʌmɪt 〕 *n.* 顛峰；山頂
  (= *mountaintop*)；高峰會議
  adj. 高階層的
  After a long, hard climb the mountaineers reached the *summit*.
  【片語】 *a summit conference* (高峰會議)

‡ **sun**[1] 〔 sʌn 〕 *n.* 太陽
  On a clear day, the *sun* shines brightly in the sky.

‡ **Sunday**[1] 〔'sʌndɪ , -de 〕 *n.* 星期天
  (= *Sun.*)

‡ **sunny**[2] 〔'sʌnɪ 〕 *adj.* 晴朗的
  (= *bright*)；開朗的

Yesterday was very bright and *sunny*.

* **super**[1] 〔'supə 〕 *adj.* 極好的
  (= *extremely good*)；超級的
  We had a *super* time.

* **superior**[3] 〔 sə'pɪrɪə , su'pɪrɪə〕 *adj.* 較優秀的 (= *better*)；有優越感的
  n. 上司；長官
  They consider themselves the most *superior* race in the world.
  【片語】 *be superior to* (比…優秀)
  【反義詞】 inferior (較差的)

‡ **supermarket**[2] 〔'supə,markɪt 〕 *n.* 超級市場
  Cheeses are sold in the *supermarket*.

* **supper**[1] 〔'sʌpə 〕 *n.* 晚餐
  We have *supper* in the evening.

* **supply**[2] 〔 sə'plaɪ 〕 *v.* 供給 (= *provide*)
  n. 供給 (= *provision*)
  The government *supplied* free books to schools.
  【記憶技巧】 *sup* (under) + *ply* (fill)
  　(「供給」是要滿足人類內心深處的需求)
  【比較】 demand (需求)

* **support**[2] 〔 sə'port 〕 *v.* 支持 (= *help*)；支撐；扶養　*n.* 支持
  All of us *supported* him.
  【記憶技巧】 *sup* (up) + *port* (carry)
  　(把東西帶過去，表示「支持」)

【典型考題】
The nurse ＿＿＿ the sick child because he was too weak to walk by himself.
A. begged　　　B. interested
C. supported　　D. insisted　　　[C]

* **suppose**[3] 〔səˋpoz〕v. 假定
（= *assume*）；認為（= *consider*）
Suppose he refuses. What shall we do?
【記憶技巧】*sup* (under) + *pose* (put)
（把想法放在心底，就是「假設」）

【典型考題】
It has rained every day this week, so
I _____ it will rain today as well.
A. glimpse   B. suppose
C. refer   D. notice   [B]

‡ **sure**[1] 〔ʃur〕adj. 確定的

‡ **surf**[4] 〔sɝf〕v. 衝浪；瀏覽（= *browse*）
My boyfriend is good at *surfing*.
【衍伸詞】*surf the Internet*（瀏覽網
路；上網）

* **surface**[2] 〔ˋsɝfɪs〕n. 外觀；表面
（= *covering*）v. 顯現（= *emerge*）
The desk has a smooth *surface*.
【記憶技巧】*sur* (above) + *face*

* **surgeon**[4] 〔ˋsɝdʒən〕n. 外科醫生
【比較】physician（內科醫生）

* **surgery**[4] 〔ˋsɝdʒərɪ〕n. 手術
（= *operation*）
Lydia had to stay in bed for two
weeks after her *surgery*.

‡ **surprise**[1] 〔səˋpraɪz〕v. 使驚訝
n. 驚訝
We will *surprise* Ann with a party
on her birthday.

【典型考題】
The ending of the movie did not come
as a _____ to John because he had
already read the novel that the movie
was based on.
A. vision   B. focus
C. surprise   D. conclusion   [C]

* **surrender**[4] 〔səˋrɛndɚ〕v. 放棄；
投降（= *give in*）；交出   n. 投降；
放棄
The police tried to convince the
gunman to *surrender*.
【記憶技巧】*sur* (upon) + *render*（給
予）（願意把東西交給別人，表示「投降」）

* **surround**[3] 〔səˋraund〕v. 圍繞；
環繞（= *encircle*）
When the young singer appeared,
he was *surrounded* by hundreds of
his fans.
【記憶技巧】*sur* (over) + *round*（環繞）

* **surroundings**[4] 〔səˋraundɪŋz〕n. pl.
周遭環境（= *environment*）
The girl realized she was lost when
she did not recognize her
surroundings.

【典型考題】
People who immigrate to a foreign
country have to spend some time
getting used to the new _____.
A. achievement   B. surroundings
C. exhibition   D. bulletin   [B]

* **survey**[3] 〔sɚˋve〕v. 調查
The police *surveyed* the scene of the
crime carefully for fear of missing
any clue that was related to the
murder.
【記憶技巧】*sur* (over) + *vey* (see)
（查看整個情況，就是「調查」）

* **survival**[3] 〔sɚˋvaɪvḷ〕n. 生還
（= *remaining alive*）；存活
Hopes are fading for the *survival* of
the missing mountain climbers.

S

survive[2] 〔 sə'vaɪv 〕 *v.* 生還 (= *remain alive*)；自…中生還；活得比…久
When the car crashed, only I *survived*.
【記憶技巧】 *sur* (above) + *vive* (live)
(活著站在一堆屍體上面，表示「生還」)

survivor[3] 〔 sə'vaɪvɚ 〕 *n.* 生還者

suspect[3] 〔 sə'spɛkt 〕 *v.* 懷疑
(= *suppose*)
〔'sʌspɛkt 〕 *n.* 嫌疑犯；可疑人物
I am not sure who stole the radio, but I *suspect* our neighbor's children.
【記憶技巧】 *su* (under) + *spect* (see)
(私底下觀察別人的行為，表示「懷疑」)

suspicion[3] 〔 sə'spɪʃən 〕 *n.* 懷疑
(= *intuition*)；察覺

suspicious[4] 〔 sə'spɪʃəs 〕 *adj.* 可疑的
(= *questionable*)；懷疑的

swallow[2] 〔'swɑlo 〕 *v.* 吞   *n.* 燕子
Alex refuses to take vitamins because he doesn't like to *swallow* pills.
One *swallow* does not make a summer.

swan[2] 〔 swɑn 〕 *n.* 天鵝

sway[4] 〔 swe 〕 *v.* 搖擺
They *swayed* to the music.

swear[3] 〔 swɛr 〕 *v.* 發誓 (= *vow*)；詛咒 (= *curse*)
I *swear* that I'll tell the truth.

【典型考題】
Peter _____ he will stand by us, so let's take him at his word.
A. swears   B. accepts
C. recovers   D. ignores   [A]

sweat[3] 〔 swɛt 〕 *v.* 流汗 (= *perspire*)
n. 汗水
Toby began to *sweat* as soon as he started climbing the hill.

sweater[2] 〔'swɛtɚ 〕 *n.* 毛衣
Sweaters are usually made of wool.
【記憶技巧】 *sweat* (流汗) + *er* (*n.*)
(穿了會流汗的東西，就是「毛衣」)

【典型考題】
When it gets colder, I'll wear a _____.
A. pants   B. sweater
C. seat   D. video   [B]

sweep[2] 〔 swip 〕 *v.* 掃
Mom *sweeps* the floor every morning.

sweet[1] 〔 swit 〕 *adj.* 甜的

swell[3] 〔 swɛl 〕 *v.* 膨脹；腫起來
A balloon *swells* when it is filled with air.

swift[3] 〔 swɪft 〕 *adj.* 快速的
The *swift* current nearly swept the swimmers out to sea.

【典型考題】
The moment the students felt the earthquake, they ran _____ out of the classroom to an open area outside.
A. swiftly   B. nearly
C. loosely   D. formally   [A]

swim[1] 〔 swɪm 〕 *v.* 游泳

swing[2] 〔 swɪŋ 〕 *v.* 搖擺 (= *sway*)
n. 鞦韆
The girl is *swinging* her legs.

switch[3] 〔 swɪtʃ 〕 *n.* 開關   *v.* 交換
Just press the *switch* to turn on the light.
He *switched* seats with her.

S

* **sword**[3]〔sord〕*n.* 劍
The pen is mightier than the *sword*.

* **syllable**[4]〔'sɪləbḷ〕*n.* 音節
The word "ape" has only one *syllable*.
【記憶技巧】*syl* (together) + *lable*
(hold) (把幾個音放在一起唸，就是「音節」)

** **symbol**[2]〔'sɪmbḷ〕*n.* 象徵 (= *sign*)；
符號
The dove is a *symbol* of peace.
【記憶技巧】*sym* (together) + *bol*
(throw) (「象徵」就是能把對所有事物的
印象集合在一起的東西)

* **sympathetic**[4]〔,sɪmpə'θɛtɪk〕*adj.*
同情的 (= *compassionate*)；有同感的
I gave her a *sympathetic* look to
show that I understood her situation.

* **sympathy**[4]〔'sɪmpəθɪ〕*n.* 同情
(= *compassion*)；憐憫
We expressed our *sympathy* to the
widow.
【記憶技巧】*sym* (together) + *pathy*
(feeling) (跟別人有同樣的感覺，就是
「同情」)

symphony[4]〔'sɪmfənɪ〕*n.* 交響曲
【記憶技巧】*sym* (together) + *phony*
(sound) (把各種樂器的聲音結合起來，
就是「交響曲」)

* **syrup**[4]〔'sɪrəp〕*n.* 糖漿
Gwen prefers to have *syrup* on her
pancakes rather than honey.

** **system**[3]〔'sɪstəm〕*n.* 系統
We should develop a *system* of our
own.
【記憶技巧】*sy* (together) + *ste*
(stand) + *m* (*n.*) (有關聯的程序擺在
一起，就會形成一個「系統」)

* **systematic**[4]〔,sɪstə'mætɪk〕*adj.*
有系統的
The technician assembled the
computer in a *systematic* way.

T t

** **table**[1]〔'tebḷ〕*n.* 桌子；餐桌
【衍伸詞】*a table of contents* (目錄)

* **tablet**[3]〔'tæblɪt〕*n.* 藥片；平板電腦
The *tablet* was so large that I had
trouble swallowing it.
【記憶技巧】*table* + *t*

tack[3]〔tæk〕*n.* 圖釘　*v.* 釘

* **tag**[3]〔tæg〕*n.* 標籤

【片語】*price tag* (定價標籤；價目牌)

tail[1]〔tel〕*n.* 尾巴；硬幣的反面
v. 秘密跟蹤
A monkey has a long *tail*.

** **tailor**[3]〔'telɚ〕*n.* 裁縫師
(= *dressmaker*)　*v.* 縫製；使配合
【重要知識】tailor 這個字源自從前裁縫師常做
「燕尾服」(tailcoat)。

‡**take**[1] 〔 tek 〕 *v.* 拿

***tale**[1] 〔 tel 〕 *n.* 故事 (= *story*)；傳言
My grandfather told me the *tale* of the tortoise and the hare.
【衍伸詞】 *fairy tale* (童話故事)

‡**talent**[2] 〔'tælənt 〕 *n.* 才能
She has a *talent* for cooking.
【衍伸詞】 talented (有才能的)

【典型考題】
Fred has a _____ for languages. He can speak Japanese, French and Russian.
A. brand　　　B. joke
C. report　　　D. talent　　[D]

‡**talk**[1] 〔 tɔk 〕 *v.* 說話；說服
Andrew and Alan are *talking* on the phone.
【片語】 *talk sb. into*… (說服某人…)

‡**talkative**[2] 〔'tɔkətɪv 〕 *adj.* 愛說話的

‡**tall**[1] 〔 tɔl 〕 *adj.* 高的
【反義詞】 short (矮的)

***tame**[3] 〔 tem 〕 *adj.* 溫馴的；順從的；平淡的　*v.* 馴服；抑制
The lion appears gentle now, but it is not *tame*.

***tangerine**[2] 〔ˌtændʒə'rin 〕 *n.* 橘子；柑橘
【重要知識】 tangerine 是小而容易剝皮的橘子，「大的橘子」或「柳丁」是 orange。

‡**tank**[2] 〔 tæŋk 〕 *n.* 油箱；坦克車

***tap**[4,3] 〔 tæp 〕 *v.* 輕拍　*n.* 水龍頭
My classmate *tapped* me on the shoulder and asked if he could borrow a pen.

‡**tape**[2] 〔 tep 〕 *n.* 錄音帶
He recorded the speech on a *tape*.

***target**[2] 〔'tɑrgɪt 〕 *n.* 目標 (= *goal*)；(嘲笑、批評的) 對象　*v.* 以…為目標；針對
My *target* is to save $200 a month.

***task**[2] 〔 tæsk 〕 *n.* 工作；任務
The *task* is not easy.

‡**taste**[1] 〔 test 〕 *v.* 嚐起來 (= *savor*)　*n.* 味道；嗜好；品味
This food *tastes* great.

***tasty**[2] 〔'testɪ 〕 *adj.* 美味的 (= *delicious*)

***tax**[3] 〔 tæks 〕 *n.* 稅
【衍伸詞】 tax-free (免稅的)

‡**taxi**[1] 〔'tæksɪ 〕 *n.* 計程車 (= *cab*)
You can take a *taxi* to the airport.

‡**tea**[1] 〔 ti 〕 *n.* 茶
【衍伸詞】 *black tea* (紅茶)

‡**teach**[1] 〔 titʃ 〕 *v.* 教

‡**teacher**[1] 〔'titʃɚ 〕 *n.* 老師

‡**team**[2] 〔 tim 〕 *n.* 隊伍　*adj.* 團隊的
There are eleven people on a football *team*.

【典型考題】
Soccer is a kind of _____ sport. That means you cannot play it by yourself.
A. team　　　　B. popular
C. funny　　　　D. boring　　[A]

‡**tear**[2] 〔 tɪr 〕 *n.* 眼淚　〔 tɛr 〕 *v.* 撕裂
Her eyes were filled with *tears*.

* **tease**[3] 〔 tiz 〕 *v.* 嘲弄（= *make fun of*）；
取笑；挑逗；梳理　 *n.* 戲弄他人者
（= *teaser*）；戲弄
Stop *teasing* him. He is merely a kid.

* **technical**[3] 〔'tɛknɪkḷ 〕 *adj.* 技術上的；
專業的；工藝的
There is a *technical* problem at the
television station, so it is not able
to broadcast now.
【記憶技巧】 *techn* (skill) + *ical* (*adj.*)

* **technician**[4] 〔 tɛk'nɪʃən 〕 *n.* 技術人員

* **technique**[3] 〔 tɛk'nik 〕 *n.* 技術
（= *skill*）；方法（= *method*）

* **technological**[4] 〔ˌtɛknə'lɑdʒɪkḷ 〕 *adj.*
科技的
【衍伸詞】 *technological development*
（科技的發展）

* **technology**[3] 〔 tɛk'nɑlədʒɪ 〕 *n.* 科技
Many students are interested in the
growing field of information
technology.
【記憶技巧】 *techno* (skill) + *logy*
(study)（「科技」是要研究特殊技術）

* **teenage**[2] 〔'tin,edʒ 〕 *adj.* 十幾歲的
Graduation from high school was
the highlight of his *teenage* years.

‡ **teenager**[2] 〔'tin,edʒɚ 〕 *n.* 青少年

* **teens**[2] 〔 tinz 〕 *n.* 十幾歲的年齡
【片語】 *in one's teens*（在某人十幾歲時）

* **telegram**[4] 〔'tɛlə,græm 〕 *n.* 電報；
電報訊息

* **telegraph**[4] 〔'tɛlə,græf 〕 *n.* 電報；
電報機　 *v.* 發電報

‡ **telephone**[2] 〔'tɛlə,fon 〕 *n.* 電話
（= *phone*）；電話機　 *v.* 打電話（給）

* **telescope**[4] 〔'tɛlə,skop 〕 *n.* 望遠鏡
The *telescope* is pointed at Saturn.
【記憶技巧】 *tele* (far off) + *scope*
(look)（「望遠鏡」是用來看遠處的東西）

‡ **television**[2] 〔'tɛlə,vɪʒən 〕 *n.* 電視
（= *TV*）

‡ **tell**[1] 〔 tɛl 〕 *v.* 告訴；分辨
【片語】 *tell* A *from* B（分辨 A 與 B）

* **temper**[3] 〔'tɛmpɚ 〕 *n.* 脾氣
（= *self-control*）；心情
It is a kind of virtue to keep one's
temper.
【片語】 *keep* one's *temper*（保持心平氣和）
　　　　 lose one's *temper*（發脾氣）

‡ **temperature**[2] 〔'tɛmprətʃɚ 〕 *n.* 溫度
The *temperature* is high in summer.

‡ **temple**[2] 〔'tɛmpḷ 〕 *n.* 寺廟（= *shrine*）；
太陽穴
Many people go to the *temple* to pray.

* **temporary**[3] 〔'tɛmpə,rɛrɪ 〕 *adj.* 暫時的
（= *short-term*）；短期的
The refugees found *temporary*
shelter at the church.
【記憶技巧】 *tempor* (time) + *ary* (*adj.*)
（有時間性的，表示是「暫時的」）
【反義詞】 permanent（永久的）

┌─【典型考題】──────
│ Mr. Smith's work in Taiwan is just
│ ＿＿＿. He will go back to the
│ U.S. next month.
│ A. liberal　　　　B. rural
│ C. conscious　　 D. temporary　　[D]
└────────────────

T

T

* **tend**[3] 〔 tɛnd 〕 *v.* 易於（ = *be apt* ）；
傾向於；照顧（ = *take care of* ）

Don't pay too much attention to
Joan; she *tends* to exaggerate.
【片語】 **tend to**（易於；傾向於）

【典型考題】

The baby panda Yuan Zai at the Taipei
Zoo was separated from her mother
because of a minor injury that occurred
during her birth. She was _____ by
zookeepers for a while.
A. departed　　　B. jailed
C. tended　　　　D. captured　　[C]

* **tendency**[4] 〔'tɛndənsɪ 〕 *n.* 傾向
（ = *inclination* ）；趨勢（ = *trend* ）

【典型考題】

In the past few years, juvenile crimes
have shown a _____ to increase.
A. tendency　　　B. commercial
C. motive　　　　D. profession　　[A]

* **tender**[3] 〔'tɛndɚ 〕 *adj.* 嫩的；脆弱的；
溫柔的（ = *gentle* ）　 *v.* 提出；呈交

The nurse gave the patient a *tender*
smile.

‡‡ **tennis**[2] 〔'tɛnɪs 〕 *n.* 網球

Mark is learning to play *tennis*.
【衍伸詞】 **tennis court**（網球場）

* **tense**[4] 〔 tɛns 〕 *adj.* 令人感到緊張的；
緊張的（ = *nervous* ）；拉緊的

There was a *tense* moment when it
seemed as if the two angry men
would come to blows.

* **tension**[4] 〔'tɛnʃən 〕 *n.* 緊張
（ = *nervousness* ）；緊張關係
【片語】 **relieve tension**（消除緊張）

‡ **tent**[2] 〔 tɛnt 〕 *n.* 帳篷

They had lived in *tents* for a few days.

‡ **term**[2] 〔 tɝm 〕 *n.* 用語（ = *language* ）；
名詞；期限；關係

【衍伸詞】 **business terms**（商業用語）
【片語】 **be on good terms with** *sb.*
（和某人關係良好）

‡ **terrible**[2] 〔'tɛrəbl̩ 〕 *adj.* 可怕的
（ = *dreadful* = *horrible* ）；嚴重的

Last night, the storm was *terrible*.
【記憶技巧】 **terr** (frighten) + **ible** (adj.)
（讓人害怕的，表示「可怕的」）

‡ **terrific**[2] 〔 tə'rɪfɪk 〕 *adj.* 很棒的

It was a *terrific* party.

* **terrify**[4] 〔'tɛrə,faɪ 〕 *v.* 使害怕
（ = *frighten* ）

The big snake at the zoo *terrified*
Lisa even though it was safely
behind glass.

* **territory**[3] 〔'tɛrə,torɪ 〕 *n.* 領土；領域

Some wild animals will attack
anyone who invades their *territory*.
【記憶技巧】 **territ** (earth) + **ory** (n.)
（所擁有的土地就叫「領土」）

【典型考題】

When the enemy troops invaded our
_____, we fought bravely to defend
our country.
A. stance　　　　B. territory
C. craze　　　　 D. universe　　[B]

* **terror**[4] 〔'tɛrɚ 〕 *n.* 驚恐；恐怖
（ = *fear* ）

The visitors ran out of the haunted
house in *terror*.
【片語】 **in terror**（恐懼地）

‡**test**[2] 〔 tɛst 〕 *n.* 測驗

*⃰**text**[3] 〔 tɛkst 〕 *n.* 內文（＝*body*）；
教科書　*v.* 傳簡訊（給）
Although he had read it several times,
Rick still could not understand the *text*.

⃰**textbook**[2] 〔'tɛkst,bʊk 〕 *n.* 教科書
I am studying an English *textbook*.

‡**thank**[1] 〔 θæŋk 〕 *v.* 感謝

⃰**thankful**[3] 〔'θæŋkfəl 〕 *adj.* 感激的
（＝*grateful*）

‡**theater**[2] 〔'θiətɚ 〕 *n.* 戲劇；戲院
（＝*cinema*）
We went to the *theater* last night to
watch a play.

⃰**theme**[4] 〔 θim 〕 *n.* 主題（＝*subject*）
Love has been a recurrent *theme* in
literature.
【片語】***theme park***（主題樂園）

‡**then**[1] 〔 ðɛn 〕 *adv.* 那時；然後

⃰**theory**[3] 〔'θiərɪ 〕 *n.* 理論
（＝*hypothesis*）；學說；看法
Seldom has the mathematical *theory*
of games been of practical use in
playing real games.
【片語】***in theory***（理論上）

‡**therefore**[2] 〔'ðɛr,for 〕 *adv.* 因此
（＝*thus*＝*accordingly*＝*hence*
consequently＝*as a result*）
This car is smaller and *therefore*
cheaper.

‡**thick**[2] 〔 θɪk 〕 *adj.* 厚的
I have never read such a *thick* book.
【反義詞】thin（薄的）

⃰**thief**[2] 〔 θif 〕 *n.* 小偷
A *thief* broke into the house last night.

‡**thin**[2] 〔 θɪn 〕 *adj.* 薄的；瘦的
The poor children are *thin*.

‡**thing**[1] 〔 θɪŋ 〕 *n.* 東西

‡**think**[1] 〔 θɪŋk 〕 *v.* 想；認為

‡**third**[1] 〔 θɝd 〕 *adj.* 第三的　*adv.* 第三

⃰**thirst**[3] 〔 θɝst 〕 *n.* 口渴；渴望

【典型考題】
After hiking all day without drinking
any water, the students sat down by
the stream to quench their ＿＿＿＿.
A. hunger　　　B. energy
C. thirst　　　D. nutrition　　**[C]**

‡**thirsty**[2] 〔'θɝstɪ 〕 *adj.* 口渴的；渴望的
（＝*eager*）
The baby is *thirsty*.

‡**thirteen**[1] 〔 θɝ'tin 〕 *n.* 十三

‡**thirty**[1] 〔'θɝtɪ 〕 *n.* 三十

⃰**thorough**[4] 〔'θɝo 〕 *adj.* 徹底的
We gave the house a *thorough*
cleaning before the guests arrived.

【典型考題】
After making a(n) ＿＿＿＿ inspection
of the second-hand car, he decided to
buy it.
A. thorough　　B. criminal
C. throughout　D. official　　**[A]**

‡**though**[1] 〔 ðo 〕 *conj.* 雖然
I love him *though* he doesn't love me.

T

‡ **thought**[1] 〔θɔt 〕 *n.* 思想 (= *idea*)

What's your *thought*?

【片語】 *on second thought* (重新考慮以後)

* **thoughtful**[4] 〔'θɔtfəl 〕 *adj.* 體貼的 (= *considerate*)；認眞思考的

Nancy is a very *thoughtful* person. She always thinks of the needs of her friends.

‡ **thousand**[1] 〔'θaʊzn̩d 〕 *n.* 千　*adj.* 千的

* **thread**[3] 〔θrɛd 〕 *n.* 線 (= *strand*)；一長條的東西　*v.* 穿線通過

There was a loose *thread* hanging from the man's jacket.

* **threat**[3] 〔θrɛt 〕 *n.* 威脅 (= *menace*)

That new store is a *threat* to our business.

* **threaten**[3] 〔'θrɛtn̩ 〕 *v.* 威脅 (= *menace*)；(壞事) 可能發生

‡ **throat**[2] 〔θrot 〕 *n.* 喉嚨

When we eat, food passes down our *throat*.

【片語】 *have a sore throat* (喉嚨痛)

‡ **through**[2] 〔θru 〕 *prep.* 透過 (= *by way of*)；穿過　*adv.* 完全地

* **throughout**[2] 〔θru'aʊt 〕 *prep.* 遍及 (= *all through* = *all over*)　*adv.* 自始至終

They searched *throughout* the town for the lost child.

‡ **throw**[1] 〔θro 〕 *v.* 丟 (= *fling* = *cast*)；舉行；使陷入

Richard *throws* small pieces of stone in a river.

‡ **thumb**[2] 〔θʌm 〕 *n.* 大拇指【注意發音】

【片語】 *be all thumbs* (笨手笨腳)

‡ **thunder**[2] 〔'θʌndɚ 〕 *n.* 雷

There was *thunder* and lightning last night.

【衍伸詞】 thunderstorm (雷雨)

‡ **Thursday**[1] 〔'θɝzdɪ 〕 *n.* 星期四

* **thus**[1] 〔ðʌs 〕 *adv.* 因此 (= *therefore*)

Thus they judged that he was guilty.

‡ **ticket**[1] 〔'tɪkɪt 〕 *n.* 票；罰單 (= *notice*)

Tom made a reservation for movie *tickets*.

【典型考題】

My father got three ＿＿＿＿ to the baseball game. All of us can go tomorrow.
A. jackets　　　　B. tickets
C. baseballs　　　D. gyms　　　[B]

* **tickle**[3] 〔'tɪkl̩ 〕 *v. n.* 搔癢；發癢

The baby laughed when his father *tickled* his feet.

* **tide**[3] 〔taɪd 〕 *n.* 潮水 (= *current*)；形勢

The ship will sail when the *tide* goes out.

Time and *tide* wait for no man.

‡ **tidy**[3] 〔'taɪdɪ 〕 *adj.* 整齊的 (= *neat*)；愛整潔的　*v.* 收拾；整理

Mike's room is very *tidy*.

‡‡**tie**[1] 〔 taɪ 〕 v. 綁；打（結） n. 領帶

I *tied* a bow for my younger sister.

【片語】 *tie the knot*（結婚）

‡‡**tiger**[1] 〔'taɪɡɚ 〕 n. 老虎

A *tiger* is a large animal that lives in the jungle.

***tight**[3] 〔 taɪt 〕 adj. 嚴格的；手頭拮据的；緊的（ = *close-fitting*）

I couldn't open the jar because the lid was on too *tight*.

【反義詞】 loose（鬆的）

***tighten**[3] 〔'taɪtn̩ 〕 v. 變緊（ = *strain*）；變嚴格

【反義詞】 loosen（使變鬆）

***timber**[3] 〔'tɪmbɚ 〕 n. 橫樑【可數】；木材（ = *wood* = *logs*）【不可數】

Workers unloaded the *timber* at the building site.

‡‡**time**[1] 〔 taɪm 〕 n. 時間；時代；次數

***timid**[4] 〔'tɪmɪd 〕 adj. 膽小的；膽怯的

The *timid* youngster was afraid to ask for a second helping of pie.

【記憶技巧】 *tim* (fear) + *id* (adj.)
（會害怕，表示個性是「膽小的」）

【反義詞】 bold（大膽的）

‡‡**tiny**[1] 〔'taɪnɪ 〕 adj. 微小的

You can see *tiny* stars in the sky.

‡‡**tip**[2] 〔 tɪp 〕 n. 小費；尖端；訣竅 v. 給小費

***tire**[1] 〔 taɪr 〕 v. 使疲倦（ = *exhaust*） n. 輪胎

***tiresome**[4] 〔'taɪrsəm 〕 adj. 令人厭煩的（ = *annoying*）；無聊的

Being a librarian is a *tiresome* job.

***tissue**[3] 〔'tɪʃʊ 〕 n. 面紙

【記憶技巧】 先背 issue（議題）。

‡**title**[2] 〔'taɪtl̩ 〕 n. 標題；名稱；頭銜

The *title* of the painting is "The Last Supper."

‡‡**toast**[2] 〔 tost 〕 n. 吐司；敬酒；乾杯 v. 向…敬酒

Ladies and gentlemen, I'd like to propose a *toast* to the bride and groom.

***tobacco**[3] 〔 tə'bæko 〕 n. 菸草

This shop sells cigarettes, cigars, and other *tobacco* products.

‡‡**today**[1] 〔 tə'de 〕 adv. 今天；現今

‡‡**toe**[2] 〔 to 〕 n. 腳趾

I dropped a book on my big *toe*.

【比較】 finger（手指）

***tofu**[2] 〔'to'fu 〕 n. 豆腐（ = *bean curd*）

I don't like the smell of stinky *tofu*.

‡‡**together**[1] 〔 tə'ɡɛðɚ 〕 adv. 一起

‡**toilet**[2] 〔'tɔɪlɪt 〕 n. 馬桶；廁所（ = *bathroom*）

***tolerable**[4] 〔'talərəbl̩ 〕 adj. 可容忍的（ = *endurable*）；可接受的

To many people, toothache is not a *tolerable* pain.

T

* **tolerance**[4] 〔'tɑlərəns〕 *n.* 容忍
(= *permissiveness*)；寬容

【典型考題】

The teacher showed _____ for the
noise in the classroom and continued
with his lecture as if he had not
heard anything.
A. connection   B. rejection
C. tolerance   D. involvement   [C]

* **tolerant**[4] 〔'tɑlərənt〕 *adj.* 寬容的
(= *open-minded*)

【典型考題】

Fortunately, my parents are _____
of my choice of music—reggae, never
making any complaint.
A. generous   B. jealous
C. miserable   D. tolerant   [D]

* **tolerate**[4] 〔'tɑlə,ret〕 *v.* 容忍
(= *permit*)；忍受 (= *endure*)
He moved out because he could not
tolerate his roommate's friends.

【典型考題】

In a democratic society, we have to
_____ different opinions.
A. participate   B. compensate
C. dominate   D. tolerate   [D]

‡ **tomato**[2] 〔tə'meto〕 *n.* 蕃茄
Tomatoes are used for making
ketchup.

* **tomb**[4] 〔tum〕 *n.* 墳墓【注意發音】
(= *grave*)

‡ **tomorrow**[1] 〔tə'mɔro〕 *adv.* 明天
Tomorrow is the day that comes
after today.

* **ton**[3] 〔tʌn〕 *n.* 公噸

* **tone**[1] 〔ton〕 *n.* 語調
Arthur could tell by his mother's
tone of voice that she was annoyed.

‡ **tongue**[2] 〔tʌŋ〕 *n.* 舌頭；語言
The *tongue* is inside our mouth.
【片語】 *mother tongue* (母語)

‡ **tonight**[1] 〔tə'naɪt〕 *adv.* 今晚
Let's go to see a movie *tonight*.

‡ **tool**[1] 〔tul〕 *n.* 器具；工具 (= *means*)
Mechanics use a variety of *tools*.

‡ **tooth**[2] 〔tuθ〕 *n.* 牙齒
We must brush our *teeth* every
morning and night.
【注意】複數型是 teeth。

‡ **top**[1] 〔tɑp〕 *n.* 頂端 (= *highest place*)；
陀螺   *adj.* 最高的；最重要的
He climbed to the *top* of the tree.

* **topic**[2] 〔'tɑpɪk〕 *n.* 主題 (= *subject*)
What's the *topic* of this article?

* **tortoise**[3] 〔'tɔrtəs〕 *n.* 陸龜；烏龜
【比較】turtle (海龜)
【衍伸詞】 *The Hare and the Tortoise*
(龜兔賽跑)【寓言故事】

* **toss**[3] 〔tɔs〕 *v.* 拋；投擲 (= *throw*)
The referee *tossed* the ball into the
air, beginning the game.

‡ **total**[1] 〔'totl̩〕 *adj.* 全部的；總計的

‡ **touch**[1] 〔tʌtʃ〕 *v.* 觸摸   *n.* 接觸
【片語】 *keep in touch with* (和…保持連絡)

* **tough**⁴〔tʌf〕*adj.* 困難的（= *difficult*）
   It is a *tough* job for a young girl.

* **tour**²〔tur〕*n.* 旅行（= *visit* = *trip*
   = *journey*） *v.* 旅遊；觀光；參觀
   We will go on a *tour* this summer
   vacation.
   【片語】***go on a tour***（去旅行）

* **tourism**³〔'turɪzm̩〕*n.* 觀光業

* **tourist**³〔'turɪst〕*n.* 觀光客
   【衍伸詞】***a tourist attraction***（風景名勝）

   tow³〔to〕*v.* 拖（= *draw*） *n.* 拖吊
   The truck that had a breakdown was
   towed to the garage.

‡ **toward**¹〔tə'wɔrd , tord〕*prep.*
   朝向⋯（= *towards*）
   He walked *toward* the door.

‡ **towel**²〔'tauəl〕*n.* 毛巾

‡ **tower**²〔'tauɚ〕*n.* 塔 *v.* 聳立
   There is a *tower* near the port.
   【衍伸詞】***ivory tower***（象牙塔）

‡ **town**¹〔taun〕*n.* 城鎮；城鎮生活

‡ **toy**¹〔tɔɪ〕*n.* 玩具
   Children like to play with *toys*.

* **trace**³〔tres〕*v.* 追蹤；追溯
   The phone company was unable to
   trace the call.
   【片語】***can be traced back to***（可追溯至）

* **track**²〔træk〕*n.* 痕跡（= *mark*）；
   足跡（= *path* = *footprint*）；軌道；
   曲目 *v.* 追蹤
   The hunter followed the bear *tracks*
   to the edge of the forest.

‡ **trade**²〔tred〕*n.* 貿易（= *commerce*）；
   行業；職業 *v.* 交易；用⋯交換
   There is a lot of *trade* between
   these two countries.

   trader³〔'tredɚ〕*n.* 生意人；商人
   （= *dealer* = *merchant*）

‡ **tradition**²〔trə'dɪʃən〕*n.* 傳統
   （= *convention*）；習俗（= *customs*）
   It's a Christmas *tradition* to give
   presents.
   【記憶技巧】***tra***（over）+ ***dit***（give）+
   ion（*n.*）（「傳統」是要一代傳一代的）

   【典型考題】
   It's a Chinese _____ to give children
   red envelopes on Lunar New Year's Day.
   A. holiday   B. festival
   C. party   D. tradition   [D]

‡ **traditional**²〔trə'dɪʃənl̩〕*adj.* 傳統的
   （= *conventional*）；慣例的

‡ **traffic**²〔'træfɪk〕*n.* 走私；交通
   （= *transportation*） *v.* 走私；非法
   買賣
   The *traffic* is very heavy today.
   【衍伸詞】***a traffic jam***（交通阻塞）

* **tragedy**⁴〔'trædʒədɪ〕*n.* 悲劇；不幸
   的事
   "Hamlet" is one of Shakespeare's
   famous *tragedies*.
   【反義詞】comedy（喜劇）

   【典型考題】
   The movie "Titanic" is about the
   _____ of a shipwreck.
   A. tragedy   B. wig
   C. sensibility   D. fad   [A]

* **tragic**⁴〔'trædʒɪk〕*adj.* 悲劇的（= *sad*）

* **trail**[3] 〔 trel 〕 *n.* 小徑 (= *path*)；足跡
   This *trail* leads to the top of the mountain and the other one goes to the lake.

‡ **train**[1] 〔 tren 〕 *v.* 訓練 (= *drill*)
   n. 火車；列車
   We *trained* the horse for the next race.

* **transfer**[4] 〔 træns'fɝ 〕 *v.* 調職；轉移
   (= *change location*)；轉學；轉車
   Dee decided to *transfer* to another school to be closer to her family.
   【記憶技巧】*trans* (across) + *fer*
   (carry) (越過某地運送，就是「轉移」)

* **transform**[4] 〔 træns'fɔrm 〕 *v.* 轉變
   On Halloween people wear costumes and *transform* themselves into witches, ghosts or fairy princesses.

* **translate**[4] 〔'trænslet 〕 *v.* 翻譯
   This software program will *translate* English to French.
   【比較】interpret (口譯)
   【重要知識】這個字一般字典唸〔træns'let 〕，但現在83%的美國人唸成〔'trænslet 〕。

* **translation**[4] 〔 træns'leʃən 〕 *n.* 翻譯

* **translator**[4] 〔 træns'letə 〕 *n.* 翻譯家

* **transport**[3] 〔 træns'port 〕 *v. n.* 運輸
   (= *v. carry*)
   The cars are *transported* by ship.

* **transportation**[4] 〔,trænspə'teʃən 〕
   n. 運輸 (= *shipping*)

‡ **trap**[2] 〔 træp 〕 *v.* 使困住   *n.* 陷阱
   Twelve passengers were *trapped* inside the burning bus.

‡ **trash**[3] 〔 træʃ 〕 *n.* 垃圾 (= *garbage* = *rubbish* = *litter* = *junk* = *scrap*)
   There are few *trash* cans on the street.

* **travel**[2] 〔'trævl̩ 〕 *v.* 旅行；行進
   I love to go *traveling*.
   Light *travels* much faster than sound.

* **traveler**[3] 〔'trævlə 〕 *n.* 旅行者

* **tray**[3] 〔 tre 〕 *n.* 托盤
   The waiter placed the drinks on a *tray* and carried them to the table.

* **treasure**[2] 〔'trɛʒə 〕 *n.* 寶藏
   (= *valuables*)   *v.* 珍惜
   They were looking for the *treasure* of the ship.

   ┌─【典型考題】──────────┐
   In stories, _____ is often buried underground in an old house or on a deserted island.
   A. fruit   B. kingdom
   C. shadow   D. treasure   **[D]**
   └────────────────────┘

‡ **treat**[5,2] 〔 trit 〕 *v.* 對待；治療；認為；請客   *n.* 請客
   I don't like the way he *treats* me.
   【片語】*treat* A *as* B (視 A 為 B)

‡ **tree**[1] 〔 tri 〕 *n.* 樹

* **tremble**[3] 〔'trɛmbl̩ 〕 *v.* 發抖 (= *shake* = *quake* = *shiver* = *quiver* = *shudder*)
   Anna *trembled* with fear when she stood on the stage.

* **tremendous**[4] 〔 trɪ'mɛndəs 〕 *adj.*
   巨大的 (= *huge* = *enormous* = *great* = *immense* = *vast* = *gigantic*)
   The rocket made a *tremendous* noise when it blasted off.

* **trend**[3] 〔 trɛnd 〕 *n.* 趨勢

The *trend* of prices is still upward.

* **trial**[2] 〔'traɪəl 〕 *n.* 審判 (= *judgment*)；
試驗

The sensational murder *trial* went
on for six months.

‡ **triangle**[2] 〔'traɪ͵æŋgḷ 〕 *n.* 三角形

【記憶技巧】 *tri* (three) + *angle* (角)

tribal[4] 〔'traɪbḷ 〕 *adj.* 部落的

* **tribe**[3] 〔 traɪb 〕 *n.* 部落
(= *aboriginal society*)

The *tribe* had lived in the rainforest
for several hundred years before
meeting outsiders.

【比較】 bribe (賄賂)

‡‡ **trick**[2] 〔 trɪk 〕 *n.* 詭計；騙局 (= *hoax*)；
把戲；技巧；惡作劇

I'm teaching my dog *tricks*.

* **tricky**[3] 〔'trɪkɪ 〕 *adj.* 困難的；難處理
的 (= *difficult*)；棘手的；詭計多端的

The problem is rather *tricky*.

‡‡ **trip**[1] 〔 trɪp 〕 *n.* 旅行 (= *travel*)
v. 絆倒

We went on a *trip* to Bali last week.

【片語】 *go on a trip* (去旅行)
trip on ~ (被 ~ 絆倒)

* **triumph**[4] 〔'traɪəmf 〕 *n.* 勝利
(= *victory*)

The baseball team is celebrating its
triumph with a big party tonight.

* **troops**[3] 〔 trups 〕 *n. pl.* 軍隊

The *troops* were ordered back to
the army base.

* **tropical**[3] 〔'trɑpɪkḷ 〕 *adj.* 熱帶的

You can expect the *tropical* island to
be hot and humid.

【衍伸詞】 subtropical (副熱帶的)
tropical rainforest (熱帶雨林)

‡‡ **trouble**[1] 〔'trʌbḷ 〕 *n.* 苦惱；麻煩
(= *difficulty*) *v.* 麻煩；使困擾

It will be no *trouble* to drive you to
the station.

* **troublesome**[4] 〔'trʌbḷsəm 〕 *adj.*
麻煩的 (= *bothersome*)

【記憶技巧】 -*some* 表「引起…的」的字尾。

‡ **trousers**[2] 〔'traʊzɚz 〕 *n. pl.* 褲子
(= *pants*)

Please wear *trousers* for the trip
tomorrow.

‡‡ **truck**[2] 〔 trʌk 〕 *n.* 卡車 (= *van*)；貨車

They hired a *truck* to move their
furniture.

‡‡ **true**[1] 〔 tru 〕 *adj.* 真的 (= *real*)

A *true* friend will always help you.

* **trumpet**[2] 〔'trʌmpɪt 〕 *n.* 喇叭 (= *horn*)

My brother can play the *trumpet*.

* **trunk**[3] 〔 trʌŋk 〕 *n.* 後車廂；(汽車的)
行李箱 (= *chest*)；樹幹；軀幹

* **trust**[2] 〔 trʌst 〕 *v. n.* 信任

I *trust* my parents in everything.

【典型考題】

Peter often tells lies. I cannot _____
him. He is not a person that can be
depended on.
A. depend   B. communicate
C. correct   D. trust   [D]

‡**truth**[2] 〔 truθ 〕 *n.* 事實

Just tell me the *truth*.

【片語】*in truth*（事實上）

* **truthful**[3] 〔'truθfəl 〕 *adj.* 真實的

‡**try**[1] 〔 traɪ 〕 *v.* 嘗試

I'll *try* to learn French.

‡**T-shirt**[1] 〔'ti,ʃɜt 〕 *n.* T 恤

‡**tub**[3] 〔 tʌb 〕 *n.* 浴缸（ = *bathtub* ）

* **tube**[2] 〔 tjub 〕 *n.* 管子（ = *pipe* ）；地鐵

Will squeezed the *tube* of toothpaste to get the last bit out.

‡**Tuesday**[1] 〔'tjuzdɪ 〕 *n.* 星期二

* **tug**[3] 〔 tʌg 〕 *v.* 用力拉   *n.* 強拉

Mary *tugged* on her mother's skirt, trying to get her attention.

* **tug-of-war**[4] *n.* 拔河

The participants in the *tug-of-war* used all their strength to pull the other team over the line.

* **tulip**[3] 〔'tulɪp 〕 *n.* 鬱金香

【記憶技巧】*tu* + *lip*（嘴唇）

* **tumble**[3] 〔'tʌmbḷ 〕 *v.* 跌倒

Susie tripped and *tumbled* down the stairs.

tummy[1] 〔'tʌmɪ 〕 *n.* 肚子

（ = *belly* = *abdomen* ）

My *tummy* hurts.

* **tune**[3] 〔 tjun 〕 *n.* 曲子

This is such a popular *tune* that everyone is humming it.

‡**tunnel**[2] 〔'tʌnḷ 〕 *n.* 隧道；地道

Our car went through a long *tunnel*.

‡**turkey**[2] 〔'tɜkɪ 〕 *n.* 火雞；火雞肉

People often drink white wine with *turkey*.

【比較】Turkey（土耳其）

‡**turn**[1] 〔 tɜn 〕 *v.* 轉向   *n.* 輪流

Go down the street and *turn* right.

【片語】*take turns*（輪流）

‡**turtle**[2] 〔'tɜtḷ 〕 *n.* 海龜

My younger brother has two *turtles*.

【比較】tortoise（陸龜）

* **tutor**[3] 〔'tjutɚ 〕 *n.* 家庭教師

（ = *private teacher* ）

Wendy's parents employed a *tutor* to teach her math.

【重要知識】這個字以前唸〔'tutɚ 〕，現在美國人多唸成〔'tjutɚ 〕。

‡**twelve**[1] 〔 twɛlv 〕 *n.* 十二

‡**twenty**[1] 〔'twɛntɪ 〕 *n.* 二十

‡**twice**[1] 〔 twaɪs 〕 *adv.* 兩倍；兩次

（ = *two times* ）

【比較】once（一次）

* **twig**[3] 〔 twɪg 〕 *n.* 小樹枝

The birds built a nest of *twigs* in the tree outside my window.

【記憶技巧】*twi* (two) + *g*（「小樹枝」通常會有兩個以上的分支）

【比較】branch（大樹枝）

*twin³ 〔twɪn〕 *n.* 雙胞胎之一
adj. 雙胞胎的
Glenda looks exactly like her *twin*.
【衍伸詞】twins（雙胞胎）

*twinkle⁴ 〔'twɪŋkḷ〕 *v.* 閃爍
（ = *sparkle* = *glitter* = *glisten* ）
I like to sit outside at night and
watch the stars *twinkle*.
【記憶技巧】*twink*（wink）+ *le* (*v.*)
（星光「閃爍」是因為星星在眨眼睛）

*twist³ 〔twɪst〕 *v.* 扭曲（ = *curl* ）；扭傷
n. 扭轉；扭扭舞
Her face was *twisted* with pain.
【典型考題】
Jack fell down while playing tennis
and ＿＿＿＿ his ankle very badly.
A. bent　　　　B. crippled
C. tripped　　　D. twisted　　[D]

‡type² 〔taɪp〕 *n.* 類型（ = *category* ）
v. 打字
I don't like people of that *type*.

*typewriter³ 〔'taɪp,raɪtɚ〕 *n.* 打字機

‡typhoon² 〔taɪ'fun〕 *n.* 颱風
There were five *typhoons* this year.
【典型考題】
The ＿＿＿＿ last week scared a lot of
people. Its strong winds and heavy
rains took fifty lives.
A. air pollution　B. soccer game
C. system　　　　D. typhoon　　[D]

*typical³ 〔'tɪpɪkḷ〕 *adj.* 典型的；
特有的
It is *typical* of him to make such
sarcastic remarks.
【片語】*be typical of*（是…特有的）

*typist⁴ 〔'taɪpɪst〕 *n.* 打字員

U u

‡ugly² 〔'ʌglɪ〕 *adj.* 醜的
（ = *unattractive* ）
I think this painting is very *ugly*.

‡umbrella² 〔ʌm'brɛlə〕 *n.* 雨傘
We use *umbrellas* when it rains.
【記憶技巧】*umbr*（shadow）+ *ella*
（小）（撐傘的時候，我們都會被雨傘的
小陰影遮住）

‡uncle¹ 〔'ʌŋkḷ〕 *n.* 叔叔
【比較】aunt（阿姨）

‡underpass⁴ 〔'ʌndɚ,pæs〕 *n.* 地下道

Many people don't like to use
underpasses.
【記憶技巧】*under* + *pass*（通過）
【反義詞】overpass（天橋；高架道路）

‡understand¹ 〔,ʌndɚ'stænd〕 *v.* 了解

*underwear² 〔'ʌndɚ,wɛr〕 *n.* 內衣
I prefer cotton *underwear* to linen.

‡uniform² 〔'junə,fɔrm〕 *n.* 制服
Many students in Taiwan have to
wear *uniforms*.
【記憶技巧】*uni*（one）+ *form*
（大家穿的是同一個款式，也就是「制服」）

T

*__union__³ 〔'junjən 〕 *n.* 聯盟；工會
The European *Union* is composed of several countries.
【衍伸詞】 *European Union* (歐盟)
(= *EU*)

‡__unique__⁴ 〔 ju'nik 〕 *adj.* 獨一無二的；僅有的；獨特的 (= *very special*)
This invaluable vase is *unique*.

【典型考題】
Everyone in the world is ＿＿＿; you can't find anyone who has the same appearance and personality as you have.
A. persuasive   B. basic
C. dependent   D. unique   [D]

*__unit__¹ 〔'junɪt 〕 *n.* 單位 (= *part*)
A gram is a *unit* of weight.

*__unite__³ 〔 ju'naɪt 〕 *v.* 使聯合 (= *combine*)
Their common interests *united* these two countries.

*__unity__³ 〔'junətɪ 〕 *n.* 統一 (= *unification*)

*__universal__⁴ 〔ˌjunə'vɝsl̩ 〕 *adj.* 普遍的；全世界的 (= *worldwide*)

‡__universe__³ 〔'junəˌvɝs 〕 *n.* 宇宙
Are there other *universes* besides our own?

‡__university__⁴ 〔ˌjunə'vɝsətɪ 〕 *n.* 大學
Which *university* do you go to?

*__unless__³ 〔 ən'lɛs 〕 *conj.* 除非
Unless Mark arrives soon, we will have to leave without him.

‡‡__until__¹ 〔 ən'tɪl 〕 *prep.* 直到
She worked there *until* last month.

*__upload__⁴ 〔 ʌp'lod 〕 *v.* 上傳
【反義詞】 download (下載)

‡__upon__² 〔 ə'pɑn 〕 *prep.* 在…之上
(= *on*)
He laid a hand *upon* my shoulder.

*__upper__² 〔'ʌpɚ 〕 *adj.* 上面的 (= *above*)
He took a book from the *upper* shelf.
【反義詞】 lower (下面的)

*__upset__³ 〔 ʌp'sɛt 〕 *adj.* 不高興的 (= *annoyed*)；生氣的
Peggy was *upset* after an argument with her best friend.

‡__upstairs__¹ 〔'ʌp'stɛrz 〕 *adv.* 到樓上
Jessie ran *upstairs*.

*__urban__⁴ 〔'ɝbən 〕 *adj.* 都市的
The city is plagued with the usual *urban* problems of smog and traffic congestion.
【記憶技巧】 *urb* (city) + *an* (adj.)
【反義詞】 rural (鄉村的)

*__urge__⁴ 〔 ɝdʒ 〕 *v.* 力勸；催促
Jimmy's parents are *urging* him to apply to Harvard.

*__urgent__⁴ 〔'ɝdʒənt 〕 *adj.* 迫切的 (= *compelling*)；緊急的 (= *emergent*)
The nurse left an *urgent* message for the doctor, asking him to return to the hospital right away.

【典型考題】
I placed a(n) ＿＿＿ call to the police when I heard the gunshot.
A. intimidating   B. long-distance
C. loud   D. urgent   [D]

*__usage__⁴ 〔'jusɪdʒ 〕 *n.* 用法

‡**use**[1] 〔 juz 〕 *v.* 使用

We *use* money to buy things.

* **used**[2] 〔 just 〕 *adj.* 習慣於…的

I am *used* to drinking a cup of
coffee every morning.

【衍伸詞】*be used to V-ing*（習慣於）

* **used to V.**[2] 以前常常…

We *used to* play tennis every Sunday.

‡**useful**[1] 〔'jusfəl 〕 *adj.* 有用的

* **user**[2] 〔'juzɚ 〕 *n.* 使用者

‡**usual**[2] 〔'juʒuəl 〕 *adj.* 平常的
（= *commonplace*）

I left home earlier than *usual*.

【片語】*as usual*（像往常一樣）

V v

* **vacant**[3] 〔'vekənt 〕 *adj.* 空的
（= *empty*）

This apartment has been *vacant* for
three months.

【記憶技巧】*vac* (empty) + *ant* (*adj.*)

┌─【典型考題】────────────┐
Someone is finally moving into the
_____ apartment downstairs.
A. blank   B. crowded
C. vacant   D. liberated   [C]
└──────────────────────┘

‡**vacation**[2] 〔 ve'keʃən 〕 *n.* 假期
（= *holiday*）

* **vain**[4] 〔 ven 〕 *adj.* 無用的；徒勞無功的
（= *futile*）；無意義的；自負的

He tried to save her but in *vain*.

【片語】*in vain*（徒勞無功）

‡**valley**[2] 〔'vælɪ 〕 *n.* 山谷（= *gorge*）

There is a river in the *valley*.

‡**valuable**[3] 〔'væljuəbl̩ 〕 *adj.* 珍貴的；
有價值的（= *prized* = *invaluable*）

【反義詞】 valueless（沒價值的）

* **value**[2] 〔'vælju 〕 *n.* 價值（= *worth*）
v. 重視

This painting is of great *value*.

【衍伸詞】values（價值觀）

* **van**[3] 〔 væn 〕 *n.* 廂型車；小型有蓋
貨車（= *small truck*）

We loaded the *van* with camping
gear and set out on our trip.

* **vanish**[3] 〔'vænɪʃ 〕 *v.* 消失
（= *disappear*）

With a wave of his hand, the
magician made the rabbit *vanish*.

【記憶技巧】*van* (empty) + *ish* (*v.*)
（空間變空了，表示東西都「消失」了）

┌─【典型考題】────────────┐
My keys must be here somewhere; they
didn't just _____.
A. escape   B. vanish
C. loose   D. diminish   [B]
└──────────────────────┘

* **variety**[3] 〔 vəˈraɪətɪ 〕 *n.* 多樣性
(= *diversity*)；種類
There is a great *variety* of food in
the night market.
【片語】 *a great variety of* (各式各樣的)
┌─【典型考題】─────────
This library is famous for its wide
_____ of books. You can find books
on any topic you are interested in.
A. technology   B. connection
C. variety   D. amazement   [C]
└──────────────────

* **various**[3] 〔ˈvɛrɪəs 〕 *adj.* 各式各樣的
(= *different kinds of*)

* **vary**[3] 〔ˈvɛrɪ 〕 *v.* 改變 (= *change*)；
不同
If you never *vary* your routine, you
may get bored.

* **vase**[3] 〔 ves 〕 *n.* 花瓶

* **vast**[4] 〔 væst 〕 *adj.* 巨大的
The royal family owns *vast* tracts of
land in the mountains.

‡ **vegetable**[1] 〔ˈvɛdʒətəbḷ 〕 *n.* 蔬菜

* **vegetarian**[4] 〔ˌvɛdʒəˈtɛrɪən 〕 *n.* 素食
主義者

* **vehicle**[3] 〔ˈviɪkḷ 〕 *n.* 車輛
Gasoline is used as a fuel for cars,
trucks and other *vehicles*.
【記憶技巧】 *vehi* (carry) + *cle* (*n.*)
(用來搬運的工具，也就是「車輛」)

* **verb**[4] 〔 vɝb 〕 *n.* 動詞
【比較】 adverb (副詞)

* **verse**[3] 〔 vɝs 〕 *n.* 詩 (= *poetry*)；韻文
He wrote plays in *verse*.
【比較】 prose (散文)

‡ **very**[1,4] 〔ˈvɛrɪ 〕 *adv.* 非常   *adj.* 正是
That's the *very* thing I was looking for.

* **vessel**[4] 〔ˈvɛsḷ 〕 *n.* 容器；船；(血) 管
An empty *vessel* makes the most
sound.
【衍伸詞】 *blood vessel* (血管)

‡ **vest**[3] 〔 vɛst 〕 *n.* 背心
I need to buy new *vests*.
【比較】 in<u>vest</u> (投資)

* **vice-president**[3] 〔ˈvaɪsˈprɛzədənt 〕
n. 副總統

* **victim**[3] 〔ˈvɪktɪm 〕 *n.* 受害者
The *victim* of the robbery was not
able to identify the man who took
his money.
【片語】 *fall victim to* (成爲…的受害者)

* **victory**[2] 〔ˈvɪktrɪ；ˈvɪktərɪ 〕 *n.* 勝利
Our football team won a big *victory*.
【記憶技巧】 *vict* (conquer) + *ory* (*n.*)
(征服困難，才能獲得「勝利」)
┌─【典型考題】─────────
She won a great _____ in the
competition. As a result, she is
admired by sports fans everywhere.
A. victory   B. donation
C. challenger   D. opponent   [A]
└──────────────────

‡ **video**[2] 〔ˈvɪdɪˌo 〕 *n.* 錄影帶
(= *videotape*)

* **view**[1] 〔 vju 〕 *n.* 景色；看法
I like to see the *view* of the harbor.

* **village**[2] 〔'vɪlɪdʒ 〕 *n.* 村莊 (=*suburb*)
   adj. 鄉村的

There is a small *village* located on
this island.

【衍伸詞】 *global village* (地球村)

* **vinegar**[3] 〔'vɪnɪgɚ 〕 *n.* 醋

You can use *vinegar* on salad.

【記憶技巧】 *vin* (wine) + *egar* (sour)
    (「醋」是產生酸味的酒)

* **violate**[4] 〔'vaɪə‚let 〕 *v.* 違反 (=*defy*)

If you *violate* the traffic rule, you may
be fined.

┌─【典型考題】─────────
If you ＿＿＿ a traffic law, such as
drinking and driving, you may not
drive for some time.
A. destroy   B. violate
C. attack   D. invade   [**B**]
└────────────────────

* **violation**[4] 〔‚vaɪə'leʃən 〕 *n.* 違反
   (=*breach*)；侵害

┌─【典型考題】─────────
Discrimination against women is a
＿＿＿＿ of human rights.
A. suggestion   B. demonstration
C. reservation   D. violation   [**D**]
└────────────────────

* **violence**[3] 〔'vaɪələns 〕 *n.* 暴力
   (=*brutality*)

Onlookers were alarmed by the
violence of the fight and called the
police.

* **violent**[3] 〔'vaɪələnt 〕 *adj.* 暴力的

* **violet**[3] 〔'vaɪəlɪt 〕 *n.* 紫羅蘭

‡ **violin**[2] 〔‚vaɪə'lɪn 〕 *n.* 小提琴
   (=*fiddle*)

A *violin* is smaller than a viola.

* **virgin**[4] 〔'vɝdʒɪn 〕 *n.* 處女
   (=*maiden*)

* **virtue**[4] 〔'vɝtʃu 〕 *n.* 長處；美德
   (=*good character*)

Honesty is a good *virtue* to cultivate.

* **virus**[4] 〔'vaɪrəs 〕 *n.* 病毒

There're all kinds of *viruses* affecting
computers all over the world.

┌─【典型考題】─────────
Getting a flu shot before the start of flu
season gives our body a chance to build
up protection against the ＿＿＿ that
could make us sick.
A. poison   B. misery
C. leak   D. virus   [**D**]
└────────────────────

* **visible**[3] 〔'vɪzəbḷ 〕 *adj.* 看得見的

X-rays are able to make *visible*
details that are otherwise impossible
to observe.

【記憶技巧】 *vis* (see) + *ible* (*adj.*)
【反義詞】 invisible (看不見的)

* **vision**[3] 〔'vɪʒən 〕 *n.* 視力 (=*sight*)

Ellen went to an optometrist to
have her *vision* checked.

‡ **visit**[1] 〔'vɪzɪt 〕 *v.* 拜訪 (=*call on*)；
   遊覽   *n.* 拜訪；參觀

‡ **visitor**[2] 〔'vɪzɪtɚ 〕 *n.* 觀光客；訪客

* **visual**[4] 〔'vɪʒuəl 〕 *adj.* 視覺的；視力的

* **vital**[4] 〔'vaɪtḷ 〕 *adj.* 非常重要的
（= *essential* = *crucial*)；生命的；
充滿活力的

His support is *vital* for our project.
The heart is a *vital* organ.

【典型考題】
E-mail plays a ＿＿＿ role in modern
communication.
A. vital　　　　B. violent
C. vertical　　　D. various　　　[A]

* **vitamin**[3] 〔'vaɪtəmɪn 〕 *n.* 維他命

One of the most effective ways to
stay healthy is to eat foods that are
rich in *vitamins*.

【記憶技巧】 *vita* (life) + *min* (n.)
（「維他命」可提供維持生命的物質）

* **vivid**[3] 〔'vɪvɪd 〕 *adj.* 生動的；栩栩
如生的

Jessie gave such a *vivid* description
of her house that I'm sure I'll know
it when I see it.

【記憶技巧】 *viv* (live) + *id* (adj.)
（就像活生生站在眼前一樣，表示很生動）

‡ **vocabulary**[2] 〔 və'kæbjə,lɛrɪ 〕 *n.*
字彙（= *words*)

He has a large *vocabulary* in English.

‡ **voice**[1] 〔 vɔɪs 〕 *n.* 聲音；發言權
v. 表達（= *give voice to*)

That man has a loud *voice*.

【比較】 sound（事物發出的）聲音

* **volcano**[4] 〔 val'keno 〕 *n.* 火山

Volcanoes are divided into three main
groups.

【注意】這個字不可唸成〔vɔl'keno 〕。

‡ **volleyball**[2] 〔'valɪ,bɔl 〕 *n.* 排球

* **volume**[3] 〔'valjəm 〕 *n.* 音量
（= *loudness*)；（書）冊；容量

He turned up the *volume* on the
television.
We have a set of Dickens' works in
24 *volumes*.

* **voluntary**[4] 〔'valən,tɛrɪ 〕 *adj.* 自願的
（= *intentional*)

Gina does *voluntary* work at the
hospital in her spare time.

【記憶技巧】 *volunt* (free will) + *ary*
（經由自由的意願而決定，表示「自願的」）

* **volunteer**[4] 〔,valən'tɪr 〕 *v.* 自願
（= *offer*)　　 *n.* 自願者

* **vote**[2] 〔 vot 〕 *v.* 投票（= *cast a vote*)
n. 選票（= *ballot*)

People under 18 years old are not
allowed to *vote* in an election.

* **voter**[2] 〔'votɚ 〕 *n.* 投票者

* **vowel**[4] 〔'vauəl 〕 *n.* 母音

【比較】 consonant（子音）

* **voyage**[4] 〔'vɔɪ·ɪdʒ 〕 *n.* 航行

Our *voyage* across the Atlantic lasted
nearly one week.

【記憶技巧】 *voy* (way) + *age* (n.)
（順著海的路線行走，也就是「航行」）

W w

wag³〔wæg〕*v.* 搖動（尾巴）(= *wave*)
n. 搖擺
Our dog *wags* its tail when it sees us
coming home from school.

*****wage**³〔wedʒ〕*n.* 工資 (= *payment*)
v. 發動
The workers at the factory were
paid a *wage* of nine dollars an hour.

*****wagon**³〔'wægən〕*n.* 四輪載貨馬車

*****waist**²〔west〕*n.* 腰
Jane wears a belt around her *waist*.

wait¹〔wet〕*v.* 等 (= *stay*)
n. 等候的時間
【片語】*wait for*（等待）

waiter²〔'wetɚ〕*n.* 服務生

waitress²〔'wetrɪs〕*n.* 女服務生
【記憶技巧】*-ess* 表「女性」的字尾。

wake²〔wek〕*v.* 醒來 (= *become
awake*) *n.* 痕跡；蹤跡
Jane *wakes* up at 6:00 every morning.

*****waken**³〔'wekən〕*v.* 喚醒；叫醒
(= *wake up* = *awaken*)
It's time to *waken* the children for
school.

walk¹〔wɔk〕*v.* 走 *n.* 散步
【片語】*take a walk*（散步）

wall¹〔wɔl〕*n.* 牆壁 *v.* 把…用牆
圍住 < *in* >
The robber climbed over the *wall* to
get away.

wallet²〔'wɑlɪt〕*n.* 皮夾
John carries his money in a *wallet*.
【比較】purse（錢包）

walnut⁴〔'wɔlnət〕*n.* 核桃
【比較】chestnut（栗子）

*****wander**³〔'wɑndɚ〕*v.* 徘徊；流浪
We *wandered* around the park, looking
for a good spot to enjoy our picnic.
【比較】wonder（想知道）
┌─【典型考題】─────────
│ Lost and scared, the little dog_____
│ along the streets, looking for its master.
│ A. dismissed   B. glided
│ C. wandered   D. marched   **[C]**
└──────────────────

want¹〔wɑnt〕*v.* 想要

war¹〔wɔr〕*n.* 戰爭
(= *armed struggle*)
Many people are killed in a *war*.

warm¹〔wɔrm〕*adj.* 溫暖的
Keep yourself *warm* in the winter.

warmth³〔wɔrmθ〕*n.* 溫暖
【記憶技巧】*-th* 表抽象名詞的字尾。

*****warn**³〔wɔrn〕*v.* 警告 (= *caution*)
The smoke alarm will *warn* you
when there is a fire in the building.
┌─【典型考題】─────────
│ My parents _____ me not to play
│ with candles.
│ A. discourage   B. beware
│ C. explain   D. warn   **[D]**
└──────────────────

‡**wash**[1] 〔 waʃ 〕 *v.* 洗

‡**waste**[1] 〔 west 〕 *v.* 浪費

> 【典型考題】
>
> Don't try to reason with Paul—you
> are _____ your breath.
> A. disposing　　B. wasting
> C. storing　　　D. willing　　**[B]**

‡**watch**[1] 〔 watʃ 〕 *n.* 手錶

‡**water**[1] 〔 'wɔtɚ 〕 *n.* 水　*v.* 給…澆水

‡**waterfall**[2] 〔 'wɔtɚ‚fɔl 〕 *n.* 瀑布
　(= *cascade* 〔 kæs'ked 〕 = *falls*)

‡**watermelon**[2] 〔 'wɔtɚ‚mɛlən 〕 *n.* 西瓜

‡**wave**[2] 〔 wev 〕 *n.* 波浪
　The *waves* are very high today.

***wax**[3] 〔 wæks 〕 *n.* 蠟

‡**way**[1] 〔 we 〕 *n.* 路;方式;樣子

‡**weak**[1] 〔 wik 〕 *adj.* 虛弱的
　My grandfather is very *weak*.
　【反義詞】 strong (強壯的)

***weaken**[3] 〔 'wikən 〕 *v.* 使虛弱
　【反義詞】 strengthen (增強)

***wealth**[3] 〔 wɛlθ 〕 *n.* 財富 (= *riches*);
　豐富
　Health is better than *wealth*.

***wealthy**[3] 〔 'wɛlθɪ 〕 *adj.* 富有的
　(= *rich*)

***weapon**[2] 〔 'wɛpən 〕 *n.* 武器;手段
　Swords, arrows, guns, claws, horns,
　and teeth are *weapons*.
　【衍伸詞】 *nuclear weapon* (核子武器)

‡**wear**[1] 〔 wɛr 〕 *v.* 穿;戴;磨損;使
　疲倦
　【片語】 *wear out* (穿破;使筋疲力盡)

‡**weather**[1] 〔 'wɛðɚ 〕 *n.* 天氣
　The *weather* is good here.

***weave**[3] 〔 wiv 〕 *v.* 編織
　The artisan *weaves* her own cloth.

***web**[3] 〔 wɛb 〕 *n.* 網狀物;蜘蛛網
　A spider sat in the middle of the *web*.
　【衍伸詞】 *the Web* (網際網路)

***website**[4] 〔 'wɛb‚saɪt 〕 *n.* 網站

wed[2] 〔 wɛd 〕 *v.* 與…結婚 (= *marry*)
　My sister and her fiancé decided
　to *wed* in a small church.
　【衍伸詞】 newlyweds (新婚夫婦)

‡**wedding**[1] 〔 'wɛdɪŋ 〕 *n.* 婚禮
　(= *wedding ceremony*)
　My parents' *wedding* was very
　romantic.

‡**Wednesday**[1] 〔 'wɛnzdɪ 〕 *n.* 星期三
　(= *Wed.*)

***weed**[3] 〔 wid 〕 *n.* 雜草
　The garden is full of *weeds* because
　no one has been taking care of it.

‡**week**[1] 〔 wik 〕 *n.* 星期

‡**weekday**[2] 〔 'wik‚de 〕 *n.* 平日
　The museum is open on *weekdays*
　only.

‡**weekend**[1] 〔 'wik'ɛnd 〕 *n.* 週末
　What are you going to do this
　weekend?
　【記憶技巧】 *week* + *end* (結束)

***weekly**[4]〔'wiklɪ〕*adj.* 每週的
（*= every week*） *n.* 週刊
【比較】daily（每天的）
monthly（每月的）

***weep**[3]〔 wip 〕*v.* 哭泣（*= cry = wail*）
Claire *wept* when she heard about
the accident.

【典型考題】
Maria _____ bitterly over the death
of her pet dog.
A. gasps   B. gasped
C. weeping   D. wept   [D]

‡**weigh**[1]〔 we 〕*v.* 重⋯
How much does it *weigh*?

***weight**[1]〔 wet 〕*n.* 重量
Alex needs to gain some *weight*.
【片語】*gain weight*（增加體重）
lose weight（減輕體重）

‡**welcome**[1]〔'wɛlkəm〕*v.* 歡迎
We always *welcome* guests to our
restaurant.

***welfare**[4]〔'wɛl͵fɛr〕*n.* 福利
Welfare programs for the elderly
provide senior citizens with nursing
homes and regular financial help.
【記憶技巧】*wel*（good）+ *fare*（go）
（「福利」是對人有益的東西）

‡**well**[1]〔 wɛl 〕*adv.* 很好
【片語】*may well*（很有理由⋯）
may as well（不妨；最好）

‡**west**[1]〔 wɛst 〕*n.* 西方
（*= occident*（'ɑksədənt ））
【比較】east（東方）

***western**[2]〔'wɛstən〕*adj.* 西方的
（*= occidental*）
【比較】eastern（東方的）

‡**wet**[2]〔 wɛt 〕*adj.* 濕的
（*= humid = damp = moist*）
Be careful of the *wet* floor.

‡**whale**[2]〔(h)wel 〕*n.* 鯨魚
A *whale* is the biggest animal living
in the sea.
【比較】shark（鯊魚）

‡**whatever**[2]〔hwɑt'ɛvə〕*pron.* 無論
什麼
You can do *whatever* you want.

***wheat**[3]〔 hwit 〕*n.* 小麥
【比較】rice（稻米）

‡**wheel**[2]〔 hwil 〕*n.* 輪子
Cars and buses move on *wheels*.

***whenever**[2]〔hwɛn'ɛvə〕*conj.* 無論
何時（*= whensoever*）
Whenever I see you, you always look
happy.

***wherever**[2]〔hwɛr'ɛvə〕*conj.* 無論
何處
My little brother follows me *wherever*
I go.

‡**whether**[1]〔'hwɛðə〕*conj.* 是否
I'm not sure *whether* it will rain.

‡**while**[1]〔 hwaɪl 〕*conj.* 當⋯的時候；
然而

***whip**[3]〔 hwɪp 〕*v.* 鞭打（*= lash*）
The carriage driver *whipped* the
horses to make them run faster.
【衍伸詞】*whipped cream*（鮮奶油）

*whisper[2] 〔ˈhwɪspɚ 〕 *v.* 小聲說
（ = *murmur* ）
Not wanting to disturb anyone, Kathy *whispered* to me during the movie.

whistle[3] 〔ˈhwɪsḷ 〕 *v.* 吹口哨 *n.* 哨子
Adam *whistled* and his dog came running at once.

‡white[1] 〔hwaɪt 〕 *adj.* 白色的
【衍伸詞】 *a white lie*（善意的謊言）

*whoever[2] 〔huˈɛvɚ 〕 *pron.* 無論是誰
Whoever comes in first will be given a trophy.

‡whole[1] 〔hol 〕 *adj.* 全部的；整個的
（ = *entire* ）
Richard ate a *whole* pizza for lunch.
【片語】 *as a whole*（就全體而言）
    on the whole（大體而言）

*wicked[3] 〔ˈwɪkɪd 〕 *adj.* 邪惡的
（ = *evil* ）
Nadia warned us against having anything to do with the *wicked* man.

‡wide[1] 〔waɪd 〕 *adj.* 寬的（ = *broad* ）
A *wide* road makes it easy for him to drive.
【反義詞】 narrow（窄的）
【衍伸詞】 *a wide variety of*（各式各樣的）

*widen[2] 〔ˈwaɪdn̩ 〕 *v.* 使變寬
（ = *broaden* ）

*width[2] 〔wɪdθ 〕 *n.* 寬度
The bridge is 30 meters in *width*.

‡wife[1] 〔waɪf 〕 *n.* 妻子

‡wild[2] 〔waɪld 〕 *adj.* 野生的；荒涼的；瘋狂的（ = *crazy* ）
We should protect *wild* animals.

‡will[1] 〔wɪl 〕 *aux.* 將會 *n.* 意志力
Where there's a *will*, there's a way.

*willing[2] 〔ˈwɪlɪŋ 〕 *adj.* 願意的
I am *willing* to do the job.
【反義詞】 unwilling（不願意的）

*willow[3] 〔ˈwɪlo 〕 *n.* 柳樹
There are several *willow* trees on the bank of the river.
【比較】 pillow（枕頭）

‡win[1] 〔wɪn 〕 *v.* 贏（ = *triumph* ）；獲得
Rose will do anything to *win* the game.
【反義詞】 lose（輸）

‡wind[1] 〔wɪnd 〕 *n.* 風（ = *air currents* ）
A great *wind* blew across the sea.
【衍伸詞】 windy（風大的）

‡window[1] 〔ˈwɪndo 〕 *n.* 窗戶
【典型考題】
It's so hot inside. Can you open the _____?
A. box   B. book
C. window   D. dictionary [C]

‡‡windy[2] 〔ˈwɪndɪ 〕 *adj.* 多風的
【典型考題】
It was very _____ this morning. My hat was blown away while I was walking on the street.
A. cloudy   B. dry
C. warm   D. windy   [D]

*wine[1] 〔waɪn 〕 *n.* 酒；葡萄酒
She got drunk on one glass of *wine*.

‡**wing**[2] 〔 wɪŋ 〕 *n.* 翅膀

I wish I had *wings* to fly.

***wink**[3] 〔 wɪŋk 〕 *v.* 眨眼

My uncle *winked* at me to let me know he was kidding.

‡**winner**[2] 〔ˈwɪnɚ〕 *n.* 優勝者

‡**winter**[1] 〔ˈwɪntɚ〕 *n.* 冬天

***wipe**[3] 〔 waɪp 〕 *v.* 擦（= *rub*）

George *wiped* the counter after he finished cooking.

***wire**[2] 〔 waɪr 〕 *n.* 電線；鐵絲

We had no power after the electrical *wires* were cut.

***wisdom**[3] 〔ˈwɪzdəm〕 *n.* 智慧
（= *intelligence*）

She spoke with authority as well as with *wisdom*.

‡**wise**[2] 〔 waɪz 〕 *adj.* 聰明的（= *smart*）

‡**wish**[1] 〔 wɪʃ 〕 *v.* 希望；祝…

What do you *wish* to have for Christmas?
I *wish* you a happy New Year.

***wit**[4] 〔 wɪt 〕 *n.* 機智（= *brightness*）；幽默

The actor answered the question with great *wit* and made the audience laugh.
【片語】 *out of one's wits*（驚慌失措）

***witch**[4] 〔 wɪtʃ 〕 *n.* 女巫
【比較】 wizard（巫師）

‡**with**[1] 〔 wɪð 〕 *prep.* 和…一起；用…

***withdraw**[4] 〔 wɪðˈdrɔ 〕*v.* 撤退
（= *retreat*）；提（款）

They decided to *withdraw* the troops from the front line.
【記憶技巧】 *with* (back) + *draw* (拉)

***within**[2] 〔 wɪðˈɪn 〕 *prep.* 在…之內

You should finish the work *within* two days.

‡**without**[2] 〔 wɪðˈaʊt 〕 *prep.* 沒有
【片語】 *can't do without*（不能沒有）

***witness**[4] 〔ˈwɪtnɪs〕 *n.* 目擊者
（= *eyewitness*）；證人

There were no *witnesses* to the car accident, so no one is sure how it happened.
【注意】 這個字也可當動詞用，作「目擊」解。

***wizard**[4] 〔ˈwɪzəd〕 *n.* 巫師

‡**wolf**[2] 〔 wʊlf 〕 *n.* 狼

Wolves kill sheep for food.

‡**woman**[1] 〔ˈwʊmən〕 *n.* 女人

***wonder**[2] 〔ˈwʌndɚ〕 *v.* 想知道
n. 驚奇；奇觀

I *wonder* why he didn't come.
【衍伸詞】 *the Seven Wonders of the World*（世界七大奇觀）

‡**wonderful**[2] 〔ˈwʌndɚfəl〕 *adj.* 很棒的
（= *amazing*）

Ida and I had a *wonderful* time.

【典型考題】
My daughter has done so much housework for me. She's been ＿＿＿ today.
A. wonderful   B. afraid
C. terrible   D. comfortable [A]

W

wood[1] 〔 wʊd 〕 *n.* 木頭（ = *timber* ）
The chair is made of *wood*.

wooden[2] 〔'wʊdn̩〕 *adj.* 木製的

woods[1] 〔 wʊdz 〕 *n. pl.* 森林
（ = *small forest* ）
We went for a walk in the *woods*.

wool[2] 〔 wʊl 〕 *n.* 羊毛（ = *fleece* ）
The sweater is one hundred percent
wool.

word[1] 〔 wɝd 〕 *n.* 字；話
【片語】 *have words with*（ 和…吵架 ）
in other words（ 換句話說 ）

work[1] 〔 wɝk 〕 *n.* 工作；作品
v. 起作用

worker[1] 〔'wɝkɚ〕 *n.* 工人

world[1] 〔 wɝld 〕 *n.* 世界
【片語】 *around the world*（ 在全世界 ）
（ = *all over the world* = *throughout*
the world ）

worm[1] 〔 wɝm 〕 *n.* 蟲
【比較】 warm（ 溫暖的 ）

worry[1] 〔'wɝɪ〕 *v. n.* 擔心
Don't *worry* about me.

worse[1] 〔 wɝs 〕 *adj.* 更糟的
Cindy is an even *worse* tennis player
than I am.

worst[1] 〔 wɝst 〕 *adj.* 最糟的

worth[2] 〔 wɝθ 〕 *adj.* 值得…
The book is *worth* reading.
【片語】 *be worth* + *V-ing*（ 值得~ ）

wound[2] 〔 wund 〕 *n.* 傷口
I have a knife *wound* on my arm.

wrap[3] 〔 ræp 〕 *v.* 包；裹
I will *wrap* his birthday present in
colorful paper.

wreck[3] 〔 rɛk 〕 *n.* 遇難的船；殘骸
v. 使遭遇船難
Salvage crews tried to bring the
wrecks to the surface.
【衍伸詞】 wreckage（ 殘骸 ）

wrinkle[4] 〔'rɪŋkl̩〕 *n.* 皺紋 *v.* 起皺紋
（ = *crinkle* ）
Alice has no *wrinkles* on her face.
This cloth *wrinkles*.

wrist[3] 〔 rɪst 〕 *n.* 手腕
John is wearing a beautiful watch
on his *wrist*.

write[1] 〔 raɪt 〕 *v.* 寫

writer[1] 〔'raɪtɚ〕 *n.* 作家
John Irving is a world-famous *writer*.

wrong[1] 〔 rɔŋ 〕 *adj.* 錯誤的
My answer was *wrong*, so I erased it.

X x ~ Y y

*X-ray³ 〔'ɛks're 〕*n.* X 光

yam¹ 〔 jæm 〕*n.* 蕃薯
(= *sweet potato*)

‡yard² 〔 jɑrd 〕*n.* 院子 (= *backyard*)；
天井；碼
Children are playing hide-and-seek in the front *yard*.

*yawn³ 〔 jɔn 〕*v.* 打呵欠
Barbara was tired and began to *yawn* during the movie.
【比較】snore (打呼)

‡yeah¹ 〔 jɛ 〕*adv.* 是 (= *yes*)

‡year¹ 〔 jɪr 〕*n.* 年

*yearly⁴ 〔'jɪrlɪ 〕*adj.* 每年的；一年
一次的 (= *annual*)
The computer applications show is held *yearly* in Taipei.

*yell³ 〔 jɛl 〕*v. n.* 大叫 (= *shout*)
Tony's mother *yelled* at him for watching TV instead of doing his homework.
【片語】*yell at* (對…大叫)

‡yellow¹ 〔'jɛlo 〕*adj.* 黃色的
My favorite umbrella is *yellow*.

‡yesterday¹ 〔'jɛstɚ‚de 〕*adv.* 昨天
It was raining *yesterday* but today the sky is clear.

‡yet¹ 〔 jɛt 〕*adv.* 尚 (未) (= *up till now*)；更加；然而 (= *however*)
conj. 但是 (= *but*)
The work is not *yet* finished.
【片語】*not yet* (尚未；還沒)

*yogurt⁴ 〔'jogɚt 〕*n.* 優格
Milk is not the only dairy product you can eat; you also can choose ice cream, *yogurt*, and cheese.

*yolk³ 〔 jok 〕*n.* 蛋黃
According to the recipe, you have to separate the *yolk* from the rest of the egg.
【比較】*egg white* (蛋白)

‡young¹ 〔 jʌŋ 〕*adj.* 年輕的
(= *youthful*)
Lucy is too *young* to have a baby.

*youngster³ 〔'jʌŋstɚ 〕*n.* 年輕人
【記憶技巧】*-ster* 表「人」的字尾。

‡youth² 〔 juθ 〕*n.* 年輕；年輕人
This club is for *youths*.
【片語】*in one's youth* (在年輕時期)
the youth (年輕人)

X

* **youthful**[4] 〔ˈjuθfəl〕 *adj.* 年輕的
   (= *young*)；年輕人的

* **yucky**[1] 〔ˈjʌkɪ〕 *adj.* 討厭的；
   難看的；令人厭惡的；令人反感的
   (= *disgusting* = *nasty*)

The school lunch is *yucky*.

‡‡**yummy**[1] 〔ˈjʌmɪ〕 *adj.* 好吃的
   (= *delicious* = *mouth-watering*)
   How *yummy* that cake was!

Z z

‡‡**zebra**[2] 〔ˈzibrə〕 *n.* 斑馬
   A *zebra* has black and white stripes
   all over its body.
   【衍伸詞】 ***zebra crossing*** (斑馬線)

‡‡**zero**[1] 〔ˈzɪro〕 *n.* 零
   The last digit of her telephone
   number is *zero*.

* **zipper**[3] 〔ˈzɪpɚ〕 *n.* 拉鍊
   My *zipper* got stuck when I tried to
   zip up my jacket.

* **zone**[3] 〔 zon 〕 *n.* 地帶；地區
   (= *area* = *region* = *district*)
   This is a residential *zone*, so there
   are no factories nearby.
   【比較】 o*zone* (臭氧)

‡‡**zoo**[1] 〔 zu 〕 *n.* 動物園；喧鬧混亂的
   地方
   There are many kinds of animals
   in the *zoo*.

Z